Shadow Education and Social Inequalities in Japan

Steve R. Entrich

Shadow Education and Social Inequalities in Japan

Evolving Patterns and Conceptual Implications

 Springer

Steve R. Entrich
Department for Education,
Social Science Educational Research
University of Potsdam
Potsdam, Germany

ISBN 978-3-319-88717-3   ISBN 978-3-319-69119-0   (eBook)
https://doi.org/10.1007/978-3-319-69119-0

Printed on acid-free paper

This Springer imprint is published by Springer Nature
The registered company is Springer International Publishing AG
The registered company address is: Gewerbestrasse 11, 6330 Cham, Switzerland

This work is dedicated to Miyuki.
May the AME be forever in your favor.

Preface

Since I entered the "shadow" of the Japanese education system some 6 years ago, I received a lot of strange looks when trying to explain the main topic of my current research. Apart from comparative educationalists, only few seem to value the merits of studying foreign systems of education. But even in comparative education research, outside-of-school realities are still rarely focused on. So besides a few foreign researchers, most research on the topic is likely to be carried out in Japan itself – or so I thought. Even in Japan, many looked rather puzzled when I told them that I would dedicate a whole book to Japanese "shadow education." It was always a struggle to explain why anyone from Germany would be interested to learn more about the Japanese shadow system, the "*juku*-industry." Whereas all Japanese seem to somehow know what *juku* are, only few researchers have analyzed this second schooling system. This, of course, does not help to understand why shadow education in Japan exists in the way it does, why it remains very successful, and what the existence of such a system means for the state of education in general and, in particular, for equality of educational opportunities in Japan. What is it that makes the Japanese *juku*-industry a topic not only interesting but highly relevant for Japanese and non-Japanese researchers alike?

The answer to this question is simple: Shadow education is a highly relevant topic because of its general implications. Shadow education exists worldwide. In some countries, such as my home country Germany, shadow education has been traditionally low in scale. In others, such as Japan, only few students manage to not enter *juku* or use other types of paid tutoring services. If we look at countries like Germany, we should not make the mistake of assuming that because our education system is very different from the Japanese one in several regards, private tutoring would not exist. In fact, these services have existed in Germany for as long as there exists schooling. And even though private tutoring has been low in scale traditionally, recently an increasing number of students enroll in these lessons resulting in a continuous expansion of the market. Similar expansions of private supplementary education sectors are evident in many other Western nations as well, including the United States, Canada, and the United Kingdom. If we take a look at our neighbor Poland or other Eastern European countries, or if we look further south, to Greece or Turkey, we cannot avoid being surprised to find massive shadow education systems with enrolment rates of 80 or 90% of an age cohort right at our doorstep.

The problem is we are surprised. We are surprised because we do not know much about the causes for the emergence of these parallel education systems, the factors responsible for increased enrolment worldwide. We can also only assume what implications such an increased participation in shadow education will have for education in general. This is why international research on the matter becomes increasingly important. This is also why research on advanced systems such as the Japanese *juku*-industry should be on top of the list of educationalists concerned with the outcomes of globalization, educational expansion, inequality formation, student performance, demographic change, educational reformation, and so on. Advanced in this sense means that the Japanese *juku*-market has undergone several transformations since its establishment in the 1960s and 1970s and achieved a role in Japanese education that is exemplary to other nations in terms of scale and functional diversity. By evaluating and analyzing what factors led to the emergence of the *juku*-industry and its transformations during the twentieth century based on historical developments, clear merits of an analysis of the Japanese *juku*-system for our understanding of the relationship between regular school and shadow education can be achieved. Such research might enable non-Japanese researchers to identify the factors leading to increased demand for shadow education in their home settings. It is also essential to estimate the possible implications of shadow education for education as an institution or the persistence of social inequalities. In sum, we would be in a position to assess what an increased participation in tutoring services means for students, families, teachers, and schools and how officials should deal with the emergence of such education businesses.

Of course, the emergence, development, scale, and functional diversity of any shadow education sector depend on the specifics of the mainstream education system of a country based on cultural and societal characteristics. And I would like to add that the way these nation-specific factors are articulated through actions of corporate (state, organizations) and primary actors (families, teachers, students) shapes education as a whole. Whereas the state primarily shapes formal education, private actors particularly shape the informal parts of education. The question is whether we are bystanders to this development or whether we try to influence this change in education. Because change is happening – whether we want to see it or not. Thus, the aim of this book can only be to shed light on a long dismissed subject in educational and social sciences and its most pressing implications focusing on an exemplary case study: shadow education and social inequality in Japan.

The results of this work not only clarify the (often mystical) role of shadow education in Japan but allow drawing conclusions about the implications of shadow education in other national settings as well. This is due to the fact that in Japan, shadow education already occupies a position that might become trendsetting for other nations. In fact, the continuous expansion of shadow education systems across the globe and the increasing similarities between these systems imply a convergence towards a world model of shadow education, resembling the Japanese model. This book now provides a deep insight into the Japanese model of shadow education urging practitioners, researchers, families, and politicians to take notice of the possible implications of shadow education inside and outside of Japan. It is also a call for similar works in other national contexts, particularly Western societies without traditional large-scale shadow education markets. This work further shows the importance and urgency to deal with the modern excesses of educational expansion and education as an institution. As written down in this book on the Japanese example, shadow education inherits the potential to become indispensable for a national system of education. It seems only natural that we know what this means for education in general, before figuring out (new) ways to deal with this matter. I hope that the reader enjoys this piece of work and that the ideas and findings brought forth inspire future research in the area of study.

Potsdam, Germany
June 2017

Steve R. Entrich

Acknowledgments

This work would not have been possible without the help of several people, whom I would like to express my sincere gratitude for their kind support, guidance, recommendations, and assistance.

First of all, I would like to thank Prof. Dr. Wolfgang Lauterbach (University of Potsdam) for constantly questioning my approaches, theoretical frameworks, and empirical analyses, approaching me with numerous alternative ideas, making helpful remarks on the structure of my works, and teaching me the importance of continuously asking yourself: "What is my particular research aim and why is this important?" After knowing each other for almost 10 years and working together in many different fields, such as writing and publishing, the creation of new degree programs, the instruction and examination of students, and the joint participation in conferences, I can honestly say that I have benefitted a lot from his long experience. Not only have I gained experience in how to write a decent research paper, I came to understand just how great and exciting the work of a researcher can be. In a similar way, I have to thank my direct colleagues at the chair for social science educational research and other members of our social science educational research colloquium taking place at the University of Potsdam. The numerous discussions and debates proved fruitful for the clarification of my research attempts and its outcomes.

I am further greatly indebted to Prof. Dr. Fumiaki Ojima (Dōshisha University) for accepting me as a visiting graduate student at the Faculty of Social Studies at Dōshisha University from October 2012 to March 2013. This half year under Ojima sensei's care was some kind of a turning point in my studies on the Japanese supplementary education industry and marked the actual start of my fieldwork periods. Not only did Ojima sensei include me in one of his social science seminars, he incorporated me in the social studies PhD group at Dōshisha University, introduced me to experts and practitioners in the field of shadow education, helped me develop my own questionnaires, and invited me to join the *Hyōgo High School Students* (HHSS) survey research team. It is appropriate to say that the factual basis for this work was laid through my granted access to the data of the HHSS survey and through my inclusion in the research team of the project. In this regard, special thanks also go to all members of the HHSS research team, in particular to Prof. Dr. Sōhei Aramaki (Kyūshū University), Dr. Hirofumi Taki (Tōkyō University), and Dr. Ryōichi Nishimaru (Dōshisha University), for their guidance, help, and support in the analysis process of the HHSS data. In addition, I am utmost grateful to the whole social studies PhD student group of Dōshisha University, particularly Dr. Fang Ba and Dr. Toshiyuki Shirakawa, who accompanied me ever since I started at Dōshisha and never stopped supporting me in countless matters.

Following my stay at Dōshisha University, I was granted a scholarship by the German Institute for Japanese Studies (DIJ), Tōkyō. Due to this generous funding and the support of my fellow scholarship recipients and the members of the DIJ, I was able to continue my fieldwork and complete my own quantitative and qualitative data collection, which serves as the second main data source for this work, entitled as *Juku Student and Teacher Survey* (JSTS). I am particularly grateful to DDr. Barbara Holthus (University of Vienna), Prof. Dr. Carola Hommerich (Hokkaido University), and Dr. Phoebe Holdgruen (DIJ).

Additional support, critical remarks, and most welcome recommendations were received by several other scholars, researchers, and experts in the field of shadow education. I am sincerely grateful to Prof. Dr. Julian Dierkes (University of British Columbia) for his constant support and critical remarks regarding my studies on the Japanese *juku*-industry. In addition, I would like to thank Prof. Dr. Mark Bray (University of Hong Kong) for his support and his many suggestions on the issues connected to shadow education worldwide. Further thanks go to Prof. Dr. Peter Backhaus (Waseda University), Prof. Dr. Takehiko Kariya (University of Oxford), Prof. Dr. Emi Kataoka (Komazawa University), Prof. Dr. Keita Takayama (University of New England), Dr. Wei Zhang (University of Hong Kong), Dr. Yoko Yamato (Aoyama Gakuin University), and Haruo Kimura and Seiko Mochida (Benesse Educational Research and Development Institute). Furthermore, my sincere appreciation goes to the numerous practitioners, the *juku* principals, teachers, and students I had the pleasure of meeting and who so willingly helped me conducting my research. I have to particularly thank Hajime and Junko Shimizu, Minoru Watanabe, Mitsuharu Agemizu, Yoshikazu Sasaki, Hiroshi Tanaka, and Susumu Iwadare. Without the help and constant support from within the *juku*-industry, my research would not have been possible. Some of you have become very good friends over the last years, and I am always very much looking forward to meeting you again. Special thanks also go to Daniela Braune for all her effort in the JSTS data translation and entry process.

Finally, my utmost gratitude goes to friends and family – old and new – who accompanied me on my long journey from an idea to this final work. In your own way, each and every one of you helped me in accomplishing this task. At this point, I would like to particularly thank my friends Anna, Ben, Basti, Fang, Hajime, Kōhei, Maiko, Nanase, Ralf, Roland, Ryōko, Sebastian, and Yujirō for all the good times we shared and their support over the last years.

Last but not least, my deepest appreciation goes to my loving spouse Carolin and our daughter Miyuki, who endured several hardships but never stopped supporting me and my sometimes "crazy" ideas. You are my family, the ones giving me continuity and guidance in all my nonscientific matters. It has not always been easy for you, but that is what keeps us moving and makes us stronger in the end, I believe. It is you to whom I dedicate my work. It is you who give my life reason to continue pushing forward and never give up. Thank you. I love you.

Potsdam, Germany   Steve R. Entrich
May 2017

Contents

List of Figures

List of Tables

Chapter 1
Introduction

Shadow Education and Social Inequality in Japan

> *"It still seems reasonable to assume that prosperous families are in a position to invest in forms of tutoring which significantly promote their children's performance in the school system."*
>
> ('Private Supplementary Tutoring', by Mark Bray 2006: 523).

は
じ
め
に

Abstract Research on shadow education frequently stressed that a participation in shadow education is highly restricted by socioeconomic background, consequently fostering educational and social inequalities. Based on a literature review and a discussion of international and Japanese research findings on the subject, this chapter outlines the general problematic underlying the book and its contents and structure. In doing so, a formalized conceptual frame suited to analyze the possible negative and positive implications of shadow education on inequality is developed, called the *Shadow–Education–Inequality–Impact* (SEII) Frame. This frame draws on the four main dimensions that affect the implications of shadow education for social and educational inequalities: *Access*, *Effects*, *Continuity*, and *Change*. Since there exists a general lack of empirical verification of assumptions such as that shadow education inevitably contributes to social reproduction, two main proposals are brought forth: First, researchers shall be encouraged to make use of the introduced SEII Frame for future research on shadow education in different settings, particularly to identify possible evolving patterns in the field. Second, the Japanese model of shadow education shall be treated as an exemplary role model for such research.

© Springer International Publishing AG 2018
S.R. Entrich, *Shadow Education and Social Inequalities in Japan*,
https://doi.org/10.1007/978-3-319-69119-0_1

1.1 Problematic

It is well known that the education systems of modern societies have to be held accountable for the reproduction of educational as well as social inequalities (Becker and Lauterbach 2016). In the case of Japan, social inequality issues concerning equality of educational opportunities have not attracted much attention until the 1990s (Okada 2012: 7). In spite of an attested persistence of inequalities across numerous countries (Shavit and Blossfeld 1993; Shavit and Park 2016) including Japan (Treiman and Yamaguchi 1993; Fujihara and Ishida 2016),[1] only recently social and economic inequalities have made it onto the research agenda of scholars and sociologists (e.g., Tachibanaki 1998; Sato 2000; Kikkawa 2006; Chiavacci and Hommerich 2017b). Following the meritocratic achievement principle, the quality of the Japanese education system was often measured in terms of performance in *international large-scale assessment* (ILSA) studies. Since the implementation of these studies in the late 1950s, Japanese students consistently range among world's top performers (see Appendix, Table 1.1). In addition, the Japanese education system was repeatedly rated as one of the OECD countries that provides fairly equal educational opportunities. Japanese education has been officially praised for its high academic outcomes, equality in educational opportunities, and quality by researchers, international organizations, and governments across the world (e.g., Stigler and Stevenson 1991; Stigler and Hiebert 1999; Akiba et al. 2007). Most recently, the most prominent ILSA, the *Programme for International Student Assessment* (PISA), again verified Japanese students' outstanding performance in international comparison, while "equal access to resources" was reported concomitant with a weak impact of students' socioeconomic background on their learning outcomes. The additionally reported above-average percentage of academically resilient students, i.e., students which perform in the top quarter while being from the bottom quarter of socioeconomic stratification, further strengthened the belief that the Japanese education system provides numerous educational opportunities for students of all social strata (OECD 2012: 48–49, 2013: 197).

However, whether a truly meritocratic education system with equal educational opportunities for all students exists in Japan has been content of several debates (see LeTendre 1996; Okada 2012). Quite on the contrary to several Western observers, some researchers stressed that education in Japan has become more unequal recently (Fujita 2010; Park and Lee 2013; Kariya 2017), also raising concerns regarding possible new types of social inequalities (Urabe et al. 2013; Chiavacci and Hommerich 2017a). Whereas the strong emphasis on educational outcomes continues to dominate the education policy in contemporary Japan (Takayama 2008), the fact that

---

[1] More recently, this persistence was again questioned by several scientists, such as Breen et al. (2009), who showed that at least in the European context quantitative inequalities have not been as persistent as declared by Shavit and Blossfeld (1993). However, as shown in a recent volume introduced by Shavit and Park (2016), inequalities persisted in a horizontal rather than vertical or hierarchical way. For the Japanese case, Fujihara and Ishida (2016) showed that inequalities remained or even increased due to the high stratification within education levels in Japan.

students are extensively involved in numerous types of paid-for, extracurricular supplementary lessons outside of school, which were described as shadow education since the early 1990s (e.g., Stevenson and Baker 1992; Bray 1999; Baker et al. 2001; Bray 2009), is often purposefully overlooked. This seems negligent, since research has shown that a high dependence on shadow education has major implications for a national education system in terms of educational quality and opportunities as well as social inequality issues (Jones 2011; Bray and Kwo 2013). Consequently, research on social inequality issues in education needs to consider inside and outside of school realities to acknowledge the extent of educational opportunity provision in Japan (Schümer 1999).

As the above quotation by Mark Bray shall illustrate, a high dependence on shadow education is believed to be mostly negative. Besides robbing students of their leisure time outside of school (Bray 2009: 13), comparative studies on shadow education frequently stressed that a participation in these lessons is highly restricted by socioeconomic background, consequently fostering educational and social inequalities (e.g., Bray 1999, 2009, 2011; Baker et al. 2001; Dang and Rogers 2008; Mori and Baker 2010; Heyneman 2011). However, overall, there are two possible outcomes of investments in such services, since shadow education "can equalize educational opportunity by providing extra support to disadvantaged children, or it can deepen educational inequality by providing a market-based resource for advantaged children" (Aurini et al. 2013: xxi). The consequences of shadow education investments can either be problematic, if seen in terms of increasing social inequalities or pressure on children, or beneficial, as a contribution to the education market as a whole (Bray 2010: 11), leading to an increase in human capital (Dang and Rogers 2008).

In addition, the organization and overall influence of a national shadow education system on students' school life course sheds light on the possible shortcomings of the regular schooling system (Roesgaard 2006; Dawson 2010). Hence, it is of utmost importance to identify the working mechanisms behind social inequality formation in educational attainment by taking into consideration non-regular, outside of school education in private sectors in different national settings. Whether a national system of education actually provides a high level of equal educational opportunities is not only a matter of how formal education is designed but highly depends on initiatives in the private education sectors and their reception by the addressees of education: students and their families. To increase its attractiveness and justify its existence, especially the private education sector is in constant competition with public schools and thus strives to provide alternatives in education as a means of ensuring competitive advantages. This competition is held in academic as well as ideological terms and not at all limited to the state-recognized private schools, but equally strong in institutions in the shadow education sector, as already argued by Rohlen (1980: 210). Consequently, a high dependence on shadow education affects educational opportunity provision in two possible ways: (1) it impedes the official claim for equal educational opportunities, or (2) it provides such opportunities were they are missing in formal education. Unfortunately, we do not know much about both these possibilities; particularly, the second one remains under-researched.

1.2   International Research on Shadow Education and Inequality

The dominance of the negative implications associated with shadow education results from its informal character. In their prominent work about shadow education in Japan, Stevenson and Baker (1992) defined shadow education as "a set of educational activities that occur outside formal schooling and are designed to enhance the student's formal school career" (p. 1639). Also, shadow education is supposed to "improve student's chances of successfully moving through the allocation process [while it is] firmly rooted within the private sector" (pp. 1640–42). Extending this definition to fit as an international frame for shadow education in multiple national contexts, Bray (2010) emphasized three main points of essence: (1) shadow education is academic in nature, clearly excluding all nonacademic forms of out-of-school education from this definition, e.g., arts or sports lessons; (2) shadow education is used as a supplement and is therefore not covering classes outside the school spectrum, e.g., language classes for children with migratory background; and (3) shadow education is private, meaning all nonprofessional forms, such as parental help with homework, or unpaid remedial classes at school, are not considered here, because shadow education is commercial in nature, profit-oriented, and thus fee based (p. 4). The terms used to describe shadow education in different national settings vary, of course. Internationally, the broad terms "supplementary education," "extended education," or "out-of-school lessons" include lessons of the above definition but have room for other, e.g., free of charge lessons, as well. The most frequently used equivalent term for shadow education is "private tutoring," even though this term might include other kinds of tutoring. Besides these, a huge variety of national specific terms and definitions for the different types and forms of shadow education can be found, resulting in a lot of difficulties when analyzing this educational sphere. The bigger a national schooling system's shadow gets, the more detailed the descriptions for the different pieces of this shadow exist. Thus, before starting to analyze this vast field of shadow education, researchers should make clear what they are analyzing exactly, by orienting on a formal definition such as introduced above and by concentrating their analyses on national specific types of shadow education that correspond to this definition. In particular when empirically approaching this field, researchers need to put much care in making sure that the used items reflect the definition of shadow education. Often studies lack item definition accuracy.

This last point is especially true for analyses based on international large-scale assessment data such as PISA or TIMSS (*Trends in International Mathematics and Science Study*). These studies provide researchers with vast amounts of data on the performance of students, their social background, and in- and out-of-school educational activities. On first glance, this must seem like a good opportunity to analyze the implications of shadow education on social inequalities as well. However, these studies hold certain limitations that might result in an oversimplification or misinterpretation at best or even a total misunderstanding of the phenomenon at worst. Whereas definition accuracy of the items used in PISA has improved over time, there still remain some fundamental issues calling for more specific data to adequately analyze the phenomenon shadow education and its outcomes. Figure 1.1 is meant to illustrate these difficulties. Using data of the 2012 PISA study, the illustrated data show that in 2012 a large percentage of 15-year-old students across the world enrolled in certain types of shadow education. I concentrated my analyses on students who either pursued private tutoring lessons or fee-based classes organized by a commercial company, i.e., learning or cram schools. A third category shows students who used both these services at the same time. All three categories combined show the overall percentage of 15-year-olds enrolled in shadow education. Accordingly, 15-year-olds in Scandinavian countries generally show very low overall enrolment ratios of often below 10%. In the United States, Canada, or the United Kingdom, 20% or more 15-year-olds participated in such lessons. German 15-year-olds reached the international average of almost 40%, whereas in Poland, Brazil, and Spain every second, 15-year-old used such services in 2012. In South Korea, Singapore, and Greece, more than 60% were enrolled in 2012, in Malaysia and Indonesia 80% or more. Interestingly, most of these students use both shadow education types simultaneously.

According to these data, in Japan, only comparatively few students (less than 20%) make use of shadow education lessons. Most attend classes at commercial companies, the Japanese *juku* (17.5%). These data stand in stark contrast to the general view on Japan as possessing one of the largest shadow education systems worldwide, which, in fact, is true. Two points are important to notice: First, all 15-year-olds in Japan are already in 10th grade. At this point, students have just passed high school entrance exams and entered high school. Following this transition, many stop their investment in shadow education – at least for some time. In 9th grade, many more students are enrolled in shadow education in Japan, up to some 80%. Second, the data have some definition (paid or unpaid lessons?) and translation inaccuracy (is the translated item reflecting what the original term described?) that can lead to unreliable findings, as argued by some researchers (Bray and Kobakhidze 2014b; Entrich 2014a). Also, there are some serious nonresponse issues attached to the data that make them sometimes unreliable.

Although research efforts increased with the perceptible expansion of worldwide shadow education over time, not much attention was paid to this particular sphere of education in most countries, since researchers as well as politicians often miss to recognize the considerable implications of this growing global private tutoring market for regular schooling systems (Bray and Kwo 2014). Therefore, this field of study is still not well enough documented. The above shown PISA data have not been used or even recognized by many researchers (except Park et al. 2016; Bray 2017), let alone the public. The scale of shadow education, the term even, and the fact that it is an international phenomenon remain largely unknown. For too long, government officials refused to acknowledge the existence and, as equally important, the influence of shadow education on students' everyday lives and educational forthcoming with the argument, shadow education would fall "outside the purview of public education and its equitable provision" (Bray et al. 2013: 1). The unwillingness to accept shadow education as part of the education system often originates

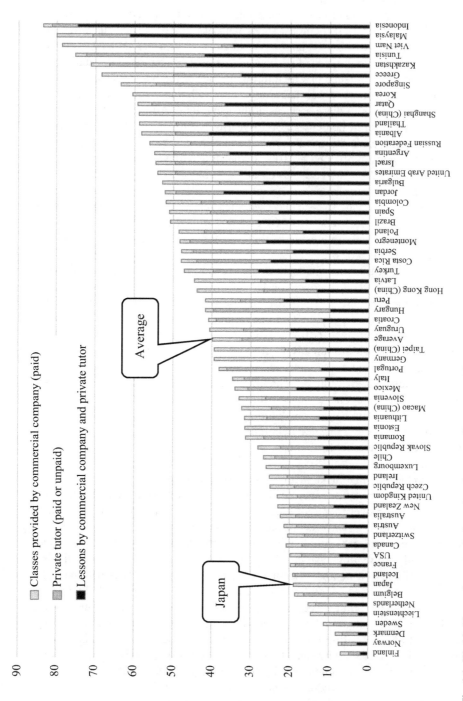

Fig. 1.1 Worldwide enrolment in shadow education, according to type, 15-year-olds, in % (PISA 2012, own calculation)

from the fact that specific problems of a national education system are best reflected in the nature and scale of its shadow education system. By officially dealing with this system, policy officials would have to admit several shortcomings of formal education (Dawson 2010: 17). In particular outside of East Asia, research findings regarding shadow education experienced less attention, wherefore the scale and implications of private tutoring are still less well understood in the Western world. Whereas the findings of the first large-scale report about worldwide shadow education as published in 1999 by the *United Nations Educational, Scientific and Cultural Organization* (UNESCO) (Bray 1999) were generally recognized in East Asian nations, the growing influence of supplementary education suppliers in Western education systems has neither led to an increased research activity nor political actions. It was not until the 2009 sequel of this publication (Bray 2009) that research outside of East Asia considerably increased as well. Today we find a growing body of literature revealing the nature, scale, and possible implications of private tutoring across numerous countries.

Although in general most studies concentrate on national systems of shadow education and avoid the look across borders, with the expansion of worldwide shadow education, comparative education research focusing on shadow education in a more and more globalized world has increased too (e.g., Baker et al. 2001; Dang and Rogers 2008; Southgate 2009; Dawson 2010; Mori and Baker 2010; Heyneman 2011; Aurini et al. 2013; Entrich 2014a, b, MacPherson et al. 2014; Park et al. 2016). The attempt to map shadow education worldwide and to show what policy implications shadow education holds for future educational development in international comparison is especially visible in the research of Mark Bray and his colleagues (Bray 1999; Silova et al. 2006; Bray 2009, 2011; Bray and Lykins 2012; Bray et al. 2013; Bray and Kobakhidze 2014a; Bray and Kwo 2014; Bray et al. 2015; Zhang and Bray 2017).

According to existing studies, the continued expansion of shadow education is generally believed to undermine the concept of equal and free education and thus represents a thread to social cohesion (Bray and Lykins 2012: 70). Shadow education might even play the most crucial role in the formation of inequality of educational opportunities due to its fee-based nature (Heyneman 2011: 185). Across the world, several studies showed that shadow education contributes to social reproduction, since an investment depends largely on whether these often expensive private tutoring types are accessible by students from disadvantaged family backgrounds or not. Among numerous works which theoretically discussed this topic (e.g., Russell 1997, 2002; Bray 1999, 2006, 2009, 2010, 2011; Dierkes 2008a, b, c; Dierkes 2009, 2010; Dawson 2010; Bray and Lykins 2012; Bray and Kwo 2013; Bray et al. 2013), empirical evidence for differing access to shadow education according to social origin was verified for low-intensity shadow education countries such as the United States (Buchmann et al. 2010; Byun and Hyunjoon 2012), Canada (Davies 2004), England (Ireson and Rushforth 2011), and Germany (Schneider 2005; Hille et al. 2016), as well as high-intensity shadow education countries such as Turkey (Tansel and Bircan 2004), parts of China (Liu and Bray 2016; Zhang and Xie 2016), South Korea (Kim and Lee 2010; Lee and Shouse 2011; Park et al. 2011), and Japan

(Seiyama 1981; Stevenson and Baker 1992; Kataoka 2001, 2015; Konakayama and Matsui 2008; Tomura et al. 2011). However, there is reason to believe that the access to shadow education is not as restricted by social origin as most studies indicate – even in high-intensity shadow education nations such as Japan. Otherwise the reported high enrolment ratios which at some points exceed 70% of a whole student population in Japan (MEXT 2008, 2014) are hard to explain in the first place. Whether the enrolment rates and intensity of shadow education participation as well as the effects of different investment strategies vary considerably across different social strata has not been in the focus of existing research. Instead, social origin variables such as highest parental education level or household income are simply controlled for. Also, most empirical research failed to appropriately differentiate between out-of-school or supplementary education and shadow education due to item definition inaccuracy and data shortcomings. Hence, there actually remains a huge gap in research about shadow education.

Following Bray's framework, shadow education cannot exist without the mainstream schooling system, which is accountable for its origin. All changes in the mainstream schooling system affect the size and shape of its shadow education system as well. However, educationalists and politicians predominantly focus on the mainstream system, avoiding to pay too much attention to educational supply in the shadow – with often unforeseeable consequences for the state of education of a country. Based on international research on the subject, we cannot avoid seeing the obvious: since the institutional model of schooling has become very similar in most nations in the course of educational expansion and due to strong internationalization trends in education, we find that the purposes, problems, and solutions in education have also become very similar in most countries – something that was already noted by the comparative educationalist Isaac L. Kandel (1933). The continuous expansion of shadow education systems across the globe has to be understood as one major, albeit unintended, outcome of international educational expansion or what some appropriately called the "education revolution" (e.g., Meyer et al. 1977; Craig 1981; Fiala and Lanford 1987; Baker 2014; Bills 2016). Whereas the major impact of this revolution in education on society has largely gone unnoticed for quite some time, societies across the world have nevertheless undergone major transformations in the course of the education revolution. According to David Baker (2014), we are now living in a world led by "schooled societies." In such schooled societies, "a wholly new social order where dimensions of education reach into and define nearly every facet of human life" (p. 8) is apparent. Today, educational credentials, academic achievements, skills, and other educational qualifications define individuals' way of acting, thinking and through this, how society as a whole is shaped. If we are aware of the fact that the way societies work across the world is influenced by education in a way unimaginable only a few decades ago, the implications of the rise of shadow education should be known, as they can hardly be overestimated. Interestingly in this context is to notice that shadow education – just as formal education – has come to share major similarities worldwide. This implies a convergence towards a *world model of shadow education*, which, as Mori and Baker (2010) argued, most likely resembles the Japanese model.

Hence, what makes the Japanese case an exemplary case for analysis is the fact that shadow education in Japan occupies a position that might become (or already is) trendsetting for other nations. It has advanced to a level where it is not the exception anymore to receive some tutoring on the side. In Japan more than 90% of the students make use of services in the shadow during their school life course. It is more appropriate to speak of shadow education as a regular feature of mass schooling. This also affects in which ways this kind of education is demanded and distributed. The extraordinary high demand for additional support outside regular classes in Japan implies that formal education leaves most families unsatisfied with the quality, contents, or organization of its schools. But is this all there is? It must be stunning for foreign researchers without experience in this field of study that shadow education in their own country might have reached a level where it has become a considerable force in education – with all its implications. The view on Japan might thus prove fruitful for our general understanding about the kind of implications shadow education can hold for education in general and social inequality in particular.

Now of course, the features of shadow education vary according to national context, since a nation's specific view on education always influences how it is dealt with supposed problems in education (Baker and LeTendre 2005: xii). Even though the worldwide growth of shadow education is based on similar causes in most countries, the intensity and functional diversity of a national system of shadow education might still depend very much on national specifics (see Bray 2009). The next section thus looks at what we supposedly know about shadow education and its implications for social inequalities in Japan.

1.3   Research on Shadow Education and Inequality in Japan

Although social inequalities might be *taken for granted* (Urabe et al. 2013: 153) by many in present Japan, there is an increased concern and awareness regarding social and educational inequalities in relation to students' out-of-school educational activities as well as growing interest in the effects and modes of operation of this *ever-expanding world* (Zeng 1999: 153). Accordingly, a growing body of Japanese literature concerning shadow education exists (e.g., Kataoka 2001, 2015; Iwase 2005, 2006, 2008; Kita 2006; Iwase 2007; Mimizuka 2007; Konakayama and Matsui 2008; Kuroishi and Takahashi 2009; Tomura et al. 2011; Tobishima 2012a, b, Minoru Watanabe 2012; Hayasaka 2013; Matsuoka 2015). The found increase in research concerned with this topic seems adequate, considering that Japan is a country with one of the largest shadow education sectors worldwide, second only to its neighbor South Korea. However, existing research has seldom focused on the issue of social inequality. The general reluctance to carry out research particularly addressing this issue might be one result of the active political ignorance towards this major education sector. As Dang and Rogers (2008) have shown, four different approaches of policy officials in dealing with shadow education can be identified internationally: prohibition, ignorance, recognition and regulation, or even active encouragement of shadow education. The South Korean government, for example, first tried to prohibit shadow education in the 1980s but failed. In the following, South Korean officials recognized shadow education as a major phenomenon in education and currently actively pursue and develop strategies to counteract the diverse effects of shadow education, particularly through the creation of after-school programs to provide all students with the opportunity to receive private tutoring and thus decrease social inequalities (Dawson 2010: 19). In contrast, even though in Japan the shadow education sector is comparably strong and influential as is the case in South Korea, similar approaches are not found. For the most part, the Japanese government ignored this educational sphere. First press announcements were made in 1999 stating that the *Ministry of Education, Culture, Sports, Science and Technology* (MEXT) was intending to tolerate the major suppliers of shadow education in Japan, the *juku* (Roesgaard 2006: 52). It was not until 2002 that the MEXT invited about 200 representatives of these privately operating, fee-based supplementary schools to discuss the possible educational opportunities that might be provided by *juku* (Dawson 2010: 18). However, whether actual change occurred in the relationship between the formal and informal education sectors in Japan is not clear. Empirical analyses focusing on changes within the *juku*-industry are nonexistent. Even though it seems that there already exist several cooperations and collaborations between regular schools and *juku* (see Dierkes 2009; Kuroishi and Takahashi 2009) and a new state-funded kind of *juku*, the so-called *mirai juku* (future *juku*, Yamato and Zhang 2017), the official view on this industry remains almost unchanged. Due to their status as companies, *juku* are officially not considered as schools, which is why not the MEXT but the *Ministry of Economy, Trade and Industry* (METI) is responsible for watching over the development of the *juku*-industry. However, since the establishment of the independent *Japanese Juku Association* (JJA) in 1988 through the authorization of the METI, government representatives perform an advisory function (Hayasaka 2013). This second schooling system therefore regulates itself and is only subject to market forces. While the regular schooling system stagnates or even shrinks due to the problems connected to the dilemma of the "aging society" Japan, the second schooling system is eager to grow further to ensure its own survival.

   As is the general opinion in international research, in Japan, shadow education is believed to contribute to educational and social inequalities also. In spite of a great variety and much diversity in shadow education supply (see Komiyama 1993, 2000; Roesgaard 2006; Manabu Watanabe 2013), former research missed to analyze whether there are differences in the access to certain kinds of lessons according to family background and how the effects of such investments differ across social strata in Japan. What is even more concerning is the fact that even though some Japanese studies acknowledged that there are three prevalent types of shadow education in Japan in general, academic *juku*, private tutors and correspondence courses (e.g., Konakayama and Matsui 2008), the existing different types of the most frequently used shadow education type, the *juku*, and the access to and outcomes of a participation according to type of *juku* were not analyzed quantitatively in a differentiated way, with only very few exceptions that remain limited in their explanatory power (e.g., Yuki et al. 1987; Mimizuka 2007). Until today, detailed quantitative and qualitative analyses with emphasis on the different functions and thus accessibility and effects of *juku* based on empirical evidence are scarce.

In Japan, the enrolment in supplementary private tutoring and "cram school" classes has become increasingly popular in the course of educational expansion following World War II. Since private schools in the shadow (*juku*) multiplied their numbers during the *juku*-boom in the 1970s (Monbushō 1977), research mainly stressed the importance of these supplementary lessons for the admission to high schools and universities by providing preparatory lessons concerning entrance examinations at the transition from one school level to the next (see, e.g., Komiyama 1993; Bray 2006). As elsewhere, considerable fees are connected to the participation in shadow education in Japan, which resulted in the strong belief that shadow education inevitably contributes to social reproduction and increases educational and thus social inequalities. This view is prevalent in Japan since the 1970s and remains the dominant opinion in the public and the sciences.[2] Based on this assumption, Seiyama (1981) formulated the so-called 'Shadow Education Investment Theory (*gakkōgaikyōiku tōshi kasetsu*, in the following SEIT), which implies that socioeconomically well-off parents are in a position to make greater investments in shadow education, thus gaining competitive advantages for their children's education level. Shadow education is thus seen as further cementing educational and social inequalities. Existing research on the subject generally supports this theory (Kataoka 2001; Konakayama and Matsui 2008; Tomura et al. 2011; Entrich 2014a) with the exception of one of Seiyama's own works (see Seiyama and Noguchi 1984). However, in particular in Japan, out-of-school lessons fill gaps and demands in all fields of education and have already created new demands. The functions of shadow education are thus very distinct as reflected in the numerous types of *juku* (Komiyama 1993, 2000; Roesgaard 2006) and other types of extracurricular education (BERD 2009). Dawson (2010) resumed that the Japanese shadow education system "goes beyond shadowing the formal system and, in effect, holds a mirror up to the formal system which reflects its shortcomings" (p. 17). A detailed comprehensive analysis of the Japanese shadow education sector thus seems promising for our understanding of the modern educational institution in all its facets and social inequality formation in modern or schooled societies. To approach this area in a comprehensive way, however, a strong theoretical groundwork should prove advantageous, as this field remains largely under-theorized until today.

---

[2] Personal conversation with Fumiaki Ojima, October 2012, Kyōto.

1.4   Approaching the Shadow: The *Shadow–Education–Inequality–Impact* (SEII) Frame

To capture the major research dimensions of shadow education and clarify possible universal causes and implications of this excess of the education revolution, a formal theoretical frame is developed, which is henceforth called *Shadow–Education–Inequality–Impact* (SEII) Frame. Specifically addressing the issue of inequalities, the major research dimensions building the basis for this formal frame are identified and brought together in the following.

As illustrated in the above literature review and discussions, any analysis concerning the implications of shadow education regarding social inequality in educational attainment needs to clarify how the *access* to shadow education supply is regulated as well as which *effects* certain shadow education investments actually produce and whether differences in the access and effects are found between students of different social strata. It goes without question that unequal access to informal education fosters educational as well as social inequalities, if students who receive additional lessons gain significant advantages over their peers. Consequently, the effects of investments in additional lessons determine whether differences in the access to such lessons actually contribute to educational inequality. To put it quite simple: only then will social inequality be affected through shadow education investments, if the access is restricted by social origin and the effects for academic achievement and educational positioning are positive and significant. In addition, the concrete conditions and circumstances under which shadow education is received and under which it produces advantages by leading to a higher education level also determine its impact on regular schooling, the competition between students, and the distribution of educational opportunities. The attested persistence of educational inequalities in several countries across the world (e.g., Shavit and Blossfeld 1993; Shavit and Park 2016) needs to be questioned by also considering the shadow education sector when discussing and analyzing educational opportunities in modern societies such as Japan. Unfortunately, this is rarely done.

Furthermore, changes regarding the connection between formal and informal education sectors have to be taken into consideration to clarify whether once existing inequalities persist, have increased, or possibly decreased. Japan experienced what was labeled "PISA shock" (Takayama 2008, 2011; Wiseman 2013), followed by highly diverse debates concerning the state of its education system, putting "education in crisis" (*kyōiku kiki*). Promptly, numerous reforms were implemented giving education a new direction (Jones 2011). Since the late 1990s, Japanese education has entered a state of continuous reformation particularly emphasizing relaxation (*yutori*) and internationalization (*kokusaika*) of education. In result, the Japanese education system has undergone rapid transformations over the last two decades. However, recent research has concentrated on analyzing the effectiveness of these reforms in terms of academic outcomes of students in national and international academic achievement tests, such as PISA. The impact of these vast changes on social inequality formation was not adequately discussed. In particular, the effects

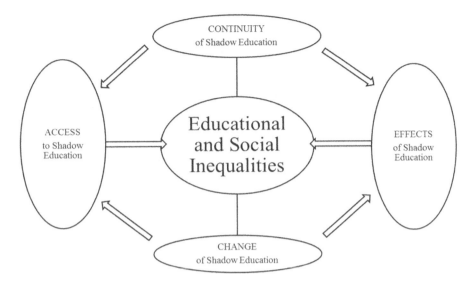

Fig. 1.2 *Shadow–Education–Inequality–Impact* (SEII) Frame: dimensions affecting the implications of shadow education for educational and social inequalities

of vast changes in the regular schooling system on its shadow (and vice versa) are not clear. Previous research avoided to empirically evaluate changes affecting formal education for its impact on the shadow education sector, wherefore new educational inequalities or opportunities might have emerged without notice. Also, it is not clear how shadow education systems such as the Japanese one manage to stay successful despite unfavorable conditions, such as decreasing student populations or educational reforms. It is thus necessary to notice evolving patterns of shadow education and the implications for social inequalities when concentrating on this field of research.

To sum this up, there are four major research dimensions we need to take into consideration to achieve comprehensive findings on the subject so as to clarify whether investments in shadow education inevitably result in inequality or might also contribute to more equality of educational opportunities. As Fig. 1.2 illustrates, both *access* to shadow education (restricted versus open) and *effects* of shadow education (positive versus negative/neutral) might stay stable (*continuity*) or *change* due to certain educational or overall societal developments which affect whether investments are made.

Each variation in the access or effects might affect the outcome for educational inequality or opportunity production. For example, if certain events cause the introduction of more opportunities for disadvantaged social strata to enter the shadow (*change → access*), while effects of such investments remain the same (*continuity → effects*), educational inequality might be reduced if the overall effects of shadow education are generally positive for participants alike. If, in stark contrast, only the access is loosened to attract more students from disadvantaged family backgrounds, while the effects of shadow education investments change into negative outcomes, inequalities might even increase, since students from disadvantaged family backgrounds make investments without increasing their chances of achieving higher educational returns.

Based on the here presented frame, a general approach to the field of shadow education research and its most feared outcome inequality is outlined, which is suited to be applied in numerous settings. Hence, researchers are encouraged to use the introduced SEII Frame for future research on shadow education in different settings. The case study presented in this volume is exemplary for such research and is meant to not only produce new knowledge on the Japanese case but provide a conceptual frame for all concerned with the matter.

1.5   Aim, Organization, and Scope of This Book

In summary, the present work attempts to provide empirical evidence on the implications of *access* to shadow education, its *effects*, the ongoing persistence (*continuity*), and possible *changes* of this market focusing on educational and social inequality and stressing the importance to recognize nation-specific features of shadow education as reflected in the diversity of its supply. The main research question thus reads as follows: does shadow education inherit the potential to function as an instrument to neutralize disadvantaged family background? In this regard, against the background of change in the Japanese world of education, this work primarily focuses on students from disadvantaged family backgrounds and how (if so) they make use of shadow education and by this gain advantages from such investments or not.

This book consists of ten chapters in total, subdivided into this general introduction to the field (Chap. 1), a theoretical part (Chaps. 2, 3 and 4), and an empirical part (Chaps. 5, 6, 7 and 8). Followed by a final conclusive chapter summarizing and discussing the findings of the foregoing chapters (Chap. 9), overall conclusions are drawn. The last chapter provides the reader with an additional excursus into recent changes in Japanese education (Chap. 10), providing much background for the change dimension.

The first chapter following this introduction (Chap. 2) aims to provide a contextual, theoretical frame for the upcoming analyses by addressing the question how the formal and informal Japanese education sectors are connected. The main focus of Chap. 2 lies on the identification of the factors driving the high dependence on shadow education and the possible implications on social inequality formation in contemporary Japan. Chap. 3 then discusses the general theoretical approaches. To clarify whether shadow education in Japan is used by socioeconomically disadvantaged students as an instrument to overcome status-specific differences in educational outcomes, this chapter identifies and outlines adequate theoretical concepts sharing one fundamental similarity: shadow education is understood as an investment resulting from a willful, rational decision of individual actors. Hence, rational choice theories (RCT) build the foundation of my theoretical framework. Before different theoretical angles are applied in each of the four empirical chapters in the upcoming empirical part of the book, Chap. 4 introduces the data basis for my calculations. Besides existing relevant studies related to the field of education in Japan and a vast amount of data drawn from reports by ministerial (e.g., MEXT, METI) and private organizations (e.g., Benesse; OECD), data of the following two surveys will be analyzed in the four empirical chapters: (1) *The Hyōgo High School Students* (HHSS)[3] surveys of the years 1997 and 2011 (Chaps. 5, 6 and 7) and (2) the 2013 *Juku Student and Teacher Survey* (JSTS) (Chap. 8).

In the second part of this book, four independent empirical chapters (Chaps. 5, 6, 7 and 8) are presented. Each of the four empirical chapters is hierarchically structured in the following way: First, the problematic related to shadow education and social inequality formation in Japan is introduced outlining the specific focus and the research question of the chapter. Second, the specific theoretical frame for the following analyses drawing on and expanding or adjusting the theoretical concepts introduced in Chap. 3 is presented, before testable hypotheses are generated. Third, the used variables and methods on which basis the analyses are carried out are outlined, followed by calculations meant to test the before formulated hypotheses. Finally, a discussion of the results of the chapter's calculations is presented. Each of my chapters builds on the Shadow–Education–Inequality–Impact Frame focusing on one of the four major dimensions of shadow education implications (see Fig. 1.2) and can be understood as independent contribution to research on shadow education, concentrating on the Japanese case. In summary, these chapters shall provide us with a throughout and deep understanding on the actual implications of shadow education for educational and social inequality formation. Consequently, each chapter addresses the main research question differently, always concentrating on the possible opportunities shadow education provides for students from disadvantaged family background.

Chapter 5 is concerned with the general *access* to shadow education in present Japan. Here the question who is involved in family decisions for shadow education in Japan and how that affects the perceived formation of educational and social inequalities is addressed. Since earlier research missed to include the agency of the student in such decisions – even though this might strongly impact the outcome of such decisions in terms of the formation of individual educational pathways and thus social inequalities – the theoretical approach presented in this chapter stresses the importance of acknowledging students as actors besides their parents rather than understanding them as simple consumers of (shadow) education. By further focusing on students with disadvantaged family backgrounds, the possibility to overcome status disadvantages as a result of access to shadow education is discussed.

Chapter 6 then focuses on the *effects* of shadow education in present Japan and addresses the question whether and under which conditions shadow education proves beneficial achieving educational goals, particularly for students from disadvantaged family backgrounds. I argue that differences in class-specific educational goals result in the persuasion of distinct educational strategies as visible in the dura-

---

[3] Original title: *Kōkōsei no shinro to seikatsu ni kansuru chōsa* = "A survey concerning the school course and school life of high school students" (see Ojima and Aramaki 2013).

tion, the type, and the purpose of study when investing in shadow education. Thus, students from disadvantageous family backgrounds who have the opportunity to make use of shadow education are likely to gain advantages enabling them to overcome socioeconomic disparities.

Chapter 7 concentrates on the persistence (*continuity*) of the shadow market, addressing the question whether the continuous high dependence on shadow education in Japan is one of the unintended consequences of educational expansion and whether disadvantaged educational strata actually benefit from this development contributing to a decrease in social inequalities. Emphasizing the role of insecurity concerning the worth and reliability of educational credentials for families' choice to make investments in shadow education and pursue entrance to high-ranked schools, changes in the impact of educational decisions for social inequality formation from the 1990s to today are discussed. I argue that the Japanese "insecurity industry" (Dierkes 2013) – the shadow education sector – managed to persist by nourishing itself on increasing insecurities among Japanese families on the one hand and by providing families with effective strategies to achieve a high education level and thus increase students' chances of gaining a high social status on the other.

Chapter 8 further focuses on the possible *change* of the shadow education industry in response to changes that affect education in general. Hence, the question is addressed how Japanese shadow education managed to maintain strong despite unfavorable circumstances since the 1990s and how this affects educational opportunities for disadvantaged educational strata. The Japanese supplementary education market remained successfully in business due to hitherto unknown and unexplored reasons. Since the implications of a high dependence on shadow education for a national system of education regarding educational opportunities and social inequality issues can hardly be overestimated, the ongoing success of the highly institutionalized Japanese shadow education market, the *juku*-industry, is explored in relation to educational changes over the last 20 years, particularly focusing on possible opportunities for students from disadvantageous family backgrounds to gain access to *juku* of different type and organization.

In Chapter 9, the findings and implications of the book are discussed. In addition, I added an excursus about the Japanese education reforms of the last 20 years (Chap. 10). This last chapter provides additional contextual information on changes in Japanese education, outlining the causes and outcomes of the *yutori* (relaxation) education reforms as the major shift in contemporary Japanese education. In particular, the question whether the *yutori* reforms have actually changed Japan's regular schooling system and by this reduced competition for high credentials and thus possibly reduced the demand for shadow education is emphasized. This chapter thus supports the SEII Frame's relational dimensions of continuity and change so as to identify possible evolving patterns of shadow education and its implications.

Finally, it has to be noted that all direct quotations and Japanese words are written in italics (e.g., *juku*), except for proper names (e.g., Dōshisha, Tōkyō). Japanese names are written in the Western way, i.e., with the last name at the end. For all Japanese terms, long vowels are marked with ‾ (e.g., *kōtōgakkō*). All used Japanese terms are listed in a glossary at the end of the book.

Appendix

Table 1.1 Japan's ranking in international large-scale assessment studies

Name and year of study	Age/grade of participants	Number of participating countries	Japan's ranking according to performance field		
			Math	Science	Reading
First international mathematics study (FIMS) 1964	13-year-olds	12	2nd	–	–
	12th grade	12	6th	–	–
First international science study (FISS) 1968–1972	10-year-olds	12	–	1st	–
	14-year-olds	14	–	1st	–
Second international mathematics study (SIMS) 1980–1982	13-year-olds	20	1st	–	–
	12th grade	15	2nd	–	–
Second international science study (SISS) 1983–1984	10-year-olds	19	–	1st	–
	14-year-olds	26	–	2nd	–
Third international mathematics and science study (TIMSS) 1995	4th grade	26	3rd	2nd	–
	8th grade	41	3rd	3rd	–
Trends in international mathematics and science study (TIMSS) 1999	8th grade	38	5th	4th	–
Programme of international student assessment (PISA) 2000	15-year-olds	32	2nd	2nd	9th
Trends in international mathematics and science study (TIMSS) 2003	4th grade	26	3rd	3rd	–
	8th grade	48	5th	6th	–
Programme of international student assessment (PISA) 2003	15-year-olds	40	6th	1st	14th
Programme of international student assessment (PISA) 2006	15-year-olds	57	10th	5th	15th
Trends in international mathematics and science study (TIMSS) 2007	4th grade	35	4th	4th	–
	8th grade	46	5th	3rd	–
Programme of international student assessment (PISA) 2009	15-year-olds	65	9th	5th	8th
Trends in international mathematics and science study (TIMSS) 2011	4th grade	52	5th	4th	–
	8th grade	45	5th	4th	–
Programme of international student assessment (PISA) 2012	15-year-olds	65	7th	4th	4th
Programme of international student assessment (PISA) 2015	15-year-olds	72	5th	2nd	8th
Trends in international mathematics and science study (TIMSS) 2015	4th grade	49/47	5th	3rd	–

References

Akiba, M., LeTendre, G. K., & Scribner, J. P. (2007). Teacher quality, opportunity gap, and national achievement in 46 countries. *Educational Researcher, 36*(7), 369–387.

Aurini, J., Davies, S., & Dierkes, J. (Hrsg.). (2013). *Out of the shadows: The global intensification of supplementary education. International perspectives on education and society.* Bingley: Emerald Publishing.

Baker, D. P. (2014). *The schooled society.* Stanford: Stanford University Press.

Baker, D. P., & LeTendre, G. K. (2005). *National differences, global similarities. World culture and the future of schooling.* Stanford: Stanford University Press.

Baker, D. P., Akiba, M., LeTendre, G. K., & Wiseman, A. W. (2001). Worldwide shadow education: Outside-school learning, institutional quality of schooling, and cross-national mathematics achievement. *Educational Evaluation and Policy Analysis, 23*(1), 1–17.

Becker, R., & Lauterbach, W. (Hrsg.). (2016). *Bildung als Privileg – Erklärungen und Befunde zu den Ursachen der Bildungsungleichheit.* Wiesbaden: VS Springer.

BERD, Benesse Education Research and Development Center. (2009). *Gakkō-gai kyōiku katsudō ni kansuru chōsa 2009 hon hōkoku-sho* [Report on the Survey concerning Out-of-School Educational Activities 2009]. Retrieved from: http://berd.benesse.jp/berd/center/open/report/kyoikuhi/webreport/index.html

Bills, D. B. (2016). Congested credentials: The material and positional economies of schooling. *Research in Social Stratification and Mobility, 43*(1), 65–70.

Bray, M. (1999). *The shadow education system: Private tutoring and its implications for planners.* Paris: UNESCO/International Institute for Educational Planning (IIEP).

Bray, M. (2006). Private supplementary tutoring: Comparative perspectives on patterns and implications. *Compare, 36*(4), 515–530.

Bray, M. (2009). *Confronting the shadow education system: What government policies for what private tutoring?* Paris: UNESCO International Institute for Educational Planning (IIEP).

Bray, M. (2010). Researching shadow education: Methodological challenges and directions. *Asia Pacific Educational Review, 11*, 3–13.

Bray, M. (2011). *The challenge of shadow education: Private tutoring and its implications for policy makers in the European Union.* Retrieved from: http://www.nesse.fr/nesse/activities/reports

Bray, M. (2017). Schooling and its supplements: Changing global patterns and implications for comparative education. *Comparative Education Review, 61*(3), 469–491.

Bray, M., & Kobakhidze, M. N. (2014a). The global spread of shadow education: Supporting or undermining qualities of education? In D. B. Napier (Ed.), *Qualities of education in a globalised world* (pp. 185–200). Rotterdam/Boston/Taipei: Sense Publishers.

Bray, M., & Kobakhidze, M. N. (2014b). Measurement issues in research on shadow education: Challenges and pitfalls encountered in TIMSS and PISA. *Comparative Education Review, 58*(4), 590–620.

Bray, M., & Kwo, O. (2013). Behind the façade of fee-free education: Shadow education and its implications for social justice. *Oxford Review of Education, 39*(4), 480–497.

Bray, M., & Kwo, O. (2014). *Regulating private tutoring for public good. Policy options for supplementary education in Asia.* Hong Kong: Comparative Education Research Center (CERC).

Bray, M., & Lykins, C. (2012). *Shadow education: Private tutoring and its implications for policy makers in Asia.* Comparative Education Research Center (CERC) and Asian Development Bank: Hong Kong.

Bray, M., Mazawi, A. E., & Sultana, R. G. (Hrsg.). (2013). *Private tutoring across the Mediterranean: Power dynamics and implications for learning and equity.* Rotterdam/Boston/Taipei: Sense Publishers.

Bray, M., Kwo, O., & Jokic B. (Hrsg.). (2015). *Researching private supplementary tutoring: Methodological lessons from diverse cultures.* Hong Kong: Springer/Comparative Education Research Center.

Breen, R., Luijkx, R., Müller, W., & Pollak, R. (2009). Nonpersistent inequality in educational attainment: Evidence from eight European countries. *American Journal of Sociology, 114*(5), 1475–1521.

Buchmann, C., Condron, D. J., & Roscigno, V. J. (2010). Shadow education, American style: Test preparation, the SAT and college enrollment. *Social Forces, 89*(2), 435–462.

Byun, S.-y., & Hyunjoon, P. (2012). The academic success of East Asian American Youth: The role of shadow education. *Sociology of Education, 85*(1), 40–60.

Chiavacci, D., & Hommerich, C. (2017a). After the banquet. New inequalities and their perception in Japan since the 1990s. In D. Chiavacci & C. Hommerich (Eds.), *Social inequality in post-growth Japan. Transformation during economic and demographic stagnation* (pp. 3–26). London/New York: Routledge.

Chiavacci, D., & Hommerich, C. (Hrsg.). (2017b). *Social inequality in post-growth Japan. Transformation during economic and demographic stagnation*. London/New York: Routledge.

Craig, J. E. (1981). The expansion of education. *Review of Research in Education, 9*, 151–213.

Dang, H.-A., & Rogers, F. H. (2008). The growing phenomenon of private tutoring: Does it deepen human capital, widen inequalities, or waste resources? *World Bank Research Observer, 23*(2), 161–200.

Davies, S. (2004). School choice by default? Understanding the demand for private tutoring in Canada. *American Journal of Education, 110*(3), 233–255.

Dawson, W. (2010). Private tutoring and mass schooling in East Asia: Reflections of inequality in Japan, South Korea and Cambodia. *Asia Pacific Educational Review, 11*, 14–24.

Dierkes, J. (2008a). Japanese shadow education: The consequences of school choice. In M. Forsey, S. Davies, & G. Walford (Eds.), *The globalisation of school choice?* (pp. 231–248). Oxford: Symposium Books.

Dierkes, J. (2008b). *Single-sex education in the Japanese supplementary education industry*. Paper presented at the Comparative and International Education Society Annual Conference, New York.

Dierkes, J. (2008c). Supplementary education: Global growth, Japan's experience, Canada's future. *Education Canada, 48*(4), 54–58.

Dierkes, J. (2009). Privatschulen und privatwirtschaftliche Zusatzschulen in Japan: Bildungspolitische Lückenbüßer und Marktlücke [Private schools and private-sector supplementary schools: Education political stopgap and gap in the market]. *Zeitschrift für Pädagogik, 55*(5), 732–746.

Dierkes, J. (2010). Teaching in the shadow: Operators of small shadow education institutions in Japan. *Asia Pacific Education Review, 11*(1), 25–35.

Dierkes, J. (2013). The insecurity industry: Supplementary education in Japan. In J. Aurini, S. Davies, & J. Dierkes (Eds.), *Out of the shadows: The global intensification of supplementary education* (International perspectives on education and society, Vol. 22, pp. 3–21). Bingley: Emerald Publishing.

Entrich, S. R. (2014a). Effects of investments in out-of-school education in Germany and Japan. *Contemporary Japan, 26*(1), 71–102.

Entrich, S. R. (2014b). German and Japanese education in the shadow – Do out-of-school lessons really contribute to class reproduction? *IAFOR Journal of Education, 2*(2), 17–53.

Fiala, R., & Lanford, A. G. (1987). Educational ideology and the World Educational Revolution, 1950–1970. *Comparative Education Review, 31*(3), 315–332.

Fujihara, S., & Ishida, H. (2016). The absolute and relative values of education and the inequality of educational opportunity: Trends in access to education in postwar Japan. *Research in Social Stratification and Mobility, 43*(1), 25–39.

Fujita, H. (2010). Whither Japanese schooling? Educational reforms and their impact on ability formation and educational opportunity. In J. A. Gordon, H. Fujita, T. Kariya, & G. K. LeTendre (Eds.), *Challenges to Japanese Education. Economics, Reform, and Human Rights* (pp. 17–53). New York: Teachers College Press.

Hayasaka, M. (2013). Juku no jishu kisei to shitsu hoshō: Shadanhōjin zenkoku gakushū juku kyōkai no setsuritsu katei to torikumi o tegakari to shite [The Self-regulation and Quality Assurance of the Juku: Referring to the Establishment Process of "The Japan Juku Association" and its Performance]. *Gakkō Kyōikugaku Kenkyū Ronshū, 27,* 11–23.

Heyneman, S. P. (2011). Private tutoring and social cohesion. *Peabody Journal of Education, 86,* 183–188.

Hille, A., Katharina Spieß, C., & Staneva, M. (2016). Immer mehr Schülerinnen und Schüler nehmen Nachhilfe [More and more students receive private tutoring]. *DIW-Wochenbericht, 2016*(6), 111–121.

Ireson, J., & Rushforth, K. (2011). Private tutoring at transition points in the English education system: Its nature, extent and purpose. *Research Papers in Education, 26*(1), 1–19.

Iwase, R. (2005). Shingaku juku ni okeru gakushū keiken no kōzō [The organization of learning experiences in a Shingaku Juku]. *Tōkyōdaigaku Daigakuin Kyōikugakukenkyūka Kiyō, 44,* 1111–1118.

Iwase, R. (2006). Shingaku juku ni okeru kodomo no kōi yōtai: Kodomo ni yoru chōsei ronri no keisei to sono sayō [The acting of children in Shingaku Juku: The formation of an arbitration logic by children and its effect]. *Tōkyōdaigaku Daigakuin Kyōiku Kenkyū-ka Nenpō, 8,* 69–78.

Iwase, R. (2007). Gendai nihon ni okeru juku no tenkai: Juku o meguru shakai-teki imi no hensen katei [The development of Juku in modern Japan: The transformation of the social importance of Juku]. *Tōkyōdaigaku Daigakuin Kyōikugakukenkyūka Kiyō, 46,* 121–130.

Iwase, R. (2008). Sōgō juku ni okeru jugyō katei no tokushitsu-teki yōtai to shakai-teki imi: Senku-teki jirei ni miru sōgō-ka to chūgaku juken to no kankei no kōsatsu [The social importance of Sōgō Juku and their specific teaching process aspects: Considering the relationship between middle school entrance exam and the pioneering case of synthetization]. *Tōkyōdaigaku Daigakuin Kyōikugakukenkyūka Kiyō, 48,* 81–91.

Jones, R. S. (2011). *Education reform in Japan* (OECD Economics Department Working Papers 888).

Kandel, I. L. (1933). *Studies in comparative education.* Boston: Houghton Mifflin.

Kariya, T. (2017). Understanding structural changes in inequality in Japanese education. In D. Chiavacci & C. Hommerich (Eds.), *Social Inequality in post-growth Japan. Transformation during economic and demographic stagnation* (pp. 149–165). London/New York: Routledge.

Kataoka, E. (2001). Kyōiku tassei katei ni okeru kazoku no kyōiku senryaku: Bunka shihon kōka to gakkōgai kyōiku tōshi kōka no jendāsa o chūshin ni [Family strategy in educational attainment process in Japan: Effects of cultural capital and investment in extra-school education]. *Kyōikugaku Kenkyū, 68*(3), 259–273.

Kataoka, E. (2015). Gakkōgaikyōiku-hi shishutsu to kodomo no gakuryoku [Expenses for out-of-school education and academic achievement of students]. *Komazawadaigaku Bungakubu Kenkyū Kiyō, 73,* 259–273.

Kikkawa, T. (2006). *Gakureki to Kakusa-Fubyōdō: Seijukusuru Nihongata Gakureki Shakai* [Education and social inequality: Contemporary educational Credentialism in Japan]. Tokyo: Tōkyō Daigaku Shuppankai.

Kim, S., & Lee, J.-H. (2010). Private tutoring and demand for education in South Korea. *Economic Development and Cultural Change, 58*(2), 259–296.

Kita, K. (2006). Gakkōgai kyōiku riyō ni tsuite no nenrei, jendā-betsu no tokusei to kaisōteki yōin [Age, gender specifics and class determinants of out-of-school education utilization]. *Kyōiku Jissen Kenkyū, 14,* 1–7.

Komiyama, H. (1993). *Gakurekishakai to juku – datsu juken kyōsō no susume.*[Credentialist society and Juku –stop the entrance examination competition!]. Tokyo: Shinhyōron.

Komiyama, H. (2000). *Juku: Gakkō surimuka jidai wo maeni* [Juku: Before the Era of Downsizing schools]. Tokyo: Iwanami Shoten.

Konakayama, A., & Matsui, T. (2008). Gakkōgai kyōiku tōshi no gakuryoku ni oyobosu eikyō ni kansuru ikkōsatsu [An empirical study on how extra school education affects academic achievement of Japanese high school students]. *Tōkaidaigaku Seiji Keizaigakubu Kiyō, 40*, 131–158.

Kuroishi, N., & Takahashi, M. (2009). Gakkō kyōiku to juku sangyō no renkei ni tsuite no ichikenkyū: Genjō no bunseki to kongo no tenbō [A study on collaborations between the Cram-school industry and public education: From present circumstances to future proposals]. *Kyōiku Sōgō Kenkyū, 2*, 1–14.

Lee, S., & Shouse, R. C. (2011). Impact of prestige orientation on shadow education in South Korea. *Sociology of Education, 84*(3), 212–224.

LeTendre, G. K. (1996). Constructed aspirations: Decision-making processes in Japanese educational selection. *Sociology of Education, 69*(3), 193–216.

Liu, J., & Bray, M. (2016). Determinants of demand for private supplementary tutoring in China: Findings from a national survey. *Education Economics, 2016*, 1–14.

MacPherson, I., Robertson, S., & Geoffrey, W. (2014). *Education, privatisation and social justice – Case studies from Africa, South Asia and South East Asia*. Oxford: Symposium Books.

Matsuoka, R. (2015). School socioeconomic compositional effect on shadow education participation: Evidence from Japan. *British Journal of Sociology of Education, 36*(2), 270–290.

MEXT, Ministry of Education, Culture, Sports, Science and Technology. (2008). *Kodomo no gakkōgai de no gakushū seikatsu ni kansuru jittai chōsa hōkoku* [National report concerning the out-of-school learning activities of children]. Retrieved from: http://www.mext.go.jp/b_menu/houdou/20/08/08080710.htm

MEXT, Ministry of Education, Culture, Sports, Science and Technology. (2014). *Kodomo no gakushūhi chōsa* [Survey concerning children's learning expenses]. Retrieved from: http://www.mext.go.jp/b_menu/toukei/chousa03/gakushuuhi/kekka/1268105.htm

Meyer, J. W., Ramirez, F. O., Rubinson, R., & Boli-Bennett, J. (1977). The World Educational Revolution, 1950–1970. *Sociology of Education, 50*(4), 242–258.

Mimizuka, H. (2007). Shōgakkō gakuryoku kakusa ni idomu: Dare ga gakuryoku o kakutoku suru no ka [Determinants of children's academic achievements in primary education]. *Kyōiku Shakaigaku Kenkyū, 80*, 23–39.

Monbushō, Ministry of Education. (1977). *Daijin kanbu chōsa tōkei-ka: Zenkoku gakushū juku toi no jittai* [Ministerial Executive Research Statistics: Actual Situation of the National Juku Problem]. Tokyo: Ministry of Education.

Mori, I., & Baker, D. P. (2010). The origin of universal shadow education – What the supplemental education phenomenon tells us about the Postmodern Institution of Education. *Asia Pacific Educational Review, 11*, 36–48.

OECD, Organisation for Economic Co-operation and Development. (2012). *Strong performers and successful reformers in education: Lessons from PISA for Japan*. Retrieved from: https://doi.org/10.1787/9789264118539-en

OECD, Organisation for Economic Co-operation and Development. (2013). *PISA 2012 results: Excellence through equity: Giving every student the chance to succeed (Volume II)*. Retrieved from: https://doi.org/10.1787/9789264201132-en

Ojima, F., & Aramaki, S (Hrsg.). (2013). *Gendai kōkōsei no shinro to seikatsu*. Kyoto: Doshisha University Press.

Okada, A. (2012). *Education policy and equal opportunity in Japan*. New York/Oxford: Berghahn Books.

Park, H., & Lee, Y.-J. (2013). Growing educational inequality in Japan during the 2000s. In G. DeCoker & C. Bjork (Eds.), *Japanese education in an Era of globalization: Culture, politics, and equity* (pp. 131–146). New York: Columbia University Press.

Park, H., Byun, S.-y., & Kim, K.-k. (2011). Parental involvement and students' cognitive outcomes in Korea: Focusing on private tutoring. *Sociology of Education, 84*, 3–22.

Park, H., Buchmann, C., Choi, J., & Merry, J. J. (2016). Learning beyond the school walls: Trends and implications. *Annual Review of Sociology, 42*, 231–252.

Roesgaard, M. H. (2006). *Japanese education and the Cram school business: Functions, challenges and perspectives of the Juku*. Copenhagen: NIAS Press.

Rohlen, T. P. (1980). The Juku Phenomenon: An exploratory essay. *Journal of Japanese Studies*, *6*(2), 207–242.

Russell, N. U. (1997). Lessons from Japanese cram schools. In W. K. Cummings & P. G. Altbach (Eds.), *The challenge of Eastern Asian education: Implications for America* (pp. 153–170). New York: State University Press.

Russell, N. U. (2002). The role of the private sector in determining national standards: How Juku undermine Japanese education authority. In G. DeCoker (Ed.), *National standards and school reform in Japan and the United States* (pp. 158–176). New York: Teachers College Press.

Sato, T. (2000). *Fubyōdō Shakai Nihon* [Inequality Society Japan]. Chūō Koron Shinsha.

Schneider, T. (2005). Nachhilfe als Strategie zur Verwirklichung von Bildungszielen. Eine empirische Untersuchung mit Daten des Sozio-oekonomischen Panels (SOEP) [Private tutoring as a strategy for achieving educational goals. An Empirical Study based on the German Socio-Economic Panel (SOEP)]. *Zeitschrift für Pädagogik, 51*(3), 363–379.

Schümer, Gundel (1999). Mathematikunterricht in Japan: Ein Überblick über den Unterricht in öffentlichen Grund- und Mittelschulen und privaten Ergänzungsschulen [Mathematics education in Japan: An overview of instruction in public elementary and secondary schools and private supplementary schools]. In V. Schubert (Ed.), Lernkultur – Das Beispiel Japan [Learning culture – the example of Japan] (pp. 45–76). Weinheim: Deutscher Studien Verlag.

Seiyama, K. (1981). Gakkōgai kyōiku tōshi no kōka ni kansuru ichikōsatsu [A study of the effects of out-of-school educational investment]. *Hokudai Bungakubu Kiyō, 30*(1), 171–221.

Seiyama, K., & Noguchi, Y. (1984). Kōkō shingaku ni okeru gakkōgai kyōiku tōshi no kōka [The effects of outside of school educational investments at the transition to high school]. *Kyōiku Shakaigaku Kenkyū, 39*, 113–126.

Shavit, Y., & Blossfeld, H.-P. (1993). *Persistent inequality: Changing educational attainment in thirteen countries*. Boulder: Westview Press.

Shavit, Y., & Park, H. (2016). Introduction to the special issue: Education as a positional good. *Research in Social Stratification and Mobility, 43*(1), 1–5.

Silova, I., Budiene, V., & Bray, M. (2006). *Education in a hidden marketplace: Monitoring of private tutoring. Overview and country reports*. Budapest: Education Support Program (ESP) of the Open Society Institute.

Southgate, D. E. (2009). *Determinants of shadow education – A cross-national analysis*. Ohio: Ohio State University.

Stevenson, D. L., & Baker, D. P. (1992). Shadow education and allocation in formal schooling: Transition to University in Japan. *American Journal of Sociology, 97*, 1639–1657.

Stigler, J. W., & Hiebert, J. (1999). *The teaching gap: Best ideas from the world's teacher's for improving education in the classroom*. New York: Free Press.

Stigler, J. W., & Stevenson, H. W. (1991). How Asian teachers polish each lesson to perfection. *American Educator, 15*(1), 12–20.

Tachibanaki, T. (1998). *Nihon no keizai kakusa* [Japan's economic inequality]. Tokyo: Iwanami Shoten.

Takayama, K. (2008). The politics of international league tables: PISA in Japan's achievement crisis debate. *Comparative Education, 44*(4), 387–407.

Takayama, K. (2011). OECD's PISA, media sensationalism, and education reform in Japan. *Asia Pacific Memo* (2011-01-13). Retrieved from: http://www.asiapacificmemo.ca/pisa-media-japan

Tansel, A., & Bircan, F (2004). *Private tutoring expenditures in Turkey* (Turkish Economic Association Discussion Paper 13).

Tobishima, S. (2012a). Gakuryoku no kaisōsa no kakudai to kazoku no kyōiku senryaku: Gakkōgai kyōiku tōshi ni yoru kakusa kakudaisetsu no saikentō [The role of shadow education in the growing inequality in academic achievement]. *Shakaigaku Kenkyū, 91*, 195–214.

Tobishima, S. (2012b). Kōkōsei no gakushū jikan ni taisuru sōki gakkōgai kyōiku tōshi no eikyō [Impact of early outside of school education on learning time of high school students]. *Nenpō Shakaigaku Ronshū, 25*, 144–155.

Tomura, Akihito, Ryōichi Nishimaru & Teruya Oda (2011). Kyōiku tōshi no kitei yōin to kōka: Gakkōgai kyōiku to shiritsu chūgaku shingaku o chūshin ni [Determinants and effects of investments in education: Focusing on out-of-school education and the transition to private middle schools]. In Y. Satō & F. Ojima (Eds.), Gendai no kaisō shakai: Kakusa to tayōsei [Modern class society: Disparity and diversity] (pp. 267–280). Tokyo: University of Tokyo Press.

Treiman, D. J., & Yamaguchi, K. (1993). Trends in Educational Attainment in Japan. In Y. Shavit & H.-P. Blossfeld (Eds.), *Persistent Inequality – Changing Educational Attainment in Thirteen Countries* (pp. 229–249). Boulder/San Francisco/Oxford: Westview Press.

Urabe, M., Ono, A., & Acosta, S. A. (2013). The consequences of changing education policies on social inequality: The case of Japan. In M. Windzio (Ed.), *Integration and inequality in educational institutions* (pp. 153–163). Dordrecht/Heidelberg/New York/London: Springer.

Watanabe, M. (2012). *Gakushū juku ni okeru zatsudan: Jukuchō e no shitsumonshichōsa kara* [Chatting about Academic Juku: Findings from a questionnaire survey of Juku heads]. Paper presented at the 64th Conference of the Japan Society of Educational Sociology, Doshisha University, Kyoto.

Watanabe, M. (2013). *Juku: The stealth force of education and the deterioration of schools in Japan*. North Charleston: CreateSpace Independent Publishing Platform.

Wiseman, A. W. (2013). Policy responses to PISA in comparative perspective. In H.-D. Meyer & A. Benavot (Eds.), *PISA, power, and policy: The emergence of global educational governance* (pp. 303–322). Oxford: Symposium Books.

Yamato, Y. & Zhang, W. (2017). Changing schooling, changing shadow: Shapes and functions of juku in Japan. *Asia Pacific Journal of Education, 37*(3), 329–343.

Yuki, M., Sato, A., & Hashisako, K. (1987). *Gakushū juku – Kodomo, oya, kyōshi wa dō miteiru ka [Academic Juku – How do children, parents, and teachers view them?]*. Tokyo: Gyōsei.

Zeng, K. (1999). *Dragon gate, competitive examinations and their consequences*. London/New York: Cassell.

Zhang, W., & Bray, M. (2017). Micro-neoliberalism in China: public-private interactions at the confluence of mainstream and shadow education. *Journal of Education Policy, 32*(1), 63–81.

Zhang, Y., & Xie, Y. (2016). Family background, private tutoring, and children's educational performance in contemporary China. *Chinese Sociological Review, 48*(1), 64–82.

Part I
Theoretical and Contextual Framework

理論的分析枠組み

Chapter 2
The Setting

The Two Sides of the Japanese Schooling System

*"Doryoku o sureba, nantoka naru
– Everybody can make it, if only
they try hard enough"*

(Former famous postulate behind
Japanese education)

場
面
設
定

Abstract The specific features of any regular schooling system affect whether and in what ways parents and students develop a demand for shadow education. Addressing the question how the formal and informal Japanese education sectors are connected, the main focus of this chapter lies on the identification of the factors driving the high dependence on shadow education and the possible implications of such a dependence for social inequality formation in contemporary Japan. Based on a literature review and secondary analyses drawing primarily on ministerial data, first, the basic structure of the regular schooling system in Japan, its postwar historical developments, and the general role of private schools are outlined. Second, the role of shadow education in contemporary Japan and its possible impact on social inequality formation is evaluated. Based on the author's fieldwork, the following findings are presented:

(1) Shadow education in Japan has to be understood as one major outcome of postwar educational expansion.
(2) The high stratification of the upper secondary and tertiary education levels as caused by the entrance examination system introduced heavy educational competition into Japanese education. This caused families' extraordinarily high demand for private supplementary lessons as a means to achieve competitive advantages in the educational race or simply avoid falling behind.
(3) Gaps in the regular schooling system's provision of education further justify the existence of this vast market.
(4) The participation of most students in such lessons and the diversity of supply imply that shadow education in Japan provides disadvantaged students with numerous educational opportunities.

2.1   Problematic

This chapter aims to provide the reader with a profound understanding of the specifics of Japanese education, its development, and the role shadow education occupies in this system. The above-quoted catchphrase "doryoku o sureba, nantoka naru" stands for the deep-rooted belief that every student has the potential to become a top performer and achieve a high societal position based on merit alone. Thus, students have to study hard while telling themselves *ganbarimasu* ("I can do it!") over and over again. This so-called *ganbari*-ism (effort-ism; see Takeuchi 1997) follows the principles of meritocratic education and equal educational opportunities for all students but does not take into account differences in starting conditions and the varying availability of supplementary educational opportunities between students of different social origin. According to theories of social reproduction (Boudon 1974; Bourdieu and Passeron 1977), educational success strongly depends on socioeconomic as well as cultural origin. However, whether students have equal access to education inside and outside of school clearly affects their chances of achieving high educational credentials and thus has major implications for social inequality formation.

Comparative education researchers stressed that solutions to educational problems remain influenced by a nation's specific view on education (e.g., Baker and LeTendre 2005: xii). Following National Education Development Theories, unique national specifics of education systems determine educational opportunities (Hans 1958; Baker and LeTendre 2005; Lenhardt 2008). As Ramirez and Boli (1987) have argued, the formation of national societies due to economic, political, and cultural developments across the world caused the need of every modern nation to implement mass education into its education system. Consequently, "[t]he nationally rooted state, secularizing earlier religious ideas and institutions, everywhere incorporated mass education as a main enterprise" (Meyer et al. 1992: 129). In contrast, the development of shadow education systems was not predestined. Even though the worldwide growth of shadow education is based on similar causes in most countries, the intensity and functional diversity of a national system of shadow education depend on national specifics (see, e.g., Bray 2009). There is empirical evidence that the specific features of the regular schooling system affect whether and in what dimension parents and students develop a demand for shadow education (Dawson 2010; Park et al. 2011). A common reason for a consideration of supplementary lessons is seen in students' weak performances in school or the shortcomings of the regular schooling system. Either the regular schooling system lacks high-quality teachers and innovative/effective teaching methods, sufficient teaching materials, and overall resources or simply does not prepare students with the expected quality of education: if parents' or students' demands and subjective expectations are not met, additional support outside of school is taken into consideration worldwide (Rohlen 1980: 224, Sato 2005, Roesgaard 2006: 53, Bray and Lykins 2012: 67).

In the case of Japan, private education markets occupy a major role in the education system. To increase its attractiveness and justify its existence, especially the private education sectors are in constant competition with public schools and thus strive to provide alternatives in education. This competition is held in academic as well as ideological terms and not at all limited to the state-recognized private schools but equally strong in institutions in the shadow education sector. As a result, changes in either one of the three domains affect the others as well and therefore shift the balance in favor of one of the competitors (Rohlen 1980: 210). Focusing on the Japanese case, this chapter addresses the question how the formal and informal Japanese education sectors are connected. The main focus of this chapter lies on the identification of the factors driving the high dependence on shadow education and the possible implications on social inequality formation in contemporary Japan. Based on secondary analyses drawing primarily on ministerial data of the Japanese *Ministry of Education, Culture, Sports, Science and Technology* (MEXT), first, the basic structure of the regular schooling system in Japan, its postwar historical developments, and the general role of private schools are outlined. In the following, special emphasis is laid on the specifics of the entrance examination system and the societal context in which education takes place. Second, the role of shadow education in contemporary Japan and its possible impact on social inequality formation is evaluated. Finally, based on the foregoing discussions and the author's fieldwork as carried out from 2012 to 2014, the interdependence of the formal and informal education sectors in Japan is discussed to draw final conclusions.

2.2   Formal Education in Japan: Developments and Specifics

Since shadow education is believed to mimic the regular schooling system (Bray 1999, 2009; Bray and Lykins 2012; Bray et al. 2013), it is of utmost importance to pay attention to the specifics of any national system of education to understand the mechanisms underlying the formation, organization, and expansion of its shadow education system. We have to be aware of the fact that "[a]s the content of mainstream education changes, so does the content of the shadow. And as the mainstream grows, so does the shadow" (Bray and Lykins 2012: x). The reasons for the formation of the Japanese system of supplementary education are hence found in the formation of the regular national education system. Therefore, a short introduction to the development of the modern Japanese education system and its specifics will be given in the following subchapters, before the role shadow education occupies in this system will be discussed.

2.2.1   The Structure of the Japanese Education System

Today, Japan has a single-track comprehensive school system inspired by the US model (Fig. 2.1). Compulsory education ranges from 1st to 9th grade. Japanese students stay at primary school (*shōgakkō*) for 6 years before they have to go on to a middle school (*chūgakkō*). Although high school is not compulsory, after 3 years at middle school, basically every student (about 98%) enters high school (*kōtōgakkō*) for another 3 years (MEXT 2017b). By attending high school regardless of its

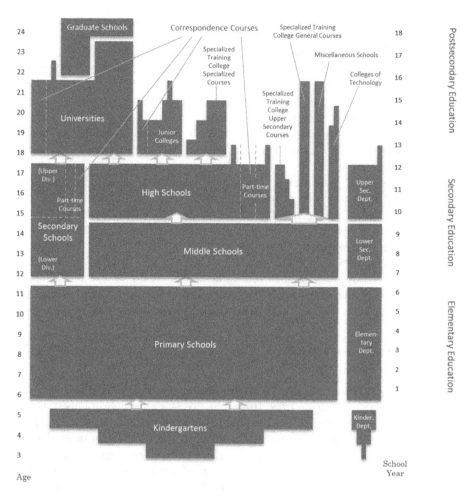

Fig. 2.1 Structure of the formal Japanese education system (MEXT 2007)

designation as vocational (*senmongakko*) or academic course (*futsūka*), every student has the opportunity to access higher education. In addition, early childhood education is provided for children from age 0–5 by childcare centers (*hoikuen*) as well as for children from age 3–5 by kindergartens (*yōchien*) (Jones 2011: 8–9).

Basically, this modern system was established during the second wave of educational reform in Japan during the American occupation (1945–1952) following World War II. In the aftermath of the devastating war, postwar reforms targeted the whole education system with the aim to democratize the Japanese people by "westernizing" the education system according to American standards and ideals of education. In cooperation with Japanese officials, the *Education Division* experts of the occupying forces emphasized the great importance of equal opportunities in education. Based on the pedagogical principles of John Dewey (1925), reformers aimed to prevent that the access to education continues to be determined by "family background, economic status, social position and sex" (Trainor 1980: 337). Due to significant changes achieved during the American occupation of Japan, this fundamental education reform is considered one of the most important education reforms ever carried out, remaining most significant for Japanese education and society.[1]

In summary, the following major changes where achieved during the occupation:

1. The former fundamental moral-ethical guidelines in education as formulated in the *Kyôiku ni kansuru chokugo* (Imperial Rescript on Education) in 1890, which were believed to have laid the foundation for the later militarization of education, were finally abolished, marking a turning point in Japanese education.
2. Instead, the fundamental right on education was established by law (*Kyōiku-Kihon-Hō*), guaranteeing every citizen "equal opportunities to receive education according to their abilities, [which] shall not be subject to discrimination in education on account of race, creed, sex, social status, economic position, or family origin" (Fundamental Law of Education, Article 4-1; in Beauchamp and Vardaman 1994).
3. The introduction of the comprehensive American school system, extending compulsory education to 9 years consisting of 6 years of primary school and 3 years of middle school, followed by another optional 3 years of high school and 4 years of tertiary education (6-3-3-4 system).
4. The reform of the curriculum and course contents with the goal of developing the full personality of a student.
5. The creation of new textbooks.
6. The opening of universities.
7. The merging of the upper and higher vocational schools to create the *New Daigaku* (new university).
8. The long-term reeducation of teachers by transferring teacher training to universities, with the goal to professionalize teacher training (Rosenzweig 1998; Hentschke 2001; Shibata 2005; Krämer 2006; Entrich 2011).

Although the occupying forces succeeded in most of their reform attempts, the Japanese were also successful in implementing the reforms in their own way, making their new education system seem American from the outside (e.g., structure) by keeping it "Japanese" from within. This means that some of the main goals of the American occupying forces were not put into practice or reversed after the occupation had ended as a result of the resistance of Japanese educationalists who were supposed to cooperate with the occupying forces. At the very beginning of all reform measures, most of the above-stated points were recommended by the *US Education Mission to Japan*. However, there were several points, such as the reform of the Japanese Language,[2] which could not be implemented due to the resistance of

---

[1] The first wave of educational reform in Japan took place during the Meiji Restoration (1868–1912) and marked the beginning of a national education system following Western standards.

[2] The complex Japanese writing system consists of three different alphabets: the Hiragana, the Katakana, and the Kanji. Whereas the Kana (Hiragana and Katakana) consisted of 50 characters

Japanese officials and some experts of the *Education Division*, which called it a topic "almost entirely outside the competence of any member of the visiting group" (Trainor 1980: 82). Clearly this reform would have been a major interference into Japanese culture and identity. Another major reform that was actually achieved during the occupation era was the decentralization of the Japanese education system by implementing "boards of education" (*kyōiku iinkai*) following the American model. This reform was also an attempt to weaken the power of the *Ministry of Education* (*Monbushō*). However, during the past occupation years (1952–1960), conservative forces within Japan promoted a revisionist course and reinstated the Ministry of Education as the central organization in education (Entrich 2011).

Consequently, the *Monbushō*, whose administrative responsibility was extended by merging with the *Science and Technology Agency* (*Kagakugijutsuchō*) in 2001 to form the new *Ministry of Education, Culture, Sports, Science and Technology* (MEXT or *Monbukagakushō*), remained the central institution for education steering. Nevertheless, prefectural and local education boards were not abolished and exist until today in each of the 47 prefectures and their municipalities. On the one hand, boards of education function as enforcement agencies of the MEXT. On the other hand, the relatively independent education boards represent the municipalities' view on education against the MEXT and might slow down the implementation of education reforms or directives as brought forth by the MEXT (Von Kopp 2000a: 155–157). Therefore, the Japanese education system is also characterized as "fairly decentralized" (M. Watanabe 2013: 115), even though the MEXT still possesses the central power in all matters concerned with education in Japan.

2.2.2   Postwar Educational Expansion

In the postwar era, the Japanese education system expanded significantly (Fig. 2.2). While all students were enrolled in primary schools since the beginning of the twentieth century, following the end of World War II, practically every student completed 9 years of compulsory education. Since the American occupation, especially the advancement rate to high school and higher education increased continuously. Due to an incredibly fast educational "upgrading" of the Japanese people, the Japanese educational expansion came to be known as "Japanese education miracle" (Arnove and Torres 2007: 5).

In the 1970s, nearly all students (95%) advanced to high school. Whereas in 1955 approximately 10% of all high school graduates enrolled at universities, this

---

each, including all used syllables, the Kanji are actually of Chinese origin, and 3160 of them were deemed obligatory to read continuous texts. The US Education Mission to Japan recommended abolishing all Kanji in order to shorten the learning period to master this language. However, due to the resistance of American and Japanese education experts, it was finally agreed to keep the traditional writing system and only reduce the number of characters to 46 for the Kana and 1850 for the Kanji. The lists for obligatory Kanji which have to be mastered by all Japanese learners are continuously updated by the MEXT and consist of 1945 Kanji today (Entrich 2011: 60–62).

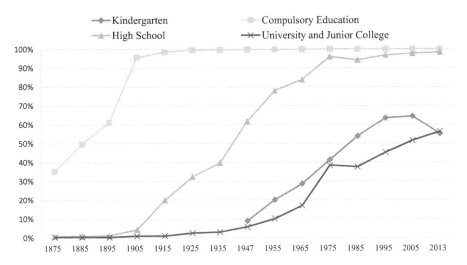

Fig. 2.2 Development of educational enrolment rates in Japan, 1875–2013 (Monbushō 1978: 16; MEXT 2005a, 2017b)

percentage continuously increased reaching its first saturation in the mid-1970s (37–38%). After the Japanese bubble economy collapsed in the late 1980s and the economy faced the greatest depression since the war, students' demand for university access increased dramatically in the early 1990s, initiating the fourth wave of educational expansion. This trend continued until today, where more than 55% of the 18-year-old age cohort enters university or junior colleges.

However, the existing education system faced problems dealing with the rapidly increasing number of high ambitious students in terms of public facilities and teachers. Not only the percentage of students who aimed to enter secondary and tertiary education had risen; the two postwar baby boom generations increased the total number of students dramatically (Fig. 2.3).

Whereas only about 1.2 million high school students were counted in 1948, this number reached five million in 1965, when the first baby boomer generation reached high school level. The second baby boomer generation further increased high school enrolment numbers reaching 5.6 million students in the mid-1980s. In the following, the post-baby boomer phase set in, characterized by a continuously decreasing fertility rate, staying at approximately 1.3 since the 1990s (Schad-Seifert 2006: 5). In the same way, the number of university students increased from 12.000 in 1948 to one million in the mid-1960s and continued to increase continuously, reaching almost 2.9 million in 2010. Hence, although the enrolment rates at the primary, middle, and high school level reached their saturation and thus limited the further expansion of these school types, it is not clear whether the last wave of educational expansion is gradually coming to a halt in the near future. If we include all types of higher education institutions, the enrolment rate of students in higher education already topped 76% in 2005 (MEXT 2007: 10) and is now at a record high of 80% (MEXT 2014c). Whereas high school diplomas have become must-haves for all

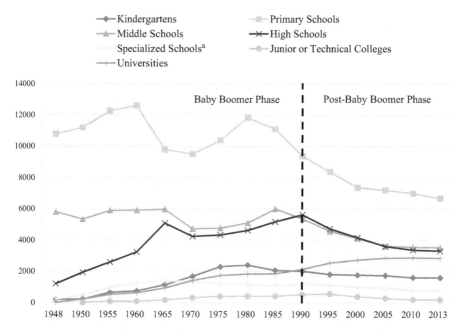

Fig. 2.3 Development of total educational enrolment in Japan, in thousands, 1948–2013 (MEXT 2005a, 2017b). ^aConsists of miscellaneous schools and specialized training colleges. For a detailed description of the presented school types (See MEXT 2017a)

students since the late 1970s, tertiary education has become somehow obligatory for Japanese students as well – not despite but because of the steadily decreasing number of students.

2.2.3   *Extending Compulsory Education for All: The Role of Private Schools*

To respond to the high aspirations of the Japanese people and to also cover the demand for well-trained workers, i.e., increase the pool of human capital, the government tried to decrease the run on universities by establishing 2-year junior colleges (*tanki daigaku*) and 5-year public colleges of technology (*kōtōsenmongakkō*) for middle school graduates, which were concomitant with increasing tuition fees (Haasch 2000a: 135). However, this was by far not enough to get a hold of the situation. State provision of higher education remained insufficient. Consequently, another strategy was pursued. Politicians and Ministry of Education officials attached utmost importance to the field of general education (1st to 9th grade) and left non-compulsory education mostly to market forces. This explains the prevalence of private education suppliers in all education sectors, which are not deemed compulsory. Private schools (*shiritsu gakkō*) have considerably increased in

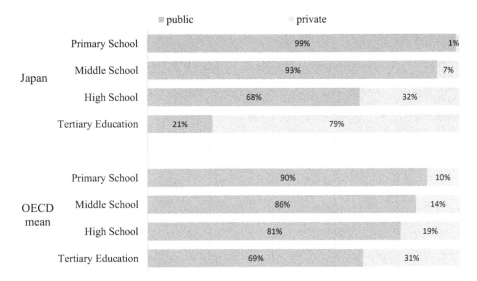

Fig. 2.4 Distribution of students according to public and private education sectors in Japan, in %, 2013 (OECD 2015: 319–320)

numbers since the end of the American Occupation in 1952 – especially in the pre-school, secondary, and tertiary education sectors. As shown in Fig. 2.4, private primary and middle schools are still more of an exception, whereas more than 30% of all high schools are privately run.

In addition, most institutions in higher education are privately organized (79%). In contrast, most OECD countries provide generally more public institutions in non-compulsory sectors and exert stronger influence on these institutions as well. The same is true for preschool education. Although by age 5 nearly all children (98%) are enrolled in kindergartens or childcare centers, a high percentage of these providers are found in the private education sector (kindergartens, 60.7%; childcare centers, 47.8%) (Jones 2011: 8–9).

Of course, there are positive aspects which show that private schools are actually a valuable addition to the public system. On the one hand, private high schools can function as a valuable alternative to public schools, because of a different pedagogical approach or learning climate. On the other hand, in the Japanese context, public schools are generally believed to provide higher teaching quality than private schools. The entrance to private high schools might still provide an advantage for students: private high schools are often affiliated to private universities, which use them to preselect their later students (*fuzoku kōtōgakkō*). This means, students who enter these *fuzoku kōtōgakkō* will have easier access to the affiliated university as well (Haasch 2000c: 168).

However, the possible advantages of choosing a private instead of a public school are overshadowed by the costs families have to pay. According to a recent estimation, public high schools charge approximately ¥118.800[3] as well as an additional

---

[3] In 2014, ¥100 equals approximately US$93 or €0.78.

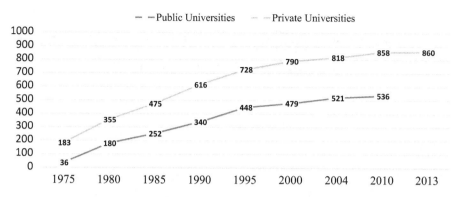

Fig. 2.5 Annual tuition fee for public and private universities in Japan, in 1000 Yen, 1975–2013 (MEXT 2005b, 2010, 2013)

¥5.650 for admission. The more prestigious national high schools charge a higher admission fee of ¥56.400. In contrast, private high schools charge ¥320.000 for tuition and ¥330.000 for admission (Kōkōjuken-Nabi 2014). The same applies for universities. There is a significant difference, though: Whereas most high school graduates (have to) enter private universities, most middle school graduates (70%) still have the opportunity to enter the cheaper public high schools.

As Fig. 2.5 shows, private universities also charge much higher costs compared to public universities. Even though the yearly tuition fees have risen independently of the type of institution, the difference between public and private universities remained. Today, the yearly tuition fee for public universities is approximately ¥536.000, whereas students have to pay about ¥860.000 on average for private universities. Additionally, public and private universities levy about the same fees for admission (about ¥280.000) and for the participation in entrance examinations (about ¥33.000; MEXT 2013).

Although the differences in tuition fees are already significant, tuition fees for private universities vary considerably according to the faculty one is eager to enter. Whereas students in the humanities are charged ¥742.500 on average, Science courses are charged with ¥1.043.000, and for medicine and dental courses the fee is as high as ¥2.765.000 per year. This means, students might have to pay not only higher tuition fees at private universities, they sometimes pay double or even five times the fee they would be charged at public universities (MEXT 2013). Therefore, most students – in particular students from disadvantaged family backgrounds – will try to enter a public university to cut corners financially. However, of the 770 universities in Japan only 86 national and 83 public universities exist, leaving 601 private universities in total (MEXT 2014b). Thus, the application rates for public universities are extraordinarily high.

2.2.4 Allocating Students to Schools: The Entrance Examination System

To sort out university applicants, a central selection instrument was introduced to the Japanese education system very early in its development. With the modernization of the education system according to Western standards during the Meiji Restoration, desirable and privileged positions required a diploma from non-compulsory private and higher middle schools as well as the passing of a special examination. In contrast, university graduates were permitted to enter these prestigious professions without taking this examination (M. Watanabe 2013: 7–9). However, higher schools or universities were almost nonexistent. Tōkyō University, the first national (imperial) Japanese university, was founded in 1877, whereas other imperial universities followed in 1897 (Kyōto University), 1907 (Tōhoku University), and 1910 (Kyūshū University). Private universities were only formally accepted by the government in 1918 (Haasch 2000b: 82–83). Hence, university degrees were highly valued, and thus an entrance examination (*nyūgaku shiken*) system was implemented to sort out applicants according to their academic achievement level. Until today, most universities and their professors view entrance examinations as the "most effective and convenient insurance that students will be of high ability, and hence easier to educate" (Amano and Poole 2005: 693). And since only merit counts in these examinations, theoretically all students are eligible to apply. Nevertheless, the implementation of this allocation instrument led to extreme competition between students in their attempt to enter prestigious universities. Thus, students were put under high pressure, leading to the emergence of what was called "exam hell" (shiken or juken jigoku, e.g., Foster 1973, Rohlen 1980, Stevenson and Baker 1992, Zeng 1999) – a term describing the intense preparation period before gaining entrance to university. Since their establishment, universities provided separate preparation courses or had affiliated preparatory schools where future students could obtain the required university entrance authorization, a sort of access certificate. However, these courses and schools were later converted into basic courses of study and completely incorporated into university faculties (Haasch 2000b: 81–82). At first the universities themselves had to ensure sufficient preparation for their applicants, before this role was shifted to the private education sector following the occupation years. Private preparatory schools, the *yobikō*, emerged and filled the gap between high school graduation and university entrance (see Mamoru Tsukada 1988, Mamoru Tsukada 1991).

Until the 1960s, however, the *shiken jigoku* was limited to a small number of students, whereas this major side-effect of educational expansion became a mass phenomenon in the further postwar era (M. Watanabe 2013: 7–9). It was no longer but a small elite that applied for university. Since the 1970s, a high percentage of high school graduates strived to enter university, whereas today this applies to the majority of students (see Fig. 2.2), making university attendance the most often pursued post-high school educational goal.

Attempts to abolish this system or change the content of the entrance examinations have not been very popular. During the postwar occupation of Japan, the American occupational forces introduced an additional IQ test in order to bring the entrance exams to a new level. However, they failed. The Japanese abolished this test as soon as the occupation ended and concentrated on the assessment of academic achievement only, to measure their students' eligibility for university or high school. Soon after the occupation, universities returned to the ways entrance examinations were held in prewar Japan: Universities simply designed their own entrance exam tests, to make sure students were academically eligible according to the universities' premises. To simplify and rationalize this system, the *Joint First-Stage Achievement Test* (JFSAT or *kyōtsū ichiji*) was introduced in 1979. Even though this new test was only mandatory for national universities, it was a first general approach to "eliminate excessively difficult test-questions, and to eradicate the 'examination hell'" (Zeng 1999: 82). However, the JFSAT did not achieve these goals. Instead, the hierarchical ranking of universities was growing. As a consequence, Prime Minister Nakasone made it one of his premises to reform the entrance examination system during the 1980s. Nakasone also believed that the JFSAT was responsible for the rigidity of the Japanese education system, which prevents students from exploring their own creativity. In the following, the current *National Center Test for University Entrance Examinations* (*daigaku nyūshi sentā shiken*) – the so-called *sentā* ("center") – was implemented and for the first time carried out in 1990 (ibid: 75–83).

The *sentā shiken* is a central achievement test which is held annually at a weekend in the midst of January – about 2 months before high school graduation. During the last decade, every year about half a million applicants took the test (see also Chap. 10, Fig. 10.1). In 2014, 560.673 students applied, from which a total of 532.987 showed up. On the first day, exams in the fields Japanese Language, Geography/History, Civics, and Foreign Languages are held, followed by exams in Mathematics and Science on the second day. Although the designation of this test as being "central" might indicate that all applicants have to take exams in all fields, this is not the case (Table 2.1).

The displayed eight testing fields are further subdivided into no less than 31 subfields. It would prove nearly impossible to take part in all these exams in only 2 days. Also, it proves unnecessary to pass all subsections of the tested fields, since all examinees have to decide on the faculty they are going to enter before taking the entrance examinations. Hence, the chosen major the applicants are eager to study determines to some degree which fields and subsections will become the core area of their individual entrance examination. In general, the *sentā shiken* contains from four to six subjects, with Japanese Language, Mathematics and English annually included and responsible for the greatest share of points (Guest 2006: 1183). Almost every applicant will thus have to prepare for these three fields intensely. In 2014, for example, 94.6% of all examinees were tested in Japanese Language, 75% in Mathematics (1) and 68% in Mathematics (2), with applicants taking either both Mathematics sections or only one of them, and approximately 98% took the test in the English Language sections. Even though the foreign language section is subdivided into the five categories English, German, French, Chinese, and Korean, in

Table 2.1 Participation ratios in the 2014 *sentā shiken*, according to testing fields (DNC 2014a, b)

Testing fields	Japanese language	Geography/ History	Civics	Mathematics (1)	Mathematics (2)	Science	Foreign languages (writing)	Foreign languages (listening)	Total
Subsections to this field	1	6	4	2	5	6	5	1	34
Maximal score points per subsection	200	100	100	100	100	100	200	50	950
Number of examinees	503.750	375.266	205.461	398.626	363.665	389.320	526.286	519.338	532.350
Participation ratio (in %)	94.6	70.5	38.6	74.9	68.3	73.1	98.9	97.6	–

2014 only 891 applicants took the test in one of the four languages besides English. In comparison, 525.217 applicants took the test in English. Following these three main fields, Science (73.1%) and Geography/History (70.5%) are of high relevance, where examinees spread out more evenly across the several subsections. The same can be said for the Civics section, even though this field is less relevant for most applicants; only 38.6% took the test in this section in 2014 (DNC 2014b).

The most interesting difference to the JFSAT is that the *sentā shiken* is not only used by national and public universities, for which it is mandatory; a high proportion of private universities also use this central examination to preselect their later students. However, following this center test, additional independent exams are held one or two weeks after the *sentā shiken* by each university. Only those students can take the second stage examination (*niji shiken*), which have obtained a certain score in the *sentā*. The final decision concerning whether an applicant is eligible to enter a university is made by weighting the results of the *sentā* and the *niji* by mostly 40–60% or 50–50%. Some universities might put more weight on their own assessments though (Wu 1993; Guest 2008). The *niji* is thus some kind of insurance for all universities – the insurance of the academic quality level of future students according to universities' own standards. This makes it hard to profoundly change the national *sentā* exam without the support of the majority of universities. Students always have to prove their academic eligibility – through the *sentā* or the *niji*.

After entrance exams are finished, all third year high school students have to pass their high school graduation exams. To succeed in this examination race, profound preparation is of essence. Consequently, the *kyōiku kyōsō* (educational competition) at the transition to university is one of the main motivators for families to pursue additional support outside of school. There exists a strong connection between the university entrance examination system and the preparation for these exams in and outside of high school. On the one hand, it became custom for universities and high schools to cooperate on these exams. Murphey (2004) reports that "changes needed to be agreed upon 2 years in advance so that high school teachers could be notified in time to prepare their students" (p: 705). In contrast, whereas the MEXT is eager to revise the contents of the *sentā* steadily to meet new educational guidelines, the annual change of the personal composition of the committee in charge of the *niji* exams makes it nearly impossible to implement content changes flexibly (ibid). Thus, for the *niji shiken* only recommendations are made by the MEXT (Guest 2008: 87). Besides teachers of regular schools, who need to be informed about the contents that await their students in the upcoming entrance exams; the operators of shadow education institutions have a great interest in these kinds of information as well. Every change in the *sentā* or *niji shiken* leads to a change in the preparation contents. This means, especially for the shadow education industry it is vital to know about the contents of entrance examinations of universities in advance, to satisfy the demands of students and parents. Thus, cooperations between universities and schools in the shadow are prevalent.

What is often overlooked in the discussion about entrance examinations in Japan is the fact that these examinations are not only found at the transition to university, but at every school transition point. Consequently, students' first experience with the *shiken jigoku* is unlikely to be at the end of high school, but much earlier than that. At the transition points from preschool education to primary school as well as primary school to middle school, entrance exams play but a secondary role, since public schools at the compulsory education level demand no preselection in general. Still, entrance examinations exist even for kindergartens. However, at the compulsory school level, entrance exams have mostly become popular for private middle schools (see Tsuneyoshi 2013). Even though the percentage of elementary school graduates who take the exam has risen since the mid-1980s, due to the still comparably small share of private middle schools as reported above (Fig. 2.4), entrance exams at this transition point remain but a local phenomenon, mostly found in urban areas. Especially for the Tōkyō metropolitan area, comparatively high entrance exam participation rates are reported (1986: 8.5%; 2006: 18%) – in some subdistricts the advancement rate is as high as 30%. Students who take these exams at the end of primary school also strive to avoid taking entrance examinations for high school and – if possible – university entrance by entering private middle schools, which are attached to high schools and often universities as well. These private middle schools have higher tuition fees but enable students to skip another round of examination hell (M. Watanabe 2013: 148–149).

Since only few students have the opportunity to avoid exam hell, most students advance to high school and higher education in the normal fashion: they take the entrance exam in order to get accepted into their school of choice. To achieve this goal, profound preparation and support is necessary. Because of that, students with high ambitions not only try to enter high-ranked universities in the end; they need to enter high-ranked middle and – more importantly – high schools as well. In general, higher-ranked schools have a higher success rate (*gōkakuritsu*), i.e., these schools are believed to provide better teaching quality and exam preparation ensuring that a large percentage of their students get accepted by prestigious universities. Consequently, the transitions to high school and university depend very much on the rank of the attended middle or rather high school (Okada 2012b: 122). The competition for university entrance is thus shifted to the high school entrance level, which was rightfully labeled the "Great Divide" by Tsuneyoshi (2013). At the end of 9th grade, a central exam for all high school applicants is held annually at the same day among all high schools. Just like universities, high schools may have a distinct specialization and several courses which demand a differently composed entrance exam to enter (LeTendre 1996: 198). Hence, every student has to prepare for the chosen school's exam differently. This shows that although the Japanese schooling system is of single-track structure, it is in fact highly stratified – especially at the high school level. Here schools are ranked predominantly by the prestige the schools accumulated according to the percentage of graduates that enter high-ranked universities by passing the difficult entrance examinations (Stevenson and Baker 1992: 1641, Ojima and von Below 2010: 277).

According to Mamoru Tsukada (2010), several types of high schools can be identified, which show significant differences in terms of their dominant curriculum orientation (focusing either on the preparation for university entrance examinations or emphasizing life guidance for the students) as well as the level of educational controlling of students' school life in a democratic or hierarchical way. The ranking of high schools is obvious for all of the involved actors: students, parents, and teachers. According to a high school teacher in Aichi prefecture, "those students who are good at academics, have a high level of interest in cultural activities, have leadership, and have talent in sports all tend to come to High school A" (ibid: 74) – in other words, the highest-ranked high school type. Whatever variable was found to be characteristic, the best measure to rank high schools is actually the academic achievement level of students. In the end, all high schools are ranked according to students' academic performance level. High-ranked high schools are eager to ensure a high academic level of their students and thus keep the difficulty level of their entrance examinations comparably high to assemble only the bright and eager students in their rows. In addition, these schools lay great emphasis on supporting their students with extracurricular courses on school grounds to enhance their students' chances to enter prestigious universities – also ensuring that the school keeps its own reputation high. These mostly urban elite and nonurban traditional high schools often orient towards university entrance preparation and strongly support their students so they will successfully enter high-ranked universities as well. In contrast, other high schools lack these strong support facilities or try to compete with the elite by cutting all nonacademic activities and pressuring their students to learn hard and aim high. The downside to this ranking system is only natural: where top schools exist, also bottom schools are found. At these low-ranked schools, mostly students from low socioeconomic family backgrounds assemble who showed below average grade points during middle school and in the entrance exams. Furthermore, the comparably high number of "problem student"' makes a profound instruction and preparation for university more difficult, and thus dropout rates are sometimes as high as 30%. Vocational high schools and night schools are categorized likewise. A low academic level is prevalent. However, vocational high schools differ in their student composition, since vocational high school students are less often resorting to delinquent behavior and are thus not labeled "problem students." Even though the learning motivation is also low here, the study purpose is different from general academic high schools. Vocational high school students also have the opportunity to access universities after graduation, but their first choice should be to accumulate a number of practical vocational certificates and enter the job market after graduation instead of going to university (ibid). However, it may occur that the "highest ranked nonacademic high schools [...] have a generally higher reputation than the lowest ranked academic high schools" (Fukuzawa and LeTendre 2001: 27).

To sum this up, we have to acknowledge that the high school ranking system in Japan produces a high educational competition for the majority of students. Only students which have no intention of entering tertiary education are somehow spared the examination hell (shiken jigoku), if they give up their hopes very early. These students are but more of an exception in the current system. Quite the contrary is true for more and more students: With the constantly rising percentage of students aiming to enter university, an upward trend is connected. All these students have to join the shiken jigoku, if they do not find ways to avoid taking the exams. Since entrance examinations are meritocratic in nature and promise high returns to education if a student succeeds, the participation in the keen competition for access to the favored schools is generally deemed worth it. An analysis of data from 1950 to 2009 showed that more than 40% of all students ever admitted to Tokyo University came from the top 30 high schools (Tsuneyoshi 2013: 170). Hence, this effort promises high educational returns through admission to top universities. Even though this "entrance examination war" (juken sensō; Rohlen 1980: 220) results in long study hours inside and outside of school, the list of alternatives is short in the Japanese *gakureki shakai* (credentialist society), where educational certificates are viewed essential for obtaining social status (Kikkawa 2006).

In conclusion, it appears safe to say that the school choice at the transition to high school is the most important educational decision made within the educational life course of Japanese students. Entrance examinations are "central to the allocation process" (Stevenson and Baker 1992: 1640), since they are few in number and decisive for the educational career of a student. However, it seems highly debatable whether entrance examinations are actually a healthy component of this system and a suitable instrument to allocate students to schools. The postulated equal distribution of educational opportunities of the Japanese schooling system becomes impeded by the entrance examination system and its major consequence, the ranking of schools and universities. But of course, there are reasons for the long insistence of this system – as well as there are heavy consequences to the produced *kyōiku kyōsō* and its examination hell, as I will discuss in the next section.

2.2.5   The Root of the Educational Competition: Credentialist Society

In summary, two main arguments are brought forth to explain why entrance examinations are viewed essential to the existing system: (1) Students have to be prepared for university as best as possible to be of high academic level and thus easy to educate (Amano and Poole 2005: 693); additionally (2) they have to endure the hardships of learning to also become determined, diligent, and self-sacrificing workers when they leave the education system. Students' suffering caused by intense preparation for exams "is seen not just as necessary evil but […] part of the whole character-building purpose of the learning process" (Aspinall 2005: 201). Only workers who endured hard competition during their educational life course are believed to provide Japan with the human capital to keep its economy competitive. This view is especially strong among industry representatives and government officials, which demand the training of a highly skilled workforce from universities.

Contrary to this belief, critics argue that this system produces too much pressure on children and robs them of their leisure time as the example of the high participation rates in shadow education illustrates. Critics of the university education system can be subdivided into insider, university students and professors, and outsider, parents, media, government, and economy. Whereas students first protested actively against the existing university system in the late 1960s, their protests became passive after the student movement did not show any hoped for results in form of reforms. It was not before the 1980s that universities acknowledged the seriousness of the state of affairs and took a reform course. At that time also professors, mostly of private universities, began to question whether the exam competition should be lessened. In particular since the 1990s, when the declining birth rate caused a steady decline in potential applicants, several university authorities did some rethinking. However, the majority of universities and their professors did not consider the entrance examination system to be easily replaceable (Amano and Poole 2005: 691–698).

The student in his role as an insider critic was mostly concerned with the ills inside the university, whereas outsider critics, especially parents and the media, focused on the competition caused by entrance exams. The root of this competition is, however, the *gakureki shakai* (credentialist society). The term *gakureki shakai* describes the important role education plays in the social consciousness of Japanese citizens. Kikkawa (2006) argued that it is the education level one has achieved and the values and attitudes connected to educational degrees rather than the occupational status which determines the social status in Japan. The Japanese thus became to value educational certificates exceptionally high (Kariya 1995; Kikkawa 2006). The rapid educational expansion in Japan was accompanied by vast economic success on an unknown scale, and thus education was highly rewarded economically (Shimizu 2001: 194). Hence, students who make it into one of the top rank universities increase their chances to get into high societal positions. Ono (2005: 5) reported that 49% of all CEOs of companies listed in the Tōkyō Stock Exchange were graduates from the top five ranking universities in the late 1990s. Similar results were found for other executives, politicians, and high-level bureaucrats. In addition, the possibility to get hired by a major company and thus have a stable job and earn higher wages generally increases with the rank of university one has graduated from. The demand for high educational credentials has thus increased significantly in the postwar era. However, in order to maintain a high academic level of university students, entrance examinations seemed to be the best instrument to sort out "the political and social elite [despite] Japan was a forerunner in adopting equal-opportunity education as the primary determinant of social mobility" (Foster 1973: 16). It is therefore noteworthy that the Japanese entrance examination system was not implemented by the government but by the universities themselves. For a long time, all universities designed their very own entrance exams and continue to do so despite the existence of the *sentā shiken*.

The reason for the implementation of entrance examinations as the central allocation instrument was theoretically explained also. In his classic work *The Diploma Disease*, John Dore (1976) called this kind of rapid educational expansion the "late development effect." According to Dore's conceptualization, in a country that starts modernization comparatively late, educational certificates gain importance on the job market, and greater emphasis will be laid on examinations as an instrument of allocation. This is exactly what happened in Japan. After the Ministry of Education regained its central authority in education after the end of the occupation, an "egalitarian but uniform system" (Amano 1998: 162) was established and thus increased the first and most important variable for the acquirement of educational credentials: opportunity, meaning "availability of schools and parental financial support" (Kariya and Dore 2006: 139). With the equalization of opportunities due to rising incomes, more families became able to afford to let their children participate in non-compulsory education as well, particularly sending them to high school and university. In addition, the "meritocracy score," as Kariya and Dore (2006: 139–140) called it, was also determined by the equalization of aspirations among the population and the conviction and effort to achieve a high academic level (ability), supported by the homogenization of students' home backgrounds and out-of-school learning support. As Rohlen (1983) has put it, educational success of Japanese students "means high average achievement in a range of subjects, distributed with relative equity over students' age population at relatively low public cost" (p. 225).

On the one hand, the blending of equality of opportunities and the prevailing competition caused by the *gakureki shakai* and its entrance examination system led to the incredible success of the Japanese education system by providing the country with a highly trained workforce. On the other hand, the *gakureki shakai* brought forth some major problems Japanese education has to deal with since the 1980s (Amano 1998: 162). The competitive exam culture and its "exam hell" as well as the creativity opposing rigid school system were believed to have brought forth school disorder phenomena such as school violence (*kōnai bōryoku*), bullying (*ijime*), student suicides, child abuse, vandalism, juvenile crimes, school absenteeism or refusal, *gakkyū hōkai* (the breakdown of school class discipline or class disruption), and psychological disorder and were thus believed to put Japanese schools and education in danger by also leading to a decline in academic achievement (Azuma 2002: 14, Fujita 2010: 22, Dierkes 2013: 3), resulting in far-reaching public debates by media and researchers concerning the failing of the public education system (Knipprath 2005: 23). In particular, the high financial burden put on families through the high costs of public and private education (including shadow education) led to additional criticism on the rights and wrongs of this system. Whereas Dore (1976) critiques the entrance exam culture in general, researchers like Rohlen (1983) also highlighted the positive effects such a system has in store for its participants: the chance for every student to actually achieve a high social status by entering a prestigious university on the basis of skills alone. In the following, the role shadow education occupies in the Japanese education system will be outlined, followed by an assessment of the connection between the two sides of Japanese education.

2.3 Japan's Second Schooling System: The Role of Shadow Education

In addition to regular public and private schooling, Japanese students of all ages are extensively involved in out-of-school educational activities. Consequently, Yuki et al. (1987) characterized the Japanese education system as twofold, possessing a dualistic structure (*kyōiku no nijūkōzō*), consisting of (public and private) schools and private supplementary schools, the *juku*. Unfortunately, recent Japanese research failed to investigate the background, purposes, and impacts as well as possible policy implications of this educational sphere in more detail. Until today, there are continuous efforts to avoid recognizing shadow education as a major part of the education system by ministry officials, resulting from its informal character. Even though there are assumed positive effects of shadow education for students, which range from the possible increase in students' academic achievement and educational forthcoming by contributing to human capital development, a high dependence on shadow education within a country is believed to increase educational and thus social inequalities and rob students of their leisure time outside of school (Bray 2009: 14). As a result, the Japanese shadow education system, the *juku*-industry, was ignored by the government until 2002, when the MEXT first invited about 200 *juku*-representatives to discuss the possible educational opportunities that might be provided by *juku* with the introduction of the 5-day school week (Asahi Shinbun 2002, in Dawson 2010: 18). First press announcements were made in 1999 stating that the MEXT was intending to tolerate *juku* (Roesgaard 2006: 52), but not much has changed since then. In this subchapter, I will first give a differentiated definition of shadow education in Japan, before literature and data regarding the history and scale of shadow education in Japan are reviewed.

2.3.1   *Extracurricular Activities in Japan: More than a Stopgap*

Even though supplementary education in Japan was attested an education-political stopgap function (Dierkes 2009), education outside of school is a broad and highly diverse field with numerous functions. In general, education outside regular school classes can be characterized as academic and nonacademic and either organized in a professional or nonprofessional way (Fig. 2.6). This classification applies to out-of-school education in any setting, not just the Japanese one.

Besides education that is not related to school nor professionally organized, there are other fields which might aim at supporting academic achievement of students but are not given by professional, meaning somehow qualified teachers charging tuition fees. This kind of education is most natural, since support such as help with homework is given by parents, family, friends, or acquaintances – people in a student's social environment. Also, professionally organized education in the nonacademic field is used and generally paid. This very diverse field of out-of-school education includes all sorts of sports and arts lessons and is entitled as *naraigoto* ("things concerned with learning"). *Naraigoto* are afternoon activities often organized in clubs (*bukatsudō*) directly taking place on school grounds. Many students come together to build teams and train with each other in sports such as baseball or soccer. Other students explore their musical and artistic skills in singing and dancing classes or take piano lessons. Also, classes are popular where students learn to

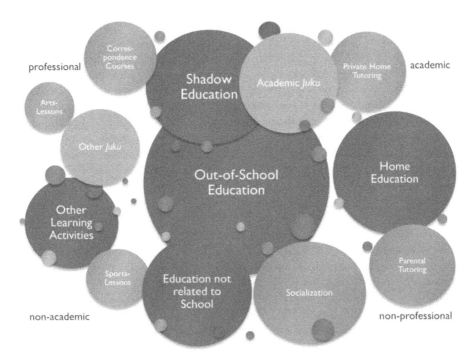

Fig. 2.6 Dimensions of out-of-school education in Japan

use the Japanese abacus (*soroban*), train calligraphy, or are instructed in martial arts (*budō*) (see Von Kopp 2000b: 180, MEXT 2008: 15).

However, all of these activities are also found at private schools, the *juku*. Whereas these *juku* are nonacademic in nature, the term *juku* is mostly associated with the academic types of these schools, the *gakushū juku*. *Gakushū* is a wider term that describes all kinds of learning activities and is therefore not bound to academic subjects in school; whereas the term *juku* was originally used to describe a private school or academy established in the Tokugawa era (1603–1868) providing all kinds of learning courses, sometimes offering courses in basic skills but also highly specialized knowledge. These approximately 1500 *shijuku* (private *juku*) sometimes only consisted of 5–10 students but could also count more than 1000 students. Major *shijuku* often accumulated a high level of prestige competing with governmental schools (Harms 1997: 27, 30). Modern research mostly failed to find a suitable definition of *juku*. These institutions are generally only mentioned but not clearly defined. It is necessary to differentiate between two major types of *juku*: academic *juku* (*gakushū juku*) and nonacademic *juku*. In previous research and public discussions, a suitable translation for *gakushū juku* is missing. These schools are often simply referred to as "cram schools" (Russell 1997, Kwok 2004, Sato 2005, Roesgaard 2006, R. Watanabe 2007). To be precise, academic *juku* provide classes which are related to academic subject contents and charge tuition fees. These schools offer private one-on-one tutoring, enrichment, as well as remedial classes or the preparation for tests and (entrance) exams. The variety of supply ranges from simple help with homework to courses that let students expand their knowledge beyond their peers' education level (Komiyama 1993: 82–87, Roesgaard 2006: 17, Dierkes 2010: 26–27). Consequently, academic *juku* are much more than cram schools; there are numerous types with different functions (for a detailed typology of *juku*, see Chap. 8). Nonacademic *juku* are also liable to costs but related to school subjects in arts, sports, or other nonacademic fields (i.e., *naraigoto*). Even though it is only natural that academic lessons outside of school are found in the nonprofessional field as well, in general school subject-related lessons are professionally organized, meaning they are privately financed and used with the aim to supplement school education. Thus, this kind of education is concurrent with our definition of shadow education (see Chap. 1, following Bray 2009, 2010).

Particularly in Japan, the investment in out-of-school classes at *juku* has become a regular feature in students' school life. Taking classes at these private supplementary schools has become very popular among students ever since the great *juku*-boom in the 1970s (Rohlen 1980). A survey conducted by the Ministry of Education (*Monbushō*) found that more than 60% of the evaluated 1000 *juku* were founded within 10 years, from 1966 to 1976 (Fig. 2.7). Whereas *juku* were almost nonexistent before the occupation years, in 1976 Ministry of Education officials further estimated that the whole market consists of approximately 22.000 schools already (Monbushō 1977: 46). This *juku*-boom continued until the dawn of the millennium, when the number of *juku* had reached its saturation with approximately 50.000 separate schools (BERD 2007: 2). Over the last 15 years or so, no further increase of this market in terms of total number of schools was reported. But also no decrease is visible.

This drastic increase of *juku*-lesson utilization in postwar Japan consumed more and more effort and time and is believed to have led to an increasing number of students who were not able to cope with the demands. This educational overstraining of students was viewed as the main cause for the concurrently emerging school disorder problems in the 1970s, leading to massive debates and the introduction of the so-called *yutori kyōiku* (no-pressure education) reforms beginning in 1977 (see Chap. 10). In response to the "examination competition problem" (*juken kyōsō no mondai*), which was recognized as producing heavy cramming on a societal level (Roesgaard 2006: 2–3), this third wave of Japanese educational reform was launched to decrease the prevalent intense competition between students, lessen the pressure on students, and give them "more time to explore their own interests" (Okada 2012a:

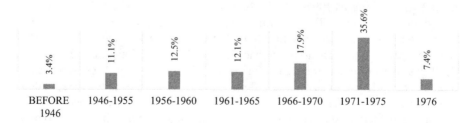

Fig. 2.7 The establishment of *juku* until 1976, in % (Monbushō 1977: 46)

139). In the same year, the Ministry of Education publicized its first national report on the "*juku*-problem" (Monbushō 1977).

The establishment and steady expansion of the Japanese *juku*-industry is one of the unintended consequences of the rapid educational expansion. These private schools were an answer to the extraordinary high increase of educational aspirations of the Japanese population after World War II. With the end of the American occupation in 1952, educational credentials were ascribed major importance, and thus the enrolment rate in high school exceeded 90% as early as the 1970s. High school became quasi-compulsory, leading to the *kyōiku no kanetsu* – overheating of education. In particular, private middle and high schools tried to place more and more students into prestigious high schools or universities by expanding their course contents and increasing the speed of learning, leading to what was called *shinkansen kyōiku* – education going as fast as the bullet train *shinkansen* (Haasch 2000d: 195, Dierkes 2010: 26). To keep up in school, students were in need of supplementary education. Instead of the Japanese government, which did not meet the educational needs of worried parents, private operators offered educational support (Haasch 1979: 43–46, Drinck 2002: 263). As I will discuss in Chap. 8, in spite of several attempts to reduce educational competition (see Chap. 10) and continuously decreasing student populations, which were believed to make shadow education in Japan superfluous (Okada 2012a: 145), the Japanese shadow education system has not considerably shrank since it has reached its peak in the 1990s but remains remarkably successful.

As Fig. 2.8 reveals, today there are even more *juku* (almost 50.000) in Japan than regular schools combined. The number of employees (280.477) is also comparable to the number of all teachers at middle or high schools. Even though the total number of *juku* might slowly decline, the industry is still expanding.

According to a recent estimation by the Yano Research Institute, the whole Japanese supplementary education industry[4] generated about ¥2.5 trillion (approximately US$20.3 billion) in 2015. Even though the overall yearly income of this

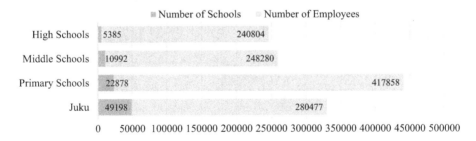

Fig. 2.8 Number of institutions and teachers in Japan, *juku* and regular schools (BERD 2007: 2)

---

[4] The Japanese supplementary education market consists of the following education businesses: (1) *juku*-industry, consisting of academic *juku* and university entrance exam preparatory schools, the *yobikō*, (2) language schools (mostly for English), (3) e-learning market, (4) correspondence courses and learning materials, and (5) further/advanced education or training (Yano Research Institute 2016).

industry decreased slightly in the 2000 years, a further increase can be seen since 2009 (Yano Research Institute 2010, 2016). Of this market, the biggest share of approximately ¥957 billion (approximately US$7.8 billion) is held by *gakushū juku* (including *yobikō* schools), showing a constant yearly market growth of 2%. However, the shadow education sector niche with the biggest yearly market growth is the language school sector (particularly English language schools). In 2015, this niche acquired more than ¥310 billion, a possible outcome of the Abe government's stronger internationalization policy in education (see Chap. 10). This field has even become more important than the correspondence education market, which has decreased in revenues since 2012, but was still accounting for ¥218 billion in 2015. Another market that has gained importance over the last years is the corporate business training service market. With the crumbling of perspectives on the job market, not only educational credentials have become more important, and thus university enrolments have increased; university students who are engaged in *shūkatsu* (job hunting), usually in their last year of university, increasingly enroll in special training schools, which support them in their struggle to find a suitable job. Hence, this market shows constant growth over the last years, forming the second largest supplementary education business market in Japan after the *juku*-industry with annual revenues of ¥497 billion in 2015. However, since this type of education is not school subject related or solely academic in nature, it lies outside the purview of this study. Another sector showing incredible high growth rates is the e-learning market. This market supposedly reached ¥177 billion in 2016.

Besides lessons taking place at *juku*, lessons given by private home tutors (*katei kyōshi*) are another very well-known and possibly the most traditional shadow education type. Private tutors are generally teaching on a one-to-one basis in the home of a student. In addition, correspondence courses (*tsūshin tensaku*), which were not existent before the 1990s, wherefore they were not mentioned in earlier studies and reports (e.g., Kondō et al. 1963; Monbushō 1977; Rohlen 1980), have also become one of the most popular shadow education types in Japan since the 1990s. These courses are provided by big companies, which either send students study material and exam sheets or provide students with online tutorials at home in exchange for fees. Students thus have to study by themselves. To evaluate their learning progress, students can send their exam sheets back to their providers and receive an evaluation. According to a national representative study carried out by the MEXT in 2007, in present Japan, the majority of students are involved in these three types of shadow education and the nonacademic *naraigoto* during compulsory school (see MEXT 2008).

Figure 2.9 shows the enrolment ratios of students in out-of-school education from 1st to 9th grade in 2007. Unfortunately, MEXT officials only considered students enrolled in compulsory education and excluded students at the preschool, high school, and tertiary education levels. However, within these 9 years of compulsory education, one trend is outstanding: With the increased enrolment in academic *juku*, the participation in *naraigoto* steadily decreases. Students shift their focus from activities which they chose based on their own ambitions and interests to lessons which are believed to provide them with the skills they need to be prepared for their future educational life course. While in primary school at least two thirds of all students participate in *naraigoto*, this percentage decreases drastically following the

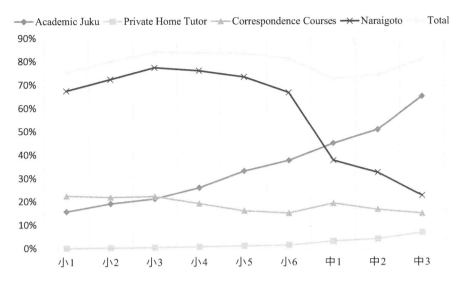

Fig. 2.9 Enrolment in out-of-school education in Japan, according to grade, in %, 2007 (MEXT 2008: 6–7). Abbreviations: 小=primary school grade; 中=middle school grade

enrolment in middle school. In 9th grade only about 23% of students are still engaged in *naraigoto*. In contrast, 65% take classes at *juku* in the last grade of middle school. Alongside, some students receive tuition from private tutors or in the form of correspondence courses. While correspondence courses are generally used more often in earlier grades, they remain on a relatively stable level and are lowest in 9th grade (15%).

Correspondence courses became popular in the early 1990s and recorded continuously increasing average enrolment rates for primary (1993, 11.7%; 2007, 19.5%) and middle school students (1993, 11.8%; 2007, 17.1%). These courses are often used as an alternative to *juku*-classes or private tutoring, which resulted in a small decrease in the enrolment rates at *juku* since the 1990s. Whereas in 1976 on average only 12% of all primary and 38% of all middle school students were enrolled at *juku*, this percentage increased to an average 23.6% for primary and 59.9% for middle schools in 1993. Data of the year 2007 show that on average even more primary school students attended *juku* (25.9%), whereas the enrolment ratio of middle school students (53.5%) decreased. In contrast to correspondence courses and *juku*-classes, the average enrolment in *naraigoto* in primary school (1985: 70.7%; 2007: 72.5%) and middle school (1985: 27.4%; 2007: 31.2%) as well as the traditional private tutoring (primary school: ~1%; middle school: ~5%) remained more or less stable (see Appendix, Fig. 2.18).

Private tutoring received at home on a one-to-one basis is still the least frequently used shadow education type in Japan (up to a maximum of 7% in 9th grade). This might be due to the high costs associated with this particular type of supplementary lessons. However, as Fig. 2.10 reveals, the average monthly expenses for private tutors and *juku*-classes are comparably high and range from approximately ¥12.000 to ¥13.000 on average per month during the first 3 years of primary school. During

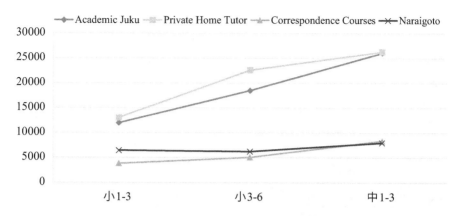

Fig. 2.10 Monthly expenses for out-of-school educational activities in Japan, according to grade, in Yen, 2007 (MEXT 2008: 6–7). Abbreviations: 小=primary school grade; 中=middle school grade

middle school, these expenses double to an average ¥26.000 yen. In contrast, expenses for *naraigoto* are comparatively low, and so are expenses for correspondence courses. Hence, correspondence courses seem to provide a comparably cheap alternative to *juku* and private home tutors. The trend of increasing expenses for shadow education continues in high school as well. According to a recent estimation, the average expenditure for high school students' out-of-school education varies between ¥132.000 (public school students) to ¥176.000 (private school students) on average per year (Kōkōjuken-Nabi 2014).

These expenses alone might not seem extraordinary high. However, it becomes clear how willingly Japanese parents pay high amounts of money for their children's education when taking a look at students' total educational expenses during high school. If we consider all tuition fees parents have to pay for their students' education, the amount of expenses is considerably higher: In total, students at public high schools pay approximately ¥580.000 (corresponding to US$5730) per annum, including the fee for tuition (¥118.800) and admission (¥5.650) of their high school; other expenses in their daily school life (¥325.000), such as school uniforms, learning materials, excursions, etc.; and additional out-of-school education (¥132.000). In comparison, for students at private high schools, these costs are already doubled: ¥1.177.000 (corresponding to US$11.625) are paid each year, including the yearly tuition (¥320.800) and admission fees (¥330.000), additional expenses (¥450.000), and approximately ¥176.000 for shadow education and *naraigoto*. In addition, parents are expected to donate an additional ¥100.000 to private high schools (Kōkōjuken-Nabi 2014). Even though the monthly costs for out-of-school education at the high school level seem smaller compared to the average expenses during middle school, we have to acknowledge that the proportion of students who continue to pursue shadow education during high school is much smaller, not least due to the increased costs for such lessons. Only those families will generally continue their investments, who aim to let their child enter university, particularly if they aim for prestigious universities. These families will mostly resort to *yobikō*, university entrance exam preparatory schools, which generally charge the highest tuition fees. Hence, the expenses for shadow education during high school are actually much higher compared to middle school expenses (see also Chap. 8).

Clearly, the financial burden on families is significant. According to MEXT data, since the end of the 1990s, the annual expenses for *juku*-classes have even increased for middle and high school students. In general, families whose children attend private schools have higher expenses than those families with children in the public sector. In particular, parents of children attending private high schools seem to accept much higher costs on average (2012: private, ¥333.000; public, ¥249.000; see Appendix, Fig. 2.19). Parents' willingness to pay these tuition fees seems exaggerated from a Western point of view. However, Japanese parents have a different consciousness regarding educational expenses. It is only natural to pay for these services and to take advantage of the possibilities the private education sectors provide. In the *gakureki shakai*, educational credentials are all that counts. Consequently, parents' insecurity concerning the unforeseeable future of their children results in additional investments in education besides the regular schooling systems' provision. A well-developed shadow education system reflects the shortcomings of the regular education system which it shadows. An education course laying more emphasis on relaxation (as introduced through the *yutori* reforms in the late 1990s, see Chap. 10) is more likely to increase the investment in shadow education because of parents' fear that their children will be unable to enter prestigious schools due to a lack of preparation. Secondly, Japan is a low-tax country. Families pay much lower taxes than families in countries such as Germany, where the taxes are very high and used to keep the education system free from tuition. In addition, in Germany, private schools are virtually nonexistent. In this regard, the general high expenses for education in Japan seem natural. Nevertheless, the high expenses for shadow education somewhat contradict the principle of equality of educational opportunities, if some students gain considerable advantages from investments in shadow education and others do not. Consequently, in Japanese educational and sociological research, shadow education is generally viewed as contributing to social reproduction or even as a factor that increases existing educational and social inequalities (Seiyama 1981; Seiyama and Noguchi 1984; Kataoka 2001; Konakayama and Matsui 2008). In general, the Japanese regular schooling system should be able to provide its students with everything they need to survive in the *kyōiku kyōsō*. But this seems not to be the case. The shadow education sector has become somehow indispensable to ensure sufficient education according to the needs of the students (and parents).

2.3.2   Families' Reasons to Enter the Shadow

The operators of this supplementary school system lure students with the promise for better pedagogical concepts that give parents a way out of an educational misery – successfully as it seems (Dierkes 2010: 25). But what do these schools provide exactly? To understand what makes this industry attractive for the majority of families in Japan, in the following, I will examine this industry's range of supply to get

an understanding about the niches shadow education occupies in the present system
and where it possibly closed gaps of regular schooling.

Besides supply in nonacademic fields (*naraigoto*), the supplementary education
system provides students with assistance in the five core academic subject areas
(Japanese, Mathematics, Social Studies, Science, and English). Figure 2.11 illustrates the distribution of *jukusei* (students enrolled at *juku*) according to subject
area.

Compulsory school students of different grades have different needs and demand
support in different academic subjects. One trend is visible for all three major types
of shadow education in Japan: Most students take lessons in more than one subject
area. However, independent of their grade, most students who pursue shadow education seem to be in need of constant support in Mathematics, wherefore enrolment
rates at *juku* in this subject ranges from 66.3% (1st grade) to 90.8% (9th grade),
from 61.4% (early grades) to 83.6% (9th grade) for private tutors, and 98.3% (early
grades) to 92.8% (9th grade) for correspondence courses (see Appendix, Fig. 2.20).
Recalling the general enrolment rates of Japanese students in the different types of
shadow education (see Fig. 2.9), these data show that more than every second middle school student demand additional instruction in Mathematics. The second most
demanded subject is Japanese Language, which is used by most of the enrolled
students during primary school (*juku*, ~61%; private tutor, ~54%; correspondence
courses, ~97%) and middle school as well (*juku*, ~49%; private tutor, ~39%; correspondence courses, ~ 91%).

However, during middle school, most of the students pursuing shadow education
lay greater emphasis on additional instruction in English Language (*juku*, ~88%;
private tutor, ~76%; correspondence courses, 90%). Here almost every *jukusei* is
enrolled in English Language classes. Even though English has not been compulsory in primary school grades before the school curriculum revision in 2008 (see
Chap. 10, Table 10.1), there are a considerable number of shadow education students taking classes in English Language from 1st to 6th grade, too (*juku*, up to

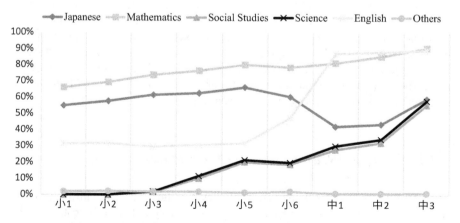

Fig. 2.11 Participation in *juku*-lessons, according to grade and subject, in %, 2007 (MEXT 2008:
12). Abbreviations: 小=primary school grade; 中=middle school grade

47.7% in 6th grade; private tutor, ~22%; correspondence courses, up to 18% in the last years of primary school).

In addition, the subjects Science and Social Studies are chosen by an increasing number of students during the second half of primary school. Whereas approximately 20% of 5th to 6th grade students enrolled at *juku* or receiving lessons by a private tutor choose Social Studies or Science, this percentage is much higher for students using correspondence courses (73%). The same applies to middle school students enrolled in supplementary lessons focusing on Social Studies (*juku*, up to 55.7% in 9th grade; private tutor, ~35%; correspondence courses, ~86%) and Science (*juku*, up to 58.2% in 9th grade; private tutor, ~39%; correspondence courses, ~86%). Hence, students enrolled at *juku* or receiving lessons by a private tutor mostly concentrate on the subjects Mathematics, Japanese, and English, whereas correspondence courses are used nearly equally frequently for all five core subjects. In conclusion, students are generally preparing for more than only one subject. Especially before the transition to high school, more students study several subjects at once in the shadow education sector. The demand for instruction in the five core subjects rises before the transition to high school indicating an increasing demand for exam preparation at the end of middle school. However, the actual attractiveness of this industry's services is best understood by taking a look at parents' and students' reasons for an enrolment in *juku*-classes, as I will describe in the following.

The reasons to attend *juku*-classes differ considerably between parents and students. Even though there are a lot of reasons to not send children to *juku*, most parents cannot avoid enrolling their children at these schools for several reasons. Parents who will not send their children to *juku* might argue that studying at school is sufficient, that the tuition fees for *juku* are too much a burden for the family, and that their children need leisure time besides school and for club and community activities (*bukatsudō* and *chiiki katsudō*) (MEXT 2008: 48). However, as shown in Fig. 2.12, parents sending their children to *juku* often do so because they themselves are unable to look after their children's learning progress outside of school (up to 31% when child is in 9th grade) or because the child is not studying when alone (up to 33% when child is in 9th grade). In addition, parents are particularly concerned about regular schools' instruction quality and stated they are sending their children to *juku* because they cannot keep up with the pace in regular school classes (up to 24% when child is in 9th grade). This indicates a need for remedial teaching. A general trend is also visible: When students enter higher grades, parents' concerns regarding school education increases. In 9th grade, prior to the child's transition to high school, these concerns reach their maximum. However, "only" about one third of all parents who send their 9th grade children to *juku* stated that they think school lessons are not sufficient enough to prepare their children for the upcoming entrance exams. At the end of middle school, several other reasons become almost equally important, particularly individual (19%) or remedial support (24%), parents' inability to look after their children (31%), or their child's perceived inability to study alone (33%). Also, the *juku* is viewed as a valuable provider of information, which is believed to be essential to succeed in entrance examinations and make the right school choices (26%). The described high stratification of the higher secondary and

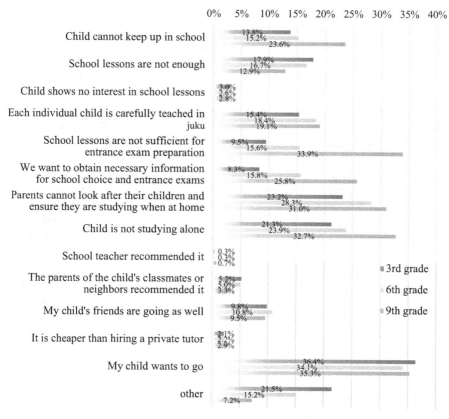

Fig. 2.12 Parents' reasons to send their children to *juku*, according to grade, in %, 2007 (MEXT 2008: 44)

tertiary education levels in Japan is actually best illustrated by taking a look at so-called distribution tables. Based on former entrance exam applicants' results in mock examinations (*mogi shiken*) carried out extensively at schools in the shadow education sector, high schools and universities are categorized according to mock examination or Z-scores (*hensachi*). Distribution tables show the needed mock examination score to pass the entrance examination of a certain high school or university and provide families with the possible range of schools or universities where the student would be eligible to apply (LeTendre 1996: 202, Takeuchi 1997: 185, M. Watanabe 2013: 51–65). For example, in 2014, the ranking of universities based on *hensachi* ranged from 50 to 74 average score points (Daigaku Juken 2014). According to data of one of the biggest operating companies in the Japanese shadow education industry, *Kawaijuku*, a ranking list of the top 30 universities was created using four components: "research funding, citations of research publications, entrance exam difficulty, and a reputation survey" (Ward 2003). Information on the difficulty level of a university's entrance exam is of major importance to families and thus one major predictor for entering the shadow education market. Besides entrance exam preparation and gaining information on school transition (in total

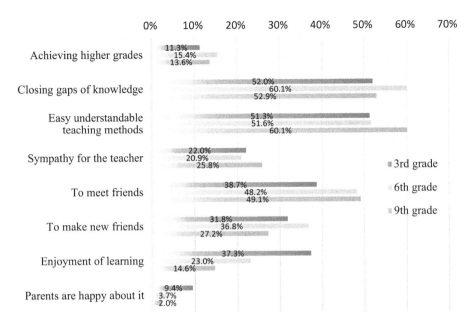

Fig. 2.13 Students' motives to attend of *juku*, according to grade, in %, 2007 (MEXT 2008: 34)

60% in 9th grade), the willingness of the child to attend a *juku* is another very important factor pushing families to consider shadow education investments. Therefore, we have to consider that students are equally important parties in the decision-making process concerning the enrolment in such lessons, as I will further discuss and empirically test in Chap. 5.

As illustrated in Fig. 2.13, students' motives to attend a *juku* are often more personal. Just a mere 11% to 15% of Japanese students attend additional classes at *juku* to achieve higher grades in school. Whereas remedial lessons seem to play but a minor role in this system, in low-intensity shadow education nations in Northern and Western European countries (e.g., Germany, United Kingdom) or North America (e.g., Canada, United States), remediation is still the major reason to invest in shadow education (e.g., Baker et al. 2001; Southgate 2009; Entrich 2014). In a German survey, more than 90% of parents and students were found to use shadow education as a means to improve the students' grades in school, for example (Jürgens and Dieckmann 2007). With higher age, fewer students join *juku*-classes because they actually like to study. However, the two main reasons of students to attend *juku* are the need to close gaps of knowledge, on the one hand, and to receive easy understandable lessons (by teachers they like) on the other hand. This clearly points to shortcomings of the regular schooling system.

Nearly equally important is the *juku* as a place to meet friends. Almost every second student in 6th to 9th grade intends to meet friends or make new ones (up to 37% in 6th grade) by attending a *juku*. In contrast, students receiving private tutoring or correspondence courses miss these last advantages. For privately tutored students, it is of higher importance that they like their teacher (primary school, ~41%;

middle school, ~42%) and whether his or her teaching methods are easy under-standable (primary school: ~70%; middle school: ~78%) (MEXT 2008: 35). This, of course, plays no role for students receiving correspondence courses. These students main motivation to choose this kind of extracurricular education is the flexibility of study time: Students can study whenever they feel like it (primary school, ~63%; middle school, ~79%) (ibid: 36). *Naraigoto* are generally only attended if students like to (ibid: 37).

In contrast to the presented data in Figs. 2.12 and 2.13 referring to the motives for participating in supplementary lessons, central reasons seem to be missing. No student explained that he or she attends a *juku* to prepare for entrance examinations, which is commonly perceived to be the main reason to attend "cram schools" in East Asian countries (Bray and Lykins 2012: 23–25). The whole discussion concerning the entrance examination race and *shiken jigoku* is based on the assumption that students are involved in intense study before the transition to the next higher school level due to entrance examinations. But is this assumption actually true? In reality, the preparation for entrance examinations amounts for only one part of the whole supplementary business, as illustrated in Fig. 2.14.

There is no general *juku* course for all students. Every student has his or her own needs, and thus every family pursues instruction according to these needs. The MEXT identified three main fields of instruction content and left one category open. Whereas 10–12% of all primary and 17–20% of all middle school students receive instruction at *juku* to catch up in school, the highest proportion of students are enrolled in courses with school-related contents, ranging from simple help with homework over preparation of school lessons to repetition and strengthening of

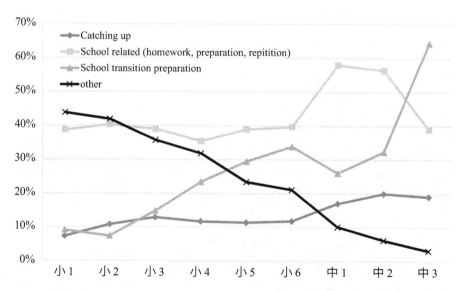

Fig. 2.14 Content of *juku*-lessons, according to grade, in %, 2007 (MEXT 2008: 18). Abbreviations: 小=primary school grade; 中=middle school grade

school curriculum contents. In primary school, approximately 35–40% of the students draw on these lessons to support their school career. In 7th and 8th grades, this percentage increases to approximately 57% of all students, only going down again to 39% in 9th grade. During the last grade of middle school, indeed most students prepare for entrance examinations and school exams (64.4%) to successfully enter a chosen high school. However, this kind of tutoring content is less important in earlier grades and most frequently used before the transition to middle and high school. Other *juku* course contents, which were not described in more detail here, are relatively often received in earlier grades but lose importance when students grow up. In contrast to lessons at *juku*, correspondence courses are almost only used for school-related needs during primary (~88%) and middle school (grade 7, 82%; 8, 76%; 9, 64%). Exam preparation only plays a major role in middle school (up to 51% in 9th grade). The same can be said for private tutors, with the addition that a high proportion receives lessons in order to catch up in school (up to 52% in 8th grade). In conclusion, the found three categories of course contents reflect families' actual educational needs and allow conclusions regarding the state of regular education. It seems as if the Japanese shadow education industry has filled central gaps in education, which were not met by regular schools. Since a high proportion of students is participating in lessons of different tuition and supposed effects outside of school and seems to not only aim to catch up to the average achievement level of their class or confront learning problems but aim to achieve competitive advantages in education, major implications for social inequality issues are connected to the existence of this educational sphere. How far-reaching the impact of shadow education on the education system as a whole proves will be evaluated in the following.

2.4 Interdependence of Regular Education and Shadow Education in Japan

Because of its high embeddedness in Japanese society, the shadow education industry was awarded a non-negligible share in the economic success of the country by Western observers (e.g., Dohmen et al. 2008: 121). The general view on these Japanese education businesses, however, changed: most researchers feel that the pressure on students has decreased and, with it, the dependence on shadow education. The presented data provide us with a different picture. Even though this market might have reached its peak in the 1990s, the Japanese shadow education industry is still highly influential economically and educationally. In spite of the assumed decline in competition between students as a result of the low fertility rate and recent reforms (see Chap. 10), the shadow education industry in Japan remains strong. Whereas the concrete reasons for the continuous high dependence on shadow education in Japan are further discussed and analyzed in Chaps. 7 and 8, the aim of this chapter was to identify in which ways the formal and informal education sectors in Japan are connected and how this might affect the formation and persistence of social inequalities in contemporary Japan. To achieve final conclusions, in the following the structure and contents of the regular schooling system and the *juku*-industry are compared based on my own fieldwork as carried out from 2012 to 2014. Whereas the main purpose of the different fieldwork periods was to conduct the *Juku Student and Teacher Survey* (JSTS) by collecting quantitative and qualitative data at *juku* of different specialization, size, and organization through two questionnaire surveys (one for students, one for teachers) and semi-structured interviews with the *juku*'s principals (for a detailed description of the JSTS, see Chap. 4), additional conversations with students, parents, *juku*-operators, and researchers in this field served to get a greater understanding about functions and implications of the Japanese *juku*-industry and its relation to formal education. However, to grasp the level of connectedness between formal and informal education and to what degree something like an interdependence between both sectors exists, materials such as advertisement, websites, and object characteristics of *juku* of different size and organization are evaluated. Based on content analyses, the organization and the bandwidth of supply as reflected in the provided programs in the shadow of the regular schooling system are analyzed to achieve a structuring of the shadow education system in Japan, which will be compared to the structure of the regular schooling system thus allowing final conclusions.

First of all, the carried-out analyses revealed that all three before outlined main types of shadow education in Japan, i.e., classes at academic *juku*, private tutoring at home, and correspondence courses, are generally provided by the same operators: the *juku sangyō* (*juku*-industry). Correspondence courses and private tutors are only outlined separately by researchers because of their obvious differences in the mode of instruction and the design of lessons, but they are actually only certain types of *juku*-lessons. Thus, a detailed analysis of the Japanese shadow education market can only concentrate on *juku* and their supply, taking into account that private tutors and correspondence courses are two types of lessons which have been outsourced by *juku* and are thus not directly taking place on *juku* school grounds. According to my analyses, the following general modes of instruction are found: one-on-one tutoring settings (e.g., private tutors at home or at *juku*), self-study settings (e.g., correspondence courses or self-study sessions at *juku*), classroom settings at *juku* (e.g., frontal teaching in small, medium, and big size classes, child-centered teaching in groups), interactive settings (e.g., video-on-demand lessons at home or at *juku*), and innovative settings (e.g., hands-on learning including experimental classes or outdoor camps) (for a similar categorization, see M. Watanabe 2013: 93–100). These different settings show the bandwidth of teaching modes and designs of lessons.

Second, there are major differences in the organization of *juku*: Whereas this industry originally started with small neighborhood schools providing lessons given by one or two teachers in a domestic environment, today huge joint-stock corporations[5] dominate the market. Hence, *juku* can be categorized into the following three major organizational types: *ōte juku* (major corporations), *chūshō juku* (*juku* of

---

[5]According to Toyo Keizai Online, there are the approximately 20 *juku*-companies declared as joint-stock companies, half of them showing record profits caused by so far unseen growth (Tomioka 2013).

small or medium size), and *kojin juku* (small owner-operated *juku*) (see also
Nishimura 2009: 15–16, METI 2010: 6). *Ōte juku* are generally franchising to reach
a larger student population of a whole city or on a prefectural, regional, or even
national level. These *juku* often operate like chain corporations comparable to
McDonald's: Similar *kyōshitsu* (study rooms) or *seminā* (seminar classrooms) are
set up to establish a net of *juku*-branches promoting one particular "product"
following the teaching and organization guidelines of the company. These big play-
ers are either specialized on special study purposes like entrance examination preparation (e.g., *yobikō*) or provide a wide range of classes for students of all ages,
including adults. Additionally, *ōte juku* are the major producer of teaching and study
material thus providing the basis for instruction within the industry themselves.
Whereas *ōte juku* often produce their own study material, the smaller *juku* usually
have contracts with teaching material suppliers owned by these big *juku*-companies
(Komiyama 1993: 83). Popular *ōte juku* are the so-called big three of the *juken
sangyō* (exam preparatory industry), which dominate the national market:
Kawaijuku, *Sundai*, and *Yoyogi Seminar* (Aspinall 2005: 211). Whereas *yobikō* such
as these are somehow regulated school corporations receiving preferential taxation,
a fourth big player emerged operating as a conventional company to remain independent: *Nagase Brothers Inc.* This company runs two very successful chains, the
Tōshin Eisei Yobikō and the *Toshin High School*. Whereas these companies focus
primarily on entrance exam preparation, other major companies operating on a
regional (e.g., *Seiki Community Group*), national (e.g., *Eishinkan*), or even international level (e.g., *Kumon Kyōshitsu* or *Benesse Corporation*) concentrate on different programs and thus provide a wide range of programs with all possible study foci.
Hence, *ōte juku* are often companies that run more than one *juku*-"track." Different
juku-chains might thus belong to the same parent company and form some kind of
conglomerate of different *juku*-tracks (including *yobikō*). According to a survey
conducted by the *Ministry of Economy, Trade and Industry* (METI) in 2010, only
17% of the 81 participating *juku*-companies were counted as major corporations. As
shown in Fig. 2.15, with more than 1000 enrolled students per company, 53.5% of
the students in the METI survey attended *ōte juku*. In contrast, only approximately
32% of the *juku* were still individually managed. These *kojinkeiei* or owner-operated
juku are generally run by their founders, who are not only school principal; they are
the school's manager and head teacher. In addition, most of these small *juku* hire

Fig. 2.15 Number of
students per *juku*, in %,
2010 (METI 2010: 7)

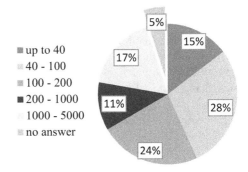

Fig. 2.16 Type of
instruction received by
juku students, in %, 2010
(METI 2010: 7)

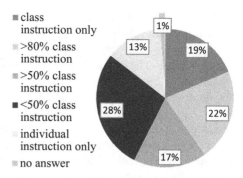

- class
  instruction only
- >80% class
  instruction
- >50% class
  instruction
- <50% class
  instruction
- individual
  instruction only
- no answer

part-time or full-time teachers, sometimes even staff members. The number of teachers varies and depends largely on the teaching approach. *Juku* focusing on individual instruction (*kobetsu shidō*) naturally need much more teachers (Dierkes 2010: 31). *Chūshō juku* thus account for the majority of *juku* (51%). These small- and medium-sized *juku* are comparable to *kojin juku*, but not managed by their owner exclusively anymore (METI 2010: 6, 7, 31). These three categories show the extremes of this market, ranging from very small single-handedly managed schools to huge companies with more than 100 branches, generally following different teaching approaches and study purposes. In between these extremes, educational diversity flourishes. The prevalent picture of *juku* as cram schools with stressed-out students sitting in large classes is only one facet of this industry. As Fig. 2.16 shows, today most *juku* provide individual (*kobetsu shidō*) and class (*shūdan shidō*) instruction. Even though class instruction predominates, only 17% of all primary and middle school students receive teaching in classes only. In contrast, more than 12% of students receive individual instruction only. According to a recent survey by the Zen Nihon Gakushūjuku Renraku Kaigi (2012), an association of Japan's whole *juku*-industry with annual meetings and conferences, individual one-on-one instruction amounts to 40% of the whole shadow education market. To make studying more attractive and up to date, technical innovations such as games and smartphone applications have been invented as well (see also M. Watanabe 2013: 93, 94, 98).

According to the Toyo Keizai Online which is titled *Juku, why record profits despite low birth rates?* (Tomioka 2013), more profits are made by less competitors in the *juku*-market. Each year 20–30 companies vanish from this industry, but still the profits increase. According to the annual reports of the Yano Research Institute focusing on education businesses in Japan, the size of the entire supplementary education industry remained unchanged in 2015 if compared to previous years. However, certain sectors have been expanding or heavily shrinking over the last years (Yano Research Institute 2010, 2016). In the case of the *juku*-industry, an increasing oligopolization of the market can be watched, which can be described as *yūshōreppai* – the survival of the fittest, resulting in a stronger competition between *juku*-companies. It appears that while *kojin* and *chūshō juku* have to fight for survival after an existence of often more than 30 years, the *big juku* can afford to hire the best teachers, buy the best equipment, and even invest in their own research (often these corporations have their own research facilities).

Based on the discussions and the evaluation and analysis of JSTS data, websites, advertisement, and object characteristics of shadow education providers in Japan, the range of diversity and supply within this market is summarized in Fig. 2.17. According to my research, the Japanese *juku*-industry has become a perfect shadow of the regular schooling system. When examining the actual supply of this vast market, it becomes clear that shadow education provides much more than help with homework and preparation for exams. I hereby argue that the prevalent traditional view on shadow education in Japan is too narrow minded and has to be rethought. As illustrated, the supply ranges from preschool to higher education and beyond. Children of all ages are targeted, really carrying out the idea of lifelong learning, which is actively promoted by several major corporations within the *juku*-market.

It is not without a certain irony that the *juku*-industry seems committed to realize national education reform plans such as the idea of lifelong learning or the improvement of overall English Language proficiency skills among students, which the formal education system's institutions struggle to accomplish. However, how successfully *juku* have become in realizing certain reform agendas is under-researched to say the least (e.g., English language education, see Lowe 2015).

Chapter 8 will discuss such issues, after the main topic concerning whether shadow education stronger contributes to social inequalities or educational opportunities is quantitatively approached in the Chaps. 5, 6 and 7.

In conclusion, this overview illustrates the strong position of shadow education in Japan. It is safe to say that among today's adolescents and young adults, there are only very few who have never seen the inside of a *juku* in their life. Especially those with high ambitions are most unlikely to achieve their goals without additional support received from the shadow. According to a recent study, even non-Japanese families generally do not succeed avoiding to purchase additional support in the shadow (Cook 2012). The very few exceptions underline the general importance of shadow education in Japan and its deep embeddedness into the Japanese education system and society. Accordingly, *juku* are "necessary organizations" (Harnisch 1994: 330), which have gained their righteous position in the education system of Japan due to their gap-closing function. However, *juku* seem to have expanded their supply beyond simple gap-closing and provide alternatives in education thus supporting the assumption that shadow education in Japan might contribute to both: educational reproduction and opportunities.

2.5 Discussion

In Japan, shadow education is a major phenomenon and hardly comparable to Western shadow education systems in terms of its scale and functions. A barely existent shadow education sector with only supportive function, e.g., providing remedial teaching for students with learning deficits on a basic level as found in the

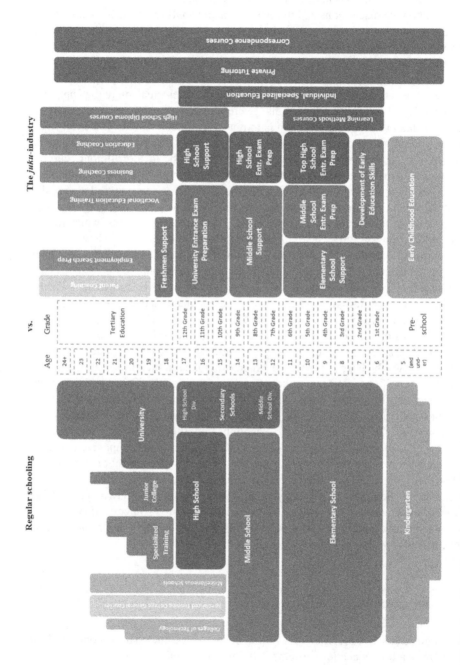

Fig. 2.17 The two sides of the Japanese schooling system

Northern European countries (Bray 2011), will only have but minor influence on the regular schooling system and the provision of equal educational opportunities for students. As was discussed in this chapter, the high dependence on shadow education services in Japan has nation-specific causes, in particular the intense educational competition for educational credentials as caused by the *gakureki shakai* increases and further drives the demand for shadow education. In addition, there seem to exist huge gaps in the regular schooling system's provision of education that further justify the existence of this vast supplementary education market. Also, we have to acknowledge that *juku* have become a major institution in the Japanese world of education – an institution that challenges regular schools' primary functions of educating and allocating students and thus heavily influences the education system's selection function. This has major implications for the formation of competition, but also implies mechanisms of closure and differentiation. The participation of most students in these lessons in the shadow and the diversity of supply make it difficult to estimate whether the shadow education system inherits real educational opportunities for students from disadvantaged family backgrounds even though it seems to primarily support educational differentials. It is possible that a high percentage of students from disadvantaged family backgrounds are in a position to use shadow education as an instrument to neutralize socioeconomic disadvantages and achieve a high social status. This issue cannot be clarified at this point and will accompany us throughout the book.

In summary, the following three major findings can be derived from the above analysis: (1) The postwar Japanese *gakureki shakai* (credentialist society) is founded on an intense "diploma disease" in the form of an entrance examination system, which causes and continues to drive heavy educational competition between students and schools and thus created families' extraordinarily high demand for private supplementary lessons to achieve a competitive advantage in the educational race. (2) The Japanese shadow education system has reached a level where not only all possible educational gaps of the schooling system are covered; supply beyond that point is offered. (3) The postulated equality of educational opportunities in Japanese education hinged on the educational opportunities provided by the shadow education industry.

The presented analysis also showed that generally there seems to exist a strong interdependence between regular schooling system and shadow education system in Japan. By identifying and describing the specifics of the two sides of Japanese education, this chapter provides a contextual, theoretical frame for the upcoming four empirical chapters (Chaps. 5, 6, 7 and 8), which will concentrate on one specific angle of the question whether shadow education in Japan actually stronger contributes to educational and social inequalities or educational opportunities. To approach this issue adequately, general theoretical concepts to explain social inequality formation applicable for analyses focusing on shadow education in Japan are introduced in the following Chap. 3, before the data bases for my analyses are outlined in Chap. 4.

Appendix

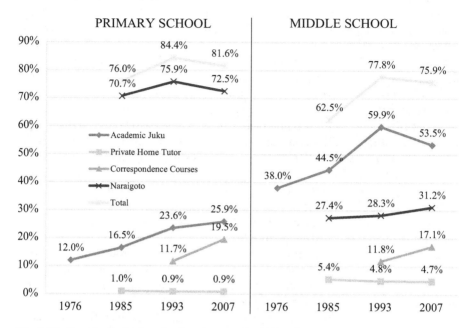

Fig. 2.18 Out-of-school education in primary and middle school, in %, 1976–2007 (Monbushō 1977: 29; MEXT 2008: 8)

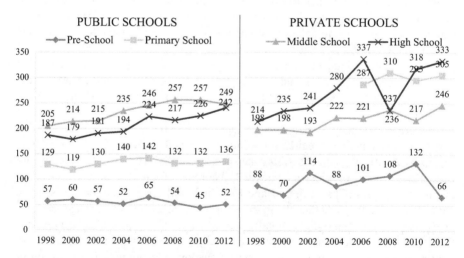

Fig. 2.19 Development of average annual expenses of public and private school students for academic *juku*-classes, in 1000 Yen, 1998–2012 (MEXT 2014a)

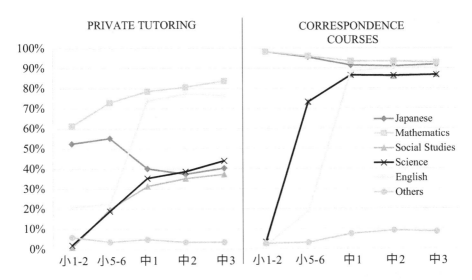

Fig. 2.20 Private tutoring lessons and correspondence courses, according to grade and subject, in %, 2007 (MEXT 2008: 14). Abbreviations: 小=primary school grade; 中=middle school grade

References

Amano, I. (1998). Postwar Japanese education: A history of reform and counterreform. In E. R. Beauchamp (Ed.), *Education and schooling in Japan since 1945* (pp. 152–167). New York: Routledge.

Amano, I., & Poole, G. S. (2005). The Japanese University in Crisis. *Higher Education, 50*(4), 685–711.

Arnove, R. F., & Torres, C. A. (Hrsg.). (2007). *Comparative education: The dialectic of the global and the local*. Lanham/Boulder/New York/Toronto/Plymouth: Rowman & Littlefield.

Aspinall, R. (2005). University entrance in Japan. In J. S. Eades, R. Goodman, & H. Yumio (Eds.), *The 'Big Bang' in Japanese higher education. The 2004 reforms and the dynamics of change* (pp. 199–218). Melbourne: Trans Pacific Press.

Azuma, H. (2002). The development of the course of study and the structure of educational reform in Japan. In G. DeCoker (Ed.), *National standards and school reform in Japan and the United States* (pp. 5–19). New York: Teachers College Press.

Baker, D. P., Akiba, M., LeTendre, G. K., & Wiseman, A. W. (2001). Worldwide shadow education: Outside-school learning, institutional quality of schooling, and cross-national mathematics achievement. *Educational Evaluation and Policy Analysis, 23*(1), 1–17.

Baker, D. P., & LeTendre, G. K. (2005). National differences, global similarities. *World culture and the future of schooling*. Stanford: Stanford University Press.

Beauchamp, E. R., & Vardaman, J. M. (1994). *Japanese education since 1945 – a documentary study*. New York: M. E. Sharpe, East Gate Book.

BERD, Benesse Education Research and Development Center. (2007). *Chōsa dēta kurippu! Kodomo to kyōiku: Juku, naraigoto – dai 1 kai* [Survey data clip concerning children and education: Juku and other learning activities, Part 1]. Retrieved from: http://berd.benesse.jp/berd/data/dataclip/clip0006/clip0006a.pdf

Boudon, R. (1974). *Education, opportunity, and social inequality: Changing prospects in western society*. New York: Wiley.

Bourdieu, P., & Passeron, J. C. (1977). *Reproduction in education, society and culture*. Beverly Hills: Sage.

Bray, M. (1999). *The shadow education system: Private tutoring and its implications for planners.* Paris: UNESCO, International Institute for Educational Planning (IIEP).

Bray, M. (2009). *Confronting the shadow education system: What government policies for what private tutoring?* Paris: UNESCO International Institute for Educational Planning (IIEP).

Bray, M. (2010). Researching shadow education: Methodological challenges and directions. *Asia Pacific Educational Review, 11*, 3–13.

Bray, M. (2011). *The challenge of shadow education: Private tutoring and its implications for policy makers in the European Union.* Retrieved from: http://www.nesse.fr/nesse/activities/reports

Bray, M., & Lykins, C. (2012). *Shadow education: Private tutoring and its implications for policy makers in Asia.* Hong Kong: Comparative Education Research Center (CERC) and Asian Development Bank.

Bray, M., Mazawi, A. E., & Sultana, R. G. (2013). *Private tutoring across the mediterranean: Power dynamics and implications for learning and equity.* Rotterdam/Boston/Taipei: Sense Publishers.

Cook, M. (2012). *Multicultural families and supplementary education (Juku) in Japan.* Paper presented at the Fourth Asian Conference on Education, Osaka.

Juken, D. (2014). *Daigaku Hensachi Jōhō 2014* [University entrance score deviation information 2014]. Accessed: Retrieved from: http://daigakujyuken.boy.jp/

Dawson, W. (2010). Private tutoring and mass schooling in east Asia: Reflections of inequality in Japan, South Korea and Cambodia. *Asia Pacific Educational Review, 11*, 14–24.

Dewey, J. (1925). *Democracy and education.* New York: MacMillan.

Dierkes, J. (2009). Privatschulen und privatwirtschaftliche Zusatzschulen in Japan: Bildungspolitische Lückenbüßer und Marktlücke [Private schools and private-sector supplementary schools: Education political stopgap and gap in the market]. *Zeitschrift für Pädagogik, 55*(5), 732–746.

Dierkes, J. (2010). Teaching in the shadow: Operators of small shadow education institutions in Japan. *Asia Pacific Education Review, 11*(1), 25–35.

Dierkes, J. (2013). The insecurity industry: Supplementary education in Japan. In J. Aurini, S. Davies, & J. Dierkes (Eds.), *Out of the shadows: The global intensification of supplementary education* (International perspectives on education and society, Vol. 22, pp. 3–21). Bingley: Emerald Publishing.

DNC, National Center for University Entrance Examinations. (2014a). *Heikinten-tō ichiran* [Summary of point average etc]. Retrieved from: http://www.dnc.ac.jp/data/shiken_jouhou/h26/

DNC, National Center for University Entrance Examinations. (2014b). *Heisei 26-nendo daigaku nyūshi sentā shiken jisshi kekka no gaiyō* [Overview of the final results of the national center test for University admissions]. Retrieved from: http://www.dnc.ac.jp/data/shiken_jouhou/h26/

Dohmen, D., Erbes, A., Fuchs, K., & Günzel, J. (2008). *Was wissen wir über Nachhilfe? Sachstand und Auswertung der Forschungsliteratur zu Angebot, Nachfrage und Wirkungen.* Bielefeld: Bertelsmann.

Dore, R. (1976). *The diploma disease. education, qualification, and development.* California: University of California Press.

Drinck, B. (2002). Marktorientierung im japanischen Bildungssystem [Market orientation in the Japanese education system]. *Zeitschrift für Erziehungswissenschaft, 5*(2), 261–278.

Entrich, S. R. (2011). *Die Grundlegung des modernen japanischen Bildungssystems – Joseph C. Trainor und die amerikanischen Bildungsreformen nach dem Zweiten Weltkrieg* [The foundation of the modern Japanese education system – Joseph C. Trainor and the American education reforms in Japan following World War II]. Hamburg: Diplomica.

Entrich, S. R. (2014). Effects of investments in out-of-school education in Germany and Japan. *Contemporary Japan, 26*(1), 71–102.

Foster, E. (1973). "Exam Hell" in Japan. *Change, 5*(6), 16–19.

Fujita, H. (2010). Whither Japanese schooling? Educational reforms and their impact on ability formation and educational opportunity. In J. A. Gordon, H. Fujita, T. Kariya, & G. K. LeTendre (Eds.), *Challenges to Japanese education. economics, reform, and human rights* (pp. 17–53). New York: Teachers College Press.

Fukuzawa, R. E., & LeTendre, G. K. (2001). *Intense years: How Japanese adolescents balance school, family and friends*. New York: Routledge.

Guest, M. (2006). Teaching progressively... for the Senta Shiken! In K. Bradford-Watts, C. Ikeguchi, & M. Swanson (Eds.), *JALT2005 conference proceedings*. JALT: Tokyo.

Guest, M. (2008). A comparative analysis of the Japanese University entrance Senta Shiken based on a 25-year gap. *JALT Journal, 30*(1), 85–104.

Haasch, G. (1979). *Japanisches und Deutsches Bildungssystem – Versuch eines Systemvergleichs* [The education systems of Japan and Germany – an attempt to compare both systems]. Tokyo: OAG.

Haasch, G. (2000a). Bildungsreformen und Reformversuche als Antwort auf die "Überhitzung der Erziehung" (*kyōiku no kanetsu*) [Educational reforms and attempts of reformation in response to the "overheating of education" (*Kyōiku no Kanetsu*)]. In G. Haasch (Ed.), *Bildung und Erziehung in Japan* [Education in Japan] (Vol. 1, pp. 136–143). Berlin: Ed. Colloquium.

Haasch, G. (2000b). Der Aufbau eines modernen Bildungssystems in der Meiji-Zeit (1868–1912) [The construction of the modern education system in the Meiji Era (1868–1912)]. In G. Haasch (Ed.), *Bildung und Erziehung in Japan* [Education in Japan] (Vol. 1, pp. 66–92). Berlin: Ed. Colloquium.

Haasch, G. (2000c). Die Struktur des Allgemeinbildenden Schulwesens [The structure of the compulsory schooling system]. In G. Haasch (Ed.), *Bildung und Erziehung in Japan* [Education in Japan] (Vol. 1, pp. 161–171). Berlin: Ed. Colloquium.

Haasch, G. (2000d). Problembereiche des allgemeinen Bildungswesens – Überhitzung der Erziehung (*kyōiku no kanetsu*) [Problem Areas of General Education – Overheating of Education (*Kyōiku no Kanetsu*)]. In G. Haasch (Ed.), *Bildung und Erziehung in Japan* [Education in Japan] (Vol. 1, pp. 195). Berlin: Ed. Colloquium.

Hans, N. (1958). *Comparative education. A study of educational factors and traditions* (Vol. 3). London: Routledge & Kegan Paul.

Harms, A. (1997). *Lernen, wie Japan von anderen lernte: Ausländische Einflüsse auf das japanische Bildungswesen im ausgehenden 19. Jahrhundert* [Learning how Japan learned from others: Foreign influences on Japanese education in the late 19th century]. Münster/New York/München/Berlin: Waxmann Verlag.

Harnisch, D. L. (1994). Supplemental education in Japan: *Juku* schooling and its implication. *Journal of Curriculum Studies, 26*(3), 323–334.

Hentschke, F. (2001). *Demokratisierung als Ziel der amerikanischen Besatzungspolitik in Deutschland und Japan, 1943–1947* [Democratization as the goal of American occupation policy in Germany and Japan, 1943–1947]. Münster/Hamburg/London: LIT Verlag.

Jones, R. S. (2011). *Education reform in Japan* (OECD Economics Department Working Papers 888).

Jürgens, E., & Dieckmann, M. (2007). *Wirksamkeit und Nachhaltigkeit von Nachhilfeunterricht: Dargestellt am Beispiel des Studienkreises* [Effectiveness and sustainability of private tutoring: As illustrated by the example of the Studienkreis]. Frankfurt am Main: Peter Lang.

Kariya, T. (1995). *Taishū kyōiku shakai no yukue: Gakureki shugi to byōdo shinwa no sengo-shi* [The future of mass education society: The postwar history of the myth of equality and the degreeocracy]. Tokyo: Chūō Kōron Shinsha.

Kariya, T., & Dore, R. (2006). Japan at the meritocracy frontier: From here, where? *The Political Quarterly, 77*(1), 134–156.

Kataoka, E. (2001). Kyōiku tassei katei ni okeru kazoku no kyōiku senryaku: Bunka shihon kōka to gakkōgai kyōiku tōshi kōka no jendāsa o chūshin ni [Family strategy in educational attainment process in Japan: Effects of cultural capital and investment in extra-school education]. *Kyōikugaku Kenkyū, 68*(3), 259–273.

Kikkawa, T. (2006). *Gakureki to Kakusa-Fubyōdō: Seijukusuru Nihongata Gakureki Shakai* [Education and social inequality: Contemporary educational credentialism in Japan]. Tokyo: Tōkyō Daigaku Shuppankai.

Knipprath, H. (2005). *Quality and equity: Japanese education in perspective*. Antwerpen: Garant.

Kōkōjuken-Nabi. (2014). *Kōkō no gakuhi* [High school expenses]. Accessed 29 Apr 2014. Retrieved from: http://www.zyuken.net/term/gakuhi/

Komiyama, H. (1993). *Gakurekishakai to juku – datsu juken kyōsō no susume* [Credentialist society and Juku –stop the entrance examination competition!]. Tokyo: Shinhyōron.

Konakayama, A., & Matsui, T. (2008). Gakkōgai kyōiku tōshi no gakuryoku ni oyobosu eikyō ni kansuru ikkōsatsu [An empirical study on how extra school education affects academic achievement of Japanese high school students]. *Tōkaidaigaku Seiji Keizaigakubu Kiyō, 40*, 131–158.

Kondō, M., Nogaki, Y., Harada, A., & Takahata, M. (1963). Shingaku junbi kyōiku no kenkyū. Gakushūjuku – kateikyōshinado ni kansuru chōsa hōkoku [A study of out-of-school education preparing for entrance examinations. Report of the Gakushū Juku and private tutoring survey]. *Kyōiku Shakaigaku Kenkyū, 18*, 239–355.

Krämer, H.-M. (2006). *Neubeginn unter US-amerikanischer Besatzung? Hochschulreform in Japan zwischen Kontinuität und Diskontinuität, 1919–1952* [Fresh start under US-occupation? Higher education reform in Japan between continuity and discontinuity, 1919–1952]. Berlin: Akademie Verlag.

Kwok, P. (2004). Examination-oriented knowledge and value transformation in East Asian cram schools. *Asia Pacific Education Review, 5*(1), 64–75.

Lenhardt, G. (2008). Vergleichende Bildungsforschung. Bildung, Nationalstaat und Weltgesellschaft [Comparative education research. Education, national state and world society]. In W. Helsper & J. Böhme (Eds.), *Handbuch der Schulforschung* [Handbook of school research] (pp. 1009–1028). Wiesbaden: VS Verlag.

LeTendre, G. K. (1996). Constructed aspirations: Decision-making processes in Japanese educational selection. *Sociology of Education, 69*(3), 193–216.

Lowe, R. J. (2015). Cram schools in Japan: The need for research. *The Language Teacher, 39*(1), 26–31.

METI, Ministry of Economy, Trade and Industry. (2010). *"Gakushūjuku kōshi ginō kentei shiken" no setsuritsu ni muketa – Gakushūjuku kōshi nōryoku hyōka shisutemu kōdo-ka jigyō* [Towards the establishment of an "exam concerning the ability of Juku teachers" – The industry for the further development of the Juku teachers' ability evaluation system]. Retrieved from: www.meti.go.jp/policy/servicepolicy/contents/management_support/H21%20gakusyujyuku%20report.pdf

MEXT, Ministry of Education, Culture, Sports, Science and Technology. (2005a). *Enrollment and advancement rate, 1948–2005*.Retrieved from: http://www.mext.go.jp/english/statistics/1302870.htm

MEXT, Ministry of Education, Culture, Sports, Science and Technology. (2005b). *Kokuritsu daigaku to shiritsu daigaku no jugyō-ryō-tō no suii* [Changes in tuition fees, etc. of national and private Universities]. Retrieved from: http://www.mext.go.jp/b_menu/shingi/kokuritu/005/gijiroku/06052921/005/002.htm

MEXT, Ministry of Education, Culture, Sports, Science and Technology. (2007). Japan's education at a glance 2006. Retrieved from: http://www.mext.go.jp/english/statistics/1303013.htm

MEXT, Ministry of Education, Culture, Sports, Science and Technology. (2008). *Kodomo no gakkōgai de no gakushū seikatsu ni kansuru jittai chōsa hōkoku* [National report concerning the out-of-school learning activities of children]. Retrieved from: http://www.mext.go.jp/b_menu/houdou/20/08/08080710.htm

MEXT, Ministry of Education, Culture, Sports, Science and Technology. (2010). *Kokuritsu daigaku no jugyō-ryō, nyūgaku-ryō oyobi kentei-ryō no chōsa kekka ni tsuite* [FY 2010 survey results concerning tuition, admission and examination fees at national Universities]. Retrieved from: http://www.mext.go.jp/a_menu/koutou/houjin/1293385.htm

MEXT, Ministry of Education, Culture, Sports, Science and Technology. (2013). Shiritsu daigaku nyūgaku-sha ni kakaru shonendo gakusei nōfu-kin. Retrieved from: http://www.mext.go.jp/a_menu/koutou/shinkou/07021403/__icsFiles/afieldfile/2014/04/07/1346053_01_1.pdf

MEXT, Ministry of Education, Culture, Sports, Science and Technology. (2014a). *Kodomo no gakushūhi chōsa* [Survey concerning children's learning expenses]. Retrieved from: http://www.mext.go.jp/b_menu/toukei/chousa03/gakushuuhi/kekka/1268105.htm

MEXT, Ministry of Education, Culture, Sports, Science and Technology. (2014b). *Kōritsu daigaku ni tsuite* [Concerning public Universities]. Retrieved from: http://www.mext.go.jp/a_menu/koutou/kouritsu/index.htm

MEXT, Ministry of Education, Culture, Sports, Science and Technology. (2014c). School basic survey 2014. Retrieved from: http://www.mext.go.jp/english/topics/1361507.htm

MEXT, Ministry of Education, Culture, Sports, Science and Technology. (2017a). *Education.* Retrieved from: http://www.mext.go.jp/english/introduction/1303952.htm

MEXT, Ministry of Education, Culture, Sports, Science and Technology. (2017b). *Statistics.* Retrieved from: http://www.mext.go.jp/english/statistics/

Meyer, J. W., Ramirez, F. O., & Soysal, Y. N. (1992). World expansion of mass education, 1870–1980. *Sociology of Education, 65*(2), 128–149.

Monbushō, Ministry of Education. (1977). *Daijin kanbu chōsa tōkei-ka: Zenkoku gakushū juku toi no jittai* [Ministerial executive research statistics: Actual situation of the national Juku problem]. Tokyo: Ministry of Education.

Monbushō, Ministry of Education. (1978). Education in Japan. *A graphic Presentation.* Tokyo: Gyosei.

Murphey, T. (2004). Participation, (Dis-) identification, and Japanese University entrance exams. *TESOL Quarterly, 38*(4), 700–710.

Nishimura, N. (2009). *Naze uchi no ko dake gōkaku suru no ka? Chūgaku juken 'kashikoi juku no tsukaikata'* [Why do only our children pass the test? The smart way to use Juku for middle school entrance]. Tokyo: Eijipress.

OECD, Organisation for Economic Co-operation and Development. (2015). *Education at a glance 2015: OECD indicators.* Retrieved from: https://doi.org/10.1787/eag-2015-en

Ojima, F., & von Below, S. (2010). Family background, school system and academic achievement in Germany and in Japan. In J. Dronkers (Ed.), *Quality and inequality of education* (pp. 275–297). Dordrecht: Springer.

Okada, A. (2012a). *Education policy and equal opportunity in Japan.* New York/Oxford: Berghahn Books.

Okada, A. (2012b). Education reform and equal opportunity in Japan. *Journal of International and Comparative Education, 1*(2), 116–129.

Ono, H. (2005). *Does examination hell pay off? A cost-benefit analysis of "Ronin" and college education in Japan* (SSE/EFI working paper series in economics and finance 346).

Park, H., Byun, S.-y., & Kim, K.-k. (2011). Parental involvement and students' cognitive outcomes in Korea: Focusing on private tutoring. *Sociology of Education, 84*, 3–22.

Ramirez, F. O., & Boli, J. (1987). The political construction of mass schooling: european origins and worldwide institutionalization. *Sociology of Education, 60*(1), 2–17.

Roesgaard, M. H. (2006). *Japanese education and the cram school business: Functions, challenges and perspectives of the Juku.* Copenhagen: NIAS Press.

Rohlen, T. P. (1980). The Juku phenomenon: An exploratory essay. *Journal of Japanese Studies, 6*(2), 207–242.

Rohlen, T. P. (1983). *Japan's high schools.* Berkeley/Los Angeles: University of California Press.

Rosenzweig, B. (1998). *Erziehung zur Demokratie? Amerikanische Besatzungs- und Schulreformpolitik in Deutschland und Japan* [Education towards democracy? American occupation and education reform policy in Germany and Japan]. Stuttgart: Franz Steiner Verlag.

Russell, N. U. (1997). Lessons from Japanese cram schools. In W. K. Cummings & P. G. Altbach (Eds.), *The challenge of eastern Asian education: Implications for America* (pp. 153–170). New York: State University Press.

Sato, M. (2005). "Juku Boom:" Cram schools cash in on failure of public schools. *The Japan Times,* July 28th, 2005. http://www.japantimes.co.jp/life/2005/07/28/life/cram-schools-cash-in-on-failure-of-public-schools/#.U4nEtCiOz3A

Schad-Seifert, A. (2006). *Japans kinderarme Gesellschaft – Die niedrige Geburtenrate und das Gender-Problem* [Japan's children poor society – the low birth rate and the gender issue] (DIJ-Working Paper 6(1)).

Seiyama, K. (1981). Gakkōgai kyōiku tōshi no kōka ni kansuru ichikōsatsu [A study of the effects of out-of-school educational investment]. *Hokudai Bungakubu Kiyō, 30*(1), 171–221.

Seiyama, K., & Noguchi, Y. (1984). Kōkō shingaku ni okeru gakkōgai kyōiku tōshi no kōka [The effects of outside of school educational investments at the transition to high school]. *Kyōiku Shakaigaku Kenkyū, 39*, 113–126.

Shibata, M. (2005). *Japan and Germany under the U.S. occupation. A comparative analysis of post-war education reform.* Lanham/Boulder/New York/Toronto/Oxford: Lexington Books.

Shimizu, K. (2001). The pendulum of reform: Educational change in Japan from the 1990s onwards. *Journal of Educational Change, 2*, 193–205.

Southgate, D. E. (2009). *Determinants of shadow education – a cross-national analysis.* Ohio: Ohio State University.

Stevenson, D. L., & Baker, D. P. (1992). Shadow education and allocation in formal schooling: Transition to University in Japan. *American Journal of Sociology, 97*, 1639–1657.

Takeuchi, Y. (1997). The self-activating entrance examination system – its hidden agenda and its correspondence with the Japanese "salary man". *Higher Education, 34*(2), 183–198.

Tomioka, K. (2013). Gakushūjuku, shōshikademo saikō eki rasshu no naze [Academic Juku, why record profits despite low birth rates?]. *ToyoKeizai Online* (2013-02-25). Retrieved from: http://toyokeizai.net/articles/-/13024

Trainor, J. C. (1980). *Educational reform in occupied Japan – trainors memoir.* Tokyo: Meisei University Press.

Tsukada, M. (1988). Institutionalised supplementary education in Japan: The Yobiko and ronin student adaptations. *Comparative Education, 24*(3), 285–303.

Tsukada, M. (2010). Educational stratification, teacher perspectives on school culture and the college entrance examination. In J. A. Gordon, H. Fujita, T. Kariya, & G. K. LeTendre (Eds.), *Challenges to Japanese education. economics, reform, and human rights* (pp. 67–86). New York: Teachers College Press.

Tsukada, M. (1991). *Yobiko life: A study of the legitimation process of social stratification in Japan.* Berkeley: Institute of East Asian Studies, University of California.

Tsuneyoshi, R. (2013). Junior high school entrance examinations in metropolitan Tokyo: The advantages and costs of privilege. In G. DeCoker & C. Bjork (Eds.), *Japanese education in an era of globalization: Culture, politics, and equity* (pp. 164–182). New York: Teachers College Press, Columbia University.

Von Kopp, B. (2000a). Aufbau, Organisation und Finanzierung des Schulwesens [Structure, organization and financing of education]. In G. Haasch (Ed.), *Bildung und Erziehung in Japan* [Education in Japan] (Vol. 1, pp. 155–161). Berlin: Ed. Colloquium.

Von Kopp, B. (2000b). Schulisches Leben und schulische Sozialisation [School life and school socialization]. In G. Haasch (Ed.), *Bildung und Erziehung in Japan* [Education in Japan] (Vol. 1, pp. 175–187). Berlin: Ed. Colloquium.

Ward, N. (2003). *About Japanese Universities.* Retrieved from: http://www.nigelward.com/japan/index.html. Accessed 10 Oct 2012.

Watanabe, M. (2013). *Juku: The stealth force of education and the deterioration of schools in Japan.* North Charleston: CreateSpace Independent Publishing Platform.

Wu, L.-E. E. T. (1993). *Japanese University entrance examination – problems in mathematics.* Mathematical Association of America: Washington, DC.

Yano Research Institute. (2010). *Kyōiku sangyō ichiba ni kansuru chōsa kekka 2010* [Survey results on the education industry market 2014]. Retrieved from: https://www.yano.co.jp/market_reports/C52110700

Yano Research Institute. (2016). *Kyōiku sangyō ichiba ni kansuru chōsa kekka 2015* [Survey results on the education industry market 2016]. Retrieved from: https://www.yano.co.jp/market_reports/C58109800

Yuki, M., Sato, A., & Hashisako, K. (1987). *Gakushū juku – Kodomo, oya, kyōshi wa dō miteiru ka* [Academic Juku – how do children, parents, and teachers view them?]. Tokyo: Gyōsei.

Zen Nihon Gakushūjuku Renraku Kaigi. (2012). *Gakushū juku hyaku-nen no rekishi – Juku dantai gojūnenshi* [100 years history of academic Juku – 50 years history of Juku associations]. Tokyo: Zen Nihon Gakushūjuku Renraku Kaigi.

Zeng, K. (1999). *Dragon gate, competitive examinations and their consequences.* London/New York: Cassell.

Chapter 3
Theoretical Approach

How to Theoretically Grasp the Implications of Shadow Education on Educational and Social Differentials in Japan?

"[F]amilies […] want to avoid for
their children any position in life
that is worse than the one
from which they start"

('Explaining Educational Differentials', by
Breen and Goldthorpe 1997: 283).

理論的アプローチ

Abstract The field of shadow education research remains generally under-theorized. Only seldom do studies apply distinct theoretical concepts to capture the causes and implications of shadow education investments for social inequality. Addressing the question whether there are adequate theoretical concepts to explain the possible implications of shadow education investments on educational and social inequality formation suited to be applied in the Japanese context also, based on an international literature review, the following three major concepts are identified and outlined:

(1) Rational Choice Theory (RCT), particularly Relative Risk Aversion and Subjective Expected Utility Theories,
(2) Shadow Education Investment Theory (SEIT), and
(3) Neo-Institutionalist Theory (NIT). These concepts are evaluated for their usability for analyses of the four dimensions outlined in the *Shadow–Education–Inequality–Impact* (SEII) Frame: *Access*, *Effects*, *Continuity*, and *Change* of shadow education investments for social inequalities. In conclusion, the outlined concepts share one fundamental similarity: The demand for shadow education is understood as an investment based on rational cost–benefit considerations of forward-looking individuals, whereas the outcomes of such investments are believed to foster social inequalities.

3.1   Problematic

This chapter serves to identify and outline adequate theoretical concepts suited to explain the possible implications of shadow education investments on educational and social inequality formation in the Japanese context. The question addressed here is whether there are adequate theoretical concepts which can be derived from international research on the subject that prove to be applicable in the Japanese context also?

Surprisingly, empirical studies on shadow education often miss concrete theoretical conceptualizations from which hypotheses are derived and tested. Most studies explore the field primarily focusing on the development, scale, and functions of shadow education in a certain national context (see Bray 1999, 2009; Aurini et al. 2013) or its policy implications (e.g., Bray 1999, 2009, 2011; Bray and Lykins 2012; Bray and Kwo 2014). This proves necessary given the fact that this field of research is comparatively new and has not attracted much attention by researchers until recently. Even though numerous studies analyze the causes, demands, and effects or outcomes of shadow education utilization across a huge variety of countries, it is rather rare that researchers apply a certain theoretical concept to achieve a deeper understanding on the mechanisms that lead to shadow education investments and its outcomes at macro-, meso-, and micro-levels of analysis. As a consequence, the opportunity to use the example of shadow education to expand our knowledge on theories of educational mobility or social reproduction is unfortunately generally missed.

To explain educational inequality formation in several national contexts, Western research concentrated on micro-level models, particularly Rational Choice Theories (in the following RCT), based on the classic work of Boudon (1974). However, such research on educational decision-making primarily focuses on school transition decisions (e.g., Erikson and Jonsson 1996; Breen and Goldthorpe 1997; Esser 1999; Jonsson and Erikson 2000; Stocke 2007; Breen et al. 2014). Only few (German) researchers have recently applied RCT to shadow education investments, understanding such investments as decisions which are based on rational cost–benefit considerations (see Schneider 2005; Guill 2012; Luplow and Schneider 2014). This Western discussion on educational decision-making based on RCT has also found its way into Japanese scientific discourses and is one of the main foundations to also explain class differentials in contemporary Japan (see Okano 1995; Furuta 2011; Sato 2013, 2017). Particularly the "Relative Risk Aversion" Theory (in the following RRAT) of Breen and Goldthorpe (1997) as one prominent version of RCT received attention in the Japanese context (see, e.g., Fujihara 2011; Hamamoto 2015; Sato 2017) and thus seems fitting to explain class differentials in Japan. The above quoted phrase by Breen and Goldthorpe has come to reflect the general understanding about families' strive for higher educational credentials and is a logical explanation for educational expansion in the Western hemisphere, but no less in Japan, where high educational aspirations have caused and continue to drive the educational expansion. However, these Western concepts on educational decision-making were not used to try to explain Japanese families' continuous high investments in shadow education. Even though shadow education in Japan is often described as a security strategy to avoid risks and was even labeled as "insecurity industry" (Dierkes 2013), particularly valuable additions to RCT such as RRAT or Subjective Expected Utility Theory (in the following SEUT; Esser 1999) have not found their ways into empirical analyses on the issue in Japan. Whereas a few Western observers such as Stevenson and Baker (1992) based their theoretical argumentation on theories of social reproduction, such as educational allocation theories (see Bourdieu and Passeron 1977), Japanese researchers mostly follow a prominent theoretical approach that was developed in the Japanese context to explain the implications of shadow education for educational and social inequality. The so-called "Shadow Education Investment Theory" (in the following SEIT; Seiyama 1981) remains the dominant theoretical frame to analyze the relation between shadow education investments and inequality formation in Japan, as several case studies show (e.g., Seiyama and Noguchi 1984; Kataoka 2001; Konakayama and Matsui 2008; Akimoto 2013).

In contrast to these more traditional views understanding shadow education as an instrument of social reproduction, Mori and Baker (2010) recently stressed that the worldwide development of shadow education and its implications for social inequalities in several national contexts has to be understood as an outcome of the vast expansion of mass education or what they refer to as "education revolution" (see Ramirez and Boli 1987; Meyer et al. 1992; Baker and LeTendre 2005). Based on "New Institutional Theory" (in the following NIT), the authors argue that "shadow education is produced by the education culture of a schooled society, and is itself part of the constructing force of education" (Mori and Baker 2010: 40). In fact, Japan was described as one of these "schooled societies" (see also Baker 2014) and as a possible role model regarding the further development of shadow education systems, whose status might slowly change from illegitimate to legitimate education sectors. According to Mori and Baker (2010), governments increasingly consider making use of shadow education to ensure more equality of educational opportunities for all students, which is believed to result in the introduction of "mass shadow education for societal progress" (p. 46) in the not so far future. However, detailed empirical research on such developments of shadow education and thus possibly changing implications for social inequalities or rather the provision of educational opportunities are nonexistent.

In the following, the three mentioned theoretical concepts (RCT, SEIT, and NIT) will be shortly outlined for their explanatory power regarding the implications of shadow education for social inequalities or rather educational opportunities in Japan.

3.2   RCT: Shadow Education as a Rational Choice?

3.2.1   Classic Rational Choice Theory

According to social educational research, the future career of a student is strongly affected by the sum of investments in his or her educational pathway. This pathway is distinguished by a number of transitions to the next education level (Maaz et al. 2006). Therefore, the choices made in the educational attainment process are deci- sive in determining which step on the social ladder a student will end up on. Following Rational Choice Theories (RCT) based on the classic work of Boudon (1974), educational decisions are made by individuals who intend to make the best choices of the available educational options considering the expected costs and ben- efits. Individuals are thus understood as forward-looking. However, it is well under- stood that such individual educational decisions made within the context of a certain education system cause educational inequality. Primary as well as secondary effects of social stratification can be identified as factors influencing the educational path- way of students (Fig. 3.1).

As an example of a primary effect, students from disadvantaged family back- grounds, i.e., families possessing comparably small amounts of economic, social, and cultural capital (Bourdieu 1983), show less academic achievement than stu- dents from advantaged backgrounds. These status-specific differences in learning habits are likely to increase the chances of class reproduction. As an example of a secondary effect, different social classes have different educational aspirations, which results in different cost–benefit considerations, and thus, educational deci- sions vary according to social origin. The interaction of both primary and secondary effects leads to the final choice between the given educational options (Boudon 1974: 29–31; Maaz et al. 2006: 301–304; Becker and Lauterbach 2016: 10–12).

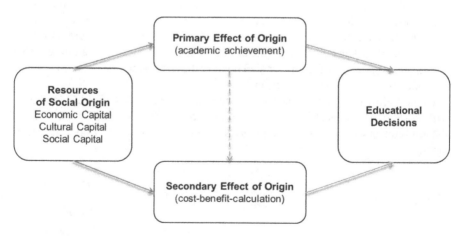

Fig. 3.1 *Simple Decision Theory Model* (Boudon 1974; Becker and Lauterbach 2004: 12)

However, in international comparison it was shown that differences in educational opportunities are more closely associated to the national characteristics of education systems than to the socioeconomic status (SES) of a student (Marks 2005). Although the effect of SES on educational attainment is long known and has aptly been characterized as 'persistent' (Shavit and Blossfeld 1993), a variation within the level of dependence of students' academic standing on the SES of their parents was proven for different countries as well as for students of different age (Jonsson and Erikson 2000). In particular, the structure of a country's education system and its institutional framework strongly determine the possible outcomes of decision-making processes regarding children's educational pathways. Primary effects become more powerful for social reproduction if the performance-related selection of an education system is very rigid. An education system with a high level of stratification and segmentation of its educational courses, a high number of educational obstacles, and educational opportunities at transition points places more weight on educational aspirations (secondary effect) (Becker and Lauterbach 2016: 13–14). As discussed before (see Chap. 2), the Japanese education system shows such high stratification levels, particularly at the secondary and tertiary education levels. Consequently, educational decisions in the Japanese context highly depend on educational aspirations (*shinro kibō*). Therefore, differences in educational aspirations according to social origin are a major cause for educational and thus social inequality reproduction.

3.2.2   RRAT: The Impact of Risk Aversion on Educational Decisions

Of the numerous works in the field of RCT, the micro-theoretical approach which came to be known as "Relative Risk Aversion Theory" (in the following RRAT) by Breen and Goldthorpe (1997) seems most promising to explain why high educational inequality persists despite massive educational expansion as reported before (Chap. 2).

The RRAT mechanism is supposed to play an important role for the secondary effect of social origin when making educational decisions. The authors make a general distinction between two educational options: staying or leaving the education system. If a student stays, two outcomes are possible: success or failure. The decision for continuation or leaving is affected by (1) the costs associated with further training, (2) the likelihood of success, and (3) the utility attached to each of the three options. Each outcome increases the possibility to enter or stay in one of three social classes: service class, working class, or underclass. Thus, by choosing to continue with education and successful graduation, the chances to enter the service class increase. If an individual encounters failure, the chances to enter the underclass increase. Students who start working immediately after school are more likely to enter the working class. Following Boudon (1974), the authors argue that students' ability level and their family's resources to meet educational costs differ according to social class (primary effect). Further, in particular, the relative risk aversion mechanism is supposed to play an important role for the making of educational decisions (secondary effect). Breen and Goldthorpe (1997) conclude that "identical relative risk aversion" is found across all social strata, meaning that parents "want to avoid for their children any position in life that is worse than the one from which they start" (p. 283). In order to avoid "downward mobility," "the educational strategy pursued by parents in the service class is to maximize the chances of their children acquiring a position in this class" (ibid). Hence, upper classes follow a status maintenance motive, whereas middle and low social strata have also the opportunity to advance socially. However, actual risk taking based on the individual's risk aversion level varies across social strata. Students from advantaged social backgrounds are more likely to choose academic-oriented programs promising high returns after school despite high risk aversion; under the same circumstances, students from low social strata tend to choose programs with lower returns. Socially disadvantaged strata where found to show less educational aspirations, because of fewer prospects of success, as well as less willingness to invest in education compared to advantaged social strata (Hillmert 2005: 176). This concept is well suited to analyze two major types of social inequality in Japan, as elsewhere: "self-organizing inequality," meaning inequality caused by class-specific differences of individual actors' choices in spite of having the same actual options due to performance etc. and inequality created by institutions, whose constraints hinder disadvantaged strata to achieve the same education levels as their advantaged peers (Sato 2017: 34). Unfortunately, this classic model does not take into account underclass families and class-specific social values. In the following, meaningful extensions to RCT and RRAT are thus shortly introduced.

3.2.3 SEUT: The Impact of Insecurity on Educational Decisions

Against the rationality of basic RCT, researchers have brought forth doubt based on the fact that different educational options include possible consequences nobody is able to fully assess. Educational decisions are made against the background of a complex interaction of several factors. Esser (1999) further formalized RCT by stressing that educational decisions are made based on individuals' educational motivation and investment risk level. Educational motivation depends on the expected level of educational returns and the expected loss of status if a suboptimal decision is made. In addition, the investment risk increases with individuals' insecurity level concerning educational success, while costs remain constant. Only if educational motivation outweighs investment risk, the decision for the educational option with the higher costs is made. According to this "Subjective Expected Utility

Theory" (SEUT), one decisive additional factor in educational decision-making is a general insecurity about future prospects.

Following Hillmert (2005), insecurity is understood as a general uncertainty regarding the costs, length, and returns connected to educational options. This insecurity is generally caused by a lack of information regarding the available educational options. The level of information regarding educational options and returns is believed to vary across social strata – as do insecurities (p. 175). As outlined above, rational decisions are based on cost–benefit calculations. In general, as long as the expected returns to education exceed the costs, investments seem reasonable (Becker and Lauterbach 2016: 15). But, if it is not certain anymore whether these returns will exceed the costs, insecurity may contribute to a different educational decision than originally envisaged. Calculations are made based on the number of available options, the modality and probability of educational success, and the modality and probability of educational consequences. Particularly, the amount of expected educational return in relation to the costs and preferences as well as the individual background contributes to these considerations. If an individual is uncertain whether some of the possible or assumed consequences will occur, insecurity becomes a major factor for decision-makers. This insecurity is connected to the risks which are related to the decision one has to make. From an individual perspective, only the subjective benefit is relevant. According to the relative risk aversion mechanism, the individual actor always tries to avoid unnecessary risks when making decisions (Breen and Goldthorpe 1997: 283). In general, the amount of insecurity is related to economic, social, and cultural resources as well as individual time management and available knowledge on educational options and their returns. Different individual resources (including social capital such as information about educational options etc.) and the institutional terms and conditions of an education system determine the decision-making frame. Educational institutions determine to what degree individual actors are permitted to decide for themselves based on their own considerations and how much weight is given to other authorities, such as teachers, schools or commissions. In Japan, the decision for high school and university is generally left to families, which have to also consider additional investments in shadow education to achieve certain educational goals. In addition, institutions act as guarantors of stability – they are supposed to guarantee that formerly promised returns to education connected to certain educational certificates will still exist at the time when students finish a chosen course of study. However, in the era of globalization, we find continuous institutional change (Hillmert 2005: 176–180). Today, increased convergence in education policy across national schooling systems due to progressing international standardization of education is prevalent (Meyer and Benavot 2013). New educational goals result in changes in the contents of educational certificates and thus confront parents, students, and teachers with new requirements. Moreover, national labor markets are increasingly affected by globalization. The concomitant institutional transformation causes new risks which have to be considered by individual decision-makers. Not being able to fully assess these risks, insecurities are created among families.

In conclusion, if risks become unpredictable, insecurity about future prospects increases. Insecurity then becomes a major factor in the formation of individual educational pathways. In the Japanese context, such insecurities might prove a decisive factor for the continued high familial investment in shadow education.

3.3   SEIT: Shadow Education as an Investment Strategy (The Japanese Viewpoint)

Partly due to the high costs and the assumed positive effects of shadow education on students' academic achievement, the belief that an investment in shadow education inevitably increases educational and thus social inequalities remains the prevalent opinion among the Japanese public and in Japanese academic research (Konakayama and Matsui 2008). To find a theoretical frame to empirically analyze this thesis and possibly disprove it, the Japanese educational sociologist Kazuo Seiyama (1981) introduced the *Shadow Education Investment Theory* (in the following SEIT).

In response to the 1970s' *juku*-boom (see Rohlen 1980), it became a necessity to create a theoretical frame to accurately analyze the Japanese shadow education sector based on empirical evidence. The SEIT underlies the strong belief among researchers as well as the public that investments in shadow education lead to a higher education level by taking advantage of the socioeconomic background of a student, consequently fostering educational inequality. Supposedly, parents with a higher SES are especially likely to use shadow education to increase their children's academic achievement and thus their education level, implying a causal connection between SES, amount of investment in shadow education, and students' academic achievement and future education level (Seiyama 1981: 173–178, Seiyama and Noguchi 1984: 113–114, Konakayama and Matsui 2008: 132). The model displayed in Fig. 3.2 shows the central relationships between the relevant variables of concern for this theory.

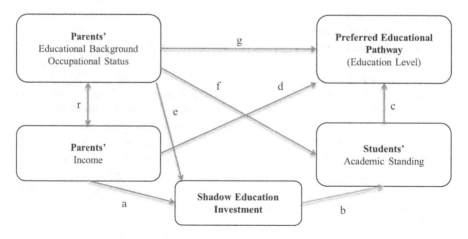

Fig. 3.2 *Shadow Education Investment Theory Model* (Seiyama 1981)

In summary, Seiyama (1981) outlined five different theory paths:

1. *Strong shadow education investment thesis* (path a → b): assumes that parents' income is causally related to students' academic achievement, since investments in shadow education are believed to be positively related to academic achievement but affordable only by few.
2. *Less strong shadow education investment thesis* (path r → e → b): reflects a similar connection but includes also the educational as well as occupational status of the parents.
3. *Culture thesis* (path r → f): assumes that students are able to acquire a high academic achievement level due to high cultural stimulation within their home, originating from their parents' high educational background and societal position.
4. *Income thesis* (path d): depicts the classical inequality of educational opportunities caused by income inequality.
5. *Aspiration thesis* (path g): assumes an increase of students' education level due to an increased educational motivation as well as higher educational aspirations because of parents' high educational and societal status and thus aspirations for their children.

The SEIT is still the predominant view in Japanese social science research concerned with shadow education. Similar to Western theories about social reproduction (Boudon 1974; Bourdieu and Passeron 1977; Bourdieu 1983), in particular the above-introduced RCT approaches, the SEIT assumes that shadow education in Japan is a choice that parents make based on their economic (*income thesis*: path d) as well as social and cultural capital (*culture thesis*: path r → f) and their own future aspirations for their children (*aspiration thesis*: path g). The central difference of SEIT in comparison to RCT is that students' academic achievement level in school is generally understood as an outcome rather than the cause of shadow education investments. Further, the SEIT assumes that the final education level of a student is determined by academic achievement, implying that any increase in academic standing automatically results in higher chances to achieve a high education level. Hence, it is assumed that parents use shadow education as an educational strategy to increase their children's chances of achieving a high education level by enhancing children's academic achievement level, particularly by procuring entrance exam preparation for high-ranked schools (*strong* and *less strong shadow education investment theses*: paths a → b and r → e → b).

Research generally detected a strong influence of parents' SES on investment in shadow education[1] (e.g., Kataoka 2001, 2015; Konakayama and Matsui 2008; Tomura et al. 2011) and found generally positive effects of shadow education on

---

[1] Seiyama and Noguchi (1984) found differences between male and female middle school students in how the SES of parents affected shadow education investment in a *juku*. A positive correlation between SES and *juku* attendance in 8th grade was found for male students but not for female students, whose family background did not affect whether or not they participated in *juku*-classes.

academic achievement or educational forthcoming (e.g., Seiyama and Noguchi 1984; Kataoka 2001; Kita 2006; Mimizuka 2007; Konakayama and Matsui 2008; Yamamoto and Brinton 2010; Entrich 2014), thus strengthening the belief that shadow education contributes to social reproduction. Whether students from disadvantaged family background find ways to access shadow education and whether the effects of shadow education vary for students from different social strata remains to be scrutinized.

3.4 NIT: Shadow Education as a Changing Institution in Japan

Recent publications in the field of comparative education stressed that development and shape of regular and shadow education systems are increasingly affected by a "global culture of education" and education reforms (Baker and LeTendre 2005; Baker 2014). In Japan, political forces driving educational reformation strongly adapt to new international preferences in education (Takayama 2013), wherefore the Japanese shadow education industry is expected to have experienced a transformation reflecting progressing educational globalization as well (Mori and Baker 2010). However, it was not yet empirically verified whether shadow education "goes beyond shadowing the formal system" (Dawson 2010: 17).

To find a theoretical frame to explain whether change within the Japanese shadow education industry has occurred, the New Institutionalism provides a reasonable and applicable theoretical foundation. According to Baker and LeTendre (2005), institutions are understood as "a set of rules for behavior and social roles [which are] powerful in [controlling] human behavior through the production of shared meaning in all realms of human existence" (p. 9). Consequently, social – and in this sense also educational – change happens through the changing of institutions (ibid: 11–12). The existent main division of this theoretical perspective into the culture and the rational choice approach offers two logical explanations. According to the culture approach, institutions are understood as a mirror of social values, norms, and structures, which provide orientation and aim to ensure the stability of social order. Following this approach, institutions are based on certain, generally shared social ideas and beliefs which result in the development of specific action patterns. Through institutions, values and ideas are transmitted from one generation to the next. However, the perception, interpretation, and implementation of these transferred norms, ideas, and moral concepts are content to variation and change. On the one hand, institutions affect individual and social actions. On the other hand, institutions also can be affected by individual actors and their actions (Maurer and Schmid 2002: 21). Japan is a country that was characterized as holding a unique position in Asia, because of being a Western-like industrial state while possessing a very different cultural heritage (Shimizu 2001: 194). In this sense, the formation of the Japanese shadow education system was a direct response to cultural specifics in conjunction with Western education structures and educational ideals as implemented following World War II.

In contrast to the cultural approach of the new institutionalism, the representatives of the rational choice approach tend to explain the formation of institutions as reaction to the actions of rationally acting individuals in response to changing circumstances or arising challenges. Here individual cost–benefit calculations are the reason for efforts that generate and maintain institutions. In turn, institutions function as frame for these individual cost–benefit considerations (Maurer and Schmid 2002: 21). Through their actions, individuals (e.g., students and parents) have the potential to change existing boundaries in the institutional world of education or create new institutions. In this regard, the formation of the *juku*-industry itself must be understood as a direct outcome of families' changed rationales concerning the education of their children. Instead of the Japanese government, which did not meet the educational demands of parents in the postwar era, private operators offered educational support (Haasch 1979: 43–46; Drinck 2002: 263). Since the 1970s' *ran-juku jidai* (period of *juku* overflow; Mawer 2015), the *juku*-industry continuously expanded its supply until its consolidation during the 1990s. During the mid-1990s, this industry reached its peak – in terms of prevalence, impact, and possibly level of specialization. Rohlen (1980) summarized this very appropriately, when writing that "[j]uku are expressions par excellence of 'middle class' ambition. Their popularity reflects the extent to which 'middle class' attitudes about education permeate Japan" (p. 238).

According to the NIT, recent changes affecting the education system of Japan, such as decreasing student populations as a result of consistently low birth rates and the *yutori kyōiku* (no-pressure education) reforms, which aimed at the relaxation of the highly competitive and rigid education system (see Chap. 10), should also show remarkable impact on the shadow education market. Following the rationale of the New Institutionalism, changed demand for shadow education should result in changes within the structure and contents of the *juku*-industry. Such changes might hold valuable and significant explanations for persisting inequalities or increasing educational opportunities through shadow education.

3.5   Summary

This chapter's aim was to identify and evaluate adequate theoretical concepts suited to explain the possible implications of shadow education investments on educational and social inequality formation in the Japanese context. In the end, all here described theoretical approaches share one major similarity: they understand the demand for shadow education as a result of rational cost–benefit considerations of forward-looking individuals, whereas the outcomes of such investments are believed to foster social inequalities. Based on the above discussions, the following basic points build the foundation for my theoretical discussions in the upcoming empirical part of this book:

1. The investment in shadow education is a *willful decision* made by rationally acting, forward-looking individuals.
2. School choice and the decision for shadow education are *close-knit* in Japan.
3. *Primary and secondary effects of social origin* influence the decision for school and shadow education alike and thus the educational pathway and future social status of students. The structure of the Japanese education system and its institutional framework place more weight on the secondary effect, wherefore educational aspirations have a major impact on educational decisions, including the decision for shadow education.
4. All social strata mean to avoid downward social mobility and thus have *identical relative risk aversion*. To maintain their social status, families with advantaged social backgrounds consider shadow education investments an effective security strategy (*status maintenance motive*), whereas such investments are also considered by more disadvantaged social strata, which then need to take into account higher risks of possible failure, if they intend to climb up the social ladder (*status advancement motive*).
5. *Insecurity* concerning the worth of educational credentials affects whether educational motivation outweighs investment risk and thus whether investments in shadow education are considered.
6. The Japanese shadow education industry is an institutionalized education market that is bound to the regular schooling system and its development. *Institutional change* in this industry happens through changes in the formal education system, which result in new educational demands of families based on rational cost–benefit considerations and cultural specifics (i.e., extraordinary high educational ambitions). Such demands are translated into decision-making, which affects the formation of educational and social inequalities.

In sum, in accordance with the macro–micro–macro model of Social Theory (Coleman 1990), on the one hand, macro-level conditions place high pressure on micro-level decisions in Japan. On the other hand, micro-level decisions show a decisive impact for macro-level inequality formation (on the development of Western sociology in Japan, see also Srubar and Shimada 2005). To clarify whether investments in shadow education inevitably result in inequality or equal educational opportunities, in my upcoming empirical chapters (Part II of the book), the four main dimensions affecting the implications of shadow education for inequality formation as introduced in the SEII Frame (see Chap. 1, Fig. 1.2) are analyzed based on the above theoretical considerations, applying the introduced concepts where applicable (Fig. 3.3).

It has to be noted though that in each of the subsequent empirical chapters, further significant amendments to the here outlined general concepts will be made to derive hypotheses fit for analysis. This is due to the fact that these theories were not meant for analyzing shadow education and its possible impact on social inequalities but stem from traditional views on education as regular schooling. This way, new versions of these theoretical concepts that are suited to be applied to the analysis of

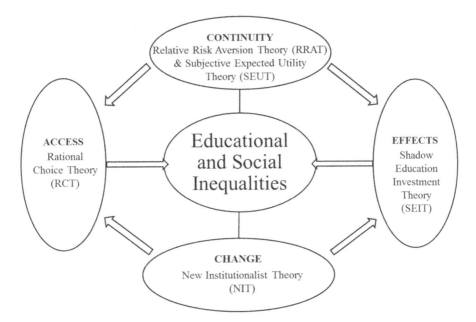

Fig. 3.3 Theoretical concepts as applied in the *Shadow–Education–Inequality–Impact* (SEII) Frame

shadow education become possible, thereby enabling us to enlarge our knowledge on this informal education sector and its implications.

For this specific study, the following concepts will be primarily used in the upcoming chapters, as shown in Fig. 3.3: As for the *access* to shadow education, particular emphasis is laid on RCT (Chap. 5). The analysis concerning the *effects* places stronger weight on SEIT (Chap. 6). To explain the *continuity* of the shadow education industry, particularly RRAT and SEUT will serve as basis for discussion (Chap. 7), before the *change* of the industry is discussed based on NIT (Chap. 8).

References

Akimoto, T. (2013). *Gakkōgaikyōiku to gakuryoku kakusa ni kansuru kenkyū – Gakuryoku kakusa e no yūkōna seisaku to wa* [Research on out-of-school education and the academic achievement gap – What are effective policies concerning the achievement gap]. Tokyo: Hitotsubashi University.

Aurini, J., Davies, S., & Dierkes, J. (Hrsg.). (2013). *Out of the shadows: The global intensification of supplementary education* (International perspectives on education and society). Bingley: Emerald Publishing.

Baker, D. P. (2014). *The schooled society*. Stanford: Stanford University Press.

Baker, D. P., & LeTendre, G. K. (2005). *National differences, global similarities. World culture and the future of schooling*. Stanford: Stanford University Press.

Becker, R., & Lauterbach, W. (2004). Dauerhafte Bildungsungleichheiten – Ursachen, Mechanismen, Prozesse und Wirkungen [Persistent educational inequalities – Causes, mechanisms, processes and outcomes]. In R. Becker & W. Lauterbach (Eds.), *Bildung als Privileg? Erklärungen und Befunde zu den Ursachen der Bildungsungleichheit* [Education as a privilege? Observations and findings on the causes of educational inequality] (pp. 9–40). Wiesbaden: VS Verlag.

Becker, R., & Lauterbach, W. (2016). Bildung als Privileg – Ursachen, Mechanismen, Prozesse und Wirkungen [Education as a privilege – causes, mechanisms, processes and outcomes]. In R. Becker & W. Lauterbach (Eds.), *Bildung als Privileg – Erklärungen und Befunde zu den Ursachen der Bildungsungleichheit* [Education as a privilege. Observations and findings on the causes of educational inequality] (Vol. 5, pp. 3–53). Wiesbaden: Springer VS.

Boudon, R. (1974). *Education, opportunity, and social inequality: Changing prospects in western society*. New York: Wiley.

Bourdieu, P. (1983). Ökonomisches Kapital, kulturelles Kapital, soziales Kapital [Economic capital, cultural capital, social capital]. In R. Kreckel (Ed.), *Soziale Ungleichheiten* [Social inequalities] (pp. 185–199). Göttingen: Otto Schwartz Verlag.

Bourdieu, P., & Passeron, J. C. (1977). *Reproduction in education, society and culture*. Beverly Hills: Sage.

Bray, M. (1999). *The shadow education system: Private tutoring and its implications for planners*. Paris: UNESCO/International Institute for Educational Planning (IIEP).

Bray, M. (2009). *Confronting the shadow education system: What government policies for what private tutoring?* Paris: UNESCO/International Institute for Educational Planning (IIEP).

Bray, M. (2011). *The challenge of shadow education: Private tutoring and its implications for policy makers in the European Union*. Retrieved from: http://www.nesse.fr/nesse/activities/reports

Bray, M., & Kwo, O. (2014). *Regulating private tutoring for public good. Policy options for supplementary education in Asia*. Hong Kong: Comparative Education Research Center (CERC).

Bray, M., & Lykins, C. (2012). *Shadow education: Private tutoring and its implications for policy makers in Asia*. Hong Kong: Comparative Education Research Center (CERC) and Asian Development Bank.

Breen, R., & Goldthorpe, J. H. (1997). Explaining educational differentials – Towards a formal rational action theory. *Rationality and Society, 9*(3), 275–305.

Breen, R., Werfhorst, H. v. d., & Jæger, M. M. (2014). Deciding under doubt: A theory of risk aversion, time discounting preferences, and educational decision-making. *European Sociological Review, 30*(2), 258–270.

Coleman, J. S. (1990). *Foundations of social theory*. Cambridge: Harvard University Press.

Dawson, W. (2010). Private tutoring and mass schooling in East Asia: Reflections of inequality in Japan, South Korea and Cambodia. *Asia Pacific Educational Review, 11*, 14–24.

Dierkes, J. (2013). The insecurity industry: Supplementary education in Japan. In J. Aurini, S. Davies, & J. Dierkes (Eds.), *Out of the shadows: The global intensification of supplementary education* (International perspectives on education and society, Vol. 22, pp. 3–21). Bingley: Emerald Publishing.

Drinck, B. (2002). Marktorientierung im japanischen Bildungssystem [Market orientation in the Japanese education system]. *Zeitschrift für Erziehungswissenschaft, 5*(2), 261–278.

Entrich, S. R. (2014). Effects of investments in out-of-school education in Germany and Japan. *Contemporary Japan, 26*(1), 71–102.

Erikson, R., & Jonsson, J. O. (1996). Explaining class inequality in education – The Swedish test case. In R. Erikson & J. O. Jonsson (Eds.), *Can education be equalized? The Swedish case in comparative perspective* (pp. 1–63). Boulder: Westview Press.

Esser, H. (1999). *Soziologie – Spezielle Grundlagen. Band 1: Situationslogik und Handeln* [Sociology – Special Foundations. Volume 1: Situational Logic and Action]. Frankfurt a.M: Campus Verlag.

Fujihara, S. (2011). Breen ando Goldthorpe no aitaiteki risuku kaihi kasetsu no kenshō: Chichioya no kodomo ni taisuru shokugyō kyōiku kitai o mochiita keiryō bunseki [Empirical test of Breen and Goldthorpe's relative risk aversion hypothesis in the Japanese society: Data analysis of a father's occupational and educational expectations for his child]. *Shakaigaku Hyōron, 62*(1), 18–35.

Furuta, K. (2011). Kyōikukikai no kaisōsa ni kansuru rirontekisetsumei no kentō [On the mechanisms of class difference in educational attainment]. *Ōsakadaigaku Daigakuin Ningen Kagaku Kenkyū-ka Kiyō, 37*, 193–213.

Guill, K. (2012). *Nachhilfeunterricht. Individuelle, familiäre und schulische Prädiktoren* [Tutoring. Individual, Familial and School Predictors]. Münster/New York/München/Berlin: Waxmann.

Haasch, G. (1979). *Japanisches und Deutsches Bildungssystem – Versuch eines Systemvergleichs* [The education systems of Japan and Germany – An attempt to compare both systems]. Tokyo: OAG.

Hamamoto, S. (2015). Gōri-teki sentaku to kyōiku kikaifubyōdō: Shitsuteki sai o kōryo shita sōtai risuku kaihi moderu no jōshiki-ka [Explaining educational differentials with rational action theory: Formalizing relative risk aversion under qualitative differentials]. *Tōhokudaigaku Daigakuin Kyōikugakukenkyūka Kenkyū Nenpō, 63*(2), 1–21.

Hillmert, S. (2005). Bildungsentscheidungen und Unsicherheit: Soziologische Aspekte eines vielschichtigen Zusammenhangs [Educational decisions and uncertainty: Sociological aspects of a multifaceted relationship]. *Zeitschrift für Erziehungswissenschaft, 8*(2), 173–186.

Jonsson, J. O., & Erikson, R. (2000). Understanding educational inequality: The Swedish experience. *L'Année Sociologique, 50*, 345–382.

Kataoka, E. (2001). Kyōiku tassei katei ni okeru kazoku no kyōiku senryaku: Bunka shihon kōka to gakkōgai kyōiku tōshi kōka no jendāsa o chūshin ni [Family strategy in educational attainment process in Japan: Effects of cultural capital and investment in extra-school education]. *Kyōikugaku Kenkyū, 68*(3), 259–273.

Kataoka, E. (2015). Gakkōgaikyōiku-hi shishutsu to kodomo no gakuryoku. [Expenses for out-of-school education and academic achievement of students]. *Komazawadaigaku Bungakubu Kenkyū Kiyō, 73*, 259–273.

Kita, K. (2006). Gakkōgai kyōiku riyō ni tsuite no nenrei, jendā-betsu no tokusei to kaisōteki yōin. [Age, gender specifics and class determinants of out-of-school education utilization]. *Kyōiku Jissen Kenkyū, 14*, 1–7.

Konakayama, A., & Matsui, T. (2008). Gakkōgai kyōiku tōshi no gakuryoku ni oyobosu eikyō ni kansuru ikkōsatsu [An empirical study on how extra school education affects academic achievement of Japanese high school students]. *Tōkaidaigaku Seiji Keizaigakubu Kiyō, 40*, 131–158.

Luplow, N., & Schneider, T. (2014). Nutzung und Effektivität privat bezahlter Nachhilfe im Primarbereich [Utilization and effectiveness of private tutoring in primary school]. *Zeitschrift für Soziologie, 43*(1), 31–49.

Maaz, K., Hausen, C., McElvany, N., & Jürgen, B. (2006). Stichwort – Übergänge im Bildungssystem. Theoretische Konzepte und ihre Anwendung in der empirischen Forschung beim Übergang in die Sekundarstufe [Keyword – transitions in the education system. Theoretical concepts and their application in empirical research on the transition to the secondary school level]. *Zeitschrift für Erziehungswissenschaft, 9*(3), 299–327.

Marks, G. N. (2005). Cross-national differences and accounting for social class inequalities in education. *International Sociology, 20*(4), 483–505.

Maurer, A., & Schmid, M (2002). Die ökonomische Herausforderung der Soziologie? [The economic challenge of sociology?]. In A. Maurer & M. Schmid (Eds.), Neuer Institutionalismus: Zur soziologischen Erklärung von Organisation, Moral und Vertrauen [New institutionalism: Concerning a sociological explanation of organization, morale and confidence] (pp. 9–38). Frankfurt am Main: Campus.

Mawer, K. (2015). Casting new light on shadow education – Snapshots of Juku variety. *Contemporary Japan, 27*(2), 131–148.

Meyer, H-D., & Benavot A. (Hrsg.). (2013). *PISA, power, and policy: The emergence of global educational governance.* Oxford: Symposium Books.

Meyer, J. W., Ramirez, F. O., & Soysal, Y. N. (1992). World expansion of mass education, 1870–1980. *Sociology of Education, 65*(2), 128–149.

Mimizuka, H. (2007). Shōgakkō gakuryoku kakusa ni idomu: Dare ga gakuryoku o kakutoku suru no ka. [Determinants of children's academic achievements in primary education]. *Kyōiku Shakaigaku Kenkyū, 80*, 23–39.

Mori, I., & Baker, D. P. (2010). The origin of universal shadow education – What the supplemental education phenomenon tells us about the postmodern institution of education. *Asia Pacific Educational Review, 11*, 36–48.

Okano, K. (1995). Rational decision making and school-based job referrals for high school students in Japan. *Sociology of Education, 68*(1), 31–47.

Ramirez, F. O., & Boli, J. (1987). The political construction of mass schooling: European origins and worldwide institutionalization. *Sociology of Education, 60*(1), 2–17.

Rohlen, T. P. (1980). The Juku phenomenon: An exploratory essay. *Journal of Japanese Studies, 6*(2), 207–242.

Sato, Y. (2013). Rational choice theory. *Sociopedia.isa, 2013*, 1–10.

Sato, Y. (2017). Institutions and actors in the creation of social inequality. A rational choice approach to social inequality. In D. Chiavacci & C. Hommerich (Eds.), *Social inequality in post-growth Japan. Transformation during economic and demographic stagnation* (pp. 29–36). London/New York: Routledge.

Schneider, T. (2005). Nachhilfe als Strategie zur Verwirklichung von Bildungszielen. Eine empirische Untersuchung mit Daten des Sozio-oekonomischen Panels (SOEP) [Private tutoring as a strategy for achieving educational goals. An empirical study based on the German Socio-Economic Panel (SOEP)]. *Zeitschrift für Pädagogik, 51*(3), 363–379.

Seiyama, K. (1981). Gakkōgai kyōiku tōshi no kōka ni kansuru ichikōsatsu [A study of the effects of out-of-school educational investment]. *Hokudai Bungakubu Kiyō, 30*(1), 171–221.

Seiyama, K., & Noguchi, Y. (1984). Kōkō shingaku ni okeru gakkōgai kyōiku tōshi no kōka [The effects of outside of school educational investments at the transition to high school]. *Kyōiku Shakaigaku Kenkyū, 39*, 113–126.

Shavit, Y., & Blossfeld, H.-P. (1993). *Persistent inequality: Changing educational attainment in thirteen countries*. Boulder: Westview Press.

Shimizu, K. (2001). The pendulum of reform: educational change in Japan from the 1990s onwards. *Journal of Educational Change, 2*, 193–205.

Srubar, I., & Shimada, S. (Hrsg.). (2005). *Development of sociology in Japan*. Wiesbaden: Springer.

Stevenson, D. L., & Baker, D. P. (1992). Shadow education and allocation in formal schooling: Transition to university in Japan. *American Journal of Sociology, 97*, 1639–1657.

Stocke, V. (2007). Explaining educational decision and effects of families' social class position: An empirical test of the Breen–Goldthorpe model of educational attainment. *European Sociological Review, 23*(4), 505–519.

Takayama, K. (2013). Untangling the global-distant-local knot: The politics of national academic achievement testing in Japan. *Journal of Education Policy, 28*(5), 657–675.

Tomura, A., Nishimaru, R., & Oda, T. (2011). Kyōiku tōshi no kitei yōin to kōka: Gakkōgai kyōiku to shiritsu chūgaku shingaku o chūshin ni. [Determinants and effects of investments in education: Focusing on out-of-school education and the transition to private middle schools]. In Y. Satō, & F. Ojima (Eds.), Gendai no kaisō shakai: Kakusa to tayōsei [*Modern class society: Disparity and diversity*] (pp. 267–280). Tokyo: University of Tokyo Press.

Yamamoto, Y., & Brinton, M. C. (2010). Cultural capital in East Asian educational systems: The case of Japan. *Sociology of Education, 83*(1), 67–83.

Chapter 4
Data and Methods

How to Empirically Grasp the Implications of Shadow Education on Educational and Social Differentials in Japan?

> *"[Q]ualitative and quantitative methods should be viewed as complementary rather than as rival camps"*
>
> ('Mixing Qualitative and Quantitative Methods: Triangulation in Action', by Todd D. Jick 1979: 602)
>
> データ

Abstract The field of shadow education research remains largely empirically unexamined. Existing empirical studies often remain very limited in their explanatory power due to the use of inadequate data sources and limited methodical approaches. In addressing the question which data and methods are best suited to achieve empirically founded comprehensive findings when empirically analyzing the implications of shadow education for social inequalities, first, existing data sources are evaluated. Second, by understanding the mixing of methods as beneficial instead of mutually exclusive, two surveys are introduced, which complement each other and allow both quantitative and qualitative analyses. Whereas the *Hyōgo High School Students* (HHSS) surveys of the years 1997 and 2011 allow for quantitative analyses of the demanding side of shadow education and across student cohorts and times, the *Juku Student and Teacher Survey* (JSTS) of the year 2013 allows for qualitative analyses from the angle of providers of shadow education as well. Third, the importance to use alternative estimates besides odds ratios, etc. to achieve comparable findings, is stressed. Finally, it is shown in which of the four dimensions outlined in the Shadow-Education-Inequality-Impact (SEII) Frame (*Access*, *Effects*, *Continuity*, and *Change*) the introduced data can be used.

© Springer International Publishing AG 2018
S.R. Entrich, *Shadow Education and Social Inequalities in Japan*,
https://doi.org/10.1007/978-3-319-69119-0_4

4.1   Problematic

To achieve empirically founded comprehensive findings, a suitable data is of essence. In the process of evaluating existing data sources that have been used to analyze the phenomenon of shadow education in the Japanese or any other context, inevitably the question whether these data are actually fit for empirical analyses concerning the implications of shadow education for social inequalities occurred. For this work, thus, the question which data would be best suited to realize reliable findings concerning the issue of social inequality and shadow education in the Japanese context is central. In addition, fitting methods to achieve the intended findings based on the chosen data proves essential. These are hurdles all researchers have think more about when researching this topic in any context, whether local, regional, national, or international. Reliable findings bearing the potential to increase our knowledge on social inequality in educational attainment in all its forms can only be produced, if much care is put into the problematic of fitting theory and data.

As I outlined in the Shadow-Education-Inequality-Impact (SEII) Frame (Chap. 1, Fig. 1.2), to achieve reliable and convincing findings on the subject, the used data should provide the opportunity to analyze determinants for the *access* to shadow education and its *effects* for individual educational pathways in present Japan. To further understand the relative impact of shadow education on social inequalities, analyses over time focusing on the possible determinants for the *continuity* and *change* of this industry are necessary. On first glance, international large-scale assessment studies such as PISA and TIMSS seem to provide the best suited data for analyzing shadow education in different national contexts including Japan. Until now, however, only few international educationalists drew on these large, representative student samples with the aim to analyze the determinants or effects of shadow education (or rather out-of-school time lessons; e.g., Baker et al. 2001, Darby E. Southgate 2009, Ojima and von Below 2010, Entrich 2013, Park 2013, Darby E. Southgate 2013, Entrich 2014a, b, Matsuoka 2015). In fact, as is the case with all studies, a number of limitations is apparent, which are not only of methodological nature. Besides cultural patterns, the questionnaires' item styles, and sample variations between countries (Hamano 2011: 3–4), we find definition and translation inaccuracy regarding the items used to capture shadow education (particularly for Japan), whereas the focus of these studies on certain student cohorts in the middle of their school careers (e.g., either 4th or 8th graders in TIMSS or 15-year-olds in PISA) does not allow to draw overall conclusions on the impact of shadow education for final educational success or participation across students' whole school life courses (see also Entrich 2014a: 83–84, 96–97). Hence, to analyze shadow education and its implications for social inequalities in Japan, nation-specific datasets are better suited.

After reviewing several promising Japanese datasets such as the *Social Stratification and Mobility* (SSM) surveys,[1] I decided to use the *Hyōgo High School*

[1] The SSM is the most prominent dataset in Japanese social sciences, conducted every 10 years since 1955.

Students (HHSS)[2] surveys of the years 1997 and 2011 as the main data basis for my quantitative analyses, because this dataset allows for broad analyses of the phenomenon of shadow education in Japan, as I will explain further in the subsequent part of this chapter. However, since even the HHSS data did not include all the necessary information to capture the implications of shadow education participation for educational and social inequalities, I designed and carried out an additional survey in 2013, called *Juku Student and Teacher Survey* (JSTS). In contrast to the HHSS data, the JSTS includes quantitative and qualitative data, allowing for generalizations based on "hard" data while "explaining the participants' perspectives and developing an understanding of the meanings they attach to the phenomena of interest" (Fairbrother 2014: 76). As the above quotation by Todd D. Jick shall illustrate, I view the mixing of methods as beneficial instead of being mutually exclusive.

In this chapter, the purposes, specifics, and advantages of both surveys will be shortly introduced followed by an introduction of the variables used in the later carried-out analyses. Following this, I will discuss the specifics of the later applied methods and estimations. Finally, a brief summary is provided.

4.2   HHSS: *Hyōgo High School Students Survey*

The HHSS survey is a cooperative research project of several universities across Japan and was conducted under the guidance of professors Fumiaki Ojima (Dōshisha University) and Sōhei Aramaki (Kyūshū University).[3] Targeting students at the end of their school life course (end of 12th grade), this survey provides a great amount of valuable data regarding the school life of high school students, their social backgrounds, and their expectations about life after school. Of particular interest for this work are students' experiences with shadow education, which have been surveyed in detail. Furthermore, several items were conducted in retrospective, thus allowing for calculations across students' whole school life courses.

The first HHSS survey has been carried out in 1981 on the largest of the four main Japanese islands, Honshu, in the prefecture Hyōgo, west central Japan. Hyōgo prefecture is not only part of the Kansai area, Japan's second largest economical and second most populated area following the conurbation Tōkyō; it also consists of urban and rural parts ranging from the Sea of Japan in the North to the Inland Sea in the South, where the capital Kōbe is located. Kōbe is the sixth largest city in Japan with a population of 1.5 million people. Along with Ōsaka and Kyōto, Kōbe is part of the Kyōto-Ōsaka-Kōbe metropolitan center of the Kansai region. Consequently, Hyōgo prefecture reflects the average Japanese population and is

---

[2] Original title: *Kōkōsei no shinro to seikatsu ni kansuru chōsa* = "A survey concerning the school course and school life of high school students."

[3] Thanks to Professor Ojima, I was directly included in the data evaluation process in 2012 and 2013. For further information about this survey, see Ojima and Aramaki (2013).

thus a good area to conduct data on the Japanese schooling system as well. Here, differently ranked high schools across the prefecture have been chosen in order to reflect the current school life situation of high school students in this prefecture and to show the diversity not just between students but schools as well. Basically similar surveys were repeated in 1997 and 2011 using comparable questions on the core items, such as social background. Thus, cross-temporal comparisons are possible.

As shown in Fig. 4.1, the first survey included 18 schools (2.782 students), the second survey was carried out at 15 schools (2.397 students), whereas the third survey included 17 schools (3.826 students). Even though each survey includes different schools, ten schools remained constant in all three surveys. However, in spite of its high relevance, the prevalence of shadow education and its impact on social inequality formation has not been a prominent research subject for a long time and was rather neglected in earlier research. Therefore, the first HHSS survey includes no questions on shadow education participation at all. This changed in the second round of the survey, where questions concerning students' participation in shadow education of several types during primary and middle school were included, before students' experiences with shadow education during their high school years were added in the 2011 survey as well. Hence, certain cross-temporal comparisons are possible and may shed light on changes in the access to shadow education against the background of major societal and educational changes from the early 1990s to the late 2000s. In addition, students were asked about their future plans as well as their experiences in retrospective, e.g., their post-high school graduation plans. This provides us with valuable data regarding the whole school life course of students of the late baby boomer generation attending the school system in the 1990s in comparison to students of the post-baby boomer generation who attended school in the 2000 years.

In the following, the variables used in the upcoming analyses of part two are shortly introduced. The focus lies primarily on data of the 2011 HHSS survey, complemented by data of the 1997 survey, where applicable. Based on the theoretical

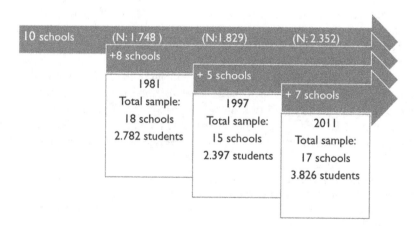

Fig. 4.1 HHSS 1981/1997/2011 – sample overviews (Ojima 2001; Ojima and Aramaki 2013)

discussion presented in Chap. 3, of particular importance for the later carried-out analyses are students' experiences with shadow education, their family background, educational aspirations, academic achievement, and the institutional and structural schooling context as reflected in school ranking. Accordingly, these variables are briefly introduced in the following.

4.2.1 Shadow Education Participation

Based on the discussion by Stevenson and Baker (1992), Bray (2010) defined shadow education as academic, supplementary, and private (see Chap. 1). The HHSS data provides us with information on the three major types of shadow education in Japan, which comply with this definition of Bray (2010): *gakushū juku* (academic *juku*, including *yobikō*), *katei kyōshi* (private home tutors), and *tsūshin tensaku* (correspondence courses). In the 2011 survey, students were asked whether they have participated in these three types of supplementary education during their primary, middle, and high school years or not. Students' experiences with shadow education were separately encoded as dummy variables (1 = yes; 0 = no) for each type and for total participation experience.

4.2.1.1 Total Enrolment

As illustrated in Fig. 4.2, a high percentage of the 12th grade students who participated in the 2011 survey received shadow education lessons from 2000 to 2005, when they were in primary school (61%), and from 2006 to 2008, when they attended middle

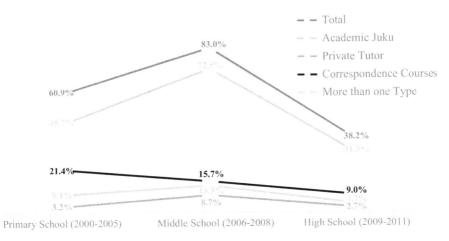

Fig. 4.2 High school students' experience with different types of shadow education during their primary, middle, and high school years, multiple responses possible, in % (HHSS 2011)

school (83%), but to a lesser extent from 2009 to 2011, during their high school years (38%). While correspondence courses were used more often in earlier grades (21%), the investment rates for private tutors (9%) and academic *juku* (73%) were highest in middle school, where the peak of out-of-school lesson attendance is reached.

However, since multiple responses were possible, we also find students who participated in more than one type of shadow education concurrently during their school life, but this only applies for students who aimed for a university. In total, 9.1% of all students participated in more than one type of shadow education during primary school, 13.5% during middle school, and 4.7% in high school. Most multiple users supplemented attendance at a *juku* with correspondence courses (7.8% in primary, 9.1% in middle, and 4.1% in high school). In contrast, students who participated in all three types of shadow education at the same time are almost nonexistent (<1%).

Although it seems reasonable to assume that the growth of the Japanese *juku*-industry is already beyond its peak, the participation in shadow education has only decreased partially. When comparing the student cohorts of 1997 and 2011, who were enrolled at the same high schools (Fig. 4.3), we find a slight but overall decrease of the student population's enrolment in shadow education in primary and middle school.

Of the 1997 cohort who attended primary school from 1986 to 1991, in total 66% participated in shadow education, whereas 88% of the same student cohort were enrolled in shadow education during their middle school years (1992–1994).

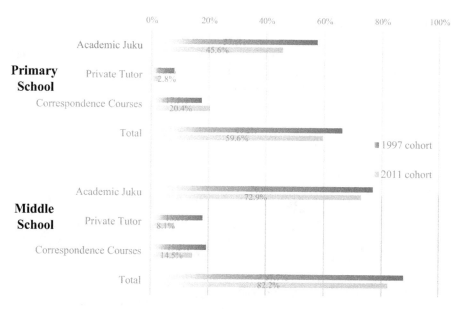

Valid responses: Only students of those schools (n=10) where considered, which took part in both surveys. HHSS 2011: n(students)= 2342 (primary school); 2341 (middle school); HHSS 1997: n(students)= 1792 (primary school); 1728 (middle school).

Fig. 4.3 High school students' experiences with different types of shadow education in the 1990s and 2000s, in % (HHSS 1997/2011)

In comparison, of the 2011 student cohort which attended primary school from 2000 to 2005, in total 60% participated in shadow education, whereas still 82% of the same student cohort reported to have participated in shadow education during their middle school years (2006–2008).

In general, our data report a decrease in enrolment rates in all fields of shadow education except for the utilization of correspondence courses during primary school, where a slight increase of 3% is found. Despite the low fertility rate and the carried-out reforms in education (see Chap. 10), the still high enrolment ratios during middle school might reflect the high concerns of families regarding admission to high ranked schools and thus social status maintenance. According to Takehiko Kariya, one of the leading Japanese sociologists in education, due to low birth rates simply more parents nowadays have the resources and the will to pay for their child's additional learning support.[4] Also, this indicates an unchanged difficulty level of certain entrance examinations and that the Japanese entrance examination hell is far from being overcome. According to our data, students in Hyōgo prefecture show generally similarly high enrolment ratios in shadow education in the 1990s and 2000s when compared to national data of the MEXT (see Chap. 7, Figs. 7.2 and 7.5).

4.2.1.2   Length of Enrolment

In addition to these numbers, we find considerable differences in the intensity of shadow education enrolment as measured in terms of length of enrolment. Table 4.1 gives an overview regarding students' long-term and short-term investments in shadow education according to period of participation and type of shadow education. In total, 88% of all students of the 2011 cohort have shadow education experience, and most of these students made long-term investments, either over their whole school life course (from primary to high school, 33%) or until entrance to high school was achieved (from primary to middle school, 31%). Considerable differences in investment periods are apparent according to type of supplementary lessons though: whereas almost two thirds of the students who have participated in *juku*-classes at some point during their school life course made long-term investments, students who decided for lessons given by private tutors or correspondence courses mostly followed short-term investment strategies.

4.2.1.3   Study Purposes

The generally found high participation ratios, however, do not account for students' actual study goals, meaning the educational goal they want to achieve. To measure students' study purposes when pursuing shadow education lessons during high school, I used students' higher education entrance intentions (i.e., the chosen entrance methods to enter a university or college). In general, students can either enter the higher education sector or the job market following high school graduation. If the

---

[4] Personal communication, November 2013.

Table 4.1 Long-term and short-term investments in shadow education, in % (HHSS 2011)

	Period of participation	Total	Academic *juku*	Private tutor	Corr. courses
Long-term	High, middle, and primary school	**32.6**	21.9	2.1	13.2
	High and middle school	9.0	13.9	9.0	5.8
	Middle and primary school	31.4	**28.4**	6.4	18.9
	Total	73.0	64.2	17.5	37.9
Short-term	Only high school	0.8	2.2	9.9	6.7
	Only middle school	21.1	26.8	**55.4**	15.4
	Only primary school	4.1	5.6	15.9	**35.3**
	High and primary school	1.0	1.3	1.4	4.9
	Total	27.0	35.9	82.6	62.3
Valid responses		*3308*	*2982*	*435*	*1112*
Percentage of all valid responses (*N* = 3748)		88.0	79.6	11.6	29.7

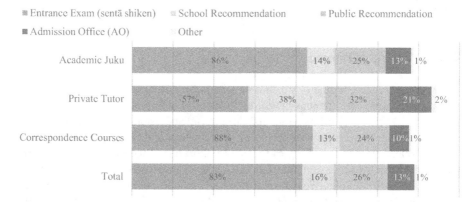

Valid responses: n(schools)=17; n(students)= 2923.

Fig. 4.4 High school students' experience with shadow education, according to the type and planned university entrance method, multiple responses possible, in % (HHSS 2011)

decision for staying in the education system is made, different entrance methods can be chosen. In the HHSS 2011 survey, students who responded that they would pursue an academic career following high school graduation (see also educational aspirations) were additionally asked how they intend to enter higher education.

Figure 4.4 shows the distribution of high school students according to used type of shadow education during high school (2009–2011) and planned entrance method to higher education at the end of 12th grade. Accordingly, the primary study focus of high school students using shadow education was preparation for entrance examinations (83.3%). Particularly students who participated in *juku*-classes and correspondence courses intended to enter higher education by taking the central entrance examination tests, the *sentā shiken*. In contrast, students receiving lessons from a private tutor at home more often seem to wish for entrance to higher education without taking the *sentā*. This kind of shadow education is only used by a very small proportion of students, though.

In general we see that students consider an investment in shadow education a probate strategy to enter higher education by succeeding in entrance exams. As an adequate alternative strategy, entrance by recommendations or through admission office (AO) has become prevalent also. Recent ministerial data showed that the percentage of students entering higher education by alternative entrance methods has increased since the 1990s for entrance through AO, but not for other alternative university entrance methods (M. o. E. MEXT, Culture, Sports, Science and Technology 2012: 1, 4). However, the total number of students taking the *sentā* has remained stable since the 1990s (see Chap. 10, Fig. 10.1). Hence, students who intend to enter higher education continue to participate in shadow education to prepare for a university and college entrance exams at the end of high school and are very likely to take the central entrance exam (*sentā shiken*). Consequently, the main study focus of students attending *juku* or other types of shadow education at the end of high school is to succeed in the central university entrance exam. These students' study focus emphasizes the traditional ways of school "transition" (*shingaku*). Still, a considerable proportion of students also continues to receive remedial and other supplementary lessons without focus on entrance exams. These students are thus understood as pursuing a general "supplementation" strategy (*hoshū*). In addition, we find a high percentage of students who do not confine themselves to using only one of the above study goals and thus follow a "comprehensive" approach (*sōgō*). Chapter 6 further discusses these main study purposes of students pursuing shadow education.

Based on the 2011 HHSS data, all high school students who stated that they intend to enter a university or college in the old-fashioned way by taking the central entrance exam are classified as having a *shingaku* study goal. Students who received supplementary lessons without intentions to enter higher education at all or via entrance exams were classified as pursuing a *hoshū* study goal. Students pursuing shadow education considering both strategies were classified as following an *sōgō* study purpose (Fig. 4.5).

According to our data, most students participate in shadow education during high school to prepare for university entrance exams (*shingaku*, 22%). Only about 7% of all students receive shadow education without having the intention to enter a university or college the traditional way (entrance exam) but pursue either alternative entrance methods or attempt to enter the job market after graduation (*hoshū*). An additional 9% of all high school students purchase lessons in the shadow with the intention to enter higher education through entrance exam or alternative methods (*sōgō*).

4.2.2   Social Origin

To measure the social origin of students as the most important explanatory variable in an analysis that is concerned with the identification of a possible increase of inequalities as an outcome of investments in shadow education, several different variables will be considered, which reflect certain dimensions of social origin fit for our analyses.

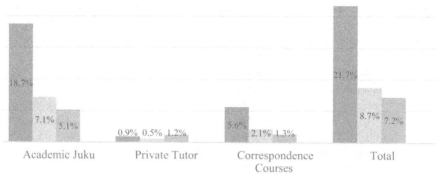

Valid responses: n(schools)=17; n(students)= 3729 (high school)

Fig. 4.5 High school students' experience with shadow education, according to study goal, in % (HHSS 2011)

4.2.2.1   Economic, Social, and Cultural Status (ESCS)

Following Bourdieu (1983), students' social origin is composed of different forms of parental human capital, which was defined as economic, social, and cultural. To reflect students' economic, social, and cultural status (ESCS), we created a variable including parents' highest occupational status[5] and highest education level,[6] as well as household possessions[7] and number of books[8] as the cultural component. Figure 4.6 shows the proportion of students participating in different types of shadow education across different social strata, ranging from the lowest quartile (low ESCS or underclass) over the two mediocre quartiles (middle ESCS or middle class) to the highest quartile (high ESCS or upper class).

The displayed distribution of students according to the four quarters of socioeconomic and cultural background (ESCS) shows significant differences in the participation rates in different types of shadow education from primary to high school.

---

[5] Parents' occupational status is encoded as (1) leading positions in companies with at least five employees, (2) regular full-time employees (such as *sarariiman*), (3) part-time employees, (4) self-employed with less than four employees, (5) helping out in the family business, (6) others, and (7) unemployed men or full-time housewives.

[6] Parents' education level is encoded as (1) university degree or higher, (2) junior college, (3) technical college, (4) high school diploma, and (5) middle school diploma (see also the following subsection).

[7] The home possessions variable is a score variable consisting of the following 11 variables asking about students' and their households' possessions: Q20-1, own room (including a room shared with siblings); Q20-2, own passport; Q20-3, Blu-ray/DVD recorder; Q20-4, digital camera; Q20-5, LCD/Plasma television; Q20-6, air cleaning machine; Q20-7, own computer; Q20-8, own mobile telephone; Q20-9, dishwasher; Q20-10, piano; and Q20-11, water filter machine.

[8] The definition of books in this survey excludes comic books, magazines, school textbooks, or reference books.

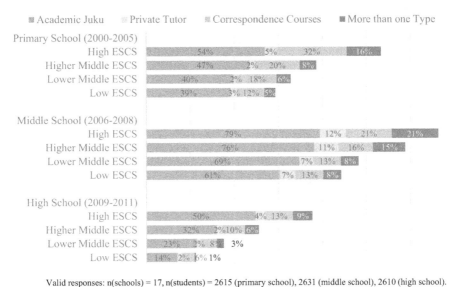

Valid responses: n(schools) = 17, n(students) = 2615 (primary school), 2631 (middle school), 2610 (high school).

Fig. 4.6 High school students' experiences with different types of shadow education during their primary, middle, and high school years, according to ESCS, multiple responses possible, in % (HHSS 2011)

With decreasing ESCS background, the participation in shadow education seems to decrease as well. Low ESCS students (bottom quarter) are generally participating in all kinds of shadow education to a lesser extent. Particularly during high school (2009–2011), most low strata students stopped their investment in shadow education.

Our data further suggests that the length of enrolment is depending on the ESCS of a student. Low ESCS strata seem to generally pursue short-term investment strategies, whereas high ESCS strata can afford to make long-term investments more often, in particular in the cases of *juku*-classes and correspondence courses. This supports the argument that low ESCS students who pursue shadow education follow purposeful and goal-oriented investment strategies. Because low ESCS students do not possess the resources to make long-term investments, short-term investments simply have to pay off (see Appendix, Fig. 4.14). Furthermore, significant differences in the proportion of students which pursue certain study goals when participating in shadow education in high school are found across ESCS groups. Almost one third of all high ESCS students pursue *shingaku*-oriented *juku* (focus on entrance exam preparation), whereas only 7% of low ESCS students invest in these kinds of lessons. The same general discrepancy is found for correspondence courses and private tutors. Besides these general differences in enrolment rates, similarities are also detected. If low ESCS strata find ways to participate in *juku*-classes during high school, they will mostly attend *shingaku* programs. Correspondence courses are more often pursued using *shingaku* programs but also *sōgō* programs (focus on entrance exam preparation and remediation). In contrast to each other, high ESCS strata use private tutors mostly with *shingaku* focus; low ESCS strata mostly receive such lessons with *hoshū* purposes (focus on remediation) (see Appendix, Fig. 4.15).

4.2.2.2 Highest Parental Education Level

Bukodi and Goldthorpe (2013) stressed that social origin needs to be "decomposed" to get a better understanding of how certain components of social origin might affect students' educational attainment. The authors proposed using components such as class, status, and education of parents separately when analyzing educational inequalities, especially when making comparisons over time to assess whether stability or change occurred in the impacts of social origins on educational attainment. Since the education level strongly determines social status in Japan (Kikkawa 2006), the parental education level is supposed to play a crucial role for social reproduction and thus is the most important component of the ESCS in the Japanese context. Also, this measure of social origin is very well suited for comparisons across time, since there are no variations within its definition and measurement.

In both HHSS surveys (1997 and 2011), parents' highest education level was measured separately for fathers and mothers using a five-degree scale ranging from the highest education level to the lowest. Category one thus includes all parents holding a university (*daigaku*) degree of at least four years study, including parents with a master or doctor degree also. Following this, parents who have obtained a degree from a junior college (*tanki daigaku)* are placed. These institutions differ from universities particularly in terms of length of study, which is only about 2–3 years. Another level of tertiary training is achieved at the technical colleges, which show a stronger focus on vocational training. The fourth category consists of those parents who did not enter tertiary education but completed high school. The lowest education level is the middle school diploma. When comparing the enrolment ratios for parents from the 1997 and 2011 cohorts (see Appendix, Table 4.8), our data reflects the earlier verified ongoing educational expansion (see Chap. 2, Fig. 2.2). In particular, mothers of the 2011 cohort are more often enrolled in tertiary education. Only few parents remain with a middle school diploma. Most parents have achieved a high school diploma or higher.

To represent parents' highest education level in each household, an additional variable for both parents' education level was computed reflecting the highest level of education achieved by both parents. Accordingly, in 2011 in almost 44% of all households, at least one parent holds a university diploma, whereas almost 21% have at least a college diploma, leaving about 36% without tertiary education training. In comparison, in 1997 a considerably higher percentage of households are found where no parent holds a college or university diploma (53%).

This categorization of parental education level allows the construction of three educational strata, from which students originate: (1) advantaged educational background (parents possess a university degree), (2) mediocre educational background (parents possess a college degree), and (3) disadvantaged educational background (parents have no tertiary education training). Similar to the found differences in

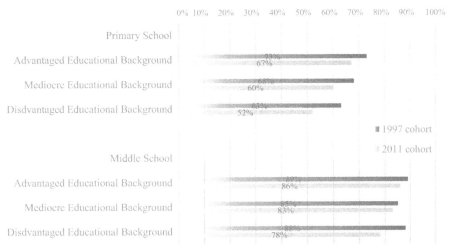

Valid responses: HHSS 2011: n(schools): 17,n(students)= 2863; HHSS 1997: n(schools): 15, n(students)= 1743.

Fig. 4.7 Students' experiences with shadow education, according to educational stratum, in % (HHSS 1997/2011)

participation rates according to ESCS quartile, differences according to educational stratum are to be expected. However, as Fig. 4.7 shows, even though such differences are apparent, they are not extreme.

Students who went to middle school in the 1990s (1992–1994) show no particular differences in enrolment in shadow education at all (advantaged educational background, 89%; disadvantaged educational background, 88%). In contrast, a smaller proportion of students from disadvantaged educational background who received shadow lessons during their middle school years in the 2000s (2006–2008) is detected (78%). Nevertheless, enrolment ratios during middle school remain considerably high across all educational strata.

4.2.2.3 Number of Siblings

To reflect households' varying sizes and distribution of income, the number of siblings[9] will be considered as another social origin category in some of my analyses. Previous research indicates that students without siblings are more likely to attend out-of-school classes since their parents can concentrate their resources on only one child (e.g., Tomura, et al. 2011). The number of siblings should thus affect whether and in what dimension investments in shadow education are affordable. This variable is encoded as possessing the following values: 1 = no siblings, 2 = one sibling,

---

[9]This variable is recoded into a variable with three values: 1 = no siblings, 2 = one sibling, and 3 = two or more siblings. These categories seem adequate, since only 7.5% of the students had more than two siblings in 2011.

and 3 = two or more siblings. These categories seem adequate, since only 7.5% of the students had more than two siblings in 2011. According to our data (see Appendix, Fig. 4.16), there seem to be almost no differences in the proportion of students with or without siblings using shadow education during middle school. However, during primary and high school, students with more siblings are less often enrolled in extracurricular lessons in the shadow. It has to be mentioned here that 10% of the whole 2011 HHSS student sample reported to have no siblings at all, whereas most students had one sibling (58%).

4.2.2.4 Parents' and Students' Educational Aspirations

Following Rational Choice Theory (RCT) and Shadow Education Investment Theory (SEIT) approaches (see Chap. 3), particularly educational aspirations are decisive for the making of educational decisions and thus the formation of educational and social inequality. However, existing research refrained from measuring aspirations separately and focused their analyses on constant social origin variables such as highest parental education level, occupation status, cultural resources, etc. (e.g., Erikson and Jonsson 1996, Jonsson and Erikson 2000, Fujihara 2011, Breen, et al. 2014). Hence, besides "decomposing social origins" into classic measures such as education level, class, and status as proposed by Bukodi and Goldthorpe (2013), I argue that especially in the Japanese case, educational aspirations need to be included in analyses concerned with educational choices or investments, as they determine the reproduction of social inequality.

To measure educational aspirations, I use the future pathway goals (*shinro kibō*) parents have for their children and students' own career ambitions, respectively. To collect such data, in the 1997 and 2011 HHSS survey, students were asked about their post-high school graduation plans. Students could choose between (1) start working (including working at home) immediately after graduation (*shūshoku*), (2) four-year university (*daigaku*), (3) junior college (*tanki daigaku*), (4) technical college (*senmongakkō*), (5) some other institutions, or (6) undecided. Using the same scale, students were asked whether they know about their parents' aspirations for them. If students were not sure or did not know their parents' aspirations, their answers were included in the "undecided" category. The final aspirations of parents and students were categorized on a five-degree scale from highest to lowest educational aspiration, omitting aspirations for other institutions (see Appendix, Table 4.9).

Since all participating students were in 12th grade, the percentage of students still undecided regarding their future career was marginal (2.6%). The majority of all parents and students aim for university entrance (>50%). However, there is also a considerable percentage of students who did not know or were not sure about their parents' expectations. In particular, the father's wish for his child's future career is often unknown by the child (23.9%). This suggests that parents' influence on students' aspirations for life after school was not very strong in these cases, and thus students themselves might have greater say in general decision-making, as I will

Table 4.2 Educational aspirations of students and planned university entrance method, in %
(HHSS 2011)

	Primary school (2000–2005)	Middle school (2006–2009)	High school (2009–2011)	Planned entrance method	
				Exam	Others[b]
University	8.5	24.0	59.3	40.4	19.0
Definitely top university	–	–	13.8	11.7	2.2
If possible top university	–	–	21.3	15.0	6.3
Average university is enough	–	–	24.1	13.7	10.5
College[a]	1.0	4.3	17.8	5.3	14.6
Job	1.4	6.3	19.7	–	–
No decision yet	89.1	65.4	0.9	–	–
Valid responses	3365	3365	3388	3358	

[a]This category consists of junior and technical college
[b]This category includes admission by recommendation (by school or publicly offered), admission office, and other possibilities

further discuss in Chap. 5. As for parents' aspirations, we assume that these were already present when their children attended primary school (2000–2005) and have remained relatively stable. I thus use the reported final aspirations throughout my analyses. In contrast, students' aspirations are formed over the courses of their school lives. Most students remain insecure regarding their future career until they reach high school (Table 4.2). Still, we find considerable proportions of students who knew where they wanted to go after graduating from high school at the early stages of their educational lives, ranging from approximately 11% in primary school to 35% in middle school.

In addition to general aspirations, we have data on students' concrete goals concerning their entrance to university. Almost 60% of students have university aspirations, and the majority aims at first-class universities (35%). However, only a few students think they can enter top universities without taking the entrance examination (8.5%). Careful preparation is thus essential, and an investment in shadow education promises a higher pass probability in these exams.

In accordance with theories on social reproduction, students' educational aspirations vary considerably across social strata (Fig. 4.8).

Not only does a higher percentage of high ESCS students pursue the highest educational track following high school graduation (university), these students also tend to make this decision earlier than their peers from less advantageous background. During middle school, 43% of students from high ESCS backgrounds have already decided to enter university following high school, whereas only 13% of low ESCS students have made the same decision at this point. In contrast, low ESCS students favor entering the labor market to a higher degree compared to other social strata (low ESCS, 10% in middle school and 23% high school; high ESCS, 2% in middle school and 11% in high school; similar results are found for educational

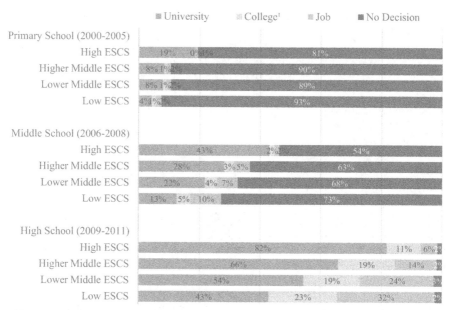

¹ This category consists of junior and technical college.

Valid responses: n(schools) = 17, n(students) = 2533 (primary school), 2533 (middle school), 2624 (high school)

Fig. 4.8 High school students' educational aspirations in primary, middle, and high school, according to ESCS, in % (HHSS 2011)

Table 4.3 Students' educational aspirations in the 1990s and 2000s, in % (HHSS 1997/2011)

		University	Junior college	Technical college	Other	Still uncertain	Job	Valid responses
Primary school	1991	7.3	0.9	0.3	0.2	90.0	1.3	1734
	2005	8.3	0.1	0.9	0.1	89.1	1.6	1967
Middle school	1994	20.1	2.8	2.4	0.4	63.4	10.8	1734
	2008	21.1	0.4	3.4	0.1	67.0	7.9	1967
High school	1997	47.1	11.1	12.3	3.2	1.7	24.7	1773
	2011	55.4	4.1	14.8	0.5	2.5	22.7	2055

Only students of those schools ($n = 10$) were considered, which took part in both surveys

strata; see Appendix, Table 4.10). Whether ambitious students from disadvantaged ESCS backgrounds can actually increase their chances of entering university by benefitting from gaining access to shadow education remains to be scrutinized.

Taking into account differences in educational preferences over time, Table 4.3 shows students' educational aspirations in the 1990s compared to the 2000s. In particular, the percentage of high school students aiming for university increased by more than 8% from 1997 to 2011. However, future educational opportunities are already predominantly predestined at the end of high school, since the rank of the high school a student attends largely determines whether certain educational goals can be achieved. Therefore, educational aspirations at the end of middle school play

Table 4.4 Percentage of students who participated in shadow education during middle school, according to educational aspirations, 1992–1994 and 2006–2008 (HHSS 1997/2011)

	University	College[a]	Still uncertain	Job	Valid responses
1992–1994	93.5	83.1	87.5	81.1	1637
2006–2008	87.5	77.6	65.0	79.8	1958

Only students of those schools ($n = 10$) were considered, which took part in both surveys
[a]This category consists of junior and technical college

a major role for future opportunities and thus students' chances to achieve a high education level. In addition, at this stage in students' educational life course, students and their families are often still uncertain which future pathway they should pick. This uncertainty concerning future prospects slightly increased from 1994 to 2008 (by more than 3%), thus leaving 67% of all middle school students insecure about their future educational pathway.

To increase their chances of gaining entrance to high-ranked high schools, shadow education is pursued by most middle school students. However, from 1994 to 2008 the percentage of students participating in shadow education decreased partly (Table 4.4). In particular, students which are uncertain which pathway to follow have considerably less often received lessons in the shadow in 2008 (65%) compared to 1994 (88%).

It seems that while students with high aspirations generally continue to make investments in shadow education, students without clear goals more often question whether such an investment is necessary.

4.2.3   High School Stratification

4.2.3.1   High School Ranking

In Japan, all high school graduates have the opportunity to access higher education. However, two major high school tracks can be divided: a general academic (*futsūka*) and a vocational track (*senmongakka*). But, as stated earlier, the Japanese academic high school system is also highly stratified through the prestige high schools have gathered according to the percentage of students that attain entrance into high-ranked universities (Stevenson and Baker 1992: 1641, Ojima and von Below 2010: 277). Following Shirakawa (2013), the academic track was subcategorized using the expected advancement ratio of students to higher education, students' socioeconomic background, and their academic standing in middle school to create a variable to depict the ranking of Japanese high schools. Following this, the 17 high schools of this study were classified into four different ranks: Academic A, B, and C as well as vocational high schools. In accordance with the expected outcomes of educational expansion, a higher percentage of the 2011 cohort attended Academic A high schools (1997, 17%; 2011, 26%), whereas fewer students entered vocational high schools (1997, 24%; 2011, 21%; see Appendix, Table 4.11). Taking into account this high school stratification, we are able to differentiate students'

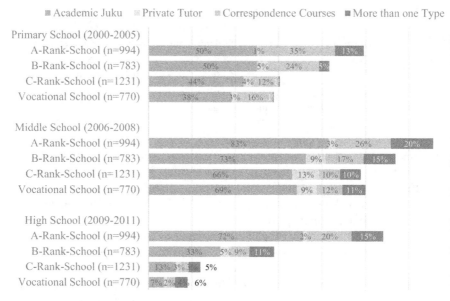

Valid responses: n(schools) = 17, n(students) = 3778 (primary school), 3806 (middle school), 3763 (highschool)

Fig. 4.9 High school students' experiences with different types of shadow education in primary, middle, and high school, according to high school ranking, multiple responses possible, in % (HHSS 2011)

participation ratios in shadow education. Figure 4.9 shows the percentage of students who participated in shadow education at the time they were in primary, middle, and high school according to the rank of high school they finally attended.

During middle school, most parents seem to somehow manage the high costs for the participation in shadow education, as it appears to have become an accepted part of children's school life. In high school, however, a high diversity can be found. Clearly students that attend Academic A high schools have more experience with shadow education in general and continue to invest far more in these lessons after middle school (80.4%) than students in Academic C (17.9%) or vocational high schools (11.6%), where the majority quits their investment. This indicates that the additional financial, time and effort investments are no longer considered worthwhile for students in Academic C high schools or vocational schools, since career aspirations make such an investment unnecessary.

4.2.3.2   Type of High School's Administration

In addition to this ranking, we need to consider whether students attend private or public schools, since students' participation ratios in shadow education vary between those school types (MEXT 2014). Hence, a dummy variable for administrative type of school (1 = public, 2 = private) is included. According to the 2011 HHSS survey data, on average twice as many public high school students (44%)

Valid responses: n(schools): 17,n(students)= 3763.

Fig. 4.10 High school students' experiences with shadow education in high school, according to location, in % (HHSS 2011)

participated in shadow education lessons during their high school years (2009–2011) than students attending private institutions (22%).

4.2.3.3   Location of High School

Furthermore, previous research has shown that the location of a school has effects on whether or not students participate in shadow education, because there might be less availability in rural areas (Stevenson and Baker 1992: 1647–1650). Also, differences in the effects of shadow education were verified according to residential area (Entrich 2014a). Based on our data, we classified three areas: metropolitan (high-density areas with more than one million residents and more than 4000 residents per square kilometer), urban (semi-dense areas with more than 100,000 but less than one million residents and more than 900 residents per square kilometer), and rural (less than 100,000 residents and less than 900 residents per square kilometer). As shown in Fig. 4.10, participation in shadow education is highest in urban areas, not metropolitan areas. In fact, more students of rurally located high schools pursue supplementary lessons than students living in metropolitan regions. For the latter students, especially correspondence courses are more valued, as these lessons are easily accessible in rural areas where only few *juku* exist.

4.2.4   Post-High School Status

After entrance to high school is achieved, students and their families need to make up their minds regarding future options and decide which pathway to follow. Besides leaving the schooling system by entering the job market after high school graduation, all high school graduates have the opportunity to enter higher education. As data of the national Ministry of Education show, approximately 57% of the 18-year-old cohort proceed to higher education in present Japan (MEXT 2017). However, due to the still existing entrance examination system, a hierarchical ranking of universities exists. To calculate whether students achieve a higher education status as a result of shadow education investments, calculations need to focus on transition to university differentiating the university level into different ranks. However, in the HHSS survey, we did not directly measure whether students actually entered a certain university. Since our data was surveyed at the end of high school, we only measured whether students aspire to enter a certain kind of university or leave the schooling system. As described above (see educational aspirations), students were first asked to give details about their post-high school career plans, ranging from entering university to joining the workforce. Additionally, all students aspiring for higher education were asked whether they intend to enter a top university or not. Of course, these categories only reflect what students actually aspire, but not, how certain it is that they will actually achieve their goal. Because of that, a further item was included in the questionnaire asking whether students are sure that they will realize their set goal. On a three-degree scale, the respondents could choose between: (1) I will definitely realize my goal; (2) I might realize my goal, if I am capable enough; and (3) I do not attach to much value to the realization of my goal. According to our data, at the end of 12th grade, most students (82%) are sure that they will achieve their chosen post-high school goal (see Appendix, Table 4.12). Particularly students who intend to enter top universities following high school graduation are generally sure that nothing stands between them and the realization of their goal (approximately 90%). For this analysis, only the latter students are considered as possessing "realistic future goals," since for the rest of the cohort, a high probability remains that they will not enter their chosen school. These "realistic future goals" of students are used as a proxy for students' post-high school education status, i.e., whether students enter a top university (1), an average university (2), a college of different sort (3), or the job market (4). This assumption seems justified considering that families have to decide very early whether a certain kind of university is pursued and how to prepare for the entrance, as I will further discuss in Chap. 5.

Using the created variable reflecting students' post-high school status, Table 4.5 verifies that students who will enter high-ranked universities pursue mostly lessons concentrating on the preparation of entrance examinations (*shingaku*, 78%) during high school. Also, lessons where students prepare for entrance examinations and, at the same time, aim for alternative university entrance methods by improving their grades, etc. (*sōgō*, 63%) are considerably often used. In contrast, students focusing on the improvement of school grades or with remedial needs (*hoshū*) also often aim for college (26%) or sometimes the job market (13%). Hence, only those students who are certain to enter higher education following high school graduation will enroll in *shingaku* or *sōgō* lessons. The generally few students pursuing shadow education during high school knowing that they will enter the job market after graduation are likely to only enroll in *hoshū* lessons due to certain study difficulties. For these and other students who chose *hoshū* and *sōgō* lessons, catching up in certain academic subjects might be the major reason for participation. The impact of shadow education on transition to higher education is thus very likely varying according to the pursued study goal, as I will investigate in Chap. 6.

Table 4.5 Students' post-high school status in relation to their participation in shadow education in high school, according to type and purpose, in % (HHSS 2011)

Type and study purpose of shadow education in high school		Post-high school status				
		Top university	Average university	College[a]	Job	Total
All types	*Shingaku*	77.5	20.8	1.7	–	525
	Sōgō	62.5	29.1	8.4	–	275
	Hoshū	32.8	28.4	25.5	13.2	204
Academic juku	*Shingaku*	78.7	19.7	1.5	–	456
	Sōgō	66.2	27.1	6.7	–	225
	Hoshū	32.0	29.9	25.9	12.2	147
Private tutor	*Shingaku*	69.6	21.7	8.7	–	23
	Sōgō	53.3	33.3	13.3	–	15
	Hoshū	34.5	27.6	31.0	6.9	29
Cor. courses	*Shingaku*	75.2	24.8	–	–	133
	Sōgō	49.3	41.8	9.0	–	67
	Hoshū	30.6	33.3	16.7	19.4	36
Valid responses		1053	609	508	470	2640

[a]This category consists of junior and technical college

4.2.5   Academic Achievement

Because of the merit-based class consciousness in Japan (Rohlen 1983: 311), the academic achievement of students is believed to be decisive for educational success in general. The transition from one school level to the next is meritocratic in nature and thus highly determined by academic performance. Accordingly, generally high-achieving students are believed to automatically enter higher-ranked schools, since they are able to pass more difficult entrance examinations or will get a recommendation for a high-ranked school. Also, RCT research stresses that the academic achievement level of students is critical in making educational decisions. This includes the decision for shadow education, since students' participation was found to depend on academic standing in school, i.e., students grade point average (GPA; e.g., Seiyama and Noguchi 1984, Stevenson and Baker 1992), and thus students' academic standing needs to be included as an influential determinant to predict whether shadow education is pursued or not. Previous research has stressed that different types of shadow education are chosen according to academic standing and purpose of study (e.g., Rohlen 1980, Komiyama 1993, 2000, Roesgaard 2006). Also, SEIT argues that the primary outcome of investments in shadow education is the improvement of academic achievement level, i.e., school grades or performance in entrance exams. However, empirical evidence is scarce. In my upcoming analyses, students' academic standing will thus be included.

   The HHSS data includes the participating 12th graders' GPA during high and middle school. This GPA is generally coded on a five-degree scale ranging from 5 (= high academic standing) to 1 (= low academic standing). Using the same scale, we are able to differentiate students into five main achievement groups, according to their participation in shadow education in their respective school levels (see Appendix, Fig. 4.17). Of our sample, 91% of all students with a high GPA in middle school responded to have participated in shadow education during this period. With lower academic achievement level, participation rates in middle school decrease. A similar clear tendency is not found for students' high school years. Apparently, students' academic achievement level in high school is strongly related to the rank of high school. Accordingly, participation rates vary much stronger between high schools than general academic achievement level.

As is general usage in social sciences, I will treat this ordinal variable as if it was metric in nature in my upcoming analyses.

4.2.6 Gender

Since Japanese parents traditionally have different ideas about the future of boys and girls and generally tend to invest more in the education of boys (Schultz Lee 2010: 1582), a dummy variable concerning gender (1 = male, 2 = female) is generally included in my upcoming analyses.

4.3 JSTS: *Juku Teacher and Student Survey*

In addition to the *Hyōgo High School Students* survey, I designed the *Juku Student and Teacher Survey* (JSTS) to complement the existing data by targeting a different population: *jukusei*, students enrolled at private schools in the shadow education sector, as well as the operators of this industry, *jukuchō* (*juku* principals), and their teachers (*jukukōshi*). Based on a multi-sequence-multimethod design (Teddlie and Tashakkori 2006), this survey was carried out by the author during several fieldwork periods from 2012 to 2014 following a two-stage random sampling method:

First, *juku* were chosen based on the following premises:

1. Specialization: *Juku* of different types were chosen.
2. Success: Following the *yūshōreppai* (survival of the fittest) principle, only *juku* were targeted, which are at least 30 to more than 50 years in business, thus managing to stay competitive and successful due to specific reasons.
3. Size: *Juku* of different sizes and organizations were chosen, thus including small- or middle-sized *juku* (*kojin/chūshō juku*) and major corporations operating as chain *juku* (*ōte juku*).
4. Location: *Juku* in Japan's metropolitan centers Kansai (Kyōto, Ōsaka) and Tōkyō (Setagaya) and in two less populated prefectural cities outside these metropolitan areas (Shiga prefecture: Kusatsu; Fukushima prefecture: Iwaki) were chosen.

Before collecting the data in the form of a questionnaire-based survey early in 2013, contacts to *juku* were established on the basis of personal recommendations and introductions. After winning general interest of several *juku* for my research, meetings were set. In these meetings, I usually first sat down for an interview with the head of the school (*jukuchō*), before taking a tour through the school, visiting the classrooms, taking a look at the teaching approaches and methods, and getting in contact with teachers and students. The exploratory semi-structured interview with the *jukuchō* followed several guiding questions to deliver basic information about the *juku*, its teachers, students, supply, and general development, while leaving room for the interviewee to talk about issues they feel are important. Following this first meeting, generally a second visit was paid to provide the school with the needed questionnaires for *jukusei* (students attending a *juku*) and *jukukōshi* (teachers at a *juku*), including *jukuchō*.

Second, a questionnaire survey following a simultaneous design, i.e., simultaneous collection of quantitative and qualitative data (Gürtler and Huber 2012: 39), was carried out from January to March 2013. The eight *juku* that took part in the survey represent five *kojin/chūshō juku* (JukuA to JukuE) and three chain *juku* (JukuF to JukuH) with numerous branches. In total, 20 *juku* schools participated, of which 500 *jukusei* and 102 *jukukōshi* filled in the questionnaire (Table 4.6). JukuF and JukuG are two different chain *juku* belonging to the same parent company, a local big player operating in the prefectures Kyōto, Ōsaka, Hyōgo, Shiga, and Nara. JukuH is another large joint stock company operating nationwide. Hence, at these two *ōte juku*, the number of students and teaching staff was too large to include everybody in the sample. After setting the targets, we decided on a suitable number of questionnaires to be given out. It was, however, not always possible to get as much participants as originally envisaged due to certain circumstances, such as the *juku*'s time schedule, individual timetables, and seasonal variation in study periods.

As shown in Table 4.6, return rates of *jukusei* vary from 50 to 78%, whereas return rates of *jukukōshi* vary considerably as well. However, apart from JukuC and JukuG, where the *jukuchō* did not want to be responsible for the missed study time of their *jukusei*, at all schools, a suitable student sample was achieved. The samples of *jukukōshi* are generally smaller, since their responses are meant to provide general information on the *juku* and their connection to regular schools and to complement these data with open items to get qualitative statements of the operators' side about reactions to recent changes in the regular schooling system and decreasing student populations. In addition to the questionnaire survey, personal conversations with students, parents, *juku*-operators, and researchers in this field served to get a greater understanding about functions and implications of the Japanese *juku*-industry and its relation to formal education. Follow-up research was carried out in August and September 2013 as well as in June 2014.

Since the quantitative data of the student survey will be used to predict why families choose a certain *juku*-type over another, certain variables need introduction. Particularly important for our analyses prove, again, social origin and school ranking variables. In addition, the JSTS provides us with the opportunity to include concrete reasons for choosing a certain *juku*.

Table 4.6 JSTS 2013 – sample overview and return ratios

		kojin/chūshō juku					ōte juku			
		JukuA	JukuB	JukuC	JukuD	JukuE	JukuF	JukuG	JukuH	Total
Juku	Official classification	*Shingaku*	*Doriru*	*Sōgō*	*Hoshū*	*Shingaku*	*Shingaku*	*Sōgō*	*Yobikō*	Total
	Number of branches	1	1	1	1	1	>50	>70	>100	>200
	Sample	1	1	1	1	1	4	2	9	20
Jukukōshi	Total number	6	2	15	4	10	>100	>200	>100	>500
	Targeted population	6	2	10	4	10	80	20	20	152
	Sample	5	1	2	4	9	61	14	9	102
	Return ratio	83%	50%	20%	100%	90%	76%	70%	45%	67%
Jukusei	Total number	120	50	350	90	80	>1000	>1000	>10000	>10000
	Targeted population	80	50	80	80	40	200	100	300	930
	Sample	45	38	0	62	31	100	0	224	500
	Return ratio	56%	76%	0%	78%	78%	50%	0%	75%	54%

Table 4.7 Highest parental education level, distribution in % (JSTS 2013: Student Survey)

	Graduate school	University	College[a]	High school	Middle school	Valid responses
Father	8.2	64.3	6.9	19.5	1.1	437
Mother	2.2	42.8	28.4	25.3	1.3	451
Parents[b]	9.1	67.0	9.1	14.1	0.7	460

[a]This category consists of junior and technical college
[b]At least one of both parents holds a degree in this category

4.3.1   Social Origin

To measure the social origin of students, gender and educational stratum are considered. Similar to the variables concerning gender and educational stratum in the HHSS survey, gender will be included as a dummy variable (1 = male, 2 = female), while educational stratum as the major indicator for students' family background was measured in terms of fathers' and mothers' highest completed education level. Both parents' highest education level was independently measured using a five-degree scale ranging from the highest education level to the lowest: (1) master's degree or a doctorate, (2) university degree, (3) technical or junior college degree, (4) high school diploma, and (5) middle school diploma. As shown in Table 4.7, the conducted sample of *jukusei* originates from more advantaged educational backgrounds for the most part (>70%).

In general, fathers have more often completed graduate school or university, whereas mothers more often hold a college degree. To represent parents' highest education level in each household, an additional variable for both parents' education level was computed reflecting the highest level of education achieved by at least one of both parents. Accordingly, the participating students' parental education level is generally considerably high. Only approximately 15% of all households have no tertiary education degree. In contrast, in 76% of all sampled cases, at least one of both parents holds a university degree.

4.3.2   School Stratification

To reflect the structural frame of the Japanese schooling system, variables concerning the stratification of schools need to be controlled for. To measure this stratification of schools, data on the reputation of a school to express the ranking of schools and their administration type (private/public) were collected. In the JSTS Student Survey questionnaire, students were asked whether the school they attend has a generally high reputation (1), an average reputation (2), or a low reputation (3) and whether they attend public schools (1) or private schools (2). According to my data, most students attend public schools (78.7%) and rate the reputation of their school as average (64.5%).

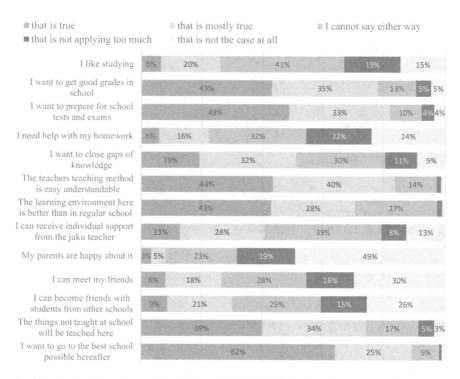

Fig. 4.11 Students' motives to attend *juku*, in % (JSTS 2013: Student Survey)

4.3.3 Unmet Demands

To find out why families choose a certain type of *juku* over another type in present Japan, particularly students' reasons to enter their *juku* and their view on school classes have been surveyed in detail. The following item seems best suited to predict the likelihood of entering a certain *juku*-type to meet new demands: "Thinking about your reasons to attend this juku, please answer to the different categories below. Please choose from [that is true] to [that is not the case at all]. Make your mark where you think it is most applicable" (Q22, Student Survey). Using a five-degree Likert scale, students could choose from *that is true* (1) to *that is not the case at all* (5). The four most applying response categories will be used as metric predictors for *juku* attendance and are displayed in Fig. 4.11.

According to these data, the main motives to attend *juku* are students' intention to perform well in school, i.e., get good grades and prepare for tests and exams. In addition, students often rate the teaching methods and the general learning environment at *juku* higher than at their school. Particularly important are further lesson contents outside the regular school curriculum and high ambitions, i.e., the transition to a high-ranked school. Only few students attend *juku* just because they like studying; most of them need help with their homework or want to meet or make new friends. Whether their parents' are actually glad that they attend such a school is of less concern to students. Some students also find it important to receive individual

■ I strongly agree   ▨ I mostly agree   ▨ I mostly disagree   ■ I strongly disagree

Fig. 4.12 Students' view on regular school's instruction quality, in % (JSTS 2013: Student Survey)

support from the teacher at *juku*. Many of these motives thus imply that students do not feel that regular school actually meets all their demands, whereas several categories point to shortcomings that might have been created through the new reform course (see Chap. 10).

In addition to students' motives to attend a *juku*, their general view on the quality of regular school's classroom instruction was measured using the four items displayed in Fig. 4.12. Accordingly, only few students actually think that school is a waste of time (16%). However, a much higher percentage of students is not sure whether school has actually prepared them sufficiently for their future life (43%) or rate class in school as not very good (55%). Also, almost one third feels that they receive not much attention when they need help during class. For my upcoming analysis in Chap. 8, the latter two variables concerning help during class ("when I need help during class, the teacher helps me") and instruction quality ("in general, class in school was not very good") will be included as dummy variables (1 = I agree; 2 = I disagree).

4.4   Methods

To achieve reliable and convincing findings, the methodological approaches used in each of the four subsequent empirical chapters are of great importance. To methodically approach the first dimension outlined in the SEII Frame (Chap. 1, Fig. 1.2), the *Access* to shadow education, binary logistic regression analyses are carried out to predict the likelihood of actually deciding for and taking part in shadow lessons based on major influential variables, such as social origin and educational aspirations of parents and students. This kind of regression analysis calculates the probability that the event occurs that students actually take part in lessons in the shadow in reference to those who do not. By applying Rational Choice Theory as a theoretical approach, these analyses are used to measure whether families actually decided to make an investment in shadow education at a certain point of time in the student's school life course or not.

To further estimate the impact of shadow education investments on educational success in Chap. 6, thus concentrating on the *Effects* dimension of the SEII Frame, multinomial logistic regression analyses are applied, allowing for similar regressions with the difference that nonbinary but nominally scaled variables, in this case the ranking of high schools and students' post-high school status, are used as independent variables reflecting educational success. Hence, in this analysis, more than two outcomes are possible, ranging from high educational returns in terms admission to an advantageous or prestigious school level to low educational returns without comparable returns.

In Chap. 7, the focus shifts to the relativity of *Access* to and *Effects* of shadow education across time, applying the *Continuity* dimension of the SEII Frame. Similar to Chaps. 5 and 6, access to and effects of shadow education are predicted using binary and multinomial regressions; only this time these analyses are meant to compare different cohorts and models across time to clarify the extent of possible inequality increase or decrease through shadow education. Hence, quantitative data of the HHSS 1997 and 2011 surveys are used.

In Chap. 8, particularly the relativity of *Access* to shadow education across time is questioned emphasizing the *Change* dimension of the SEII Frame based on quantitative and qualitative data alike. To achieve comprehensive findings, I will approach this final issue based on mixed methods, using a so-called within-method triangulation model (Jick 1979: 602–611, Gürtler and Huber 2012). Hence, in addition to quantitative descriptive and multinomial logistic regression analyses in the first part of the results section, qualitative content analyses are used to help explain the quantitative findings (Creswell et al. 2003), i.e., explain whether the found effects are an outcome of certain developments in the Japanese education system.

Furthermore, it is worth noting that all completed quantitative regression analyses attempt to test whether shadow education functions as educational opportunity for students with disadvantaged family background and thus helps these students to overcome the gap of educational starting chances. Hence, the access to and effects of shadow education are calculated for different social strata allowing for comparisons between enrolment opportunities and benefits of shadow education for students with advantaged and disadvantaged family background. However, as several colleagues have stressed, neither logit (lnOR) or probit coefficients nor the oft-displayed odds ratios (OR) are suited for comparison (e.g., Allison 1999). In fact, "LnOR and OR reflect effects of the independent variables as well as the size of the unobserved heterogeneity" (Mood 2010: 73), wherefore it is not only invalid to make comparisons between samples, but between groups within samples, models

(Allison 1999), and of course, comparisons across time (Mood 2010). Such comparisons are often misleading, as they assume "that the unobserved heterogeneity is the same across the compared samples, groups, or points in time" (Mood 2010: 73). Thus, by comparing lnOR or OR between groups or samples, misinterpretations of one's calculations including a possible over- or underestimation of certain effects is likely to occur. To solve the problem of comparing coefficients or OR between groups, Williams (2009) proposed to generally apply a more advantageous class of models, so-called heterogeneous choice models (also location-scale or heteroskedastic ordered models). These models allow to use ordinal in addition to binary-encoded dependent variables. Also, "sources of heterogeneity can be better modeled and controlled for, and insights can be gained into the effects of group characteristics on outcomes that would be missed by other methods" (Williams 2009: 531).

Following these suggestions, I use the statistical software STATA that allows the additional post-estimation of Average Marginal Effects (AME) following my regression analyses (Auspurg and Hinz 2011, Williams 2012). I am thus able to realize comparisons between models (e.g., with which probability a top high school or a low-ranking high school is chosen in reference to all other high schools), groups (e.g., students from advantaged versus disadvantaged social origin or with what likelihood a certain kind of shadow education is chosen in comparison to another), and whole samples over time (e.g., comparisons between the student cohorts of the 1997 and 2011 HHSS data surveys). In contrast to OR, which have been preferred by many social scientists for quite some time, AME show no chances for the occurrence of a certain phenomenon; they specify by how many percentage points the average probability of the represented group of one variable is different from the probability in the reference group (if used for binary logistic regressions) or from the probability of all other outcomes (if used in multinomial logistic regressions) (Auspurg and Hinz 2011: 69). For example, we are able to predict by how many percentage points the average probability that students' participate in shadow education differs from the probability that students do not participate in shadow education. Focusing on social origin, we are then able to compare whether students from advantaged social backgrounds have a higher or lower average probability to participate in shadow education compared to students from disadvantaged social backgrounds. We are also able to predict whether such investments in shadow education have a higher impact on whether students attend a high, a mediocre, or a low-ranking high school or university based on their social origin.

4.5 Summary

This chapter's aim was to introduce the purposes, specifics, and advantages of two datasets and specifics of the chosen methodical approaches. As discussed above and finally summarized in Fig. 4.13, the presented data provide us with the opportunity to make analyses concerning all dimensions outlined in the SEII Frame: *Access, Effects, Continuity*, and *Change* (see also Chap. 1). In the subsequent empirical

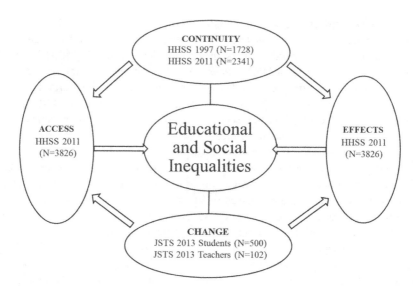

Fig. 4.13 Data used to analyze the four dimensions outlined in the *Shadow-Education-Inequality-Impact* (SEII) Frame

chapters (Chaps. 5, 6, 7 and 8), the main questions related to shadow education and its implications for educational and social inequality are comprehensively analyzed based on the here introduced data. Whereas Chaps. 5 and 6 draw on the 2011 HHSS survey data to clarify *access* to and *effects* of shadow education in present Japan, Chaps. 7 and 8 scrutinize variations in *access* and *effects* according to *continuity* and *change* of the market. Therefore, in Chap. 7 data of the 1997 HHSS survey is used in addition to the 2011 HHSS data analyzing the persistence of this market from the 1990s onward. In Chap. 8, I draw on the 2013 JSTS data to analyze how the Japanese *juku*-industry remained successfully in business despite unfavorable circumstances. All carried-out analyses will display average marginal effects instead of reporting the conventional, sometimes misleading logit coefficients and odds ratios. Hence, reliable findings are produced with the intention of achieving comprehensive findings on the discussed issues concerning shadow education and its implications for social inequalities.

Appendix

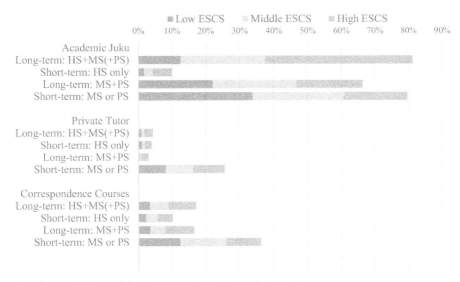

Abbreviations: PS=Primary School; MS=Middle School; HS=High School.
Valid responses: n (schools) = 17, n (students) = 648 (low ESCS), 1300 (middle ESCS), 651 (high ESCS).

Fig. 4.14 Length of enrolment in shadow education, according to ESCS groups, multiple responses possible, in % (HHSS 2011)

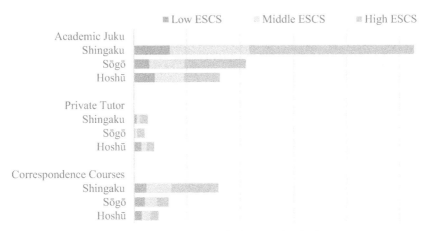

Abbreviations: PS=Primary School; MS=Middle School; HS=High School
Valid responses: n (schools) = 17, n (students) = 648 (low ESCS), 1300 (middle ESCS), 651 (high ESCS).

Fig. 4.15 Study purpose of shadow education in high school, according to ESCS groups, multiple responses possible, in % (HHSS 2011)

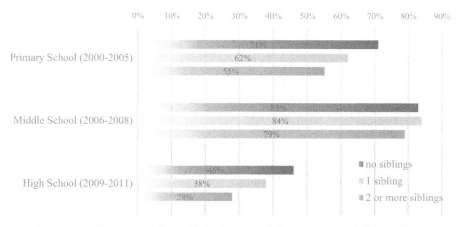

Valid responses: HHSS 2011: n(schools): 17,n(students)= 3524 (primary school), 3522 (middle school), 3480 (high school).

Fig. 4.16 Students' experiences with shadow education, according to number of siblings, in % (HHSS 2011)

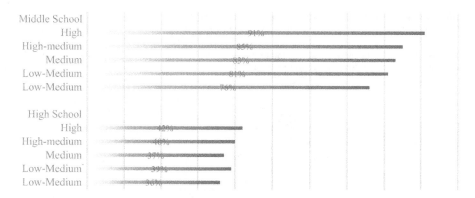

Valid responses: n(schools): 17,n(students)= 3761 (middle school),3730 (high school).

Fig. 4.17 Middle and high school students' experiences with shadow education, according to grade point average (GPA), in % (HHSS 2011)

Table 4.8 Highest parental education level, distribution in %, 1997 and 2011 (HHSS 1997/2011)

		University	College[a]	No tertiary education[b]	Valid responses
1997	Father	37.9	3.4	58.7	1487
	Mother	14.0	18.2	67.8	1524
	Parents[c]	37.8	9.3	52.9	1574
2011	Father	41.1	10.2	48.7	1821
	Mother	19.4	31.0	49.6	1932
	Parents[c]	43.5	20.9	35.6	1956

Only students of those schools (n = 10) were considered, which took part in both surveys.
[a]This category consists of junior and technical college
[b]This category consists of middle and high school diploma
[c]At least one of both parents holds a degree in this category

Table 4.9 Educational aspirations of parents and students at the end of high school, in % (HHSS 2011)

	University	Junior college	Technical college	No decision yet	Job	Valid responses
Father	51.1	3.6	7.1	23.9	14.3	3209
Mother	55.2	4.3	10.0	13.2	17.2	3396
Student	57.7	4.9	15.6	2.6	19.1	3510

Table 4.10 Students' educational aspirations, according to parents' highest education level, in %, 1994 and 2008 (HHSS 1997/2011)

Students' educational aspiration			University	College[a]	Still uncertain	Job	Valid responses
Parents' highest education level[b]	University	1994	32.6	4.6	59.4	3.4	564
		2008	32.6	2.1	60.8	4.5	822
	College[a]	1994	19.3	9.3	63.6	7.9	140
		2008	18.0	4.4	71.5	6.2	390
	No tertiary education[c]	1994	12.6	5.6	66.2	15.7	786
		2008	11.0	5.2	71.5	12.3	657

Only students of those schools (n = 10) were considered, which took part in both surveys
[a]This category consists of junior and technical college
[b]At least one of both parents holds a degree in this category
[c]This category consists of middle and high school diploma

Table 4.11 Distribution of students, according to rank of high school, in %, 1997 and 2011 (HHSS 1997/2011)

	Academic A	Academic B	Academic C	Vocational	Total
1997	16.8	27.7	31.2	24.3	2397
2011	26.1	20.6	32.8	20.5	3826

Only students of those schools (n = 10) were considered, which took part in both surveys

Table 4.12 High school students' future goals, according to level of certainty, in % (HHSS 2011)

Level of certainty	Future goals				
	Top university	Average university	College[a]	Job	Total
I will definitely realize my goal	**89.8**	**77.4**	**79.5**	**74.1**	**81.6**
I might realize my goal	9.7	17.4	18.7	19.6	15.3
I do not care about that	0.5	5.2	1.8	6.3	3.1
Valid responses	1176	801	653	652	3282

[a]This category consists of junior and technical college

References

Allison, P. D. (1999). Comparing logit and probit coefficients across groups. *Sociological Methods & Research, 28*(2), 186–208.

Auspurg, K., & Hinz, T. (2011). Gruppenvergleiche bei Regressionen mit binären abhängigen Variablen – Probleme und Fehleinschätzungen am Beispiel von Bildungschancen im Kohortenverlauf. [Group comparisons in regressions with binary dependent variables - Problems and misjudgements using the example of educational opportunities in the cohort course]. *Zeitschrift für Soziologie, 40*(1), 62–73.

Baker, D. P., Akiba, M., LeTendre, G. K., & Wiseman, A. W. (2001). Worldwide shadow education: Outside-school learning, institutional quality of schooling, and cross-national mathematics achievement. *Educational Evaluation and Policy Analysis, 23*(1), 1–17.

Bourdieu, P. (1983). Ökonomisches Kapital, kulturelles Kapital, soziales Kapital [Economic Capital, Cultural Capital, Social Capital]. In R. Kreckel (Ed.), *Soziale Ungleichheiten* [Social inequalities] (pp. 185–199). Göttingen: Otto Schwartz Verlag.

Bray, M. (2010). Researching shadow education: Methodological challenges and directions. *Asia Pacific Educational Review, 11*, 3–13.

Breen, R., Werfhorst, H. v. d., & Jæger, M. M. (2014). Deciding under doubt: A theory of risk aversion, time discounting preferences, and educational decision-making. *European Sociological Review, 30*(2), 258–270.

Bukodi, E., & Goldthorpe, J. H. (2013). Decomposing 'Social Origins': The effects of parents' class, status, and education on the educational attainment of their children. *European Sociological Review, 29*(5), 1024–1039.

Creswell, J. W., Clark, V. L. P., Gutmann, M. L., & Hanson, W. E. (2003). Advanced mixed methods research designs. In A. Tashakkori & C. Teddlie (Eds.), *Handbook of mixed methods in social and behavioral research* (pp. 209–240). Thousand Oaks: Sage.

Entrich, S. R. (2013). Causes and effects of investments in shadow education in Japan – A comparative point of view. In F. Ojima & S. Aramaki (Eds.), *Gendai kōkōsei no shinro to seikatsu* [Career and life of high school students today] (pp. 157–182). Kyoto: Doshisha Publishing.

Entrich, S. R. (2014a). Effects of investments in out-of-school education in Germany and Japan. *Contemporary Japan, 26*(1), 71–102.

Entrich, S. R. (2014b). German and Japanese education in the shadow – Do out-of-school lessons really contribute to class reproduction? *IAFOR Journal of Education, 2*(2), 17–53.

Erikson, R., & Jonsson, J. O. (1996). Explaining class inequality in education – The Swedish test case. In R. Erikson & J. O. Jonsson (Eds.), *Can education be equalized? The Swedish case in comparative perspective* (pp. 1–63). Boulder: Westview Press.

Fairbrother, G. P. (2014). Quantitative and qualitative approaches to comparative education. In M. Bray, B. Adamson, & M. Mason (Eds.), *Comparative education research. Approaches and methods* (pp. 71–93). Hong Kong: Comparative Education Research Center (CERC), Springer.

Fujihara, S. (2011). Breen ando Goldthorpe no aitaiteki risuku kaihi kasetsu no kenshō: Chichioya no kodomo ni taisuru shokugyō kyōiku kitai o mochiita keiryō bunseki [Empirical test of breen and goldthorpe's relative risk aversion hypothesis in the Japanese society: Data analysis of a father's occupational and educational expectations for his child]. *Shakaigaku Hyōron, 62*(1), 18–35.

Gürtler, L., & Huber, G. L. (2012). Triangulation. Vergleiche und Schlussfolgerungen auf der Ebene der Datenanalyse [Triangulation. Comparisons and conclusions at the data analysis level]. In M. Gläser-Zikuda, T. Seidel, C. Rohlfs, A. Gröschner, & S. Ziegelbauer (Eds.), *Mixed Methods in der empirischen Bildungsforschung* [Mixed methods in empirical educational research] (pp. 37–50). Waxmann: Münster.

Hamano, T. (2011). The globalization of student assessments and its impact on educational policy. *Japan Academic Society for Educational Policy Proceedings, 13*, 1–11.

Jick, T. D. (1979). Mixing qualitative and quantitative methods – Triangulation in action. *Administrative Science Quarterly, 24*, 602–611.

Jonsson, J. O., & Erikson, R. (2000). Understanding educational inequality: The Swedish experience. *L'Année Sociologique, 50*, 345–382.

Kikkawa, T. (2006). *Gakureki to Kakusa-Fubyōdō: Seijukusuru Nihongata Gakureki Shakai* [Education and social inequality: Contemporary educational credentialism in Japan]. Tokyo: Tōkyō Daigaku Shuppankai.

Komiyama, H. (1993). *Gakurekishakai to juku - datsu juken kyōsō no susume* [Credentialist society and Juku –Stop the entrance examination competition!]. Tokyo: Shinhyōron.

Komiyama, H. (2000). *Juku: Gakkō surimuka jidai wo maeni* [Juku: Before the era of downsizing schools]. Tokyo: Iwanami Shoten.

Schultz Lee, K. (2010). Parental educational investments and aspirations in Japan. *Journal of Family Issues, 31*(12), 1579–1603.

Matsuoka, R. (2015). School socioeconomic compositional effect on shadow education participation: Evidence from Japan. *British Journal of Sociology of Education, 36*(2), 270–290.

MEXT, Ministry of Education, Culture, Sports, Science and Technology. (2012). *Kōdai setsuzoku tokubetsu bukai (dai 4-kai) haifu shiryō - shiryō 1: AO nyūshi-tō no jisshi jōkyō ni tsuite.* [Special group concerned with the connection between high school and university education (4th Meeting). Distribution material – Material 1: Concerning the implementation of the AO entrance]. Retrieved from: http://www.mext.go.jp/b_menu/shingi/chukyo/chukyo12/shiryo/1329266.htm

MEXT, Ministry of Education, Culture, Sports, Science and Technology. (2014). *Kodomo no gakushūhi chōsa* [Survey concerning children's learning expenses]. Retrieved from: http://www.mext.go.jp/b_menu/toukei/chousa03/gakushuuhi/kekka/1268105.htm

MEXT, Ministry of Education, Culture, Sports, Science and Technology. (2017). *Statistics.* Retrieved from: http://www.mext.go.jp/english/statistics/

Mood, C. (2010). Logistic regression. Why we cannot do what we think we can do, and what we can do about it. *European Sociological Review, 26*(1), 67–82.

Ojima, F. (Ed.). (2001). *Gendai kōkōsei no keiryō shakai-gaku: shinro – seikatsu – sedai.* Tokyo: MINERVA.

Ojima, F., & Aramaki, S. (Eds.). (2013). *Gendai kōkōsei no shinro to seikatsu.* Kyoto: Doshisha University Press.

Ojima, F., & von Below, S. (2010). Family background, school system and academic achievement in Germany and in Japan. In J. Dronkers (Ed.), *Quality and inequality of education* (pp. 275–297). Dordrecht: Springer.

Park, H. (2013). *Re-evaluating education in Japan and Korea. Demystifying stereotypes.* London/New York: Routledge.

Roesgaard, M. H. (2006). *Japanese education and the cram school business: Functions, challenges and perspectives of the Juku.* Copenhagen: NIAS Press.

Rohlen, T. P. (1980). The Juku phenomenon: An exploratory essay. *Journal of Japanese Studies, 6*(2), 207–242.

Rohlen, T. P. (1983). *Japan's high schools*. Berkeley/Los Angeles: University of California Press.
Seiyama, K., & Noguchi, Y. (1984). Kōkō shingaku ni okeru gakkōgai kyōiku tōshi no kōka [The effects of outside of school educational investments at the transition to high school]. *Kyōiku Shakaigaku Kenkyū, 39*, 113–126.
Shirakawa, T. (2013). Gendai no kōtōgakkō ni okeru shinro bunka no jōken – Chii tassei shikō to jiko jitsugen shikō [Conditions for course differentiation in today's high schools]. In F. Ojima & S. Aramaki (Eds.), *Gendai kōkōsei no shinro to seikatsu* [Career and life of high school students today] (pp. 33–47). Kyoto: Doshisha University Press.
Southgate, D. E. (2009). *Determinants of shadow education – A cross-national analysis*. Ohio: Ohio State University.
Southgate, D. E. (2013). Family capital: A determinant of supplementary eduaction in 17 Nations. In J. Aurini, S. Davies, & J. Dierkes (Eds.), *Out of the shadows: The global intensification of supplementary education* (pp. 245–258). Bingley: Emerald Publishing.
Stevenson, D. L., & Baker, D. P. (1992). Shadow education and allocation in formal schooling: Transition to university in Japan. *American Journal of Sociology, 97*, 1639–1657.
Teddlie, C., & Tashakkori, A. (2006). A general typology of research designs featuring mixed methods. *Research in the Schools, 13*(1), 12–28.
Tomura, A., Nishimaru, R., & Oda, T. (2011). Kyōiku tōshi no kitei yōin to kōka: Gakkōgai kyōiku to shiritsu chūgaku shingaku o chūshin ni [Determinants and effects of investments in education: focusing on out-of-school education and the transition to private middle schools]. In Y. Satō & F. Ojima (Eds.), *Gendai no kaisō shakai: Kakusa to tayōsei* [Modern class society: Disparity and diversity] (pp. 267–280). Tokyo: University of Tokyo Press.
Williams, R. (2009). Using heterogeneous choice models to compare logit and probit coefficients across groups. *Sociological Methods & Research, 37*(4), 531–559.
Williams, R. (2012). Using the margins command to estimate and interpret adjusted predictions and marginal effects. *The Stata Journal, 12*(2), 308–331.

Part II
Results of Analyses

分析結果

Chapter 5
Access to Shadow Education

A Rational Choice? Who Decides to Invest in Shadow Education?

"Shō ga nai ne...?
– It cannot be helped
don't you think so too...?"

(Popular answer to the question
why children attend *juku*)

学校外教育の需要

Abstract This chapter analyzes the *Access* dimension outlined in the Shadow-Education-Inequality-Impact (SEII) Frame, specifically addressing the question who is involved in the decision for shadow education and how that might affect the perceived formation of social inequality. In Japan, families need to decide whether or not an investment in shadow education is necessary to increase the chances of successfully entering a chosen high school or university. Based on sociological Rational Choice Theory, thus far, socioeconomic background and parents' educational aspirations, in conjunction with students' academic achievement, have been deemed influential to such decisions in Japan. The agency of the student is rarely even considered. Basing my calculations on data of the 2011 *Hyōgo High School Students* (HHSS) survey, the following main findings are presented:

(1) students' influence on decision-making concerning shadow education increases with higher age;
(2) in high school, students' own ideas concerning their future life course determine the decision for shadow education even against their parents' wishes;
(3) considerable differences in the effects of social origin and educational aspirations on the decision for a certain type of shadow education are found; and

---

A different version of this chapter (including approximately 60% of its contents) was published under the title "The Decision for Shadow Education in Japan: Students' Choice or Parents' Pressure?" In: *Social Science Japan Journal* 18(2): 193–216 (see Entrich 2015).

(4) low social strata prefer correspondence courses, whereas high social strata prefer *juku*-lessons. The theoretical approach presented in this chapter stresses the importance of acknowledging the existence of a multitude of actors involved in each phase of the decision-making process, including the students themselves, especially when explaining inequalities in modern societies.

5.1   Problematic

Understanding investments in shadow education in Japan as willful decisions made by families in accordance with Rational Choice Theory (RCT) and Shadow Education Investment Theory (SEIT), this chapter addresses the question who is involved in such family decisions and how that might affect the perceived formation of social inequality through shadow education. As discussed earlier (Chap. 2), at the transition to high school and university, Japanese families are confronted with two major decisions regarding students' future careers. In addition to deciding which school to attend, families must decide whether or not an investment in shadow education is necessary to increase the chances of successfully entering a chosen school (Takeuchi 1997: 183–184). The above cited phrase *shō ga nai ne* implies that Japanese families do not see real alternatives to sending children to *juku*. However, a participation in shadow education requires students' time and effort and parents' money. And since no such investment is made accidentally, participation in shadow education has to be understood as the result of a willful, rational decision made by individuals.[1]

Research drawing on RCT usually shows that socioeconomic background and parents' educational aspirations in conjunction with students' academic achievement strongly influence the making of educational decisions in a student's educational life course. In the same way, SEIT research generally shows that parents' economic, social, and cultural status (ESCS) and their educational aspirations determine whether shadow education is pursued or not. It is not clear how much influence students themselves actually have on the decision for or against shadow education. Throughout the literature on educational decision-making in the Japanese context, there is no question about the fact that students make the final decision for a school. However, students are understood as being selected (*senbatsu*), rather than making a choice (*sentaku*) on their own (Kariya 2017). In the same manner, parents are the ones deemed influential for whether or not a child attends shadow education lessons (e.g., Tsuneyoshi 2013). Lauterbach (2013) recently appealed for the expansion of Boudon's classic Rational Choice Theory about social reproduction by rec-

---

[1] In this chapter, participation in shadow education is thus understood as the consequence of a decision to invest. The terms "investment," "decision," and "choice" are thus used synonymously.

ognizing students as investing actors rather than simple consumers of education. An earlier work of Gambetta (1987) also stressed the importance to consider students as active agents in educational decision-making. This acknowledgment of students' agency was neither pursued empirically very often nor was it applied to decisions outside formal education (i.e., school transition), such as the decision for shadow education. This will now be made up.

A strong impact of students' own aspirations on the final decision for schools and shadow education investments implies the need for a revision of the fundamentals of RCT and SEIT. Students who play an active or dominant part in the decision-making process describe a different cause for educational decisions than originally assumed. In this chapter, I argue that educational decisions are the cumulative outcome of all involved actors' preferences as reflected in their educational aspirations for a student's pathway. Since the decision for shadow education is believed to remain primarily with the parents, who decide whether they send their children to a *juku* based on aspirations and socioeconomic status, analyses concerning the impact of students' own career ambitions which are not based on social origin alone but are influenced by contextual factors and students' own ideas promise valuable findings for our understanding about the formation of individual educational pathways. In addition, the decision for shadow education could prove as an act of resiliency among students across different socioeconomic strata and thus provide one explanation for a comparably high proportion of disadvantaged students who manage to achieve a high academic achievement level in international comparison. Access to shadow education could thus prove as an educational opportunity enabling students to realize academic resiliency.[2]

Using data from the 2011 *Hyōgo High School Students* (HHSS) survey, this chapter provides new findings on the impact of students' educational aspirations on decision-making regarding shadow education across different social strata. Based on RCT and SEIT, a twofold decision model is constructed stressing the importance of acknowledging students as actors besides their parents and recognizing structural contextual factors which are believed to exert a strong influence on the final decision. After the theoretical framework and data are discussed, binary logistic regression analyses are carried out to show the impact of students' educational aspirations on the decision for shadow education as a possible counterweight to parents' aspirations and social origins while also comparing the choices of low and high social strata students.

---

[2] Following a definition by the OECD (2013): 194), students are classified as resilient if they are in the bottom quarter of socioeconomic stratification and perform in the top quarter of all students, after accounting for socioeconomic background.

5.2 Theoretical Framework: Shadow Education as a Family Decision

To refer to the parents as responsible decision-makers and to exclude the agency of the student for educational decisions might seem reasonable – as long as children are young of age. However, taking up a recent argumentation of Lauterbach (2013), students gain influence on the outcomes of decision-making processes as they get older. In the context of educational transitions and decision-making, it was rarely analyzed whether parental preferences keep dominating decision-making or whether adolescent children influence such decisions through divergent ideas about their own educational career. In particular within social science research on youth, it is argued that children and adolescents significantly contribute to their own socialization and development (Lange and Xyländer 2010: 23). Students themselves impact their educational careers by taking an active part in the decision-making process (Hurrelmann 2010). We have to consider the possibility that students also calculate the possible outcomes and the costs of their investment (time and effort) or simply develop divergent aspirations from their parents. Hence, a strong impact of students' own views on their future pathways could result in an alteration of the original secondary effect of social origin. By taking the initiative, students might simply follow another educational pathway than their parents had in mind and achieve a different social status than projected based on classic SEIT and RCT.

In addition, especially nonrational beliefs can contribute to divergent educational decisions than classic RCT would predict (Boudon 2003). It is quite reasonable to assume that such nonrational beliefs weigh stronger in the case of students, whose preferences are influenced by individual wishes and several other actors besides their parents, such as peers, teachers, etc. Thus, to theoretically grasp the working mechanisms behind educational decision-making in Japan, the influence of all involved actors' preferences (i.e., educational aspirations of parents and students) needs to be scrutinized against the background of further influences, such as social networks, etc. (e.g., peers, teachers), and country-specific structural factors (e.g., tracking/ranking of schools). However, existing RCT and SEIT research generally missed to separately measure the share of educational aspirations of neither parents nor students, but concentrated their analyses on constant social origin variables, particularly highest parental education level and occupational status or cultural resources (e.g., Erikson and Jonsson 1996; Jonsson and Erikson 2000; Fujihara 2011; Breen et al. 2014). Any analysis concerned with educational decisions should separately measure the share of aspirations' effects on the final decision to show how important the secondary effect of origin proves in a certain context. Additionally, factors determining educational decisions that lie outside of the individual's agency need to be taken into consideration to show what remains of the effects of social origin and educational aspirations on the decision (primary effect of social origin). Hence, following the argument put forth by Lauterbach (2013), RCT and SEIT models are merged and extended by recognizing that students are in a position to

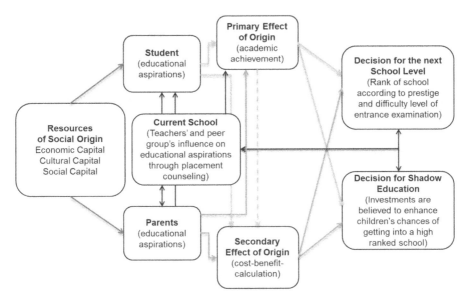

Fig. 5.1 Extension of RCT and SEIT: *Twofold Multiple Actor Decision Model* (Japanese context)

make individual decisions regarding their future careers, especially older students (Fig. 5.1).

The created rational choice model is twofold, concentrating on the two main decisions in the context of schooling in Japan: school and shadow education. Both decisions are primarily made within families, by two groups of actors: parents and students. The formation of students' educational aspirations is strongly affected by their social, economic, and cultural background and their parents' educational aspirations for them. In particular mothers' aspirations were found to show very strong effects on primary and middle school students' aspirations in regard to school choice (Hamajima and Takeuchi 2002: 5). However, there are several other factors we need to consider as influential for both parties' aspirations. Mimizuka (2009) showed that high school students' educational aspirations are more strongly affected by the rank of school attended, academic achievement, and gender than by their parents' socioeconomic status. Additionally, the shadow education sector affects students' career ambitions and thus possible differences in students' views on upcoming decisions regarding school choice or further shadow education investments. Thus, in my analysis, I control for these factors in order to reveal whether students' aspirations affect the decision for shadow education. In the following, I will outline the possible influence of parents, student, school, and *juku* on the final decision concerning shadow education.

In Japanese schools, *shinro shidō*, or placement counseling, is practiced to "construct" students' aspirations (LeTendre 1996). At the transition from middle to high school and high school to university, teachers strive to place all students in a suitable school. To achieve this goal, in addition to academic preparation, teachers provide their students with information about their future options and try to increase their students' motivation to perform well at high school and university entrance examinations. If a student fails to enter a chosen school, not only is the student blamed, but the student's family will often blame the school and its teachers as well. Hence, teachers try to point students into a direction that reflects the families' expectations and aspirations (ibid, 198–199). Since many entrance exams are held on the same days, students' choices are severely constrained. Students who cannot enter their first choice school will either have to wait until the next year or apply to a lower-ranked institution. Nowadays about 30% (up to 60% at top universities) of all high school graduates do not manage to get into their first choice university on the first try and become *rōnin* (students without a school affiliation) for at least a year (Ono 2005: 1). However, middle school graduates cannot afford to not enter a high school immediately. The same applies for the representatives of their middle schools, who would be blamed if one of their former students would not achieve entrance to a high school. The consequences might be a bad reputation for the school and a personal interrogation of the supposed responsible teacher(s). To avoid such a thing from happening, an internal selection process takes place at Japanese schools: first, "unsafe" choices are sorted out on the basis of students' academic achievement; second, recommendations for admission (*suisen nyūgakkō*) as an alternative to entrance examinations are granted to students (LeTendre 1996: 198–200). Since students can apply to several high schools and universities, they are generally advised to apply to one highly ranked and one less prestigious high school, following the *suberidome* (insurance) principle (Watanabe 2013: 41). According to a recent study, sometimes teachers also advise parents to send their children to *juku* in order to assure entrance into the school or university they desire (Cook 2013). Besides their teachers, students' peers function as a possible influence on the decision for shadow education as well. As shown in Chap. 2, in a 2007 MEXT survey, almost half of all students (6th grade, 48.2%; 9th grade, 49.1%) responded that they attend a *juku* to meet friends from school (see Chap. 2, Fig. 2.13). According to my own research, students often join classmates who already attend a *juku*. Many *juku*-operators thus need no advertisement but manage to get enough students through word of mouth.

Parents also try to directly influence the aspirations of their children at home and through their correspondence with school teachers. They tend to follow teachers' advice if they are uncertain about the decision for a certain school (LeTendre 1996: 204). However, parents' willingness to invest large amounts of money for supplementary education primarily arises from their insecurity about what would happen if their children did not participate in such lessons, as I will further discuss in Chap. 7. In the Japanese *gakureki shakai* (credentialist society), educational credentials are all that counts (Kikkawa 2006). In recent years, the PISA shock and the decline in academic achievement debates (Takayama 2008) have further contributed to parents' insecurity concerning their children's future (Bjork and Tsuneyoshi 2005: 623). Consequently, supplementary education is still considered a very effective security strategy.

The shadow education industry promises to get students into prestigious schools and into desired jobs by "guaranteeing success." To support students in their attempts to enter schools by entrance exam, the industry carries out mock exams (*mogi shiken*) showing students what schools they have a high pass probability when taking the entrance exam. Based on former applicants' results in mock examinations, Z-scores (*hensachi*) are derived nationwide, which serve to categorize high schools and universities and create distribution tables showing the needed mock examination score to pass the entrance examination of a certain high school or university (LeTendre 1994, 1996: 202, Takeuchi 1997: 185, Roesgaard 2006, Watanabe 2013: 51–65).[3] Hence, the *juku* is a place where general information concerning school choice and entrance examinations is gathered. According to the MEXT (2008: 44), parents' main reasons to send their children to *juku* are concerned with passing entrance examinations (34% in 9th grade) and to obtain information about which high school they should pick, as well as information on the upcoming entrance examinations (26% in 9th grade; see Chap. 2, Fig. 2.12).

In addition, students in Japan generally believe that there is a causal relationship between effort and academic achievement (Takeuchi 1997: 189–191). My own fieldwork confirmed the ongoing essential role of this *ganbari*-ism (effort-ism) as a mechanism underlying educational decision-making. Parents, schools, and *juku* teachers believe that only a massive investment of time, effort, and money leads to success in entering highly ranked schools. Since people in Japan generally believe that every student has the same cognitive potential, those who do not succeed in the "entrance examination war" (*juken sensō*) (Rohlen 1980: 220) have simply not put enough effort into it. Consequently, the decision for shadow education is a strategy to achieve a high education level. Whether students with less socioeconomic and cultural resources have the possibility to pursue such a strategy remains unclear.

According to a survey conducted by LeTendre (1996), approximately 95% of Japanese students believe that they alone are responsible for school choice – more than 60% wanted to attend a chosen school even if their parents or teachers were against it. It is reasonable to assume that students' determination also affects the families' decision for shadow education. Although parents' cost-benefit calculations regarding the decision for shadow education highly depend on their financial resources and aspirations, students might be less influenced by their parents' socioeconomic status than predicted by classic RCT or SEIT. In fact, in line with my own fieldwork, Cave (2016) confirmed that many students view the decision to enter a *juku* as their own. It also happens that one child enters a *juku*, while his or her siblings do not (p. 204).

---

[3] My own fieldwork revealed that mock exams remain highly important for high school and university entrance despite being banned from schools. In the same way, the use of distribution tables by schools' homeroom teachers was forbidden in 1992 (see LeTendre 1994). However, this ban only shifted more importance to the shadow education sector, which took up this part of *shinro shidō* (see also Chap. 8 for more changes in the *juku*-industry).

5.2.1   Research Hypotheses: Students' Share in the Decision
for Shadow Education

The aim of this chapter is to clarify students' possible role in educational decision-making and thus the possible divergent effects of decisions leading to social inequality, concentrating on the choice for shadow education in Japan. As discussed above, educational decisions in the Japanese context are believed to depend on social origin, parents' educational aspirations, students' academic achievement, and the attended school as roughly reflected in the rank of the school. Additionally, the shadow education sector itself plays a major role in this decision-making by providing parents and students with information on school transition and students' actual chances of entering a certain school based on mock exam outcomes. However, whether students' aspirations actually differ from parents' expectations, and thus divergent decisions are favored by the two groups, is unclear. As Lauterbach (2013) indicates, students have their own ideas about their future careers, which become stronger as they get older. It is possible that students do not follow their parents in their preferences, and in the end, decisions are made that reflect students' aspirations more than parents' aspirations. Whereas parents primarily consider the costs associated with shadow education and its assumed effects, students are in a better position to assess whether an investment is really necessary and what type of shadow education is most promising due to correspondence with their teachers and peers as well as their former and actual experiences with shadow education. Hence, students might decide for or against an investment in shadow education even against their parents' wishes or prefer a different type of shadow education. If this is the case, existing decision theories need to be reevaluated by focusing on both parties: parents and students. In addition, the question whether shadow education also provides educational opportunities for disadvantaged students to succeed against the odds shall be answered by concentrating on low strata in comparison to high strata students and their possibilities to access different types of shadow education. Thus, whether the high proportion of resilient students found in Japan can be explained through these students' high enrolment in shadow education shall be examined. In conclusion, my research hypotheses read as follows:

[H1]   Educational decisions are the cumulative outcome of all involved actors' preferences as reflected in their educational aspirations. The impact of parents' aspirations on the decision for shadow education weakens with higher age of their child, and students' aspirations become critical for the decision.

[H2]   High school students in particular have a greater say in the decision concerning shadow education, as well as what kind of shadow education is chosen. Hence, an alteration of social origin determination becomes possible, thus counteracting social reproduction.

[H3]   Shadow education is accessible by socioeconomically disadvantaged students also. By benefitting from a participation in shadow education, low socioeconomic strata possibly achieve a different education level than predicted by classic RCT. Shadow education thus provides an explanation for a high percentage of academically resilient students.

In the following, the above stated hypotheses will be tested as follows: (1) the different effects of social origin and parents' aspirations in comparison to students' aspirations on the decision for shadow education in primary, middle, and high school are calculated; (2) the detailed impact of educational aspirations and social origin in high school on the decision for different types of shadow education is predicted while also controlling for contextual variables; and (3) calculations of students at the bottom quarter and the top quarter of socioeconomic stratification are compared to predict the chances of disadvantaged students in relation to advantaged students to pursue shadow education as a strategy to achieve a high education level.

5.3   Results: The Impact of Students' and Parents' Educational Aspirations on the Decision for Shadow Education in Japan

To obtain sound conclusions, analyses are based on suitable data of the third HHSS survey, conducted in 2011. Following a short outline of the used variables, I analyze the decision for shadow education using binary logistic regression. Whereas my first analysis investigates the changing influence of social origin and parents' and students' educational aspirations on the decision for shadow education from primary to high school, my second analysis concentrates on the decision for different types of shadow education during high school by also controlling for contextual variables.

5.3.1   Data and Methods

Students' actual participation in shadow education is used as a proxy for the families' decision to invest in shadow education. Hence, in my upcoming analyses, I will use the investment in academic *juku* (including *yobikō*), private home tutors, and correspondence courses as dependent variables (encoded as 1 = yes; 0 = no). The question is what determines a family's decision to invest in supplementary lessons in general? It goes without question that if one student attends *juku*-classes once a week and another attends classes three times a week, different levels of support are received, and the latter student might have an advantage. Also, different cost-benefit calculations apply for these cases. Hence, families with less financial resources might choose a different type of shadow education, which best fits their financial background and students' supposed educational needs. Since this analysis focuses on the decision for an investment in shadow education per se, the actual intensity of participation is not included.

Existing studies on the access to shadow education in Japan revealed that investments vary according to gender (e.g., Seiyama and Noguchi 1984), number of siblings (e.g., Tomura et al. 2011), grade and school type (e.g., Kataoka 2001; Konakayama and Matsui 2008; Tomura et al. 2011; Matsuoka 2015), ranking of high schools (e.g., Tomura et al. 2011; Kariya 2013; Entrich 2014; Matsuoka 2015), students' academic standing in school (e.g., Seiyama and Noguchi 1984; Stevenson and Baker 1992), whether students have already invested a lot of time for extracurricular lessons at an early age (e.g., Tobishima 2012), and, following Cultural Capital Theory by Bourdieu (1983), cultural background (e.g., Konakayama and Matsui 2008). In addition, previous research has shown that the location of a school affects whether students have the opportunity to participate in shadow education (Stevenson and Baker 1992). As stressed in RCT, parents' economic, social, and cultural status (ESCS), their educational aspirations, and the academic achievement level of students are critical in making educational decisions. The effects of students' aspirations, as opposed to parental aspirations, on the decision of whether to invest in shadow education, remain unclear.

To understand whether students' influence on the decision for shadow education gains importance as they get older, a cross-temporal comparison of the effects of students' and parents' educational aspirations on investment in shadow education while controlling for further influential factors such as gender, ESCS, students' schooling background (such as placement counseling) as reflected in the stratification of high schools, academic standing, and former experience with shadow education will be carried out in the following.

5.3.2 Results of Analyses

To ascertain the determinants for the decision to invest in shadow education, I conducted logistic regression analyses in the following manner: First, I analyze what matters more from primary school to high school: social origin and parents' aspirations or students' aspirations [H1]? Following this, I analyze the determinants for shadow education participation in high school in more detail by adding the introduced contextual covariates and differentiating between the three different types of shadow education in Japan: private tutors, correspondence courses, and *juku*-classes [H2]. Third, educational aspirations of students from low and high social strata on the decision for a certain type of shadow education are compared to examine whether shadow education is used as a strategy of disadvantaged students to increase their chances of educational success [H3]. As discussed earlier (Chap. 4), to solve the problem of comparing coefficients between groups and samples, I calculate and display the Average Marginal Effects (AME) instead of giving out regression coefficients or odds ratios.

5.3.2.1   Decision for Shadow Education from Primary to High School

Table 5.1 shows a binary logistic regression predicting the influence of gender, family background, and educational aspirations on students' participation in shadow education during primary, middle, and high school. The aspirations of parents and students were coded according to the three major goals: staying in the education system and pursuing the highest track (1) university, staying in the education system and pursuing one of the two tracks with less risk but still high expected returns (2) junior or technical college, and leaving the education system by (3) entering the job market. This last category includes all those parents and students who were still undecided concerning these three major goals during primary, middle, and high school.

In Model 1, only the educational aspirations of parents were included to show the direct effects of social origin on decision-making as stressed by classic RCT. In Model 2, students' aspirations were added. Model 3 further differentiates between social classes, showing the impact of students' and parents' educational aspirations across ESCS groups (bottom 25%, middle 50%, top 25%).

According to Model 1, the impact of the ESCS of a student shows the strongest effect on the decision for shadow education, even though this influence varies in its intensity from primary to high school. ESCS thus explains from 38% (middle school) to 51% (high school) of the decision for shadow education. Additionally, gender seems to play a role in decision-making. Although, traditionally, parents tended to invest more in education for boys than girls (Schultz Lee 2010: 1582), this seems not to be the case anymore. In our sample, boys are up to 11% (high school) less likely to receive supplementary lessons than girls. During middle school, the difference is not as large, but it is still significant. It seems that it is no longer desirable for girls to either get married or join the workforce directly after graduation. Nowadays, first achieving a high education level and then deciding whether to pursue a career or a life as a housewife seems to be a more common security strategy. However, whether real change has occurred here will be the content of Chaps. 7 and 8.

Parents' aspirations for their children show very different effects between father and mother. Whereas the father's aspirations are not significant, mothers whose goal is to place their child in university – in comparison to mothers who favor the job market or have not made a decision yet – have a strong positive influence on the decision for shadow education, which seems to be strongest in high school (35% higher likelihood). However, by including students' own aspirations in Model 2, we find considerable differences in the effects of mothers' aspirations. The small percentage of single-minded students who had already decided to attend university when they were in primary school have an 8% higher likelihood to choose shadow education compared to their undecided peers. With higher age, the influence of students' own aspirations increases. Although no effect can be detected in middle school, where the majority of students are enrolled in shadow education apparently without having any real choice, in high school, the impact of students' aspirations becomes stronger than that of their mothers' aspirations if they have decided for university (mother, 8% increased likelihood; student, 26% increased likelihood). In

Table 5.1 Binary logistic regression analyses predicting students' participation in shadow education during primary, middle, and high school, displaying AME (HHSS 2011)

Primary school (2000–2005)

			Model 1	Model 2	Model 3[b]		
Social origin	ESCS		.46***	.44***	Low	Middle	High
	Gender	Male	−.10***	−.10***	−.08+	−.09**	−.13***
Educational aspirations	Father	University	.01	.00	.05	.01	−.14*
		College[a]	.00	.01	.08	−.03	−.05
		REF: job or no decision yet					
	Mother	University	.19***	.18***	.12+	.19**	.38**
		College[a]	.11*	.11*	.12	.14*	.18
		REF: job or no decision yet					
	Student	University		.08*	.15	.03	.09*
		College[a]		−.07	.08	−.23	n.e.
		REF: job or no decision yet					
N (valid cases)			2373		556	1187	629
Pseudo R² (McFadden)			.05	.05	.03	.03	.05

Middle school (2006–2008)

Social origin			Model 1	Model 2	Model 3		
	ESCS		.38***	.38***	Low	Middle	High
	Gender	Male	−.03*	−.03*	.02	−.06**	−.02
Educational aspirations	Father	University	−.03	−.03	−.10	−.00	−.04
		College[a]	.06*	.06*	.11+	.06	.02
		REF: job or no decision yet					
	Mother	University	.12***	.12***	.15*	.11*	.19
		College[a]	.05	.06	.10	.04	.19
		REF: job or no decision yet					
	Student	University		.00	.13*	−.03	−.01
		College[a]		−.06	.02	−.07	−.20
		REF: job or no decision yet					
N (valid cases)			2372		556	1187	629
Pseudo R² (McFadden)			.05	.05	.03	.02	.03

High school (2009–2011)

Social origin			Model 1	Model 2	Model 3		
	ESCS		.51***	.47***	Low	Middle	High
	Gender	Male	−.12***	−.11***	−.07*	−.12***	−.13**

(continued)

Table 5.1 (continued)

Educational aspirations	Father	University	.04	−.01	−.03	−.01	.07
		College[a]	−.04	.00	.08	−.02	−.09
		REF: job or no decision yet					
	Mother	University	.35***	.15***	.06	.20***	.11
		College[a]	.03	−.03	.03	.02	−.02
		REF: job or no decision yet					
	Student	University		.35***	.31***	.31***	.41***
		College[a]		.09*	.02	.11+	.16
		REF: job or no decision yet					
N (valid cases)			2354		577	1211	637
Pseudo R² (McFadden)			.17	.19	.14	.16	.12

***P<0.001; **P<0.01; *P<0.05; +P<0.10; *n.e.* not estimable
[a]This category consists of junior college and technical college aspirations
[b]The category "low" represents the students of the lowest quartile of ESCS stratification, whereas the category "high" represents the highest ESCS quartile, respectively. The category "middle" represents the 50% of students between the lowest and highest ESCS quartiles

addition, the generally strong effect of ESCS slightly decreases due to the consideration of students' aspirations, especially during high school.

In Model 3, the effects of parents' and students' aspirations on shadow education choice are differentiated according to social origin. Differences in the effects are especially visible between bottom and top quarter social stratification (ESCS) groups. During primary school, mothers' aspirations dominate the decision-making across all social strata. However, low ESCS students already show a high but insignificant impact on shadow education choice (15%). In contrast, the impact of students' aspirations is smaller for other social strata, but significant for top ESCS groups (9%). During middle school, aspirations of high ESCS groups become generally insignificant, since nearly all high ESCS students use shadow education at this time. For low social strata, students' and mothers' aspirations strongly affect whether shadow education is pursued. During high school, a strong impact of mothers' aspirations remains for middle ESCS groups only. Low and high social strata students gain the upper hand in the decision-making.

To get more accurate results regarding the influence of educational aspirations as determinants of the decision for shadow education investments, the following section concentrates on the influence of social origin and educational aspirations on students' participation in different types of shadow education during high school while also controlling for contextual covariates.

5.3.2.2   Decision for Shadow Education in High School

In Table 5.2, three models are presented, concentrating on high school only and recoding the variables concerning educational aspirations. In high school, the question is no longer whether parents or students have made their decisions regarding students' future pathways, but how much these aspirations differ. Hence, only students' and parents' aspirations for labor market entrance after graduation ("job") are used as a reference category in the following calculations. In addition, students' aspirations for university are further differentiated according to whether they intend to enter a top university or an average university and through what entrance method they intend to enter.

Model 4 again shows similarly strong influences of social origin and educational aspirations. Students with the intention to enter a first-class university by entrance exam are 53% (!) more likely to choose some kind of shadow education compared to peers with job aspirations. There are thus huge differences in the chance to take part in shadow education according to the rank of university a student intends to apply at, as well as the method of entrance he or she intends to use. If parents have high aspirations for their child (university), or are undecided about their child's future pathway, the child is either more (mother) or less likely (father) to receive supplementary lessons. This infers that fathers are either not as involved in the decision-making process for students' pathways or they do not see the necessity of attending additional lessons in the shadow education sector. Hence, the main decision-makers are students and their mothers. They both believe that an additional investment in shadow education might prove valuable if they have decided that the student should enter a university, especially if it is a first-class university, and they hope to enter via entrance examination.

By adding contextual variables in Model 5, this assumption is further supported. Contextual variables such as the diversity of high schools (ranking, administration, and location) strongly affect the decision for shadow education. In addition, families in which the student has already participated in shadow education during primary or middle school are also more likely to choose shadow education in high school. Students' current (high school) or former (middle school) academic standing shows comparably low or no effects. In contrast, the effects of social origin and educational aspirations decrease considerably, and gender differences become less obvious (−6%). In particular, the ESCS' influence decreases heavily (−13%). The student and his or her mother thus see shadow education primarily as an investment in the child's future. Hence, students who intend to enter university by an alternative entrance method and not take the entrance exam do not see the need to receive supplementary lessons such as preparatory classes at *yobikō*, but choose to concentrate more on school instead. While additional lessons might help improve academic achievement, and thus help a student obtain a recommendation from their high school to a university, such an investment would be time-consuming, and it might seem more promising to increase the time-investment in school (e.g., for club activities).

Table 5.2 Binary logistic regression analyses predicting students' participation in shadow education during high school, according to ESCS groups[a], displaying AME (HHSS 2011)

			Participation in shadow education				
			Model 4	Model 5	Model 6		
Social origin	ESCS		.35***	.22**	Low	Middle	High
	Gender	Male	−.10***	−.04**	.01	−.06**	−.02
	Siblings	0	.14***	.12***	.12*	.12**	.11+
		1	.06**	.03	−.01	.02	.06+
		REF: two or more					
Schooling background	High school ranking	Academic A school		.43***	.21*	.42***	.57***
		Academic B school		.31***	.08	.24***	.56***
		Academic C school		.21***	.11*	.16***	.35***
		REF: vocational school					
	Administration	Public school		.25***	.12*	.19***	.46***
		REF: private school					
	School's location	Metropolitan area		.11***	−.05***	.11**	.17***
		Urban area		−.02	−.07+	.02	−.04
		REF: rural area					
	Academic standing	Middle school		.02*	.04**	.02	−.00
		High school		.01	.00	.01	.02*
	Shadow education experience	Primary school		.11***	.11***	.07**	.18***
		Middle school		.21***	.14***	.26***	.19**
		REF: no participation					

(continued)

Table 5.2 (continued)

			Participation in shadow education				
			Model 4	Model 5	Model 6		
Educational aspirations	Father	University	−.12*	−.10*	−.14+	−.11	−.00
		College[b]	−.08	−.04	−.01	−.07	−.04
		no decision yet	−.11*	−.07	−.06	−.10	.00
		REF: job					
	Mother	University	.23***	.15**	.26***	.15*	−.13
		College[b]	.12+	.08	.16+	.09	−.20
		no decision yet	.16**	.14**	.17**	.14	−.11
		REF: job					
	Student	University					
Top Uni * entrance exam			.53***	.32***	.17+	.34***	.59***
Average Uni * entrance exam			.38***	.21***	.05	.23**	.52***
Uni * other entrance methods			.11*	.14**	.01	.17*	.38**
		College[b]	.06	.01	−.07	.05	.25+
		No decision yet	.06	.08	n.e.	.12	.52**
		REF: job					
N (valid cases)			2324		545	1158	616
Pseudo R² (McFadden)			.27	.42	.43	.39	.42

***P<0.001; **P<0.01; *P<0.05; +P<0.10; *n.e.* not estimable

[a]The category "low" represents the students of the lowest quartile of ESCS stratification, whereas the category "high" represents the highest ESCS quartile, respectively. The category "middle" represents the 50% of students between the lowest and highest ESCS quartiles

[b]This category consists of junior college and technical college aspirations

Model 6 differentiates between the bottom quarter ESCS group, the two middle quarter ESCS groups, and the top quarter ESCS group. In contrast to high ESCS students, the ranking of high schools does not explain the choice for participation in shadow education as strongly as for other social strata (low ESCS, 21% if they attend an Academic A school; high ESCS, 57%). Low ESCS students who achieved entrance into top-ranked high schools are still less likely to pursue shadow education compared to their peers.

If low ESCS students live in a metropolitan or urban area, their chances to choose shadow education decrease, whereas middle and high ESCS students' chances increase if they live in metropolitan areas. According to my fieldwork, this can be explained by the higher costs of shadow education in areas with a high population density. For low social strata, a high academic standing in middle school and former experience with shadow education prove to be important factors for a further decision for shadow education in high school. Also, by controlling for these contextual variables, considerable changes in the effects of low social strata's aspirations become visible if compared to Model 3. Apparently, low ESCS students' aspirations show less impact on the decision to enter shadow education in comparison to other social strata (17% if they want to enter a top university by entrance exam). In particular, top ESCS students' aspirations highly impact the choice for shadow education (up to 59% if they want to enter a top university by entrance exam). These students will even pursue shadow education with a higher likelihood of 52% if they have not yet made a decision for their future pathway compared to high ESCS peers who intend to enter the job market. Shadow education is thus used as a security strategy by advantaged students to not risk moving socially downward if the student has not committed to a clear pathway yet. Whereas mothers' aspirations do not affect the decision among the high ESCS group, aspirations of mothers of bottom ESCS students still strongly affect whether shadow education is chosen (26% if university is favored, 16% if college is favored). However, another significant difference between social strata is found as well: if the mother of a low ESCS student has not made a decision for her child's future pathway yet, the student will have a 17% higher chance to choose shadow education. Socioeconomically disadvantaged students thus have more freedom to decide for shadow education participation if their mothers have not predetermined their future pathway or simply do not involve in their students' school and after-school life as much.

In the end, (female) students aiming for a top university while attending a highly ranked public school in a metropolitan area and possessing a high ESCS but no siblings have the highest chances of entering the shadow education sector in high school, especially if they had previous experience with shadow education. However, the decision is still strongly influenced by social origin, and thus we have to ask whether social inequalities are inevitably reproduced by these decisions.

5.3.2.3 Decision for Different Types of Shadow Education in High School

Taking into account the diversity of the shadow education industry in Japan, the decision for shadow education differs considerably between the three main types as illustrated in Table 5.3, Models 7–9.

At first glance, the decision to attend a *juku* depends strongly on social origin, school background, and educational aspirations, as it does for shadow education in general (Model 7). However, a closer look reveals that gender differences are no longer found, and ESCS exerts a particularly high influence on the chance to choose *juku*, compared to shadow education in total (compared to Model 5, +13%). Moreover, fathers' aspirations play no significant role for this decision, and while the influence of students' aspirations decreased, it remains one of the strongest predictors.

In contrast, the actual determinants for private tutoring at home are hard to detect (Model 8). This might be due to the relatively small number of students who actually

Table 5.3 Binary logistic regression analyses predicting students' participation in different types of shadow education during high school, displaying AME (HHSS 2011)

			Academic *juku*	Private tutor	Correspondence courses
			Model 7	Model 8	Model 9
Social origin	ESCS		.35***	.02	−.02
	Gender	Male	−.02	.00	−.05***
	Siblings	0	.08**	.03	.05*
		1	.03	−.01	.00
		REF: two or more			
Schooling background	High school ranking	Academic A school	.38***	.01	.05*
		Academic B school	.29***	.02	.06*
		Academic C school	.19***	.01	.02
		REF: vocational school			
	Administration	Public school	.24***	.00	.08***
		REF: private school			
	School's location	Metropolitan area	.11***	.00	.00
		Urban area	−.01	−.00	−.06***
		REF: rural area			
	Academic standing	Middle school	.01	−.01	.02*
		High school	−.01	−.00	.01*
	Shadow education experience	Primary school	.08***	.01	.08***
		Middle school	.16***	.04*	.09**
		REF: no participation			
Educational aspirations	Father	University	−.08	−.00	−.00
		College[a]	−.05	−.01	.05
		no decision yet	−.10	.01	.03
		REF: job			
	Mother	University	.18***	.01	.01
		College[a]	.10	.01	.02
		No decision yet	.16**	.01	.04
		REF: job			
	Student	University			
	Top Uni * entrance exam		.23***	.02	.11***
	Average Uni * entrance exam		.13*	.01	.14***
	Uni * other entrance methods		.07	.02	.05*
		College[a]	.00	.01	−.01
		No decision yet	.03	n.e.	.04
		REF: job			

(continued)

Table 5.3 (continued)

	Academic juku	Private tutor	Correspondence courses
	Model 7	Model 8	Model 9
N (valid cases)	2324	2307	2324
Pseudo R² (McFadden)	.40	.08	.22

***P<0.001; **P<0.01; *P<0.05; +P<0.10; *n.e.* not estimable due to too small number of cases
[a]This category consists of junior college and technical college aspirations

use this kind of shadow education. Only shadow education experience during middle school significantly increases the chance of receiving lessons from a tutor. Social background does not seem to impact the choice for tutors. For correspondence courses, no significant positive effects of students' ESCS can be detected (Model 9). If a decision for correspondence courses was made, school background generally played a less significant role compared to that when choosing a *juku*. However, two very clear differences are found: the possibility to choose correspondence courses is the same in rural and metropolitan areas, and students' with high academic standing in school show a higher chance to enroll in these courses.

A detailed analysis predicting the choice for the different types of shadow education according to low and high social strata is presented in Table 5.4, Models 10–11. Since the number of cases was too small to make valid calculations, the choice for private tutors is omitted here. Concerning the choice for *juku*-lessons, across all social strata, similar effects as predicted for shadow education in general (Model 6) are found, with few exceptions.

The location of a student's school plays no role for the chance to attend *juku* for low social strata, for example. Also, academic standing in middle school seems less important for these students. More importantly, low strata students' aspirations show no significant effect for the decision to attend *juku*; only low ESCS mothers' aspirations seem to strongly impact this decision. Due to the high diversity of the *juku*-market, a final statement cannot be achieved with the given data. Detailed analyses allowing to differentiate between characteristics of different *juku*-types are necessary to satisfactorily assess whether low social strata are socially excluded from *juku*-attendance to a high degree. Thus, this issue will be picked up again in Chap. 8.

Concerning the choice for correspondence courses, contextual background plays a minor role for low social strata with the exception of area and academic standing. The chance to choose correspondence courses decreases for low ESCS students when their school is located in a metropolitan area (−12%). In contrast, for each one unit increase of the academic standing, low ESCS students' chance to demand such courses increases by 3%. High ESCS students have a higher chance to choose correspondence courses if they are female and attend a public Academic B high school. However, particularly educational aspirations of high ESCS groups impact the decision for such an investment, if students intend to enter university by entrance exams. Similar effects are found for middle ESCS groups, only to a lesser extent. For low social strata, mothers' university aspirations also show further significant effects on

Table 5.4 Binary logistic regression analyses predicting students' participation in different types of shadow education during high school, according to ESCS groups[a], displaying AME (HHSS 2011)

			Academic *juku*			Correspondence courses		
			Model 10			Model 11		
			Low	Middle	High	Low	Middle	High
Social origin	ESCS							
	Gender	Male	.02	−.05*	.01	−.03	−.06**	−.06*
	Siblings	0	.09	.06+	.06	−.01	.07*	−.01
		1	−.01	.02	.07*	.00	−.01	.02
		REF: two or more						
Schooling background	High school ranking	Academic A	.25**	.35***	.51***	−.07	.11**	.07
		Academic B	.13+	.24***	.47***	−.09	.05	.20**
		Academic C	.09*	.16***	.28***	−.01	.00	.02
		REF: vocational school						
	Administration	Public school	.14*	.18***	.40***	−.06	.07**	.19***
		REF: private school						
	School's location	Metropolitan area	.04	.09**	.19***	−.12*	.04	.00
		Urban area	−.03	.02	−.01	−.04	−.04*	−.12**
		REF: rural area						
	Academic standing	Middle school	.01	.02	.01	.03**	.00	.02
		High school	−.01	−.00	.00	.01	.01	.01
	Shadow education experience	Primary school	.04+	.06*	.17***	.06*	.08***	.10*
		Middle school	.09**	.23***	.12*	.04	.08*	n.e.
		REF: no participation						

Educational aspirations							
Father	University	−.14+	−.10	.05	.01	.00	.05
	College[b]	−.03	−.09	.02	.03	.05	.55
	No decision yet	−.09	−.14	.02	.05	.04	.10
	REF: job						
Mother	University	.20**	.19*	.05	.06*	−.01	−.24
	College[b]	.19+	.10	−.05	.02	.08	−.34
	No decision yet	.12*	.18*	.05	.05	−.00	−.08
	REF: job						
Student	University						
	Top Uni * entrance exam	.12	.29***	.34+	.05	.10*	.17**
	Average Uni * entrance exam	−.04	.19**	.25	.11*	.13*	.19**
	Uni * other entrance methods	−.07	.16*	.11	.01	.05	.07
	College[b]	−.12+	.10	.06	.01	−.03	−.02
	No decision yet	n.e.	.17	.17	n.e.	n.e.	n.e.
	REF: job						
N (valid cases)		545	1158	616	545	1152	548
Pseudo R^2 (McFadden)		.38	.38	.35	.33	.24	.18

***$P<0.001$; **$P<0.01$; *$P<0.05$; +$P<0.10$; *n.e.* not estimable due to too small number of cases

[a] The category "low" represents the students of the lowest quartile of ESCS stratification, whereas the category "high" represents the highest ESCS quartile, respectively. The category "middle" represents the 50% of students between the lowest and highest ESCS quartiles

[b] This category consists of junior college and technical college aspirations

this choice. Socioeconomically disadvantaged students generally increase their chances of receiving such courses, if they pursue entrance to average universities by entrance exams. Otherwise, no significant effects of these students' aspirations can be detected. At this moment, it is recommendable to also include the pseudo R^2 results of the three submodels used for comparison of the three ESCS groups. For the low ESCS group, I find a considerably higher R^2 (.33) compared to the other ESCS group submodels (.24 and .18). The submodel for low ESCS students thus better explains the relationship of the chosen variables. Ambitious low strata students thus exert a strong influence on the decision for correspondence courses.

In summary, we find considerable differences across social strata when choosing different types of shadow education. On the one hand, it seems that correspondence courses and private tutors generally provide alternatives for socioeconomically disadvantaged students to also benefit from supplementary education services. On the other hand, detailed analyses differentiating between social strata show that high and middle ESCS students have a greater say in the decision for *juku*- and correspondence courses, whereas the aspirations of mothers remain a strong predictor for low ESCS students' chances to enroll in *juku*-lessons and, to a lesser degree, to receive correspondence courses.

Due to the concept behind these courses, students have to learn autonomously, and students with low academic standing or learning deficits need to receive remedial tutoring and might thus encounter difficulties with the self-study approach. Families of such students are thus more likely to choose *juku* with a focus on remedial teaching (*hoshū* or *kyōsai*, see Chap. 8, p. 199) or a private tutor. However, students' aspirations show the strongest influence on the decision for correspondence courses. When choosing this kind of shadow education, it does not matter what parents actually wish for their child's pathway – students' aspirations decide. It is possible that students are free to choose these courses since they are easily accessible (mostly online) and comparably cheap, and many students work part time during high school,[4] so they might be able to pay the tuition themselves. Correspondence courses thus provide a real alternative for ambitious students across all social strata and, for students from disadvantaged backgrounds, across all school ranks.

5.4   Discussion

I will now summarize the findings and implications of my analyses, with respect to my stated research hypotheses.

Concerning [H1]: even though social origin and mothers' aspirations strongly influence the decision for an investment in shadow education, students' own influence

---

[4] Of our sample (valid responses = 3799), 22.9% responded that they work part time (*arubaito*) besides school.

on the decision increases with age when they have made up their mind about their future path.

Concerning [H2]: the decision for shadow education during high school depends more strongly on students' than parents' aspirations. When controlling for contextual variables such as school ranking and former experiences with shadow education, the effects of students' and parents' aspirations as well as social origin generally decrease but remain strong. However, the influence of social origin and educational aspirations varies according to type of shadow education: whereas an investment in *juku* depends highly on social origin, school background, and aspirations of parents and students, a decision to take correspondence courses is generally neither affected by social origin nor by parental aspirations, but mostly depends on students' own aspirations.

Concerning [H3]: the impact of family's educational aspirations and contextual variables on the decision for shadow education in general and certain types of shadow education in particular was found to vary across ESCS groups. Bottom quarter ESCS students' aspirations thus have a high impact on the choice for shadow education in middle school, if compared to peers who have not yet made a decision yet or favor the job market. Whereas ambitious students from advantageous ESCS backgrounds generally increase their chance to enter shadow education in high school independent of their parents' wishes regarding their future educational pathway, the choice to invest in shadow education among disadvantaged ESCS strata remains primarily with the mothers. Only if bottom quarter ESCS mothers have not made a decision yet, their child will use this freedom of choice and becomes more likely to choose shadow education. Top quarter social strata base their decisions very much on contextual background, such as school ranking. For bottom quarter social strata, the decision depends primarily on aspirations. Similar effects are found for *juku*-choice and the decision to receive correspondence courses, with the exception that bottom quarter social strata students have a significant say in the decision for correspondence courses also. Hence, ambitious students with sufficient academic achievement are in a position to benefit from shadow education such as correspondence courses despite disadvantageous socioeconomic background and independent of the attended school.

In conclusion, we must acknowledge that the decisions for shadow education are made within family contexts, but without much influence of fathers. Mothers are simply much more involved in their children's school and out-of-school life. Hence, the future aspirations of mothers and students are very much in line with each other. However, although the mother's influence stays strong over time, the student gains more influence over the decision for shadow education as they grow older. In high school, the student might see the need to invest in shadow education to improve his or her chances to follow a desired pathway, even if the mother is not convinced. Students thus prove very resilient when they have decided to follow a certain path. In particular, if a mother has not made a clear decision for her child's future career or if the student is unaware of her choice, the student might use this freedom to increase his or her chance of entering a highly ranked university by attending a *juku* during high school. The differences in the decision to seek a distinct type of shadow education reflect this freedom as well. Whereas enrolment in *juku* is still much more affected by social origin, the educational aspirations of parents, and school background, correspondence courses are easily accessible and affordable. Students thus do not depend as much on their parents' resources and approval to purchase these courses. In addition, students intending to enter a first-class university via entrance exam proved to be most likely to attend shadow education. These students simply convinced their parents of the importance of participating in shadow education for their future career, and they may also make different decisions concerning shadow education investments.

This analysis also shows the importance of considering contextual background, such as school ranking, administration type and location, and previous experience with shadow education, to loosen the impression that the decision to seek shadow education is a zero-sum game between parents and students. Only then, the actual impacts of social origin and educational aspirations become visible and allow us to verify whether this impact is significant against the structural background in which decisions are made. I found that highly ranked public high schools in metropolitan areas assemble a higher proportion of students who feel the need to invest in shadow education during high school. These schools push their students to enter highly ranked universities and thus ensure their own prestige stays high. The influence of students' social origin thus decreases when they are enrolled at such a highly ranked institution. However, if we believe that these schools determine where their students end up, students' own aspirations would not show the strong impact found in my analyses. Thus, even against the backgrounds of strong social origin and school influence, a clear and strong effect of students' own aspirations remains throughout all analyses.

Two surprising results outside the main focus of this study have to be highlighted as well: (1) of the different types of shadow education, only the chance to take correspondence courses increases with high academic standing in school; and (2) girls are more likely to enter shadow education than boys. While I have attempted to give reasonable explanations for these findings, detailed analyses are necessary to explain these results satisfactorily.

In sum, an expansion of Boudon's classic decision theory has been proven to be necessary, and this should be acknowledged in future research. The same is true for future Japanese research on shadow education, which needs to also acknowledge the influence of students' own choices on the decision for shadow education. Shadow education does not automatically reproduce social inequality. There are different types of shadow education, and not every type depends heavily on social origin, as we could see in the case of correspondence courses. In addition, my field-work confirmed that there is considerable diversity within the *juku*-industry. The different types of *juku* not only provide different learning opportunities but often try to increase their number of students by also launching voucher programs and creating individual curricula for those with less financial resources. Thus, this issue will be taken up again in Chap. 8 focusing on the *juku*-industry and its possible contribution to educational opportunities and inequality reproduction in detail.

Additionally, my analysis showed that students who intend to enter university via entrance exams are much more likely to feel the need to receive supplementary lessons. A recent OECD report concluded that if more weight is placed on the recognition of recommendations and extracurricular activities instead of such exams, the dependence on *juku* would diminish (Jones 2011: 33–34). Based on the findings presented here, this seems reasonable. However, as Amano and Poole (2005: 694) argued, all reforms targeting entrance examinations might be useless in a society where the brand of a product is more important than its content. The "labelization" (*gakkōreki*) of schooling institutions will not stop. In contrast, students' roles in decision-making could very possibly alter the potential impact of social origin; students could counteract social reproduction by getting involved themselves. Students from disadvantaged socioeconomic backgrounds might have the chance to achieve academic resiliency by deciding for shadow education. Thus, shadow education might be one explanation for the large proportion of academically resilient students in Japan due to the provision of opportunities outside of the regular schooling system, which are at least partly accessible by disadvantaged social strata also. However, since such resiliency is only achieved if disadvantaged strata gain similar or higher benefits from their investments in shadow education compared to advantaged strata, the effects of shadow education need further clarification. Hence, this assumption will be further explored in Chap. 8.

The findings of this chapter provide a strong argument to not overlook students as actors who might choose divergent educational pathways and thus impact educational decisions in several contexts. Whether similar findings are found in different national contexts, however, remains to be tested in future research through comparative case studies. Particularly the focus on disadvantaged socioeconomic strata promises valuable insights concerning educational inequality formation.

References

Amano, I., & Poole, G. S. (2005). The Japanese University in Crisis. *Higher Education, 50*(4), 685–711.

Bjork, C., & Tsuneyoshi, R. (2005). Education reform in Japan: Competing visions for the future. *The Phi Delta Kappan, 86*(8), 619–626.

Boudon, R. (2003). Beyond rational choice theory. *Annual Review of Sociology, 29*, 1–21.

Bourdieu, P. (1983). Ökonomisches Kapital, kulturelles Kapital, soziales Kapital [Economic capital, cultural capital, social capital]. In R. Kreckel (Ed.), *Soziale Ungleichheiten* [Social inequalities] (pp. 185–199). Otto Schwartz Verlag: Göttingen.

Breen, R., van de Werfhorst, H., & Jæger, M. M. (2014). Deciding under doubt: A theory of risk aversion, time discounting preferences, and educational decision-making. *European Sociological Review, 30*(2), 258–270.

Cave, P. (2016). *Schooling selves. Autonomy, interdependence, and reform in Japanese junior high education*. Chicago/London: The University of Chicago Press.

Cook, M. (2013). Expatriate parents and supplementary education in Japan: Survival strategy or acculturation strategy. *Asia Pacific Education Review, 14*, 403–417.

Entrich, S. R. (2014). German and Japanese education in the shadow – Do out-of-school lessons really contribute to class reproduction? *IAFOR Journal of Education, 2*(2), 17–53.

Entrich, S. R. (2015). The decision for shadow education in Japan: Students' choice or parents' pressure? *Social Science Japan Journal, 18*(2), 193–216.

Erikson, R., & Jonsson, J. O. (1996). Explaining class inequality in education – The Swedish test case. In R. Erikson & J. O. Jonsson (Eds.), *Can education be equalized? The Swedish case in comparative perspective* (pp. 1–63). Boulder: Westview Press.

Fujihara, S. (2011). Breen ando Goldthorpe no aitaiteki risuku kaihi kasetsu no kenshō: Chichioya no kodomo ni taisuru shokugyō kyōiku kitai o mochiita keiryō bunseki [Empirical test of Breen and Goldthorpe's relative risk aversion hypothesis in the Japanese society: Data analysis of a father's occupational and educational expectations for his child]. *Shakaigaku Hyōron, 62*(1), 18–35.

Gambetta, D. (1987). *Were they pushed or did they jump? Individual decision mechanisms in education.* London/New York: Cambridge University Press.

Hamajima, K., & Takeuchi, K. (2002). *Kodomo no shingaku asupirēshon no kitei yōin ni kansuru kenkyū: Toshi shōchūgakusei no 15 nenkan no henyō* [A study concerning the determinants of children's aspirations regarding the transition to a higher school level: The transformation of urban primary and middle school students over 15 years]. Paper presented at the 54th Annual Meeting of the Japan Society of Educational Sociology, Hiroshima.

Hurrelmann, K. (2010). *Lebensphase Jugend – Eine Einführung in die sozialwissenschaftliche Jugendforschung* [Stage of life: Youth – An introduction to sociological research on youth]. Juventa: Weinheim.

Jones, R. S. (2011). *Education reform in Japan* (OECD Economics Department Working Papers 888).

Jonsson, J. O., & Erikson, R. (2000). Understanding educational inequality: The Swedish experience. *L'Année Sociologique, 50*, 345–382.

Kariya, T. (2013). *Education reform and social capital in Japan: The changing incentive divide.* London/New York: Routledge.

Kariya, T. (2017). Understanding structural changes in inequality in Japanese education. In D. Chiavacci & C. Hommerich (Eds.), *Social inequality in post-growth Japan. Transformation during economic and demographic stagnation* (pp. 149–165). London/New York: Routledge.

Kataoka, E. (2001). Kyōiku tassei katei ni okeru kazoku no kyōiku senryaku: Bunka shihon kōka to gakkōgai kyōiku tōshi kōka no jendāsa o chūshin ni [Family strategy in educational attainment process in Japan: Effects of cultural capital and investment in extra-school education]. *Kyōikugaku Kenkyū, 68*(3), 259–273.

Kikkawa, T. (2006). *Gakureki to Kakusa-Fubyōdō: Seijukusuru Nihongata Gakureki Shakai* [Education and social inequality: Contemporary educational credentialism in Japan]. Tokyo: Tōkyō Daigaku Shuppankai.

Konakayama, A., & Matsui, T. (2008). Gakkōgai kyōiku tōshi no gakuryoku ni oyobosu eikyō ni kansuru ikkōsatsu [An empirical study on how extra school education affects academic achievement of Japanese high school students]. *Tōkaidaigaku Seiji Keizaigakubu Kiyō, 40*, 131–158.

Lange, A., & Xyländer, M. (2010). Bildungswelt Familie: Disziplinäre Perspektiven, theoretische Rahmungen und Desiderate der empirischen Forschung [Education in the family: Disciplinary perspectives, theoretical framing and sesiderata of empirical research]. In A. Lange & M. Xyländer (Eds.), *Bildungswelt Familie – Theoretische Rahmung, empirische Befunde und disziplinäre Perspektiven* [Education in the family – theoretical framing, empirical findings and disciplinary perspectives] (pp. 23–94). Juventa: Weinheim.

Lauterbach, W. (2013). *Is it always the family of origin? The influence of parental and teenage aspirations on status attainment in young adulthood.* Paper presented at the 2nd international conference on transitions in youth and young adulthood, University of Basel.

LeTendre, G. K. (1994). Distribution tables and private tests: The failure of middle school reform in Japan. *International Journal of Educational Reform, 3*(2), 126–136.

LeTendre, G. K. (1996). Constructed aspirations: Decision-making processes in Japanese educational selection. *Sociology of Education, 69*(3), 193–216.

Matsuoka, R. (2015). School socioeconomic compositional effect on shadow education participation: Evidence from Japan. *British Journal of Sociology of Education, 36*(2), 270–290.

MEXT, Ministry of Education, Culture, Sports, Science and Technology. (2008). Kodomo no gakkōgai de no gakushū seikatsu ni kansuru jittai chōsa hōkoku [National report concerning the out-of-school learning activities of children]. Retrieved from: http://www.mext.go.jp/b_menu/houdou/20/08/08080710.htm

Mimizuka, H. (2009). Shinro sentaku no kōzō to hen'yō [Structure and transformation of course selection]. In T. Onai (Ed.), *Kyōiku no fubyōdō* [Educational inequality] (pp. 224–239). Nihontosho: Tokyo..

OECD, Organisation for Economic Co-operation and Development. (2013). *PISA 2012 results: Excellence through equity: Giving every student the chance to succeed (Volume II)*. Retrieved from: https://doi.org/10.1787/9789264201132-en

Ono, H. (2005). Does examination hell pay off? A cost-benefit analysis of "Ronin" and college education in Japan (SSE/EFI Working Paper Series in Economics and Finance 346).

Roesgaard, M. H. (2006). *Japanese education and the Cram school business: Functions, challenges and perspectives of the Juku*. Copenhagen: NIAS Press.

Rohlen, T. P. (1980). The Juku Phenomenon: An exploratory essay. *Journal of Japanese Studies, 6*(2), 207–242.

Schultz Lee, K. (2010). Parental educational investments and aspirations in Japan. *Journal of Family Issues, 31*(12), 1579–1603.

Seiyama, K., & Noguchi, Y. (1984). Kōkō shingaku ni okeru gakkōgai kyōiku tōshi no kōka [The effects of outside of school educational investments at the transition to high school]. *Kyōiku Shakaigaku Kenkyū, 39*, 113–126.

Stevenson, D. L., & Baker, D. P. (1992). Shadow education and allocation in formal schooling: Transition to University in Japan. *American Journal of Sociology, 97*, 1639–1657.

Takayama, K. (2008). The politics of international league tables: PISA in Japan's achievement crisis debate. *Comparative Education, 44*(4), 387–407.

Takeuchi, Y. (1997). The self-activating entrance examination system – its hidden agenda and its correspondence with the Japanese "Salary Man". *Higher Education, 34*(2), 183–198.

Tobishima, S. (2012). Kōkōsei no gakushū jikan ni taisuru sōki gakkōgai kyōiku tōshi no eikyō [Impact of early outside of school education on learning time of high school students]. *Nenpō Shakaigaku Ronshū, 25*, 144–155.

Tomura, A., Nishimaru, R., & Oda, T. (2011). Kyōiku tōshi no kitei yōin to kōka: Gakkōgai kyōiku to shiritsu chūgaku shingaku o chūshin ni [Determinants and effects of investments in education: Focusing on out-of-school education and the transition to private middle schools]. In Y. Satō & F. Ojima (Eds.), *Gendai no kaisō shakai: Kakusa to tayōsei* [Modern class society: Disparity and diversity] (pp. 267–280). Tokyo: University of Tokyo Press.

Tsuneyoshi, R. (2013). Junior high school entrance examinations in metropolitan Tokyo: The advantages and costs of privilege. In G. DeCoker & C. Bjork (Eds.), *Japanese education in an era of globalization: Culture, politics, and equity* (pp. 164–182). New York: Teachers College Press, Columbia University.

Watanabe, M. (2013). *Juku: The stealth force of education and the deterioration of schools in Japan*. North Charleston: CreateSpace Independent Publishing Platform.

Chapter 6
Effects of Shadow Education

Achieving Educational Goals: Who Benefits from Investments in Shadow Education?

"Yon-tō, go-raku –
Four (hours of sleep and you)
pass, five (hours and you) fail"

(Popular saying among students who
prepare for high school or university
entrance exams)

学
校
外
教
育
の
効
果

Abstract This chapter analyzes the *Effects* dimension outlined in the Shadow-Education-Inequality-Impact (SEII) Frame, specifically addressing the question whether shadow education inherits the power to enhance all students' chances to achieve a high education level independent of socioeconomic origin. Apparently, a comparatively high percentage of academically resilient students is found in Japan, meaning students showing top performance despite disadvantaged socioeconomic background. Unfortunately, whether these students have the chance to benefit from shadow education and thus become academically resilient, thus achieving a high education level, has not been empirically researched yet. Focusing on students' shadow education investment returns as expressed in students' likelihood to enter prestigious high schools or universities and by extending Shadow Education Investment Theory, my calculations based on data of the 2011 *Hyōgo High School Students* (HHSS) survey show the following main findings:

(1) Whether investments in shadow education increase students' chances of gaining entrance to high-ranked schools depends largely on the duration, the used type, and the purpose of study and varies considerably across social strata.
(2) Whereas long-term investments in *juku*-classes focusing on transition/entrance exams prove most effective for entrance to prestigious schools, disadvantaged strata also gain significant advantages from short-term investments in shadow education.
(3) Even though well-off families have the advantage of making more use of all lessons, disadvantaged students gain generally higher benefits from their investments in transition-oriented classes. These findings imply that social inequalities in Japan are only significantly reduced if more disadvantaged students join the competition and make goal-oriented and purposeful investments.

© Springer International Publishing AG 2018
S.R. Entrich, *Shadow Education and Social Inequalities in Japan*,
https://doi.org/10.1007/978-3-319-69119-0_6

6.1   Problematic

According to the OECD, Japan is one of the countries which possesses an education system with a more equal distribution of educational opportunities for students of different social origins (OECD 2010: 30). In this regard, recent surveys by the OECD reported a high percentage of resilient students in Japan, meaning students who perform in the top performance groups in PISA despite disadvantaged socioeconomic status (OECD 2013: 194). Unfortunately, only few studies have actually researched the phenomenon of resilient students and the factors that determine educational success despite disadvantageous background (OECD 2011a: 16). The above quotation reflects the enormous pressure on and willingness of students to do well academically, especially in entrance examinations, which determine their future educational pathways and career opportunities. However, whether socioeconomically disadvantaged students have the chance to benefit from shadow education and thus become academically successful in school and beyond, thus achieving a high education level, has not been empirically researched yet and will be content of this chapter.

Even though there is empirical evidence that shadow education can lead to a higher education level (e.g., Stevenson and Baker 1992 and Kataoka 2001), such positive effects are overshadowed by the belief that due to its fee-based character, shadow education is used by socioeconomically advantaged families as an instrument of social closure (Heyneman 2011: 185). This belief is prevalent in Japan also. Following the "Shadow Education Investment Theory" (SEIT; Seiyama 1981) as introduced in Chap. 3, socioeconomically well-off families are in a position to make long-term investments in shadow education and thus gain a status advantage by increasing their children's academic achievement and by gaining entrance to prestigious schools. Shadow education is thus seen as further cementing educational and social inequalities. Existing research generally supports the assumed connection between shadow education investments and social inequality reproduction (e.g., Seiyama and Noguchi 1984; Kataoka 2001; Konakayama and Matsui 2008; Tomura et al. 2011; Entrich 2014).

However, whether shadow education can function as an instrument to overcome socioeconomic disparities by enabling disadvantaged students to achieve a higher education level than originally predicted by classic theories of social reproduction (e.g., Boudon 1974; Bourdieu and Passeron 1977) and SEIT (Seiyama 1981; Seiyama and Noguchi 1984) was not discussed or empirically tested yet. Consequently, in the following I attempt to clarify whether the benefits of shadow education are indeed limited to students from well-off family backgrounds as indicated by SEIT or whether shadow education inherits the power to enhance *all* students' chances to achieve a high education level. If the latter was true, shadow education would be one possible explanation for the reported high percentage of academically resilient students in Japan in international comparison, also.

To provide new findings on the effects of shadow education for educational success (i.e., the achievement of educational goals) against the background of social inequality formation, in this chapter I base my calculations on data of the 2011 *Hyōgo High School Students* (HHSS) survey. After the theoretical framework and the methods and data are discussed, multinomial and binary regression analyses are carried out to empirically test the effects of shadow education on students' transition to high school and university across different ESCS groups.

6.2   Theoretical Framework: Overcoming Social Background Disparities (Academic Resiliency Through Shadow Education?)

In the following, the possible impact of shadow education on academic resiliency among Japanese students will be discussed, before I will critically evaluate the suppositions of the "Shadow Education Investment Theory" (SEIT) regarding the supposed effects of shadow education on educational success in relation to social origin. Further, the results of existing empirical studies on the subject are reviewed before adjustments to the SEIT will be made. Based on this groundwork, fitting research hypotheses are formulated, which will be tested in the following analyses in part three.

6.2.1   Shadow Education as an Educational Opportunity?

One strong indicator for actual equal opportunities in education is the percentage of resilient students of a country. In general, students with a disadvantaged socioeconomic background show less academic achievement than students with an advantaged family background in accordance with theories of social reproduction and RCT. This known primary effect of social origin was again verified by results of the OECD's PISA study (OECD 2012: 49). However, considerable differences of the impact of family background on student performance are found across countries. According to a recent study carried out by the OECD, students are "classified as resilient if he or she is in the bottom quarter of the PISA index of economic, social and cultural status (ESCS) in the country/economy of assessment and performs in the top quarter of students from all countries/economies, after accounting for socioeconomic status" (OECD 2013: 194). In all countries we can find students that overcome their given status disadvantage and thus show what educational opportunities their national education system really offers. However, the classification of PISA participants according to intensity level of shadow education participation shows that in economies where shadow education is highly prevalent (high-intensity shadow education countries), a higher proportion of resilient students can be found than on average in OECD countries, as Table 6.1 shows.

Table 6.1 PISA 2006–2012: percentage of resilient students (OECD 2010: 169, 2011a: 88, 2013: 197)

PISA participants	High-intensity shadow education countries				Low-intensity shadow education countries					OECD Mean
	China (Hong Kong)	China (Shanghai)	Japan	South Korea	Australia	Finland	Germany	United Kingdom	United States	
PISA 2006[a]	24.8	–	17.6	17.7	15.5	22.2	12.6	13.5	9.9	13.0
PISA 2009	18.1	18.9	10.5	14.0	7.7	11.4	5.7	6.0	7.2	7.7
PISA 2012	18.2	19.2	11.4	12.8	6.3	8.2	7.5	5.8	5.2	6.5

[a]In contrast to the definition for 2009 and 2012 data, the percentage of resilient students resembles students who are in the bottom third of ESCS and perform in the top third

In high-intensity shadow education countries such as Japan, more than 10% of the students with a disadvantaged socioeconomic background overcome these disadvantages, a significantly higher proportion of students compared to the average OECD country. Another general trend is visible as well: countries that generally show high average scores in PISA but moderate impact of students' socioeconomic background on performance have a higher percentage of resilient students, e.g., Finland (11.4% in 2009), South Korea (14% in 2009), China (Hong Kong, 18.2% in 2012; Shanghai, 19.2% in 2012), and Japan (11.4% in 2012). In comparison, average-performing countries with higher ESCS impact on students' performance possess a generally smaller proportion of resilient students (United States 2012, 5.2%; Germany 2012, 7.5%). Considering the known high academic competitiveness of East Asian nations such as China, South Korea, and Japan, these results are not easy to explain. We have to ask how so many students are actually able to overcome their status disadvantages, in particular in East Asian nations. The deep-rooted understanding about education as the key to success founded in Confucianism and thus high educational aspirations of families are well known; but is this all there is? The high prevalence of shadow education in East Asian nations is believed to also contribute to the enormous success of East Asian students in international assessment tests (Schümer 1999: 71; Park 2013: 8; Watanabe 2013: xv-xvi). But, in addition, disparities in educational attainment and academic achievement are believed to increase due to varying investments in supplementary education according to students' socioeconomic backgrounds.

Unfortunately, only few studies have actually researched the phenomenon of resiliency among students and the factors that determine educational success despite disadvantageous background (OECD 2011a: 16). The PISA data showed that academically resilient students show a higher level of self-confidence and tend to spend generally more time in class than their peers (OECD 2011b). In addition, I assume that students in high-intensity shadow education nations such as Japan make more use of educational opportunities outside of school. But data on the issue are scarce. Also, academic resiliency through shadow education is only possible under two conditions: First, students from disadvantaged family backgrounds need to have access to shadow education services, which was discussed in the preceding Chap. 5, and, second, students from disadvantaged family backgrounds need to gain considerable academic advantages due to a participation in shadow education. In the next sections, I will discuss under which circumstances an investment in shadow education possibly results in academic advantages before deriving fitting hypotheses.

6.2.2   Purposes of Shadow Education Investment

Since the main purpose of shadow education is to increase academic achievement, it is only natural that the public ascribes shadow education an academic achievement enhancement function. For Japan, this view is also prevalent in scientific circles and became the foundation of the so-called Shadow Education Investment

Theory (SEIT) as enunciated by Seiyama (1981). According to SEIT, parents use shadow education as an educational strategy to increase their children's chances of achieving a high education level by enhancing children's academic standing in school. Due to differences in socioeconomic resources, children from well-off family backgrounds are believed to gain competitive advantages over their peers, consequently reproducing or even increasing social inequalities (see Chap. 3). This general assumption implies that any increase in academic standing automatically results in higher chances to achieve a high education level. However, this view denies the fact that there are not only different amounts of investments in shadow education, e.g., long or short term,[1] but also different goals which call for different types of support.

Investments in shadow education are used by families as a strategy to increase students' chances to pass entrance exams at higher-ranked schools by receiving professional support to prepare for such exams. However, it is not appropriate to equate the whole shadow education system with the *juken sangyō* – the exam preparatory industry, as Komiyama (1993: 83) notes. By evaluating advertisement and programs of shadow education operators during my recent fieldwork, it became obvious that there are two main fields of effects promised by *juku*-operators: (1) to ensure the transition to the next school level by primarily preparing students for entrance examinations and guiding them on, indicating that students will be able to enter a first-class school through a *juku*'s support, and (2) supplementary education to help students improve their academic standing in school, either of remediation or enrichment character. Thus, students pursue different study types to accomplish either one of these educational goals. This also means that an investment in shadow education does not necessarily result in an above-average academic standing in school or high scores in entrance exams.

Data of a national survey by the MEXT (2008) support this argumentation (see Chap. 2, Fig. 2.14). Besides entrance exam preparation (26.7% on average), during compulsory school students receive *juku*-classes either to catch up in school (13.6% on average); receive help with homework or prepare, repeat, or strengthen school lessons contents (42.8% on average); and several other undefined contents (24.1% on average). Even though the majority of students participate in preparatory lessons at the end of middle school (9th grade, 64.4%), most of the time, the highest proportion of students is enrolled in lessons with school-related content. Unfortunately, ministerial data generally only include responses for compulsory school (grades 1–9), not high school. Based on data provided by the Benesse Corporation, the majority of high school students who continue to enroll in shadow education pursue preparatory lessons to increase their chances of passing university entrance exams (see Chap. 8, Fig. 8.1, or BERD 2013).

---

[1] Long-term investments are understood as investments at more than one school level, e.g., in high, middle, and primary school or middle and primary school. Short-term investments are understood as temporally limited investments in response to certain learning problems or needs (for exam preparation and so forth), e.g., only in high school or middle school or primary school.

In contrast to classes at *juku*, most students use correspondence courses neither to prepare for entrance exams nor catch up in school, but to focus on school-related contents (repetition, preparation, homework) in primary (~88%) and middle school (7th grade, 82%; 8th grade, 76%; 9th grade, 64%). During middle school, these courses are also more often used for exam preparation (9th grade, 51%). The same can be said for students who receive lessons from private tutors, with the addition that a high proportion receives lessons in order to catch up in school (up to 52% in 8th grade) (MEXT 2008: 20–21). Since the contents of school curriculum and entrance exams actually differ very much, particularly in the case of private middle and high schools (Tsuneyoshi 2013: 176), it is important to separately measure the effects of shadow education on academic achievement in school and in entrance exams. Especially high-ranked schools need a high difficulty level of their entrance examinations resulting in contents which exceed the standard curriculum contents of the previous school level by far. Hence, different learning contents and teaching methods are found compared to lessons with the purpose to increase the academic standing or GPA (grade point average) in school. As Rohlen (1980) described it, "in popular speech, juku themselves are often differentiated in a vague manner in 'shingaku juku' where better students go and hoshū juku or schools where catch-up is the central concern" (p. 210). The here mentioned two main types of *juku* represent the two main study areas in the shadow: *shingaku* (transition) and *hoshū* (supplementation) lessons. According to their name, *hoshū juku* provide supplementary or additional tuition implying remedial purposes also, wherefore these schools are open for different kinds of lessons. The operators of such schools try to provide students with a real chance to enter higher-ranked schools through the recommendation system by improving their performance in school in several regards – not only grades. Since such recommendations are primarily made on the basis of the *naishinsho*, a personal report card in which "not only grades but also manners, conduct and dedication are evaluated" (Roesgaard 2006: 55), even students who cannot keep the pace in class (*ochikobore*) might increase their chances of gaining entrance to prestigious schools. This *juku*-type thus has a strong relation to school curriculum contents, whereas the other main *juku*-type, the *shingaku juku*, are schools concentrating on the transition from one school level to the next. The main focus thus lies on preparation for entrance exams (see Fukaya 1977; Komiyama 1993, 2000; Roesgaard 2006). Of the many other existing types of *juku* (see Chap. 8), one type exists which combines both main study purposes, the *sōgō* ('comprehensive') *juku* (Komiyama 1993, 2000). The *sōgō* approach allows students to concentrate on more than one study focus. Hence, students can follow different investment strategies at once, implying different effects on their set educational goals.

In conclusion, three major categories of study purpose can be identified: (1) improving the performance in entrance examinations to achieve the transition from one school level to the next (*shingaku*), (2) improvement of academic standing in school (*hoshū*), or (3) more than one major study goal (*sōgō*). These different study purposes indicate high differences between the expectable effects of shadow education on educational success, depending on the pursued educational goal and thus the purpose of shadow education investment. Hence, the accuracy of the SEIT and its supposition which implies that benefits of shadow education are reserved for students with high socioeconomic status is of question. Only few studies attempted to disprove that shadow education investments automatically support educational and thus social reproduction (e.g., Konakayama and Matsui 2008), and only Seiyama and Noguchi (1984) partly succeeded in doing so. However, reviewing the results of existing studies concerning the effects of Japanese shadow education on educational success might provide valuable arguments for or against the validity of the SEIT and show where possible adjustments might prove meaningful. Hence, before making suppositions about the likelihood that some students might overcome their disadvantaged family background due to shadow education investments – if they in fact have the chance to make such investments (see Chap. 5) – the state of research regarding effects of shadow education on academic success is reviewed in the following.

6.2.3 Verified Effects of Shadow Education in Japan

Research concerned with the effects of shadow education on educational success focused on the following three outcomes: (1) academic performance in international large-scale assessments (ILSA), (2) academic standing in school, and (3) the transition to the next higher school level, e.g., high school or university. However, until the 1990s (and partly beyond), Japanese schools often went so far as to forbid researchers to include questions about students' socioeconomic background in their surveys, even in international large-scale assessments (Kariya 2010: 56). Hence, only few studies focusing on the connection between the socioeconomic background of students and their academic achievement exist. In particular, studies on the differences in effects of investments in shadow education on educational success according to socioeconomic background are still scarce.

6.2.3.1 Effects of Shadow Education on Performance in ILSA

Following the prevalent belief that the high scores of Japanese students in ILSA comparisons are due to shadow education (Park 2013: 81–87), Western research focusing on the effects of shadow education on students' educational success mostly analyzed the possible effects on academic performance in ILSA such as TIMSS (e.g., Baker et al. 2001) and PISA (e.g., Southgate 2009; Ojima and von Below 2010, Park 2013; Entrich 2014). This seems somehow justified considering that the prevalence of shadow education in East Asian countries such as Japan might falsify the results of students' performances and thus make them "incomparable" to Western nations without systems depending on shadow education (Bracey 1997). Surprisingly, only few studies draw on the data of the most renowned ILSA such as PISA or TIMSS to verify or refute this often heard statement. Based on TIMSS 1995 data, Baker et al. (2001) classified the shadow education systems of 41 countries according to their primary focus on enrichment or remedial lessons or a mixed form of both based on responses of 7th and 8th grade students.[2] Whereas most countries were classified as having remedial modal strategies motivating shadow education, Japan was found to have a mixed system. Therefore, the authors concluded that whether shadow education affects Japanese students' high scoring in international comparison depends largely on the purpose of study. Copying this approach, Southgate (2009) carried out similar analyses based on responses of 15-year-old students across 36 countries, using PISA 2003 data. At first glance, the general findings of Southgate's analyses are similar to those of Baker and his colleagues. Japan was again classified as mixed in general. However, in a further step, Southgate subdivided outside of school lessons into "classes" and "tutoring" and found that out-of-school classes in Japan are primarily of enrichment nature, whereas tutoring is not. Using a different approach, Ojima and von Below (2010), Park (2013), and Entrich (2013, 2014) analyzed the PISA data of the years 2003, 2006, and 2009 respectively, focusing on Japan and either Germany or South Korea. All three studies used out-of-school lessons as explanatory variable for students' performance in PISA instead of treating it as dependent variable. The plausible value regressions of Ojima and von Below showed that a participation in out-of-school lessons exerts a general positive significant effect on students' math performance in PISA 2003. Following the logic of Baker et al., an overall positive significant effect of out-of-school lessons on performance on a national level indicates that the Japanese system would have to be classified as predominantly of enrichment nature. However, Park (2013) tried to disprove the assumption that shadow education participation contributes to the high scoring of Japanese (and Korean) students in international comparison using plausible value regression and propensity score matching. Park found significant negative effects of out-of-school time lessons on performance in PISA for Japan. According to Park's findings, out-of-school lessons do not contribute to a higher performance of Japanese students in PISA (pp. 86–88). In my recent works, I based my analyses on PISA 2009 data and carried out plausible values regression analyses as well (Entrich 2013, 2014). However, by differentiating my analyses according to the used type of out-of-school lessons and controlling for gender, SES, and ranking of schools, I found that only enrichment lessons show positive significant effects on Japanese students' performance, whereas remedial lessons showed generally negative significant effects. Additionally, these analyses revealed great differences in the effects of out-of-school lessons on PISA performance between students living in different population areas. In summary, the findings of my recent work "implicate that an out-of-school education system of predominantly enrichment character which is close-knit to the level of stratification of the high school system as found in large Japanese cities

---

[2] This classification was done using logit coefficients of the use of shadow education participation as a function of students' mathematics scores while controlling for several influential variables such as students' socioeconomic background, language, sex, community, remedial teaching, and the interaction term between socioeconomic status and mathematics performance. The shadow education systems of each country were categorized as enrichment in nature, if the logit coefficient showed a positive significant effect; as remedial, if the coefficient showed a negative significant effect; and as mixed, if the found effect was insignificant (Baker et al. 2001).

intensifies the impact social origin has on educational outcomes and results in increasing educational disparities" (Entrich 2014: 96). Whether the Japanese shadow education system provides opportunities to advance socially for students with disadvantaged family background was not empirically analyzed with ILSA data. The results of these studies generally support the SEIT. However, there are the following major shortcomings of PISA data, which are to some degree also applicable to TIMSS and other ILSA data: First, we find definition inaccuracy regarding shadow education; second, in particular in countries outside the Anglo-Saxon and European context such as Japan, translation inaccuracy is prevalent; and third, to explain this phenomenon and its effects on academic performance in several contexts, more data is needed. Due to these shortcomings, until now data of studies focusing only on the Japanese case promise more accurate results (ibid: 83–84, 96–97).[3] Since shadow education was never meant to improve students' performance in ILSA, it seems generally not very appropriate to measure for such effects using ILSA's performance scores as dependent variables. The educational strategies pursued by families when making investments in shadow education aim to achieve two possible outcomes: higher academic standing and successful school transition.

6.2.3.2   Effects of Shadow Education on Academic Standing in School

Existing empirical analyses focusing on the effects of shadow education on educational success in Japan often concentrated on analyzing such effects on students' academic standing in school or GPA (grade point average) (e.g., Seiyama 1981; Seiyama and Noguchi 1984; Kataoka 2001; Hamajima and Takeuchi 2002; Kariya and Shimizu 2004; Mimizuka 2007; Konakayama and Matsui 2008; Kariya 2013; Kataoka 2015). According to these case studies, variables representing aspects of students' economic, social, and cultural status (ESCS) exert a strong impact on students' academic standing in school in accordance with theories of social reproduction and SEIT.

Up to date, the only work that partly disproved the SEIT was carried out by Seiyama himself. In their 1984 analysis, Seiyama and his colleague Noguchi found significant differences concerning the effects of ESCS variables on the chance to invest in *juku*-lessons and the effects of such investments on academic standing during middle school between male and female students. Whereas male students' ESCS strongly affected whether an investment in *juku*-classes was pursued, such investments did not pay off for the same students, meaning no positive significant effects could be verified. On the contrary, female students seemed unaffected by family origin when pursuing *juku*-lessons, but gained significant benefits from such an investment. Kataoka (2015) found that neither investments in supplementary schools (*kyōshitsu gakushū katsudō*) nor lessons and general study at home (*katei gakushū katsudō*) exert a strong positive significant effect on primary or middle

---

[3] For general critique on using ILSA data such as TIMSS and PISA for analyses concerned with shadow education and its effects, see Bray and Kobakhidze (2014).

school students' GPA in school. However, whether shadow education proves beneficial for students' academic standing highly depends on the type and purpose of study, which were not differentiated. In their attempt to also falsify the SEIT, Konakayama and Matsui (2008) recently analyzed the effects of different types of shadow education, namely, *juku*-lessons, private tutoring, and correspondence courses, on students' GPA at the end of primary, middle, and high school. Their results suggest that receiving correspondence courses increases academic standing in middle school, whereas *juku*-lessons enhance academic standing in high school. Mimizuka (2007) and Kita (2006) further differentiated academic *juku* into two types, based on students' study purpose: *juken* or *shingaku juku* (*juku* focusing on exam preparation) and *hoshū juku* (*juku* focusing on school-related and remedial contents). For both types generally positive effects were reported, which were supposedly higher for primary and middle school students who attend *shingaku juku* compared to students attending *hoshū juku*.

In summary, there is one general problem with the findings of these studies: the carried out analyses are not eligible to actually explain effects of shadow education investments but rather show the relationship between a participation in shadow education and students' GPA. Since no longitudinal survey data was used to analyze the connection between shadow education and academic achievement improvement, most analyses are not suited to explain effects of shadow education. For example, if students who participated in *shingaku juku*-classes show significantly higher academic achievement, this could mean that they have actually improved their academic standing in school due to these lessons or that generally only students with high academic standing attend *shingaku juku*-classes. To adequately measure the effects of shadow education investments, it is necessary to measure the academic achievement of students or their GPA at two points in time: before taking shadow education lessons and afterward. Also, a control group is necessary. Only then will we be able to assess whether these additional investments caused an improvement in academic achievement. The same general problem applies to the existing studies based on ILSA data. Unfortunately, such data does not exist, at least not on a broader scale with a sufficient sample.

6.2.3.3   Effects of Shadow Education on Transition

Besides the overall effects on academic standing in school, the effectivity of shadow education might be better measured by calculating effects of shadow education on whether students actually achieve a certain educational goal or not. However, only few studies sought to explain whether students increase their chances of educational success due to shadow education by measuring the impact of a participation in such lessons on entrance to high school, entrance to university, or total years of formal schooling. In this regard, Tomura et al. (2011) predicted the influence of shadow education experience on total education years as a proxy for education level. The authors found no significant effect at the 5% level when controlling for gender, father's occupational and educational status, the rank of high school, and academic standing in 9th grade. Yamamoto and Brinton (2010) carried out a multiple step regression analysis and found strong direct effects of shadow education on total education years, which disappeared due to the inclusion of ESCS, academic standing, and high school rank variables. Particularly students' academic standing in school and the rank of the attended high school thus mediate the effects of shadow education. Hence, it seems advisable to measure students' educational success as a possible result of shadow education by calculating whether students actually increase their chances of gaining entrance to high-ranked schools: the higher the entered school's rank, the higher the chances of educational success.

Stevenson and Baker (1992) showed that the entrance to university highly depends on ESCS variables, academic standing, and high school's reputation. Whether students participated in shadow education also showed considerable effects, which varied heavily according to type. Only practice examinations (*mogi shiken*) and correspondence courses were found to positively increase the chance to enter university. Students who did not enter their university of choice on first try and became *rōnin* generally increased their chances to enter university with the number of *rōnin*-years, too (see also Ono 2005).

Up to date, only Kataoka (2001) focused her analyses concerning the effects of shadow education on three dimensions of educational success: academic standing, transition to high school, and total years of formal schooling. By controlling for ESCS variables and academic standing and differentiating her calculations according to gender, Kataoka found significant positive effects of shadow education investments in primary and middle school on students' transition to an elite high school for boys and on male students' total years of formal schooling. For girls, no such effects were verified. Differences in the effects of different types and purposes of shadow education were not taken into consideration here. However, since the contents of high school and university entrance examinations and school curriculum differ partly extreme and thus a high academic standing in school is no guarantee for educational success in terms of gaining entrance to a high-ranked high school or university, the evaluated analyses need further refinement and adjustment to actually verify or refute the SEIT and clarify whether shadow education provides students with a competitive advantage to achieve a higher education level through realizing admission to higher-ranked schools.

In summary, existing studies generally report positive effects of shadow education on educational goals and thus support the SEIT. However, most studies missed to acknowledge that different educational goals call for different support or preparation and thus analyses have to separately measure the possible effects of different types and purposes of shadow education on different academic outcomes. Only purposeful investments should result in significant advantages for achieving educational goals. In addition, the duration of such investments has not been considered in any analyses so far, even though one fundamental supposition of the SEIT is that families with a high SES gain a competitive advantage through shadow education, because they are in a position to make higher investments compared to families with lower SES. Due to the connected costs, only high ESCS families are believed to be able to afford long-term investments and thus gain higher benefits for educational success, whereas low social strata generally can only afford to make short-term investments. Also, research did not differentiate which students actually benefit from investments in shadow education, with the exception of gender and location. ESCS variables are generally used as control variables and show a strong impact on educational success thus supporting SEIT. However, whether academic resiliency among Japanese students from disadvantageous backgrounds can be explained through shadow education, which thus functions as a provider of educational opportunities, was not discussed yet. Consequently, by acknowledging that different educational goals call for different strategies when investing in shadow education to accurately pursue these goals from a rational choice point of view, adjustments to SEIT prove necessary. In the following, the SEIT will be adjusted to pay respect to these concerns, before research hypotheses are formulated.

6.2.4 Research Hypotheses: Effects of Shadow Education on Educational Success

Based on the foregoing discussions, I argue that specific investment strategies are pursued and thus investments in shadow education lead to different outcomes depending on the type (academic *juku*, private tutor, or correspondence courses), the duration (long term or short term), and the purpose of study (*shingaku*, *sōgō*, or *hoshū*). Only a fitting investment should result in the hoped for results and thus increase students' education level in the end. Whether differentiated investments inevitably result in educational and thus social inequalities is not well enough researched. As discussed above, on the one hand, shadow education is very likely used by well-off families as an instrument of social closure. On the other hand, shadow education might also provide an explanation for the percentage of academically resilient students in Japan by providing additional educational opportunities for students from disadvantaged family backgrounds. Only students who enter high-ranked schools will gain status advantages. Improvements in academic standing should generally be beneficial for such transitions, either in the way that students have a higher pass probability in entrance exams or students receive a recommendation for a high-ranked school based on a high GPA. If these benefits apply to students with disadvantaged ESCS also, shadow education can function as an instrument to neutralize disadvantaged family background. Socioeconomically disadvantaged students might somehow find ways to participate in some kind of shadow education (as discussed in Chap. 5) and through this investment increase their chances to accomplish a set educational goal. If this was the case, shadow education would contribute to a more equal provision of educational opportunities.

Due to the discussed relevance of the field, this chapter addresses the question whether and under which conditions shadow education proves beneficial achieving educational goals, particularly for students from disadvantaged ESCS backgrounds. Based on the foregoing discussions, the following adjustments to SEIT shall serve to answer my main research question by creating a fitting frame to test applicable hypotheses: First of all, to measure the actual effects of shadow education on a certain education goal, the effects of different types of shadow education need to be separately measured. Second, a further differentiation between long-term and short-term investments proves necessary. Third, the purpose of study most likely determines whether students gain actual status advantages. This should only be the case if the likelihood to achieve the second educational goal – entrance to high-ranked schools – is increased as a result of shadow education investments. Hence, SEIT only proves correct if students from advantageous family backgrounds gain entrance to prestigious schools as a result of shadow education investments, whereas students from disadvantaged family backgrounds do not. Even if students are able to increase their academic standing in school significantly, this does not mean that shadow education functions as educational opportunity that leads to overall educational success resulting in a higher societal position than originally predicted through classic SEIT or theories about social reproduction. Due to these considerations, SEIT is adjusted as shown in Fig. 6.1.

Accordingly, this model separately accounts for differences in effects of shadow education investments according to type, duration, and main study purpose on the two major educational goals students seek to accomplish: (1) increasing their academic standing in school (*hoshū*) and (2) gaining entrance to high-ranked schools to achieve a high education level (*shingaku*). To reflect differences in (1) the expected effects of social origin on investments in shadow education according to type, duration of investment (long term/short term), and main study focus of the lessons and (2) differences in the expected effects of such investments on the two major aca-

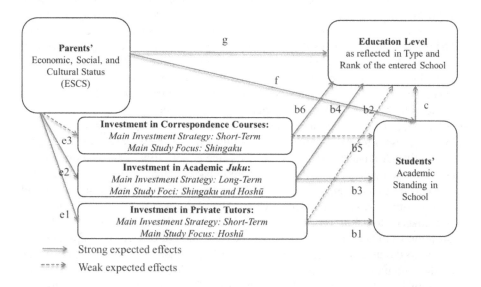

Fig. 6.1 Extension of SEIT: *differentiated investment strategy and outcome model* (Japanese context)

demic goals, the depicted paths are further differentiated into paths which represent strong or weak expected effects. Besides the *culture thesis* (path f) and *aspiration thesis* (path g), which were similarly existent in Seiyama's original SEIT, this model draws up the following hypotheses:

[H1]   *Private tutor investment strategy thesis* (paths e1 → b1 → c and e1 → b2), which is subdivided into two sub-theses:

[H1-1]   Students from advantaged parental ESCS backgrounds make long-term investments in private tutoring with primarily *shingaku* study focus and gain significant advantages for school transition.

[H1-2]   Students from disadvantaged parental ESCS backgrounds make short-term investments in private tutoring with primarily *hoshū* study focus without gaining significant advantages for school transition.

[H2]   *Academic juku investment strategy thesis* (paths e2 → b3 → c and e2 → b4), which is subdivided into two sub-theses:

[H2-1]   Students from advantaged parental ESCS backgrounds make long-term investments in *juku*-classes with primarily *shingaku* study focus and gain significant advantages for school transition.

[H2-2]   Students from disadvantaged parental ESCS backgrounds make short-term investments in *juku*-classes either primarily with *shingaku* focus or following several strategies (*sōgō* study focus) and gain significant advantages for school transition.

[H3]   *Correspondence courses investment strategy thesis* (paths e3 → b5 → c and e3 → b6), which is subdivided into two sub-theses:

[H3-1]   Students from advantaged parental ESCS backgrounds make long-term investments in correspondence courses with primarily *hoshū* study focus without gaining significant advantages for school transition.

[H3-2]   Students from disadvantaged parental ESCS backgrounds make short-term investments in correspondence courses with primarily *shingaku* study focus or following several strategies (*sōgō* study focus) and gain significant advantages for school transition.

Hypothesis [H1] underlies the assumption that private tutoring is generally more expensive compared to class lectures or correspondence courses and thus short-term investments are favored by most students. This kind of tutoring is often used for remedial purposes, to counteract learning difficulties at school or catch up to the average performance level in class. When used for *shingaku* purposes, these lessons are most expensive and thus only affordable by students from advantageous backgrounds. Hypothesis [H2] underlies the assumption that classes at *juku* are affordable by most students and a large bandwidth of classes is provided following all kinds of study purposes (see, e.g., Komiyama 1993; Roesgaard 2006). As Tobishima (2012) has shown in a recent work, students which enter *juku* early in their school life course are likely to continue investing in later age. However, since the costs for *shingaku* and *hoshū* can differ quite a lot, long-term investments following a *shingaku* study focus are more likely made by middle and high ESCS strata, whereas low ESCS strata are more likely to make short-term investments and also stronger concentrate on transition strategies besides *shingaku*. Hypothesis [H3] underlies the assumption that correspondence courses are generally cheap and thus easy accessible by all social strata. In addition, even though these courses are mostly used for homework and repetition/preparation of school-related contents (*hoshū*) in earlier grades, they also allow following a *shingaku* study purpose particularly at the end of middle school and during high school and thus possibly increase students' chances of entering high-ranked schools. Whereas high ESCS strata might use these courses as a simple supplement to their learning activities in general, for low ESCS strata, these courses are an opportunity to achieve educational goals despite disadvantages (see also Chap. 5), if they use them with *shingaku* or at least *sōgō* study focus. Hence, if socioeconomically disadvantaged students make such goal-oriented, purposeful education investments, they should be able to achieve academic resiliency and a high education level as a result of shadow education investments.

In the following, the effects of shadow education investments according to type, duration, and study purpose on students' likelihood to enter high-ranked high schools and universities will be tested for students at the bottom quarter, the mediocre quarters, and the top quarter of socioeconomic stratification in comparison to verify whether the above-stated hypotheses are correct.

6.3   Results: The Impact of Shadow Education on School Transition

To obtain sound conclusions, the stated hypotheses will be tested using data from the 2011 HHSS survey. Following a short outline of the used variables, the effects of shadow education on the transition to high school and university across different social strata are calculated.

6.3.1   Data and Methods

As reviewed before, previous research found that effects of shadow education vary according to several factors. In summary, the effects of shadow education investments on transition to high school vary according to academic standing in school; gender; economic, social, and cultural status (ESCS); type of shadow education; and purpose of study, as well as general learning time outside of school. However, as the latter variable distorts the actual effects of shadow education, it will be omitted. In the case of transition to university, the ranking of high schools is another highly influential factor. Fortunately, HHSS data includes suitable variables to control for such influences and measure the impact of shadow education investments on educational goals adequately (see Chap. 4). Also, these controls are in line with previous research on high school transition in Japan without focus on shadow education (e.g., Kariya and Rosenbaum 1987).

In addition to enhancing students' academic standing, shadow education is supposed to "improve student's chances of successfully moving through the allocation process" (Stevenson and Baker 1992: 1640–1642). To measure whether shadow education has significant positive effects on school transition, we need to assess whether students actually increase their chances to enter prestigious or higher-ranked institutions in reference to less prestigious or average schools through shadow education investments. Hence, I will use the created variables for high school ranking (Academic A, Academic B, Academic C, and vocational high schools) and students' post-high school status (top university, average university/college)[4] as dependent variables. To answer my above-stated research hypotheses, for the later carried out analyses, students' participation in different types of shadow education (academic *juku*, private tutors, correspondence courses), the duration of investments (long-term or short-term), and the pursued study goals (*shingaku*, *hoshū*, *sōgō*) are included as major explanatory variables for students' educational success. Further, variables such as gender and academic achievement will be controlled for. For my analyses concerned with the transition to university, high school ranking will be controlled (for the creation of the variables, see Chap. 4).

6.3.2   Results of Analyses

To test my above-stated hypotheses, multinomial and binary logistic regression analyses are carried out in the following manner: First, multinomial logistic regressions serve to predict the effects of long- and short-term investments in shadow education on the transition to differently ranked high schools (Model 1), before further differentiating the same model according to type of shadow education investment (Model 2) and across ESCS groups (Model 3). Second, the effects of different types of shadow education on the transition to top universities in reference to average universities and junior/technical colleges are predicted through binary logistic regressions, differentiating for investment duration (Model 4), before further differentiating these calculations according to ESCS groups (Model 5). Third, the same analyses are repeated focusing on study purposes of shadow education investments instead of investment length (Models 6 and 7). For all carried out analyses, the Average Marginal Effects (AME) are displayed to achieve comparable findings suited for interpretation.

---

[4] Since only a very small proportion of students who will enter the labor market following high school graduation actually participated in shadow education during their high school years and if, followed a *hoshū* study purpose, my analysis will omit such students and focus on those who continue their educational career in the tertiary education sector, I will concentrate on whether students enter top universities and thus achieve a competitive advantage or not.

6.3.2.1   Effects of Shadow Education on Transition to High School

Table 6.2 shows the predicted general likelihoods for gaining entrance to differently ranked high schools, meaning the school middle school students entered following graduation, by using the ranking of high schools as dependent variable. The results of Model 1 are in line with previous research. Socioeconomic background (ESCS) and academic achievement are decisive for the enrolment at a top-ranked high school (Academic A) in reference to enrolment in any of the other high schools. In particular, the strong impact of academic standing in school is without a doubt explained by the requirements of entrance examinations, where the difficulty level increases with the reputation of a school. Here students' likelihood to attend an Academic A high school in comparison to all lower-ranking high schools increases by 17% for each increase in GPA. The opposite is found for Academic C schools (-13% likelihood). Furthermore, students' ESCS is a major predictor for the attendance of high-ranked high schools (Academic A and B). Students from disadvantaged backgrounds thus primarily enter Academic C and vocational high schools.

In addition, gender differences are detected. Male students are more likely to enroll at Academic C schools, while girls are more likely to attend Academic B and, apparently, vocational schools. Model 1 additionally verifies general positive effects of a participation in shadow education on the likelihood to enter higher-ranked schools (Academic A and with limitations Academic B schools). However, such positive effects depend strongly on the length of investment, supporting the general assumption of the SEIT. However, an additional differentiation of shadow education into its main three types shows that effects vary considerably according to the used type (Model 2).

Model 2 verifies that long- and short-term investments in *juku*-classes and correspondence courses generally increase the likelihood to enter an Academic A high school, with the exception of short-term investments in primary school. Students which attended *juku*-classes during primary school are less likely to enter Academic A schools, but are much more likely to enter Academic B schools (+19%). In stark contrast, students who received lessons from private tutors are less likely to gain entrance to higher-ranked schools, but are more likely to enter Academic C schools. For students entering vocational schools, shadow education does not seem to play a role. These results support the assumption that private tutoring is primarily used with remedial (*hoshū*) purposes until the end of middle school, whereas *juku*-classes and correspondence courses also serve *shingaku* study purposes.

Whether students from disadvantaged family backgrounds benefit from these positive effects of shadow education or whether such effects are limited to high social strata is clarified in Model 3 (Table 6.3). According to my calculations, high social strata gain the highest benefits of long-term and short-term investments (when in middle school) in *juku*-classes (+9% for the likelihood to enter Academic A schools). Low ESCS strata only gain significant benefits from long-term investments in *juku*-classes. However, for high ESCS students, a participation in correspondence courses prior to high school does not positively affect their likelihood to enter top-ranking high schools; only short-term investments during primary school

Table 6.2 Multinomial logistic regression analysis predicting the rank of high school students entered, displaying AME (HHSS 2011)

Rank of high school:		Academic A		Academic B		Academic C		Vocational	
		Ref: all respective other high schools							
		Model 1	Model 2	Model 1	Model 2	Model 1	Model 2	Model 1	Model 2
Social origin	ESCS	.26***	.25***	.51***	.49***	−.50***	−.48***	−.27***	−.27***
	Gender (male)	.01	.01	−.07***	−.07***	.15***	.13***	−.08***	−.07***
Academic standing in middle school (GPA)		.17***	.17***	−.01*	−.01*	−.13***	−.13***	−.03***	−.03***
Shadow education experience Total	Long-term: MS+PS	.07**		.01		−.03		−.05+	
	Short-term: MS only	.04+		.00		−.04		−.01	
	Short-term: PS only	−.05		.19***		.00		−.14***	
	Ref: no participation								
Academic *juku*	Long-term: MS+PS		.06***		−.00		−.04+		−.02
	Short-term: MS only		.05**		−.01		−.06*		.02
	Short-term: PS only		−.08*		.19***		−.02		−.09**
	Ref: no participation								
Private tutor	Long-term: MS+PS		−.12*		.03		.18*		−.08
	Short-term: MS only		−.045		−.02		.07*		−.00
	Short-term: PS only		−.14**		.08		.13*		−.06
	Ref: no participation								
Corr. courses	Long-term: MS+PS		.06*		.01		−.04		−.02
	Short-term: MS only		.06*		.03		−.10**		.00
	Short-term: PS only		.05*		.03		−.06*		−.02
	Ref: no participation								
N (valid cases)		2584							
Model significance (chi²-test)		***	***	***	***	***	***	***	***
Pseudo R²(McFadden)		.22	.23	.22	.23	.22	.23	.22	.23

Abbreviations: *GPA* grade point average, *PS* primary school, *MS* middle school
***P<0.001; **P<0.01; *P<0.05; +P<0.10

Table 6.3 Multinomial logistic regression analyses predicting the rank of entered high school, according to ESCS groups[a], displaying AME (HHSS 2011)

	Rank of high school	Academic A			Academic B			Academic C			Vocational		
		Ref: All respective other high schools											
		Model 3											
		Low	Middle	High	Low	Middle	High	Low	Middle	High	Low	Middle	High
Social origin	ESCS Gender (male)	-.01	.01	.03	-.01	-.06**	-.13***	.18***	.09***	.18***	-.16***	-.03	-.08**
Academic standing in middle school		.12***	.17***	.21***	.02*	-.00	-.05***	-.13***	-.13***	-.11***	-.00	-.04***	-.05***
Shadow education	Academic juku Long-term: MS+PS	.05+	.07**	.09+	.01	.03	-.06	-.06	-.05	-.02	-.00	-.05	-.01
	Short-term: MS only	.04	.06*	.09+	.02	.01	-.07	-.10*	-.07*	-.02	.05	.01	.00
	Short-term: PS only	-.03	-.08	-.11	.06	.16*	.34***	.04	-.03	-.08	-.06	-.06	-.15***
	Ref: no participation												
	Private tutor Long-term: MS+PS	-.15***	-.11	-.14	-.09***	-.07	.11	.22	.33*	.06	.02	-.15	-.03
	Short-term: MS only	-.05	-.05	-.05	.04	-.02	-.04	-.01	.07	.11*	.02	-.00	-.03
	Short-term: PS only	-.09+	-.14+	-.22*	-.09***	.12	.22+	.13	.14	.09	.05	-.13	-.09+
	Ref: no participation												
	Corr. courses Long-term: MS+PS	.11*	.07*	.02	-.02	.01	.04	.01	-.05	-.06	-.10	-.03	.00
	Short-term: MS only	.09+	.08*	.02	-.01	.01	.17*	-.08	-.11*	-.12	.00	.02	-.07
	Short-term: PS only	.07	.04	.05	.03	.05	.04	.01	-.09*	-.07+	-.04	-.01	-.01
	Ref: no participation												
N (valid cases)		641	1295	648	641	1295	648	641	1295	648	641	1295	648
Model significance (chi²-test)		***	***	***	***	***	***	***	***	***	***	***	***
Pseudo R²(McFadden)		.17	.19	.27	.17	.19	.27	.17	.19	.27	.17	.19	.27

Abbreviations: *PS* primary school, *MS* middle school

***P<0.001; **P<0.01; *P<0.05; +P<0.10

[a]The category "low" represents the students of the lowest quartile of ESCS stratification, whereas the category "high" represents the highest ESCS quartile, respectively. The category "middle" represents the 50% of students between the lowest and highest ESCS quartiles

increase the likelihood of entering Academic B schools by 17%. In contrast, low ESCS students gain significant advantages from long-term (+11%) and short-term investments in middle school (+9%). A participation in private tutoring lessons is generally negatively associated with educational success in the sense that students do not gain significant benefits for entrance to higher-ranked schools. Hence, private tutors are used when students encounter difficulties keeping up at school and are in need of remedial support.

In summary, these results verify hypotheses [H3], [H1-2], and [H2-1] for the first major transition point in Japanese students' school life course. Concerning [H1], high ESCS strata do not gain benefits from long-term (or short-term) investments in private tutoring. At least until middle school graduation, this kind of tutoring seems to be used for remedial (*hoshū*) purposes only – by all social strata. Concerning [H2], low ESCS students only gain significant advantages through *juku*-classes when making long-term investments. Concerning [H3], correspondence courses prove highly beneficial for low ESCS strata, for long- and short-term investments. What seems generally important here is a contemporary investment prior to this transition. This applies to all social strata, but varies according to the used type of shadow education: short-term investments in *juku*-classes prove very beneficial for high ESCS strata, but not for low ESCS strata. In the same way, short-term investments in correspondence courses prove beneficial for low ESCS strata.

However, since no data on the study purposes during middle school are available in our dataset, final statements regarding the accurateness of the hypotheses cannot be made yet.

6.3.2.2   Effects of Shadow Education on Transition to Higher Education

Following the transition to high school, students need to make up their minds regarding their future prospects. Whether students of different social strata who continue or start their investment in shadow education during high school benefit from such investments is calculated in Table 6.4, Models 4–7. Whereas Models 4 and 5 take into account differences in shadow education type and investment duration similar to Model 3, Models 6 and 7 focus on the pursued study purpose of the used lessons. All models are limited to students who will enter higher education institutions, excluding students who will enter the labor market following high school graduation. The reason for this limitation lies in the generally lower number of students which pursue shadow education in high school and their primary study focus when doing so. As illustrated in an earlier table (Chap. 4, Table 4.5), no student with the intention to enter the labor market pursued shadow education with *shingaku* or *sōgō* study focus. Thus, to use students which will enter the job market as a reference category is redundant. To some extent the same applies to students entering college: no students used correspondence courses with *shingaku* focus. Hence, to predict which students enter top universities and which students do not, in the following the likelihood to enter top universities in reference to average universities and junior/technical colleges is calculated through binary logistic regressions.

Table 6.4 Binary logistic regression analyses predicting students' post-high school status, i.e., entrance to top university, according to ESCS groups,[a] displaying AME (HHSS 2011)

			Top university							
			Ref: Average university or junior/technical college							
Rank of university:			Model 4	Model 5			Model 6	Model 7		
				Low	Middle	High		Low	Middle	High
Social origin	ESCS		.34**				.33**			
	Gender (male)		.18***	.23***	.20***	.12**	.17***	.23***	.18***	.10*
High school	Ranking	Academic A school	.23***	.40***	.23***	.14+	.15**	.29***	.13*	.08
		Academic B school	.21***	.33**	.19**	.17*	.18***	.28**	.16**	.12+
		Academic C school	−.04	.06	−.04	−.13+	−.06	.05	−.07	−.14+
		Ref: vocational schools								
	Academic standing		.06***	.06**	.06***	.06**	.06***	.06*	.07***	.06*
Shadow education	Academic *juku*	Duration								
		Long-term: HS+MS(+PS)	.18***	.31**	.14***	.23***				
		Short-term: HS only	.15*	.30+	.08	.18+				
		Long-term: MS+PS	.03	.06	−.02	.10				
		Short-term: MS or PS	−.01	−.02	.01	−.04				
		Purpose								
		Shingaku					.28***	.38***	.26***	.28***
		Sōgō					.18***	.45***	.17**	.15*
		Hoshū					−.02	.02	−.11	.08
		Ref: no participation								

Predictor	Category	Duration: all	low	middle	high	Purpose: all	low	middle	high
Private tutor — Duration	Long-term: HS+MS(+PS)	.18+	.20	.17	.18+				
	Short-term: HS only	.05	.10	.12	-.06				
	Long-term: MS+PS	-.06	n.e.	-.10	-.06				
	Short-term: MS or PS	.00	.06	.04	-.08				
Private tutor — Purpose	*Shingaku*					.11	.01	-.01	.24*
	Sōgō					.15	n.e.	n.e.	-.04
	Hoshū					.09	.22	.04	.03
	Ref: no participation								
Corr. courses — Duration	Long-term: HS+MS(+PS)	.09+	.12	.11	.05				
	Short-term: HS only	.05	.01	.08	.02				
	Long-term: MS+PS	.10*	.04	.09	.10				
	Short-term: MS or PS	-.01	-.12	.05	-.06				
Corr. courses — Purpose	*Shingaku*					.10*	.20	.16*	.02
	Sōgō					-.03	.06	-.10	.03
	Hoshū					.07	-.01	.12	.07
	Ref: no participation								
N (valid cases)		1639	302	816	520	1639	302	813	520
Model significance (χ^2-test)		***	***	***	***	***	***	***	***
Pseudo R^2(McFadden)		.15	.22	.12	.14	.16	.23	.14	.14

Abbreviations: *PS* primary school, *MS* middle school, *HS* high school

$***P<0.001$; $**P<0.01$; $*P<0.05$; $+P<0.10$

[a]The category "low" represents the students of the lowest quartile of ESCS stratification, whereas the category "high" represents the highest ESCS quartile, respectively. The category "middle" represents the 50% of students between the lowest and highest ESCS quartiles

First, Model 4 shows the impact of students' ESCS, gender, high school ranking, academic standing, and shadow education investments according to duration on the likelihood to enter top universities. In accordance with previous research, (male) students from advantaged ESCS backgrounds, which attend a high-ranked high school (Academic A or B) and show higher academic standing in high school, are generally much more likely to enter top universities. In addition, particularly long-term investments (from primary or middle to high school) in *juku*-classes (+18%), private tutors (+18%), and correspondence courses (+9%) increase the likelihood to enter a top university significantly and thus provide students with opportunities to achieve a high education level and thus social status. Short-term investments only prove beneficial in the case of *juku*-classes during high school (+15%).

Whether all students benefit from these advantages of shadow education is calculated in Model 5. In comparison to other strata, low ESCS students' likelihood to enter top universities is strongly affected by gender and, particularly, the rank of the high school they attend. To gain entrance to high-ranked universities, students from disadvantaged backgrounds thus need to enter high-ranked high schools first. In addition, long-term investments in shadow education seem particularly beneficial for low ESCS students, but show significant advantages only for investments in *juku*-classes (+31%). A long-term participation in *juku*-classes proves to be an effective investment strategy across all social strata.

For low ESCS students, the reported AME are considerably high for short-term investments in *juku*-classes as well (+30%). High ESCS strata additionally gain significant advantages through long-term investments in private tutoring services (+18%). The calculations of Model 5 thus support my hypotheses [H1], [H2], and [H3], with the exception that significant probabilities for low ESCS students' likelihood to gain entrance to high-ranked universities are only detected for long-term and short-term (during high school) investments in *juku*-classes. However, long-term investments in correspondence courses and even private tutoring of low ESCS strata show much higher AME compared to the other ESCS groups, indicating that there are positive effects for students, but due to the too small number of cases, no significances can be verified.

To reach final conclusions, Models 6 and 7 analyze whether distinct study purposes of the pursued shadow education type show different effects on the likelihood to enter top universities. Within these models, the effects of shadow education investments during high school are measured independent of investment duration, since the purpose of study might have changed considerably over time and inconsistencies are very likely. Model 6 shows a similar impact of students' ESCS, academic standing, and gender on the transition to top universities. The effects of the ranking of high schools decreased due to the inclusion of shadow education according to study purpose. As expected, lessons with a *shingaku* purpose show generally the strongest effects on transition to higher-ranked universities (up to 28% for *juku*-classes), whereas investments in lessons with *hoshū* focus show no effects.

A further differentiation of this model according to ESCS groups reveals significant differences between the effects of lessons across social strata (Model 7). Similar to Model 5, the impact of gender and high school ranking is apparent for low ESCS students. Also, all social strata gain significant advantages through investments in *juku*-lessons with *shingaku* and *sōgō* focus, whereas private tutoring is only beneficial for high ESCS students, when using this kind of shadow education with a *shingaku* focus. Correspondence courses seem to only show benefits when used with a *shingaku* focus, and only for low and mediocre strata. There are no significances for low ESCS strata though. In addition to these findings, low ESCS students show the highest potential to increase their likelihood to enter top universities through shadow education investments: using *juku*-classes with an *sōgō* study focus increases the likelihood to enter a top university by incredible 45%.

The results of Models 5 and 7 generally verify hypotheses [H1], [H2], and [H3], with the exception that short-term investments in correspondence courses with primarily *shingaku* focus show no significant effects for low ESCS students, even though considerably high AME are reported, which indicate very positive effects.

6.4   Discussion

I will now summarize the findings and implications of my analyses, with respect to my stated research theses.

Concerning [H1], the *private tutor investment strategy thesis*, [H1-1] proved partly correct: My analyses found that students from advantaged parental ESCS backgrounds, which make long-term investments in private tutoring, will gain no advantages for the transition to high school, suggesting that this kind of shadow education serves primarily *hoshū* purposes in primary and middle school. However, if high ESCS strata students make long-term investments in private tutoring and use these lessons with a *shingaku* focus at least during high school, their likelihood to enter high-ranked universities considerably increases, thus verifying my hypothesis. [H1-2] proved correct: For students from disadvantaged parental ESCS backgrounds, private tutoring investments prove generally nonsignificant for school transition.

Concerning [H2], the *academic juku investment strategy thesis*, [H2-1] proved correct: According to my calculations, we could clarify that students from advantaged parental ESCS backgrounds make long-term investments in *juku*-classes with primarily *shingaku* study focus and gain significant advantages for the transition to high school and university. [H2-2] proved partly correct: For students from disadvantaged parental ESCS backgrounds, significant advantages of short-term investments in *juku*-classes could not be verified for the transition to high school or university, even though short-term investments in high school showed particularly high AME for the likelihood to enter top universities. The additional analysis taking into account the primary study focus of the lessons proved that particularly low ESCS strata gain significant advantages for the likelihood to enter top universities if they pursue *juku*-classes with *shingaku* or *sōgō* study focus. Therefore, [H2] is also considered verified.

Concerning [H3], the *correspondence courses investment strategy thesis*, [H3-1] proved correct: My analyses verified that students from advantaged parental ESCS backgrounds make long-term (and short-term) investments in correspondence courses without gaining significant advantages for the transition to high school or university. The prevalent pursued type of these lessons thus is of *hoshū* character. [H3-2] proved partly correct: Students from disadvantaged parental ESCS backgrounds gain significant advantages for the transition to high school if they pursue short-term (and long-term) investments in correspondence courses, indicating that these courses are used with *shingaku* purpose. In the case of the transition to top universities, no significant effects were verified. Whether low ESCS strata students gain advantages through these courses is difficult to actually verify, since the number of students which participate in correspondence courses and enter top universities is generally very small. It seems nevertheless reasonable to assume that low ESCS strata students who make long-term investments in correspondence courses following a *shingaku* purpose will increase their likelihood to also enter high-ranked universities.

In conclusion, it was shown that shadow education generally increases students' chances of achieving a high education level. Therefore, shadow education is an effective strategy to achieve a competitive advantage and gain a high education and thus social status. The initial question was, however, whether shadow education inherits the power to enhance *all* students' chances to achieve a high education level or whether the benefits of shadow education are limited to students with well-off family backgrounds as indicated by the "Shadow Education Investment Theory" (SEIT).

First of all, the results of my analyses showed that all social strata gain significant returns from investments in shadow education. Secondly, it became obvious that families pursue very different investment strategies according to socioeconomic background. On the one hand, we cannot deny the fact that the largest proportion of students who participate in shadow education originates from advantageous family backgrounds, wherefore shadow education is possibly used as an instrument of social closure. Social inequality is thus possibly reproduced as long as high ESCS students have greater access to shadow education compared to other strata. However, this fact should not neglect that students from disadvantageous family backgrounds find ways to participate in shadow education as well and through such investments potentially increase their final education level also. In general, it seems that the Japanese shadow education industry provides families with a large bandwidth of supply, enabling all families to find a fitting investment strategy to achieve a certain educational goal. Consequently, shadow education also provides educational opportunities for students from disadvantaged family backgrounds and is an explanation for the high percentage of academically resilient students in Japan.

These findings make clear that adjustments to the SEIT proved necessary, since inequalities in educational outcomes also largely depend on whether students from disadvantageous backgrounds join the competition and make goal-oriented and purposeful investments. Even if 90% of all high ESCS students invest in shadow education and only 10% of all low ESCS students make such investments, it depends on the investment strategy and its outcomes for a students' education level. For example, if the investment strategy which is pursued does not lead to significant competitive advantages for most of the students from advantageous family backgrounds, but students from disadvantageous backgrounds gain the hoped for returns, social inequality reproduction would not be supported by the shadow industry. Whereas correspondence courses are comparably cheap and easily accessible, in particular investments in *juku*-classes with a *shingaku* study focus are generally more restricted by high costs and entrance examinations, similar to exclusive private schools in the formal education system. Competitive advantages of shadow education for low ESCS students were found for *juku*-classes with a *shingaku* or *sōgō* study focus only. Hence, follow-up research needs to analyze how it is possible that students actually gain access to these lessons despite stark limitations in family resources. Clearly, equal access to shadow education does not exist. As Schlösser and Schuhen (2011: 377) argued, equal access to shadow education for all social strata would be the second best solution to the supposed increase in social inequality through shadow education. The first best solution is to dispose of the causes for shadow education demand, meaning the shortcomings of the regular schooling system. Whether a step toward this goal bears fruits has not been analyzed yet and shall thus be content of Chaps. 7 and 8. Thus, questions concerning the development of the shadow education system and the possibilities to gain access to the provided lessons are of high relevance. Unfortunately, whether the shadow education industry has changed over the last decades was not empirically analyzed yet, wherefore the following Chap. 7 will concentrate on the persistence of access restrictions from the 1990s onward. Whether certain political attempts to make shadow education superfluous showed effects will be further discussed in Chap. 8, which will also explore how students from disadvantaged family backgrounds can gain access to *juku* of different type.

Finally, the limitations of this work have to be outlined. This analysis does not allow to make statements about the actual quality of instruction in the shadow. This additional factor might explain considerable differences in the effects of a chosen course and should be drawn up in future research.

References

Baker, D. P., Akiba, M., LeTendre, G. K., & Wiseman, A. W. (2001). Worldwide Shadow education: Outside-school learning, institutional quality of schooling, and cross-national mathematics achievement. *Educational Evaluation and Policy Analysis, 23*(1), 1–17.

BERD, Benesse Education Research and Development Center. (2013). *Gakkō-gai kyōiku katsudō ni kansuru chōsa yōji kara kōkōsei no iru katei o taishō ni* [Data on the survey concerning out-of-school educational activities targeting families with students from early childhood to high school]. Retrieved from: http://berd.benesse.jp/berd/center/open/report/kyoikuhi/2013/

Boudon, R. (1974). *Education, opportunity, and social inequality: Changing prospects in Western society*. New York: Wiley.

Bourdieu, P., & Passeron, J. C. (1977). *Reproduction in education, society and culture*. Beverly Hills: Sage.

Bracey, G. W. (1997). On comparing the incomparable: A response to Baker and Stedman. *Educational Researcher, 26*(3), 16–29.

Bray, M., & Kobakhidze, M. N. (2014). Measurement issues in research on Shadow education: Challenges and pitfalls encountered in TIMSS and PISA. *Comparative Education Review, 58*(4), 590–620.

Entrich, S. R. (2013). Causes and effects of investments in Shadow education in Japan – A comparative point of view. In F. Ojima & S. Aramaki (Eds.), *Gendai kōkōsei no shinro to seikatsu* [Career and life of high school students today] (pp. 157–182). Kyoto: Doshisha Publishing.

Entrich, S. R. (2014). Effects of investments in out-of-school education in Germany and Japan. *Contemporary Japan, 26*(1), 71–102.

Fukaya, M. (1977). Shingakujuku to sono kinō: shūdan mensetsu chōsa o tegakari to shite [The Shingakujuku and its functions: Clues from a group interview study]. *Kyōiku Shakaigaku Kenkyū, 32*, 51–64.

Hamajima, K, & Takeuchi, K. (2002). *Kodomo no shingaku asupirēshon no kitei yōin ni kansuru kenkyū: Toshi shōchūgakusei no 15 nenkan no henyō* [A study concerning the determinants of children's aspirations regarding the transition to a Higher School Level: The transformation of Urban Primary and Middle School students over 15 years]. Paper presented at the 54th annual meeting of the Japan society of educational sociology, Hiroshima.

Heyneman, S. P. (2011). Private tutoring and social cohesion. *Peabody Journal of Education, 86*, 183–188.

Kariya, T. (2010). The end of Egalitarian education in Japan. The effects of policy changes in resource distribution on compulsory education. In J. A. Gordon, H. Fujita, T. Kariya, & G. K. LeTendre (Eds.), *Challenges to Japanese education. Economics, reform, and human rights* (pp. 54–66). New York: Teachers College Press.

Kariya, T. (2013). *Education reform and social capital in Japan: The changing incentive divide*. London/New York: Routledge.

Kariya, T., & Rosenbaum, J. E. (1987). Self-selection in Japanese junior high schools: A longitudinal study of students' educational plans. *Sociology of Education, 60*(3), 168–180.

Kariya, T., & Shimizu, K. (2004). *Gakuryoku no shakaigaku: Chōsa ga shimesu gakuryoku no henka to gakushū no mondai* [Sociology of academic achievement: A study showing change of academic achievement and learning problems]. Tokyo: Iwanami.

Kataoka, E. (2001). Kyōiku tassei katei ni okeru kazoku no kyōiku senryaku: Bunka shihon kōka to gakkōgai kyōiku tōshi kōka no jendāsa o chūshin ni [Family strategy in educational attainment process in Japan: Effects of cultural capital and investment in extra-school education]. *Kyōikugaku Kenkyū, 68*(3), 259–273.

Kataoka, E. (2015). Gakkōgaikyōiku-hi shishutsu to kodomo no gakuryoku [Expenses for out-of-school education and academic achievement of students]. *Komazawadaigaku Bungakubu Kenkyū Kiyō, 73*, 259–273.

Kita, K. (2006). Gakkōgai kyōiku riyō ni tsuite no nenrei, jendā-betsu no tokusei to kaisōteki yōin [Age, gender specifics and class determinants of out-of-school education utilization]. *Kyōiku Jissen Kenkyū, 14*, 1–7.

Komiyama, H. (1993). *Gakurekishakai to juku – datsu juken kyōsō no susume* [Credentialist society and Juku –Stop the entrance examination competition!]. Tokyo: Shinhyōron.

Komiyama, H. (2000). *Juku: Gakkō surimuka jidai wo maeni* [Juku: Before the Era of downsizing Schools]. Tokyo: Iwanami Shoten.

Konakayama, A., & Matsui, T. (2008). Gakkōgai kyōiku tōshi no gakuryoku ni oyobosu eikyō ni kansuru ikkōsatsu [An empirical study on how extra school education affects academic achievement of Japanese High School Students]. *Tōkaidaigaku Seiji Keizaigakubu Kiyō, 40*, 131–158.

MEXT, Ministry of Education, Culture, Sports, Science and Technology. (2008). *Kodomo no gakkōgai de no gakushū seikatsu ni kansuru jittai chōsa hōkoku* [National report concerning the out-of-school learning activities of children]. Retrieved from: http://www.mext.go.jp/b_menu/houdou/20/08/08080710.htm

Mimizuka, H. (2007). Shōgakkō gakuryoku kakusa ni idomu: Dare ga gakuryoku o kakutoku suru no ka [Determinants of children's academic achievements in Primary Education]. *Kyōiku Shakaigaku Kenkyū, 80*, 23–39.

OECD, Organisation for Economic Co-operation and Development. (2010). *Overcoming social background – Equity in learning opportunities and outcomes (volume II)*. Retrieved from: https://doi.org/10.1787/9789264091504-en

OECD, Organisation for Economic Co-operation and Development. (2011a). *Against the odds: Disadvantaged students who succeed in school*. Retrieved from: https://doi.org/10.1787/9789264090873-en

OECD, Organisation for Economic Co-operation and Development. (2011b). *PISA in focus 5: How do some students overcome their socio-economic background?* Retrieved from: http://www.oecd-ilibrary.org/education/how-do-some-students-overcome-their-socio-economic-background_5k9h362p77tf-en

OECD, Organisation for Economic Co-operation and Development. (2012). *Strong performers and successful reformers in education: Lessons from PISA for Japan*. Retrieved from: https://doi.org/10.1787/9789264118539-en

OECD, Organisation for Economic Co-operation and Development. (2013). *PISA 2012 results: Excellence through equity: Giving every student the chance to succeed (Volume II)*. Retrieved from: https://doi.org/10.1787/9789264201132-en

Ojima, F., & von Below, S. (2010). Family background, school system and academic achievement in Germany and in Japan. In J. Dronkers (Ed.), *Quality and inequality of education* (pp. 275–297). Dordrecht: Springer.

Ono, H. (2005). *Does examination Hell Pay off? A cost-benefit analysis of "Ronin" and college education in Japan*. (SSE/EFI working paper series in economics and finance 346). Stockholm: Stockholm School of Economics.

Park, H. (2013). *Re-evaluating education in Japan and Korea*. In*Demystifying Stereotypes*. London/New York: Routledge.

Roesgaard, M. H. (2006). *Japanese education and the cram school business: Functions, challenges and perspectives of the Juku*. Copenhagen: NIAS Press.

Rohlen, T. P. (1980). The Juku Phenomenon: An exploratory essay. *Journal of Japanese Studies, 6*(2), 207–242.

Schlösser, H.-J., & Schuhen, M. (2011). Führt Nachhilfe zu Wettbewerbsverzerrungen? [Does private tutoring result in distortions of competition?]. *Empirische Pädagogik, 25*(3), 370–379.

Schümer, G. (1999). Mathematikunterricht in Japan: Ein Überblick über den Unterricht in öffentlichen Grund- und Mittelschulen und privaten Ergänzungsschulen [Mathematics education in Japan: An overview of instruction in Public Elementary and Secondary Schools and Private Supplementary Schools]. In V. Schubert (Ed.), *Lernkultur – Das Beispiel Japan* [Learning culture – The example of Japan] (pp. 45–76). Deutscher Studien Verlag: Weinheim.

Seiyama, K. (1981). Gakkōgai kyōiku tōshi no kōka ni kansuru ichikōsatsu [A study of the effects of out-of-school educational investment]. *Hokudai Bungakubu Kiyō, 30*(1), 171–221.

Seiyama, K., & Noguchi, Y. (1984). Kōkō shingaku ni okeru gakkōgai kyōiku tōshi no kōka [The effects of outside of school educational investments at the transition to high school]. *Kyōiku Shakaigaku Kenkyū, 39*, 113–126.

Southgate, D. E. (2009). *Determinants of shadow education – A cross-national analysis*. Ohio: Ohio State University.

Stevenson, D. L., & Baker, D. P. (1992). Shadow education and allocation in formal schooling: Transition to University in Japan. *American Journal of Sociology, 97*, 1639–1657.

Tobishima, S. (2012). Kōkōsei no gakushū jikan ni taisuru sōki gakkōgai kyōiku tōshi no eikyō [Impact of early outside of school education on learning time of High School Students]. *Nenpō Shakaigaku Ronshū, 25*, 144–155.

Tomura, A., Nishimaru, R., & Oda, T. (2011). Kyōiku tōshi no kitei yōin to kōka: Gakkōgai kyōiku to shiritsu chūgaku shingaku o chūshin ni [Determinants and effects of investments in education: Focusing on out-of-school education and the transition to Private Middle Schools]. In Y. Satō & F. Ojima (Eds.), *Gendai no kaisō shakai: Kakusa to tayōsei* [Modern class society: Disparity and diversity] (pp. 267–280). Tokyo: University of Tokyo Press.

Tsuneyoshi, R. (2013). Junior high school entrance examinations in metropolitan Tokyo: The advantages and costs of Privilege. In G. DeCoker & C. Bjork (Eds.), *Japanese education in an Era of globalization: Culture, politics, and equity* (pp. 164–182). New York: Teachers College Press, Columbia University.

Watanabe, M. (2013). *Juku: The stealth force of education and the deterioration of schools in Japan.* North Charleston: CreateSpace Independent Publishing Platform.

Yamamoto, Y., & Brinton, M. C. (2010). Cultural capital in East Asian educational systems: The case of Japan. *Sociology of Education, 83*(1), 67–83.

Chapter 7
Persistence of Shadow Education

The Insecurity Factor: Why Shadow Education Remains Strong

"One attends a first-class juku, passes through first-class middle and high schools and enters a top university. If one has achieved this, then one can enter a first-class company and have a happy life"

('The Future of Mass Education Society', by Kariya 1995: i).

学校外教育の永続性

Abstract This chapter analyzes the *Continuity* dimension outlined in the Shadow-Education-Inequality-Impact (SEII) Frame, specifically addressing the question whether educational and thus social inequalities in present Japan have increased due to increasing insecurities concerning educational credentials and their returns, which in turn affect families' educational decision-making processes. Following rational choice and relative risk aversion theories and focusing on the first major transition point in students' school life course, families' decisions for high school and shadow education prior to high school transition in the 1990s and 2000s are analyzed particularly emphasizing the role of insecurity for families' choices. Comparative calculations based on the *Hyôgo High School Students* (HHSS) surveys from 1997 and 2011 show the following main findings:

(1) Since the 1990s, the likelihood to pursue shadow education prior to high school transition of insecure or high ambitious students from disadvantaged educational strata has generally increased.

(2) However, the likelihood of these students to enter top-ranked high schools has actually decreased since the 1990s – in spite of shadow education investments.

(3) Additional investments in shadow education have become a must-have for those who try to avoid social downward mobility and therefore hardly serve to achieve a higher social status but rather maintain an accomplished social status. As a

© Springer International Publishing AG 2018
S.R. Entrich, *Shadow Education and Social Inequalities in Japan*,
https://doi.org/10.1007/978-3-319-69119-0_7

result, the latest wave of educational expansion in Japan is gradually coming to a halt. Shadow education has become an institution that regulates access to schools and by this strongly determines access to educational credentials and future social status.

7.1   Problematic

One of the unexpected or unintentional consequences of (international) educational expansion was the increase of individual risks due to highly individualized life courses characterized by *Risikohaftigkeit* (riskiness), increasing pressure to make decisions, and the subjective construction of biographies (Beck 1986; Müller 1998: 93). In the Japanese *gakureki shakai* (credentialist society), educational credentials rather than the occupational status determine social status (Kikkawa 2006). As the above quotation by Takehiko Kariya illustrates, to attain a high social status, it is essential to achieve a high level of education by entering prestigious schools (including *juku*). Until recently, a degree from one of Japan's top universities guaranteed access to the functional elite of the society, but this security is gradually dwindling. In this chapter, I assume that the so-called insecurity industry (Dierkes 2013) – the Japanese shadow education sector – managed to persist due to the belief that investments in lessons outside of school are an effective strategy to achieve a high education level and thus increase students' chances of gaining a high social status. Thus, I argue that the Japanese shadow education industry nourishes itself on insecurities among Japanese families regarding the worth of educational credentials.

Dierkes (2013) argued that the "combination of educational reforms, along with widespread doubts cast on conventional, especially public, school systems, has placed Japanese parents in a position of great uncertainty" (p. 11). As a result of changing societal and educational circumstances, it becomes highly difficult for families to fully assess whether formerly sufficient educational courses will still ensure status maintenance. In result, insecurity concerning educational credentials and their actual worth for a student's individual pathway emerge and affect educational decisions, especially at transition points in students' educational life course. Following RCT, increasing insecurities would therefore contribute to altered goals in decision-making and changes in the formation of social inequalities (Hillmert 2005). Although the number of students is shrinking as a result of the low fertility rate (MEXT 2017) and there exist more opportunities to gain entrance to universities and high schools without taking entrance exams (Aspinall 2005), the ongoing heavy reliance on shadow education in Japan supports the assumption that educational decisions are influenced by increasing insecurities.

In fact, with the burst of the bubble economy in the early 1990s, the ongoing financial crisis as well as the "sluggish economy" and "unfairly biased, relentless policies" (Fujita 2010: 32), once existing guarantees are increasingly questioned. Over the last two decades, not only economic inequalities (*keizai kakusa*) have increased in Japan (Tachibanaki 1998, 2005); it is also assumed that educational inequalities have exacerbated (Fujita 2010; Park and Lee 2013). This must seem questionable at first, since for Japan, increased social mobility of students from the post-baby boomer generation, initiating a new wave of educational expansion, is observed. The percentage of the 18-year-old population, which enters universities, doubled since the 1990s (1990: 25%; 2010: 51%; MEXT 2017). On the one hand, the length of individual educational training periods and the associated direct investment and opportunity costs increased for a high proportion of students. On the other hand, the struggle for coveted educational degrees and the risk of failure increased as well. Whether investments and the related costs will ultimately pay off often remains unclear for many students and their families. This results in insecurity in decision-making regarding existing educational credentials and their returns. This insecurity possibly causes the continuous high enrolment in shadow education and thus increasing inequalities.

This chapter thus addresses the question whether the continuously high dependence on shadow education in Japan has to be understood as a result of changed rationales when making educational decisions in the Japanese context, consequently increasing educational and thus social inequalities.

To answer this question, this chapter aims to clarify how increased insecurity concerning educational credentials and their returns affect educational decisions concerning shadow education investments and school choice in present Japan compared to the 1990s and thus whether this has led to an increase in social inequality or not. Only if disadvantaged social strata have increased their investments in shadow education since the 1990s due to increased insecurities and gained significant advantages for their educational career and thus social status, social inequalities would have decreased since the 1990s. A comparison between the determining factors for the decisions concerning shadow education and school transition in the 1990s and the 2000s (microlevel) promises clarification regarding the formation of educational inequalities due to societal and educational changes (macro-level). The above stated research question can thus be specified by asking how individual actors (microlevel) have responded to changing societal and educational circumstances (macro-level) when making educational decisions concerning school transition and shadow education investments for social inequality formation in Japan.

To better grasp and explain the working mechanisms behind social inequality formation in present Japan, in the following, first the possible impact of societal and educational changes on insecurity formation when making educational decisions in present Japan compared to the 1990s is discussed. Based on the foregoing discussions and the introduced theories, particular the Subjective Expected Utility Theory (SEUT) and the Relative Risk Aversion Theory (RRAT) (see Chap. 3), a theoretical model concentrating on the impact of insecurity on shadow education investments and high school transition is constructed generating the later tested hypotheses of this chapter. Secondly, calculations based on the *Hyōgo High School Students* (HHSS) survey of the years 1997 and 2011 are carried out. By comparing the effects of students' educational aspirations including insecurities across different educational strata on the choices for shadow education and high school between student cohorts of the 1990s and 2000s, this chapter sheds light on the formation of social and educational inequalities in the changing society Japan over the last 20 years.

7.2 Theoretical Background: Persistent Inequalities Due to Increasing Insecurities?

Although the results of existing studies have provided extensive insights for our understanding of the formation of social inequality in different national contexts (Shavit and Blossfeld 1993; Breen et al. 2014), including Japan (e.g., Treiman and Yamaguchi 1993; Sato 2000; Kataoka 2001, 2015; Yamamoto and Brinton 2010; Fujihara 2011; Hamamoto 2015; Fujihara and Ishida 2016), insecurity regarding future educational pathways and their returns was not taken into account as an influential factor in educational decisions in empirical research. So far, based on SEUT and RRAT, it is believed that the degree of insecurity is related to the familial economic, social, and cultural resources, individual time management, and available information regarding existing educational options and their returns, which generally results in class-specific educational decisions and thus reproduces social inequalities. While the institutional framework of an educational system sets the scope for the making of decisions, familial cost-benefit calculations based on educational aspirations and level of insecurity determine the decision for one of the available alternatives. Furthermore, institutions act as guarantors of stability – they guarantee that certain returns to education can be expected when somebody finishes a certain degree program successfully (Hillmert 2005: 175–180). As Breen et al. (2014: 260) have recently put it, the "state of the world" – meaning the condition of a country's economy and the available employment opportunities in relation to the relative worth of educational credentials – determines the level of returns to education investments. However, because the "state of the world" and the institutional and contextual educational frame in which decisions are made are content of constant change, any analysis concentrating on the formation of educational inequalities has to consider the influence of such changes on individual actors and their rationality when making decisions. Since insecurities become a major factor in the formation of individual educational pathways if risks become unpredictable, insecurities should be particularly considered in educational decision-making in regard to the status motive (maintenance or advancement) underlying educational decisions.

As for the Japanese case, the "state of the world" has undergone remarkable changes over the past 20 years. To clarify whether insecurity has possibly increased in present Japan compared to the 1990s, the following changes in the state of the world in Japan (macro-level) are briefly outlined regarding their possible impact on insecurity formation for educational decision-making focusing on the choices for shadow education and high school (microlevel).

7.2.1   A Changed Context: Societal Changes Affecting Insecurity in Japan

The long predominant opinion within the public and the social sciences until the end of the 1990s, according to which Japan was believed to be a "great middle class society" with barely any income gaps (Schad-Seifert 2007: 105), proved wrong. Even though it is true that family backgrounds are still more homogeneous in Japan compared to other industrialized countries, differences in economic and cultural background are contributing to "genetic mechanisms to produce ever less real equality of opportunity" (Kariya and Dore 2006: 155–156). Meanwhile, phrases like *karyū shakai* (lower class society), *keizai kakusa* (economic inequality), and *fubyōdō shakai* (inequality society) have found their way into public and scientific discussions, not least because of several best-selling books that brought this issue to public attention (e.g., Tachibanaki 1998, 2006; Sato 2000; Miura 2005). Unfortunately, the consequences of societal changes for the younger generation and their possible implications for future inequalities are under-researched.

During the 1990s, the phenomenon of demographic change intensified Japan's economic struggles and created new problems, like the obsolescence of the Japanese society. In 2005, Japan had already become the country with the oldest population worldwide (Goodman 2012: 162–163). In contrast, the young generation decreases continuously in numbers (MEXT 2017), and thus the individual is stronger taken into responsibility for the sake of Japan's future. The partly extortionate demands of the public as well as economic and political representatives toward Japan's students and young adults create pressure that youngsters can hardly live up to. Students who try to escape examination hell are likely to become socially excluded through educational exclusion (Fujita 2010: 39). Even so, the needs and demands of the younger generation have not received much public or political attention (Toivonen and Imoto 2012: 3).

As a clear indication of rising inequalities, the increasing division of the labor market into secure and insecure employment seems applicable. Educational credentials held their power due to the spread of major corporations' "lifetime employment guarantee" (Kariya and Dore 2006: 142) – a guarantee that is increasingly perceived as vanishing. More correctly, this guarantee only applies to the regularly employed. However, despite educational expansion at the tertiary level (see Chap. 2, Fig. 2.2), the proportion of non-regular employees rapidly increased since the 1990s (1990: 20%; 2013: 37%, see Fig. 7.1) and is no longer a marginal phenomenon (JILPT 2016: 41).

Besides increasing low-wage, non-regular work and youth unemployment, several excesses of this recent development illustrate how insecure the living conditions

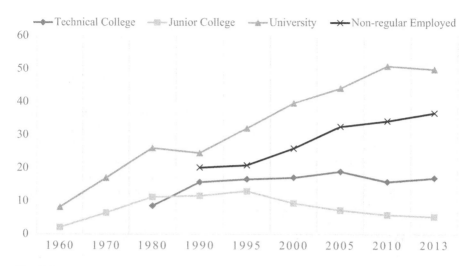

Fig. 7.1 Enrolment rates for higher education and non-regular employment ratio, 1960–2013 (JILPT 2016; MEXT 2017)

of youth and adolescents have become: NEET,[1] *furītā*,[2] *parasaito shinguru*,[3] *hikikomori*,[4] *wākingu puā*,[5] and net-café refugees[6] are some of the categories used to describe problematic, modern living conditions of adolescents. In addition, higher demands at all levels of the education system and the labor market contribute to increased competition between youth as well as higher and longer investments in education on the one hand and youth that gets "lost in transition" on the other hand. This last point refers to low-ranked high schools where most students achieve graduation, but 30% to 40% of those graduates are neither entering the labor market nor tertiary education and will also not enter the university entrance exam preparatory industry by becoming *rōnin*.[7] These graduates simply leave the education system

---

[1] The term NEET describes 15- to 34-year-olds who are "not in education, employment, or training," as well as not officially seeking a job and neither married nor included in work at home (Eswein and Pilz 2012: 511-512, see also Toivonen 2012).

[2] Freeter (Japanese: *furītā*) are 15- to 34-year-old "*free* Arbei*ter*," meaning free worker using the German word "Arbeiter." Freeter are involved in part-time jobbing or other forms of work and are generally not attached to an education institution or work at home (Eswein and Pilz 2012: 511).

[3] The term *parasaito shinguru*, meaning parasite singles, refers to young adults who still "live with their parents and rely on them financially" (Brinton 2011: 1).

[4] *Hikikomori* are socially isolated young adults, mostly men (Brinton 2011: 1).

[5] The *wākingu puā* ("working poor") are often young people who are financially disadvantaged despite working (Brinton 2011: 1).

[6] Net-café refugees are often young homeless people living in Internet cafés (Brinton 2011: 1).

[7] The term *rōnin* actually means masterless samurai of the feudal era and is used today to describe students who prepare for university or college entrance but have already graduated from high school and are thus without official affiliation.

without the attempt to make another transition. Hence, they do not even have a part-time job or, what is even more disturbing, a future perspective (Brinton 2011: xiv).

Even the recently reported record-high employment advancement rate of university graduates in 2016, of which 97.3% were able to achieve employment in April of this year (Kyodo 2016), cannot hide the fact that an increasing proportion of graduates actually enters non-regular, insecure, or unattractive jobs. Besides the fact that the actual employment advancement rate of university graduates would be accurately reported as 72% when excluding those who entered graduate school or those who failed to enter employment and decided to repeat another year (!) (ibid; the same applies to previous statistics; see Appendix, Fig. 7.4), it has become obvious that there are grave differences between jobs. In the end, "[w]hat university graduates who seek jobs desire is not simply employment, but rather decent work" (Uenishi 2013: 88). Even graduates from *Tōdai* (Tōkyō University) or any other of the most prestigious universities in Japan might encounter difficulties getting a "decent," meaning a secure, fair paid and appropriate job according to their qualifications and specialization if they fail to get a full-time position fast. In 2005, nearly every second high school graduate (47.9%) experienced a job change within 3 years after getting employed, whereas every third (35.9%) university graduate experienced the same instability (Fujita 2010: 40).

In sum, insecurity among adolescents has become prevalent, because "[l]ife-long employment, a seniority-based wage system, and collectivism […] have now crumbled to a significant extent [and] [t]he labor market and job conditions have become severe, especially for youth" (ibid: 42) in recent years. In present Japan, students have to either increase their efforts to gain access to a more limited number of attractive jobs or prepare themselves to eventually join a new economic market of low-wage jobs and increasing insecurity. Since youth without a university degree from a renowned institution is more often affected by these changes, graduating at a prestigious university is still the most securing strategy. According to the predictions of Amano (1998), the competition for access to university was believed to take a new direction, resulting in a categorization of universities into three major groups: highly selective universities, mildly competitive universities, and noncompetitive or "F-rank" (free-pass) universities (Amano and Poole 2005: 694, 706). As Kariya (2013) has verified, the considerable increase in the number of private universities over the last years (see also MEXT 2017) and substantial differences in the entrance exam scores needed for admission support Amano's assumptions. An increasing percentage of students attempts to enter institutions of higher education to increase their chances on the labor market, knowing that there are grave differences in the value of the achieved educational credentials and their worth for the labor market. As Fig. 7.1 also shows, the percentage of students aiming for universities continuously increases, whereas lower-ranked institutions in the tertiary education sector (junior and technical colleges) have lost importance recently. According to ministerial data (MEXT 2017), whereas the chances to enter employment for middle and high school graduates continuously decreased over the last decades, only higher education graduates encountered an increase in employment rates following the mid-1990s again (see Appendix, Fig. 7.4). Accordingly, Uenishi (2013) argued that "[t]oday, half of all high school graduates decide to go on to university because of the difficult employment environment that they face" (p. 89).

In the present Japanese *gakureki shakai*, the likelihood to enter prestigious and secure jobs is still highly dependent on the level of one's educational degree and the rank of the institution one has graduated from. Consequently, the hope to pass the difficult entrance examinations and gain entrance to prestigious high schools and universities and by this increase their chances to get hired for a desirable steady position in one of Japan's big companies or government agencies is a strong motivator for students to still give it their all. Therefore, most university applicants still try to enter higher-ranked, prestigious institutions by taking the central entrance examination while using F-rank institutions as security strategy (Kinmoth 2005: 119). During the last year of university, students face their last major transition point: the transition to the labor market. Recently, the competition between students in their attempt to enter attractive and secure jobs has increased. University students are forced to prepare for job-hunting (*shūkatsu*), which "is becoming the main route to employment among young people" (Uenishi 2013: 89) and remains "still tough despite economic upturn" (Kakuchi 2014). Special private *shūkatsu* preparatory schools have emerged over the last years and offer university students help in their search for suitable and stable jobs. Somehow these schools are reminiscent of *juku* or *yobikō*; only they pursue somehow different goals (even though they also concentrate on *shingaku*=transition) and apply different methods. Students are instructed to extol themselves as being a valuable addition to a company and thus achieve entrance to a renowned company. Whereas university students in their *shūkatsu* period have already reached a significant step in their life course awaiting their final transition to the labor market, whether school students make it to this final step highly depends on the choices at the preceding school transition points and with how much investment of time, money, and effort they pursue their defined goals. Along the way, it is essential to acquire the needed "armamentarium" to succeed in the *kyōiku kyōsō* and the *shiken jigoku*.

However, due to the described changes, it might not always be clear which armamentarium this is. It is thus not surprising that "the majority of high school students (is believed to be) unclear about their career goals when they apply for universities" (Tsukasa Daizen, professor at Hiroshima University, cited in Kakuchi 2013). This uncertainty concerning future job opportunities leaves students insecure only focusing on the next major step in their individual educational pathways. To increase future job opportunities and decrease insecurities, it is essential for students to enter high-ranked high schools and universities. Since the competition for university is shifted to the high school entrance level (Tsuneyoshi 2013: 165), the decision for a certain high school and the efforts that families undertake to achieve entrance to the chosen school determine students' future educational pathways and job opportunities. For families with clear and ambitious educational goals, additional investments in shadow education are viewed as an effective educational strategy and a maybe a "necessary evil" (Entrich 2013) to increase their chances of gaining entrance to prestigious schools. In contrast, for students who have decided to enter the labor market following high school graduation, investments in shadow education play but a minor role.

As shown earlier (Chap. 6), students who receive support in the shadow generally increase their chances of gaining entrance to high-ranked institutions. However, given the aforementioned changing labor market conditions, it seems likely that more and more students seek to enter university, using shadow education as a security strategy to make sure to maintain a high social status (status maintenance motive). The increased insecurity regarding educational qualifications and their returns as caused by vast societal changes should have created an increased demand for security. The shadow education industry fills that demand by promising to get students through school and into desired jobs by providing what families need – guarantees to success.

This argumentation is supported by the fact that revenues and enrolment rates of the shadow education system in Japan remained surprisingly strong and stable over the last two decades. In spite of several attempts to decrease the educational competition in the course of the *yutori* education reforms (see Chap. 10) and a steadily decreasing number of students, which were believed to make this industry superfluous until 2009 (Okada 2012: 145), current data of the Yano Research Institute and the MEXT verify a continuous high dependence on shadow education in Japan. Accordingly, a continuous increase in overall revenues of the Japanese supplementary education industry (including the *juku*-industry; see also Chap. 2) was reported for previous years, generating approximately ¥2.5 trillion in 2015 (Yano Research Institute 2010, 2016). The MEXT reported that the percentage of public school students whose parents paid for *juku*-classes in 2014 was still extremely high compared to the 1990s (Fig. 7.2): 42% of primary school students, 70% of middle school students, and 34% of high school students were enrolled in such classes in 2012.

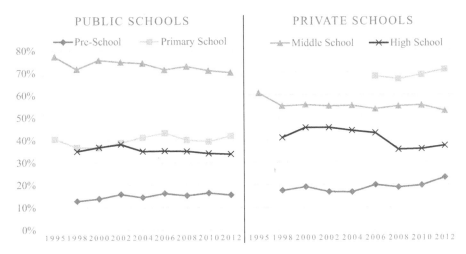

Fig. 7.2 Percentage of public and private school students whose parents paid for academic *juku*-classes, 1995–2012 (Monbushō 2001: 25, MEXT 2014)

According to these data, only small differences in the enrolment rates at *juku* are visible from 1995 to 2012. Similar trends in the development of *juku*-attendance were reported for students of private schools. In addition, correspondence courses and private tutors are frequently used as alternatives to traditional classroom instruction at *juku* (37% elementary school students; 36% middle school students; 17% high school students; see Appendix, Fig. 7.5). These data illustrate the persistence of this market, which seems largely unaffected by changes.

Whereas the concrete reasons for the ongoing success of shadow education in Japan will be discussed in the upcoming Chap. 8, this chapter suggests that the underlying cause for families to continue making investments in supplementary lessons is insecurity regarding future educational prospects. Following the introduced RCT approaches (particularly SEUT and RRAT), whether families realize the importance of this major transition point in students' school life course and decide to pursue shadow education highly depends on parents' highest education level (including their aspirations for their children) and students' own ideas regarding their future educational pathway. Previous research additionally showed that there are significant differences in the impact of parents' education level on shadow education investments and students' final education level between different age cohorts or generations. Kataoka (2001) analyzed changes in the access to shadow education and its effects across three different birth cohorts (1951–1960; 1961–1970; 1971–1980) in her attempt to predict the educational status of students based on socioeconomic background and educational strategies. Using the *Social Science and Mobility* (SSM) survey of 1995, Kataoka identified three major strategies through which families try to ensure a high educational status of their children. Besides the reduction of the number of children and a specific cultural heritage, shadow education investments were specified as one major educational strategy to avoid social downward mobility. Whereas the access to shadow education was found to be restricted by parents' education status for the two younger birth cohorts (35–49-year-olds and 20–34-year-olds), no effect was found for the 50–69-year-old cohort. In addition, shadow education investments were found to exert a significant effect on students' transition to an elite high school and their final educational status for males of the younger cohorts only. Basing their analyses on SSM data of the year 2005, Tomura et al. (2011) predicted the influence of shadow education experience of the same three birth cohorts on their later achieved total education years as a proxy for education level. The authors found no significant effect on the 5% level when controlling for gender, father's occupational and educational status, the rank of high school, and academic standing in 9th grade. These findings beg the question whether the continuous high dependence on shadow education in Japan is one of the unintended consequences of educational expansion and whether disadvantaged educational strata actually benefit from this development contributing to a decrease in social inequalities or not.

Unfortunately, existing studies failed to acknowledge individual educational aspirations reflecting families' main goal, i.e., status maintenance or social advancement, and how these goals may have changed across social strata since the 1990s due to increasing insecurities concerning educational returns. It remains unclear whether the impact of educational aspirations across different social strata changed over time and thus may provide explanations for increasing or decreasing social inequalities in present Japan.

7.2.2   Research Hypotheses: The Impact of Insecurity on Educational Decisions

Based on the discussions above, the following SEUT and RRAT approaches are extended emphasizing the importance to take into account the impact of change on insecurity concerning educational credentials and its influence on the decisions for shadow education and high school. I argue that both the institutional frame and the state of the world are content of change in every nation. However, only when major changes occur over a very limited period of time – as verified for Japan – the mechanisms underlying educational decision-making get considerably affected. The factor that impacts these mechanisms is insecurity. At times where major changes occur, individuals become increasingly insecure concerning the benefits and risks associated with educational options. Thus, the rationality of choices is bound to the insecurity level, which determines whether families primarily follow a status maintenance or social advancement motive when deciding for schools and whether or not investments in shadow education are necessary to achieve this goal. To make reasonable choices, individuals have to be aware of the risks or – in other words – the consequences associated with all possible educational outcomes of their decision. Only then they can act rationally and avoid too high risks (risk aversion, RRAT), for example.

In contrast to classic RRAT, which assumes that low social strata can only advance socially, I argue that students from disadvantaged social backgrounds in present Japan also face the risk to get socially excluded by entering the expanding sector of "bad" jobs, characterized by precarious working conditions and low wages. Hence, due to increased insecurities concerning educational credentials and their returns, students of these strata will either be more likely to follow a status maintenance motive or wait with their decision concerning their future pathway. This way students might miss the opportunity to achieve a higher education level due to missed investments, such as shadow education. In contrast, students from mediocre social background more often follow the social advancement motive if they get insecure, whereas advantaged social backgrounds need to follow the status maintenance motive and are thus more likely to either make an early decision to go to university or remain uncertain using shadow education as a security strategy to keep all possible opportunities open. In general, all strata are more likely to follow the status maintenance motive if they get increasingly insecure concerning educational credentials. However, whereas high social strata are willing to take higher risks, they will be more likely to make investments in shadow education independent of their educational aspirations. I suppose that students from low social strata will only pursue shadow education if they intend to achieve a higher social status than their parents. Whether a large proportion of students still follows the social advancement motive is of question.

In summary, this chapter addresses the question whether the continuous high dependence on shadow education in Japan is one of the unintended consequences of educational expansion and whether disadvantaged educational strata actually benefit from this development contributing to a decrease of social inequality. Figure 7.3 shows the basic relationships of the model.

The displayed model subdivides students into three educational strata based on their parents' highest education level, which determines social status in Japan's *gakureki shakai* (Kikkawa 2006): advantaged (at least one of both parents holds a university degree), mediocre (at least one of both parents holds a college degree), and disadvantaged educational stratum (both parents hold no tertiary education degree). In the same manner, students' educational aspirations are subdivided into high (university), mediocre (college), and low aspirations (job). In addition, there is the possibility that students are still uncertain which pathway they should follow due to insecurity (uncertainty). Two educational decisions are in the focus of this model: (1) high school choice, ranking from top to low rank schools, and (2) the decision for shadow education investments.

Taking into account increased insecurities concerning educational credentials and their returns since the 1990s, the following hypotheses will be tested in the upcoming results section:

[H1]   *Insecurity-shadow education investment thesis* (paths a1/b1/c1 → d2/e2 and a2/b2/c2 → g), which is subdivided into two sub-theses:

[H1-1]   Due to increased insecurities concerning educational credentials and their returns, students from advantaged educational strata continue to primarily

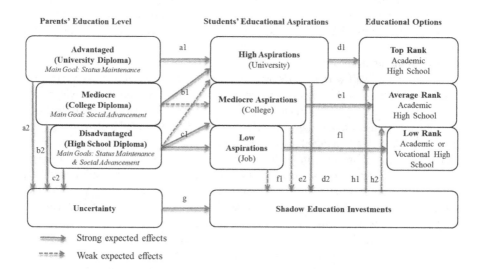

Fig. 7.3 Extension of SEUT and RRAT: *Insecurity decision model* (Japanese context)

follow the status maintenance motive and thus use shadow education as a security strategy to avoid downward social mobility similar to the 1990s.

[H1-2] Due to increased insecurities concerning educational credentials and their returns, students from disadvantaged educational strata which still follow the social advancement motive or are uncertain which pathway to pursue have become more likely to use shadow education as a strategy to achieve upward social mobility since the 1990s.

[H2] *Insecurity-shadow education impact thesis* (paths a1/b1/c1 → d2/e2 → h and a2/b2/c2 → g → h1/h2), which is subdivided into two sub-theses:

[H2-1] Due to increased insecurities concerning educational credentials and their returns, students from advantaged educational strata, which continue to primarily follow the status maintenance motive or are uncertain about their future educational pathway and have participated in shadow education prior to the transition to high school, still gain considerably higher advantages from shadow education investments for high school transition than students from disadvantaged educational strata in present Japan compared to the 1990s.

[H2-2] Due to increased insecurities concerning educational credentials and their returns, students from disadvantaged educational strata, which primarily follow the status advancement motive or are uncertain about their future educational pathway and did participate in shadow education prior to the transition to high school, gain considerably higher advantages from shadow education investments for high school transition in present Japan compared to the 1990s.

Hypothesis [H1] underlies the assumption that all educational strata want to avoid downward social mobility in accordance with RRAT. However, advantaged educational strata are generally very aware of the pathway they need to follow to preserve their status, thus showing the lowest uncertainty level. Due to major societal changes, students' of these strata continue to make investments in shadow education largely independent of their educational aspirations to avoid downward social mobility. In contrast, students from disadvantaged educational strata generally only make such investments if they want to advance socially. Hypothesis [H2] underlies the assumption that students from advantaged educational strata are in a position to make higher investments in shadow education and thus achieve a competitive advantage in the education race. Consequently, students of low educational strata are believed to be less likely to enter top high schools in spite of high aspirations and shadow education investments. As a consequence, entrance to high-ranked universities and high societal positions is likely to remain limited to students of advantaged educational strata. In the following, the formulated hypotheses will be empirically tested.

7.3   Results: Persistent Inequalities?

To obtain sound conclusions, following a short outline of the used variables, based
on data of the second and third HHSS survey, conducted in 1997 and 2011, respectively, I analyze the decision for shadow education in the 1990s and 2000s using
binary logistic regression analysis, before measuring the effects of such investments
in conjunction with insecurity on the transition to high school in the 1990s and
2000s through multinomial logistic regressions.

7.3.1   Data and Methods

To measure the varying impact of social origin on investments in shadow education
as a possible outcome of increasing insecurities from the 1990s onward, I will use
students' enrolment in shadow education during middle school in the 1990s (1992–
1994) in comparison to the 2000s (2006–2008) as dependent variables. Students'
educational aspirations, which include whether they were insecure toward the given
post-high school educational options, will serve as major explanatory variable to
clarify whether insecurities possibly play an increasing role for the decision for
shadow education in Japan. Further, educational stratum as reflected in parents'
highest education level as the major component to measure social origin in the
Japanese context, gender, and students' academic standing in middle school as one
major explanatory factor for shadow education participation and students' former
experience with shadow education (i.e., during primary school) will be controlled
for. To further measure the impact of class-specific shadow education investments
in relation to educational aspirations, again, educational stratum is included, as is an
interaction term computed from students' educational aspirations and their investments in shadow education. It will thus be measured whether students who have
received shadow lessons prior to high school transition and are uncertain about their
future prospects, (1) have experience with shadow lessons and aim for university
following high school, (2) have experience with shadow lessons and aim for junior
or technical college following high school, or (3) have not received shadow lessons
and/or aspire to directly enter the job market after high school (see also Chap. 4,
Table 4.4). Through this variable, we will be able to elaborate the actual effects of
insecure students' investment in shadow education on educational success as measured in the rank of the entered high school. Similar to Chap. 6 and in line with
previous research on high school transition in Japan, gender and academic achievement will also be controlled for (e.g., Kariya and Rosenbaum 1987).

   Before proceeding with analyzing the impact of insecurities on shadow education investments and high school entrance, further descriptive relations between
shadow education investments, students' educational aspirations including insecurity, and parental education background from the 1990s to the 2000s are visualized
in Table 7.1. First of all, we have to be aware of the fact that due to educational

Table 7.1 Distribution of educational aspirations of students who received shadow education in middle school, according to parents' educational background, in %, 1992–1994 and 2006–2008 (HHSS 1997/2011)

Parents' highest education level[c]			University	College[a]	No tertiary education[b]	Total
Educational aspirations of students participating in shadow education	1992–1994	University	31.2	18.4	12.2	20.0
		College[a]	4.0	7.4	4.8	4.7
		Uncertain	50.9	52.2	57.5	54.5
		Job	2.5	5.9	12.3	8.0
		No participation	11.4	16.2	13.3	12.8
		Valid responses	552	136	755	1443
	2006–2008	University	29.2	15.6	9.3	19.4
		College[a]	1.6	3.6	4.0	2.8
		Uncertain	51.4	56.2	55.0	53.7
		Job	3.7	4.9	6.3	4.8
		No participation	14.2	19.7	25.5	19.3
		Valid responses	819	390	655	1864

Only students of those schools ($n = 10$) were considered, which took part in both surveys
[a]This category consists of junior and technical college
[b]This category consists of middle and high school diploma
[c]At least one of both parents holds a degree in this category

expansion the distribution of students according to educational background has changed. Whereas the majority of students which attended middle school from 1992 to 1994 originated from disadvantaged educational strata, for students attending middle school from 2006 to 2008, the opposite is found: most students come from highly educated families. Furthermore, the reported decrease in shadow education investments since the 1990s (see Chap. 4, Fig. 4.3) mostly stems from a decreasing percentage of students from disadvantaged educational strata. Here the percentage of students which did not participate almost doubled from 13% in the 1990s to 26% in the 2000s. In addition, the percentage of low educated strata students with university aspirations participating in shadow education has further decreased leaving only 9%, whereas a high percentage of high educated strata students continues to have very precise ideas about their future pathway prior to high school entrance and pursues shadow education to achieve this goal (29%). However, the majority of students remain uncertain concerning future educational prospects prior to high school transition without showing considerable changes.

These data imply that the percentage of students from lower educated strata which actively pursue higher educational credentials (status advancement motive) has actually decreased, whereas advantaged educational strata still have to make sure that they avoid downward social mobility (status maintenance motive) by making additional investments in shadow education and aiming for the best schools. Educationally lower strata might still be socially excluded from high societal positions. Even if these students gain entrance to university, they might not possess the needed armamentarium to enter to the best schools.

7.3.2 Results of Analyses

To ascertain differences in the determinants for the decision to invest in shadow education between the 1990s and 2000s, I conducted logistic regression analyses predicting the impact of students' educational aspirations on their likelihood to invest in shadow education during middle school in the 1990s and 2000s (Model 1) and differentiated these analyses for parents' highest education level in a further step (Model 2) [H1]. Following this, I conducted multinomial logistic regressions predicting students' high school choice in 1995 and 2009 focusing on the likelihood of students with different aspirations and shadow education experience (Model 3), also differentiating for parents' highest education level in a further detailed analysis (Model 4) [H2]. Again, for all carried out analyses, the Average Marginal Effects (AME) are displayed.

7.3.2.1 Decision for Shadow Education: Then and Now

Table 7.2 shows binary logistic regressions predicting the influence of parents' highest education level, gender, academic standing in middle school, former experience with shadow education in primary school, and students' educational aspirations on students' participation in shadow education during middle school from 1992 to 1994 and 2006 to 2008.

The results of Model 1 show that students' educational stratum exerts a higher and partly significant influence on the likelihood to pursue shadow education in the 2000s compared to the 1990s. Whereas gender differences in the access to shadow education seem to play no role anymore, in particular, former experience with shadow education increases the likelihood to again pursue such lessons in middle school significantly (+25% in 2000s) and considerably more than in the 1990s (+15% increase). If students have high aspirations or are uncertain about their future prospects, they will be significantly more likely to pursue shadow education. In comparison, this likelihood has considerably decreased since the 1990s. This implies that the impact of increasing insecurities concerning future prospects on the likelihood to invest in shadow education has not increased – in contrast to my general assumption. It is possible that insecurities have affected certain educational strata stronger than other strata.

When differentiating my analyses according to parents' highest education level, a different picture is presented. As shown in Model 2, students from advantaged and mediocre educational strata are not significantly more likely to make investments in shadow education regardless if they have high aspirations or are uncertain concerning future prospects in reference to job aspirations, with the exception for mediocre educational strata with university aspirations (+27%). In trend perspective, students' educational aspirations seem to have lost considerable influence for high and mediocre educational strata's likelihood to pursue shadow education in middle school. Even students aiming for university are not significantly more likely to pursue

Table 7.2 Logistic regression analyses predicting students' participation in shadow education during middle school – comparison of 1997 and 2011 cohorts, displaying AME (HHSS 1997/2011)

Participation in shadow education		Model 1			Model 2								
		Basic model			Differentiation according to parents' highest education level								
					University diploma			College diploma			No tertiary education		
		1992–1994	2006–2008	Difference	1992–1994	2006–2008	Difference	1992–1994	2006–2008	Difference	1992–1994	2006–2008	Difference
Parents' highest education level	University	−.01	.05*	+.06									
	College	−.04	.02	+.06									
	Ref: no tertiary education												
Gender	Male	.09***	−.02	−.11	.12***	.01	−.11	.23**	−.08*	−.31	.05+	−.01	−.06
Academic standing	Middle school	.01	.02*	+.01	.02*	.02*	–	−.01	−.02	−.01	.00	.03*	+.03
Shadow education	Primary school	.10***	.25***	+.15	.04	.24***	+.20	.10	.24***	+.14	.14***	.27***	+.13
	Ref: no participation												
Students' educational aspirations	*Uncertain*	.09*	.08*	−.01	.08	−.02	−.10	.18	−.03	−.21	.08*	.17**	+.09
	University	.16***	.09*	−.07	.14	−.02	−.16	.27+	.05	−.22	.13**	.17*	+.04
	College	.08	.07	−.01	.11	−.02	−.13	.19	−.01	−.20	.03	.17*	+.14
	Ref: job												
N (valid cases)		1439	1845		549	812		136	385		754	648	
Model significance (chi²-test)		***	***		***	***		***	***		***	***	
Pseudo R² (McFadden)		.07	.14		.08	.13		.16	.12		.08	.13	

***$P < 0.001$, **$P < 0.01$, *$P < 0.05$, +$P < 0.10$

shadow education compared to students who want to enter the labor market. Conversely, this means that advantaged and mediocre educational strata have generally no choice anymore whether they want to pursue shadow education. In accordance with hypothesis [H1-1], for these educational strata, shadow education has become a regular feature in their school career – at least during middle school. Even if students have decided to enter the job market following high school graduation, they have the same likelihood to pursue shadow education during middle school. Here families seem to favor entrance to high-ranked schools independent of their aspirations. What counts are the increased chances of students to enter high-ranked schools due to shadow education participation and by this gain entrance to universities, colleges, or jobs of their own choice following high school.

In contrast, disadvantaged educational strata have become increasingly more likely to invest in shadow education in middle school since the 1990s, if they follow the status advancement motive and aim for higher educational credentials than their parents or remain uncertain concerning their future pathway. This implies that the shadow education industry nourishes itself particularly from increasing insecurities among disadvantaged educational strata. However, since the number of students with higher aspirations and the percentage of students who invest in shadow education among disadvantaged strata has actually decreased since the 1990s (see Table 7.1), the here presented findings only verify that lower educated families' children make more use of shadow education if they have decided for the status advancement motive in accordance with hypothesis [H1-2]. For higher educated strata, the need to avoid social downward mobility still determines investments in shadow education to a far higher degree.

This implies that either the access to shadow education has become more severe or the remaining disadvantaged educational strata have a generally lower insecurity level and follow traditional pathways as predicted by theories of social reproduction. As a consequence, educational expansion is likely to reach a new level of saturation, as indicated by the small decrease in university entrance rates from 2010 to 2013 (see Fig. 7.1). Only if students from disadvantaged educational backgrounds gain the same or higher advantages from their investments in shadow education for high school transition, social inequality is likely to be partly reduced in present Japan.

7.3.2.2 Decision for High School: Then and Now

To measure the impact of parents' highest education level and students' educational aspirations and shadow education investments on the likelihood to enter high schools of different ranking, Table 7.3 shows the results of a multinomial logistic regression using the ranking of high schools as dependent variable.

As Model 3 shows, students from advantaged educational stratum (parents possess university degree) are 10% more likely to enter Academic A high schools in reference to all other high schools and compared to students from disadvantaged educational backgrounds. The likelihood of these advantaged students even increased since the 1990s (+4%). A decrease in the likelihood to enter Academic B

Table 7.3 Multinomial logistic regression analyses predicting students' likelihood to enter high schools of different rank – comparison of 1997 and 2011 cohorts, displaying AME (HHSS 1997/2011)

| | | Model 3 | | |
		Basic model		
Entrance to Academic A high schools		**1995**	**2009**	**Difference**
Parents' highest education level	University	.06**	.10***	+.04
	College	−.02	.04+	+.06
	Ref: no tertiary education			
Gender	Male	−.05*	.01	+.06
Academic standing	Middle school	.13***	.16***	+.03
Students' educational Aspirations *shadow Education investment	*Uncertain*	.14***	.09***	−.05
	University	.27***	.19***	−.08
	College	.05	.09+	+.04
	Ref: job aspiration and/or no shadow education investment			
Entrance to Academic B high schools		**1995**	**2009**	**Difference**
Parents' highest education level	University	.13***	.08***	−.05
	College	.05+	.05*	−.01
	Ref: no tertiary education			
Gender	Male	−.31***	−.13***	+.18
Academic standing	Middle School	−.01	−.01*	−
Students' educational aspirations *shadow education investment	*Uncertain*	−.05*	.03	+.08
	University	−.04	.07*	+.11
	College	−.00	−.05	−.05
	Ref: job aspiration and/or no shadow education investment			
Entrance to Academic C high schools		**1995**	**2009**	**Difference**
Parents' highest education level	University	−.01	−.05*	−.04
	College	−.01	−.03	−.02
	Ref: no tertiary education			
Gender	Male	.24***	.23***	−.01
Academic standing	Middle School	−.15***	−.12***	+.03
Students' educational aspirations *shadow education investment	*Uncertain*	.11***	.00	−.11
	University	.16***	.02	−.14
	College	.13*	.10+	−.03
	Ref: job aspiration and/or no shadow education investment			
Entrance to vocational high schools				
Parents' highest education level	University	−.18***	−.13***	+.05
	College	−.02	−.06*	−.04
	Ref: no tertiary education			
Gender	Male	.12***	−.12***	−.24
Academic standing	Middle school	.03***	−.02**	−.05

(continued)

Table 7.3 (continued)

| | | Model 3 | | |
		Basic model		
Students' educational aspirations *shadow education investment	*Uncertain*	−.20***	−.12***	+.08
	University	−.38***	−.28***	+.10
	College	−.17**	−.14*	+.03
	Ref: job aspiration and/or no shadow education investment			
N (valid cases)		1439	1845	
Model significance (chi²-test)		***	***	
Pseudo *R²* (McFadden)		.36	.27	−.09

***$P < 0.001$, **$P < 0.01$, *$P < 0.05$, +$P < 0.10$

or C high schools if parents' education level is very high is found, though. In addition, gender differences are not detected for entrance to Academic A schools anymore, whereas the likelihood of boys compared to girls to enter Academic B schools has also considerably increased. In contrast, the probability of boys to enter vocational schools has decreased since the 1990s. A slightly higher impact of academic standing in middle school on entrance to Academic A and C schools is detected (+3%). The opposite is found for Academic B and vocational schools, though. This might be an indicator for increasing difficulty levels of entrance exams at top-ranking high schools or changed contents of entrance exams at some schools, laying greater emphasis on school curriculum contents than before. Top schools seem to try to maintain an elite position in the education system by rigorously selecting students, even more than in the 1990s (!) – implying mechanisms of social closure. This impression is supported when also considering the influence of educational aspirations and uncertainties. Not only uncertain students, who have used shadow education in middle school, show a reduced likelihood (-5%) to enter a top school in 2009 compared to 1995. This also applies for highly ambitious students with shadow education experience (−8%), who still show an almost 20% higher probability of being admitted to top schools compared to students who did not invest in shadow education and/or have lower educational aspirations.

In trend perspective, students who invested in shadow education lessons prior to high school transition were generally much more likely to enter Academic A schools in 1995 (+27%) compared to 2009 (+19%), if they aspired to enter university afterward. An opposite trend can be identified for the access probability to Academic B schools: students with similar goals are now 11% more likely to enter Academic B schools compared to the 1990s. The probability to enter Academic C or vocational schools under these conditions decreased or remains negatively associated to school entrance, implying that ambitious students who invested in shadow education generally increase their likelihood to enter higher-ranking schools. For the likelihood of uncertain students with shadow education experience in middle school to enter Academic A schools, a similar development is reported (-5% for Academic A and +8% for Academic B schools). This further supports the argument that access to top schools with correspondingly higher expected returns to education has become even more selective.

To clarify which educational strata actually benefit most from high aspirations and which effects uncertainty concerning future educational pathways and shadow education investments show for high school entrance, Model 4 further differentiates my analyses according to educational stratum (Table 7.4). According to Model 4, the detected decrease of the impact of students' university aspirations on entrance to Academic A schools concomitant with an increased probability to enter Academic B schools is verified across all educational strata. At first glance, only marginal differences between students of different educational backgrounds and their likelihood to enter top schools are found. However, even though students from disadvantaged educational strata (no parental tertiary education background) who follow a status advancement motive (university aspirations) still gained significant benefits in 2009 if they have made investments in shadow education prior to high school (+16%), their more advantaged peers' probability to enter Academic A schools was much higher (+22%). Not only have the advantages of shadow education investments decreased since the 1990s, particularly students from disadvantaged strata now show a generally smaller likelihood to enter top schools than before. Instead, they are more likely to enter Academic B schools (+9% increase since 1995 if uncertain and with shadow education experience). In contrast, students from advantaged educational backgrounds gain no advantages for entrance to Academic B schools, if they have high aspirations and shadow education experience. Overall, a general negative trend can be identified. If students' possess high educational aspirations and/or are uncertain and have invested in shadow education, a higher probability to gain admission to prestigious high schools remains, and thus higher educational returns are to be expected. Yet, the direct impact of academic performance on the likelihood to enter a high-ranked school remains significant, whereas the impact of additional investments in shadow education shrunk, particularly for students from disadvantaged educational backgrounds.

In summary, in comparison to the 1990s, students from disadvantaged educational backgrounds are less likely to achieve entrance into high-ranked schools. In fact, the differences in the impact of uncertainty and high educational aspirations in conjunction with shadow education investments on the likelihood to achieve entrance to Academic A schools are much higher for advantaged and mediocre educational strata. This means that students from advantaged and mediocre educational strata have actually to some degree converged in their demand for shadow education services independent of educational aspirations, i.e., it does not matter whether they follow a status maintenance or advancement motive.

Table 7.4 Multinomial logistic regression analyses predicting students' likelihood to enter high schools of different rank, according to educational stratum – comparison of 1997 and 2011 cohorts, displaying AME (HHSS 1997/2011)

Parents' highest education level:		Model 4								
		University diploma			College diploma			No tertiary education		
		1995	2009	Difference	1995	2009	Difference	1995	2009	Difference
Entrance to Academic A high schools										
Gender	Male	−.02	.03	+.05	.04	.02	−.02	−.08**	.00	+.08
Academic standing	Middle school	.16***	.21***	+.05	.15***	.14***	−.01	.10***	.10***	–
Students' educational aspirations	*Uncertain*	.15**	.13***	−.02	.18**	.04	−.14	.11***	.05*	−.06
	University	.27***	.22***	−.05	.27***	.23***	−.04	.26***	.16***	−.10
*shadow education investment	College	−.01	.07	+.08	.13	.07	−.06	.07	.08	+.01
	Ref: job aspiration and/or no shadow education investment									
Entrance to Academic B high schools										
Gender	Male	−.38***	−.16***	+.12	−.39***	−.15***	+.24	−.24***	−.06**	+.18
Academic standing	Middle school	−.04**	−.03***	+.01	−.02	−.01	+.01	.02*	.00	−.02
Students' educational aspirations	*Uncertain*	−.08	−.03	+.04	−.14+	.03	+.17	−.01	.08**	+.09
	University	−.14*	.01	+.15	−.07	.05	+.13	.05	.11*	+.06
*shadow education investment	College	−.01	−.21***	−.20	−.15	−.04	+.11	.05	.04	−.01
	Ref: job aspiration and/or no shadow education investment									

Entrance to Academic C high schools

		1995	2009	Difference	1995	2009	Difference	1995	2009	Difference
Gender	Male	.36***	.19***	−.17	.15**	.29***	+.14	.18***	.24***	+.02
Academic standing	Middle school	−.11***	−.12***	−.01	−.12***	−.11***	−.01	−.19***	−.13***	+.06
Students' educational aspirations *shadow Education investment	*Uncertain*	.03	.00	+.03	.20*	−.01	−.21	.14***	.02	−.12
	University	.02	.00	−.02	.13	.03	−.10	.24***	.05	−.19
	College	.07	.00	−.07	.17	.02	−.15	.14*	.18*	+.04
	Ref: job aspiration and/or no shadow education investment									

Entrance to vocational high schools

		1995	2009	Difference	1995	2009	Difference	1995	2009	Difference
Gender	Male	.05	−.05+	−.10	.19*	−.16**	−.35	.14***	−.18***	−.32
Academic standing	Middle school	−.01+	−.06***	−.05	−.01	−.04*	−.03	.08***	.02	−.06
*Students' educational aspirations *shadow education investment*	*Uncertain*	−.10*	−.11**	−.01	−.24*	−.06	+.18	−.24***	−.15***	+.09
	University	−.15**	−.24***	−.09	−.31*	−.30***	+.01	−.56***	−.32***	+.24
	College	−.05	.14	+.21	−.15	−.05	+.10	−.26**	−.30**	−.04
	Ref: job aspiration and/or no shadow education investment									
N (valid cases)		549	812		136	385		754	648	
Model significance (chi²-test)		***	***		***	***		***	***	
Pseudo R^2 (McFadden)		.37	.29	−.08	.35	.24	−.11	.30	.19	−.11

***$P < 0.001$, **$P < 0.01$, *$P < 0.05$, +$P < 0.10$

7.4   Discussion

I will now summarize the findings and implications of my analyses, with respect to
my stated research theses.

Concerning [H1], the *insecurity-shadow education investment thesis* [H1-1]
proved partly correct: according to my calculations, due to increased insecurities
concerning educational credentials and their returns, students from advantaged educational strata continue to use shadow education as a security strategy to avoid
downward social mobility. Following primarily the status maintenance motive, differences in the likelihood to participate in shadow education prior to high school
were not detected between students from advantaged educational stratum with high
(university), mediocre (college), or low aspirations (job), though. Significant differences in the likelihood to pursue shadow education could not be verified for high
strata students that are uncertain regarding their future pathway in reference to job
aspirations. Hence, the fear to lose in the educational race for the best positions and
thus risk downward social mobility remains a strong motivator to make investments
in shadow education in Japan. The generally decreasing impact of higher aspirations in reference to lower aspirations compared to the 1990s further implies that
shadow education is used to first enter a high-ranked high school and keep all
opportunities open, even if students have already decided to enter the labor market.
High strata students use shadow education as a security strategy to enter high-
ranked high schools to increase their chances of gaining entrance to university, college, or attractive jobs following high school graduation. [H1-2] proved correct
also: according to my analyses, due to increased insecurities concerning educational
credentials and their returns, students from disadvantaged educational strata which
still follow the social advancement motive (university or college aspirations) or are
uncertain which future pathway they should pursue have become much more likely
to use shadow education as a strategy to achieve upward social mobility since the
1990s. However, the overall percentage of students from disadvantaged educational
stratum decreased since the 1990s, wherefore a smaller number of students actually
enters and possibly benefits from advantages of shadow education for upward social
mobility.

Concerning [H2], the *insecurity-shadow education impact thesis* [H1-1] proved
correct: according to my calculations, due to increased insecurities concerning educational credentials and their returns, students from advantaged educational strata
which continue to primarily follow the status maintenance motive (i.e., have university aspirations) or are uncertain about their future educational pathway and have
participated in shadow education prior to the transition to high school continue to
gain considerably higher advantages from shadow education investments for high
school transition than students from disadvantaged educational strata in present
Japan compared to the 1990s. However, my analyses also revealed that the advantages of shadow education for school transition in reference to students without high
aspirations have generally decreased. This is clearly one outcome of educational
expansion and the concomitant general upgrading of the Japanese people. Also,

advantaged educational strata seem to use shadow education as a necessary security strategy even if no university or college entrance is pursued. [H1-2] proved wrong: according to my calculations, due to increased insecurities concerning educational credentials and their returns, students from disadvantaged educational strata, which primarily follow the status advancement motive or are uncertain about their future educational pathway and did participate in shadow education prior to the transition to high school, do not gain considerably higher advantages from shadow education investments for high school transition in present Japan compared to the 1990s. High aspirations and shadow education investments still result in a higher probability to achieve entrance to top high schools, but this likelihood decreased drastically. Students of these stratum significantly increased their likelihood to enter good or mediocre-ranked (Academic B) high schools since the 1990s but are less likely to enter top-ranked (Academic A) schools in present Japan.

In summary, as a result of insecurities concerning educational credentials and their expectable returns, the majority of families continue to make investments in shadow education in present Japan. Such insecurity thus contributed to the success of the Japanese shadow education industry. The presented findings indicate that social inequalities are unlikely to be reduced due to recent developments. Particularly insecure students from disadvantaged educational strata show an increased likelihood to invest in shadow education in middle school compared to the 1990s but gain less benefits from such investments. For high educated strata, investments in shadow education seem inevitable to avoid social downward mobility and maintain a high social status, even if these students are unsure where to go following their high school graduation or are determined to not enter tertiary education. For students from high educated strata, shadow education is a security strategy to ensure entrance to high-ranked high schools and by this improve their chances of admission to good universities or achieve competitive advantages on the labor market.

Overall, three trends can be identified resulting from the latest wave of educational expansion, contributing to more educational inequality: (1) Insecurities regarding educational returns increasingly induce advantaged educational strata to make investments in shadow education to maintain their social status, regardless of their educational aspirations – even though the returns to these investments seem to have decreased. This makes it even harder for disadvantaged educational strata to catch up. The continued high dependence on shadow education in Japan can thus be interpreted as a response to increasing uncertainty in decision-making processes. (2) In order to counteract a general drop in students' academic performance levels, the high selectivity of renowned schools continues to grow and makes it easier for educated families to achieve admission to high-ranked schools. Thus, upper classes are provided with new possibilities of social closure. (3) Additional investments in shadow education have become a must-have for those who try to avoid social downward mobility, whereas those who are in more need of additional support to bridge the gap in starting chances increasingly distance themselves from making such investments. Since additional investments in shadow education hardly serve to achieve a higher social status, but rather maintain an accomplished social status, the latest wave of educational expansion in Japan is gradually coming to a halt. Shadow education is therefore becoming a tool of social exclusion, as disadvantaged social classes are increasingly excluded from its utilization. Shadow education has become an institution that regulates access to schools and by this strongly determines access to educational credentials and future social status.

In conclusion, increased insecurity in educational decisions is a plausible explanation for recent developments in the upper secondary and tertiary education levels of Japan. To better grasp and explain the working mechanisms behind social inequality formation in present Japan, a focus on the formation of individual educational pathways also considering educational and societal changes and their impact on the insecurity level of families is necessary. Based on the above discussions and the findings of my analyses, the extension of existing RCT approaches stressing the importance to pay attention to changing educational and societal context and include insecurity factors into analyses proves important. The results of this chapter further suggest to extend RCT models by taking up the made propositions regarding insecurity formation and changes in different social strata's risk aversion level in future empirical research focusing on different stages of individual educational pathways in different national contexts. This way risk aversion in educational decision-making can be adequately understood, and thus persistent or new inequalities in educational attainment can be uncovered and explained. The discussions showed that particularly families' risk aversion level when making decisions seems affected by increasing insecurity concerning educational credentials and their expected returns. Comparative analyses between different cohorts prove meaningful in order to reveal trend developments in educational attainment and their outcomes concerning the impact on social inequality formation.

In the case of Japan, due to the verified devaluation of educational credentials, access to high school should actually have become less difficult for disadvantaged social strata. However, since advantaged educational strata constantly strive for ways to preserve their status by getting their children a competitive advantage, the ranking of schools within the same track (e.g., academic high schools or university) takes on the role of allocating students to different societal positions, thus providing advantaged social strata with opportunities of social closure. Investments in shadow education provide students with the opportunity to achieve a higher education level and thus social status independent of social origin if only they gain access to fitting lessons. However, only if more students from disadvantaged social strata exploit this opportunity, social inequalities will be significantly reduced. Of course, as discussed before (Chap. 5), to make use of the advantages of shadow education, opportunities to access these lessons in spite of a limited amount of resources prove essential. As shown in Chaps. 5 and 7, such opportunities seem to exist. However, the ways in which students gain access to different kinds of lessons are still unclear. In particular during high school, the pursued type of shadow education lessons might prove decisive for students' likelihood to enter high-ranked universities and actually achieve a status advantage (see Chap. 6). Hence, the following chapter finally analyzes how the diversity in supply of shadow education contributes to more equal provision of educational opportunities in present Japan and further discusses the concrete measures that enabled this supplementary education system to stay successful. As this chapter has shown, insecurities serve to keep the percentage of students from advantaged and mediocre educational strata stable. However, due to the low fertility rate, the total number of students has already considerably decreased, wherefore the number of students pursuing shadow education has decreased as well. How this industry managed to persist will thus be further explored in the upcoming Chap. 8.

Appendix

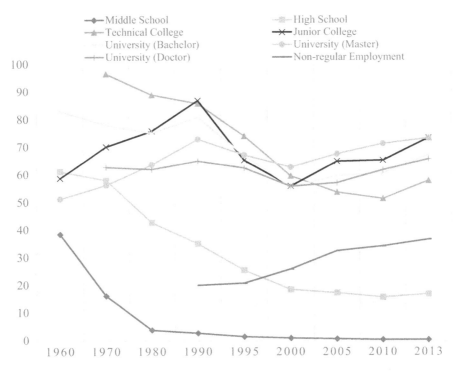

Fig. 7.4 Percentage of new graduates entering employment according to educational degree and non-regular employment ratio, 1960–2013 (JILPT 2016; MEXT 2017)

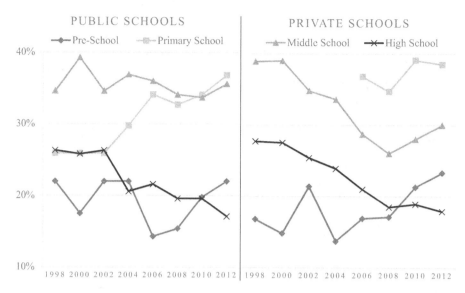

Fig. 7.5 Percentage of public and private school students whose parents paid for private tutors or correspondence courses, 1998–2012 (MEXT 2014)

References

Amano, I. (1998). Postwar Japanese education: A history of reform and counterreform. In E. R. Beauchamp (Ed.), *Education and schooling in Japan since 1945* (pp. 152–167). New York: Routledge.

Amano, I., & Poole, G. S. (2005). The Japanese University in Crisis. *Higher Education, 50*(4), 685–711.

Aspinall, R. (2005). University entrance in Japan. In J. S. Eades, R. Goodman, & H. Yumio (Eds.), *The 'Big Bang' in Japanese Higher Education. The 2004 reforms and the dynamics of change* (pp. 199–218). Melbourne: Trans Pacific Press.

Beck, U. (1986). *Risikogesellschaft – Auf dem Weg in eine andere Moderne* [Risk-society – Towards another modern age] (Vol. 1. Aufl.). Frankfurt a.M.: Suhrkamp Verlag.

Breen, R., van de Werfhorst, H., & Jæger, M. M. (2014). Deciding under doubt: A theory of risk aversion, time discounting preferences, and educational decision-making. *European Sociological Review, 30*(2), 258–270.

Brinton, C. M. (2011). *Lost in transition: Youth, work, and instability in postindustrial Japan.* New York: Cambridge University Press.

Dierkes, J. (2013). The insecurity industry: Supplementary education in Japan. In: J. Aurini, S. Davies, & J. Dierkes (Eds.), *Out of the shadows: The global intensification of supplementary education* [International perspectives on education and society, Vol. 22]. (pp. 3–21). Bingley: Emerald Publishing.

Entrich, S. R. (2013, May 21). Juku – A necessary evil? *Jukupedia.* http://blogs.ubc.ca/jukupedia/2013/05/21/guest-post-juku-a-necessaryevil/

Entrich, S. R. (2016). Zunehmende Bildungsungleichheiten in Japan? Der Einfluss von Unsicherheit auf Bildungsinvestitionen von den 1990ern bis heute [Increasing educational inequalities in Japan? The impact of insecurities on educational investments from the 1990s to today]. *Japan Jahrbuch, 39*, 227–256.

Eswein, M., & Pilz, M. (2012). Zwischen Wollen, aber nicht können und Können, aber nicht wollen: Übergangsprobleme von Jugendlichen in Japan am Beispiel der „Freeter" und „NEETs" [Between wanting to, but not having the opportunity: Transitional problems of young people in Japan using the example of "Freeter" and "NEETs"]. *International Review of Education, 58*, 505–531.

Fujihara, S. (2011). Breen ando Goldthorpe no aitaiteki risuku kaihi kasetsu no kenshō: Chichioya no kodomo ni taisuru shokugyō kyōiku kitai o mochiita keiryō bunseki [Empirical test of Breen and Goldthorpe's relative risk aversion hypothesis in the Japanese society: Data analysis of a father's occupational and educational expectations for his child]. *Shakaigaku Hyōron, 62*(1), 18–35.

Fujihara, S., & Ishida, H. (2016). The absolute and relative values of education and the inequality of educational opportunity: Trends in access to education in postwar Japan. *Research in Social Stratification and Mobility, 43*(1), 25–39.

Fujita, H. (2010). Whither Japanese schooling? Educational reforms and their impact on ability formation and educational opportunity. In J. A. Gordon, H. Fujita, T. Kariya, & G. K. LeTendre (Eds.), *Challenges to Japanese education. Economics, reform, and human rights* (pp. 17–53). New York: Teachers College Press.

Goodman, R. (2012). Shifting landscapes. The social context of youth problems in an ageing nation. In R. Goodman, Y. Imoto, & T. Toivonen (Eds.), *A sociology of Japanese youth. From returnees to NEETs* (pp. 159–173). New York: Routledge.

Hamamoto, S. (2015). Gōri-teki sentaku to kyōiku kikaifubyōdō: Shitsuteki sai o kōryo shita sōtai risuku kaihi moderu no jōshiki-ka [Explaining educational differentials with rational action theory: Formalizing relative risk aversion under qualitative differentials]. *Tōhokudaigaku Daigakuin Kyōikugakukenkyūka Kenkyū Nenpō, 63*(2), 1–21.

Hillmert, S. (2005). Bildungsentscheidungen und Unsicherheit: Soziologische Aspekte eines vielschichtigen Zusammenhangs [Educational decisions and uncertainty: Sociological aspects of a multifaceted relationship]. *Zeitschrift für Erziehungswissenschaft, 8*(2), 173–186.

JILPT, Japan Institute for Labour Policy and Training. (2016). *Labor situation in Japan and its analysis*. Retrieved from: http://www.jil.go.jp/english/lsj/index.html

Kakuchi, S. (2013). *Reform of university entrance exam sparks debate*. University World News, November 14th, 2013. http://www.universityworldnews.com/article.php?story=20130913114950164

Kakuchi, S. (2014, January 17). Graduate job hunt still tough despite Economic upturn. *University World News*. http://www.universityworldnews.com/article.php?story=20140117150414228

Kariya, T. (1995). *Taishū kyōiku shakai no yukue: Gakureki shugi to byōdo shinwa no sengo-shi [The future of mass education society: The postwar history of the myth of equality and the degreeocracy]*. Tokyo: Chūō Kōron Shinsha.

Kariya, T. (2013). *Understanding structural changes in inequality in education*. Paper presented at the DIJ-Workshop "Social Inequality in Japan: A Reassessment" DIJ Tokyo.

Kariya, T., & Dore, R. (2006). Japan at the meritocracy frontier: From here, where? *The Political Quarterly, 77*(1), 134–156.

Kariya, T., & Rosenbaum, J. E. (1987). Self-selection in Japanese junior high schools: A longitudinal study of students' educational plans. *Sociology of Education, 60*(3), 168–180.

Kataoka, E. (2001). Kyōiku tassei katei ni okeru kazoku no kyōiku senryaku: Bunka shihon kōka to gakkōgai kyōiku tōshi kōka no jendāsa o chūshin ni [Family strategy in educational attainment process in Japan: Effects of cultural capital and investment in extra-school education]. *Kyōikugaku Kenkyū, 68*(3), 259–273.

Kataoka, E. (2015). Gakkōgaikyōiku-hi shishutsu to kodomo no gakuryoku [Expenses for out-of-school education and academic achievement of students]. *Komazawadaigaku Bungakubu Kenkyū Kiyō, 73*, 259–273.

Kikkawa, T. (2006). *Gakureki to Kakusa-Fubyōdō: Seijukusuru Nihongata Gakureki Shakai [Education and social inequality: Contemporary educational credentialism in Japan]*. Tokyo: Tōkyō Daigaku Shuppankai.

Kinmoth, E. H. (2005). From selection to seduction: The impact of demographic change on private higher education in Japan. In J. S. Eades, R. Goodman, & Y. Hada (Eds.), *The 'Big Bang' in Japanese higher education. The 2004 reforms and the dynamics of change* (pp. 106–135). Melbourne: Trans Pacific Press.

Kyodo (2016, May 20). Record 97% of University Graduates land Jobs. *The Japan Times*. http://www.japantimes.co.jp/news/2016/05/20/business/economy-business/record-97-university-graduates-land-jobs/#.V5nJ26KYDcY

MEXT, Ministry of Education, Culture, Sports, Science and Technology. (2014). *Kodomo no gakushūhi chōsa* [Survey concerning children's learning expenses]. Retrieved from: http://www.mext.go.jp/b_menu/toukei/chousa03/gakushuuhi/kekka/1268105.htm

MEXT, Ministry of Education, Culture, Sports, Science and Technology. (2017). *Statistics*. Retrieved from: http://www.mext.go.jp/english/statistics/

Miura, A. (2005). *Karyū shakai: Aratana kaisō shūdan no shutsugen* [Lower class society: The emergence of a new class group]. Tokyo: Kobunsha.

Monbushō, Ministry of Education. (2001). *Kodomo no gakushūhi chōsa hōkokusho* [Report on children's learning expenses]. Tokyo: Ōkurashō Insatsukyoku.

Müller, W. (1998). Erwartete und unerwartete Folgen der Bildungsexpansion [Expected and unexpected consequences of educational expansion]. In J. Friedrichs, R. M. Lepsius, & K. U. Mayer (Eds.), *Die Diagnosefähigkeit der Soziologie* (pp. 81–112). Opladen: Westdeutscher Verlag.

Okada, A. (2012). *Education policy and equal opportunity in Japan*. New York/Oxford: Berghahn Books.

Park, H., & Lee, Y.-J. (2013). Growing educational inequality in Japan during the 2000s. In G. DeCoker & C. Bjork (Eds.), *Japanese education in an era of globalization: Culture, politics, and equity* (pp. 131–146). New York: Columbia University Press.

Sato, T. (2000). *Fubyōdō Shakai Nihon* [Inequality society Japan]. Chūō Koron Shinsha.

Schad-Seifert, A. (2007). Japans Abschied von der Mittelschichtgesellschaft: Auflösung des Familienhaushalts oder Pluralisierung der Lebensformen? [Japan's farewell to the middle-class society: Resolution of the family household or pluralisation of lifestyles?]. *Japanstudien, 19*, 105–128.

Shavit, Y., & Blossfeld, H.-P. (1993). *Persistent inequality: Changing educational attainment in thirteen countries*. Boulder: Westview Press.

Tachibanaki, T. (1998). *Nihon no keizai kakusa [Japan's economic inequality]*. Tokyo: Iwanami Shoten.

Tachibanaki, T. (2005). *Confronting income inequality in Japan. A comparative analysis of causes, consequences, and reform*. Cambridge/London: MIT Press.

Tachibanaki, T. (2006). *Kakusa shakai – nani ga mondai nano ka* [Unequal society – what are the problems?]. Tokyo: Iwanami Shoten.

Toivonen, T. (2012). NEETs – the strategy within the category. In R. Goodman, Y. Imoto, & T. Toivonen (Eds.), *A sociology of Japanese youth* (pp. 139–158). London/New York: Routledge.

Toivonen, T., & Imoto, Y. (2012). Making sense of youth problems. In R. Goodman, Y. Imoto, & T. Toivonen (Eds.), *A sociology of Japanese youth* (pp. 1–29). London/New York: Routledge.

Tomura, A., Nishimaru, R. & Oda, T. (2011). Kyōiku tōshi no kitei yōin to kōka: Gakkōgai kyōiku to shiritsu chūgaku shingaku o chūshin ni [Determinants and effects of investments in education: Focusing on out-of-school education and the transition to private middle schools]. In: Y. Satō & F. Ojima (Eds.), *Gendai no kaisō shakai: Kakusa to tayōsei* [Modern class society: Disparity and diversity] (pp. 267–280). Tokyo: University of Tokyo Press.

Treiman, D. J., & Yamaguchi, K. (1993). Trends in educational attainment in Japan. In Y. Shavit & H.-P. Blossfeld (Eds.), *Persistent inequality – Changing educational attainment in thirteen countries* (pp. 229–249). Boulder/San Francisco/Oxford: Westview Press.

Tsuneyoshi, R. (2013). Junior high school entrance examinations in metropolitan Tokyo: The advantages and costs of privilege. In G. DeCoker & C. Bjork (Eds.), *Japanese education in an era of globalization: Culture, politics, and equity* (pp. 164–182). New York: Teachers College Press, Columbia University.

Uenishi, M. (2013). Employment of new graduates. *Japan Labor Review, 10*(4), 80–89.

Yamamoto, Y., & Brinton, M. C. (2010). Cultural capital in East Asian educational systems: The case of Japan. *Sociology of Education, 83*(1), 67–83.

Yano Research Institute. (2010). *Kyōiku sangyō ichiba ni kansuru chōsa kekka 2010* [Survey results on the education industry market 2014]. Retrieved from: https://www.yano.co.jp/market_reports/C52110700

Yano Research Institute. (2016). *Kyōiku sangyō ichiba ni kansuru chōsa kekka 2015* [Survey results on the education industry market 2016]. Retrieved from: https://www.yano.co.jp/market_reports/C58109800

Chapter 8
Change of Shadow Education

Diversity in Supply: How Shadow Education Remains Strong

"For more than 30 years students come to our juku - and I think that the situation has gotten even worse. There is more pressure on them in spite of all the educational reforms..."

(Interview with a principal of a small *juku*, Nov. 2012).

学校外教育の変容

Abstract This chapter analyzes the *Change* dimension outlined in the Shadow-Education-Inequality-Impact (SEII) Frame, specifically addressing the question how Japanese shadow education managed to maintain strong despite unfavorable changes which were believed to make this industry superfluous until 2009 and how this affects educational opportunities for disadvantaged educational strata. Since the implications of a high dependence on shadow education for a national system of education regarding educational opportunities and social inequality issues are hardly overestimated, following a neo-institutionalist approach, the ongoing success of the *juku*-industry is explored. Applying a mixed-method approach basing my calculations on data of the 2013 *Juku Student and Teacher Survey* (JSTS), the following main findings are presented:

(1) Due to decreasing student populations, the reformation of the mainstream schooling system, and changed educational demands of families, the originally highly specialized *juku* have expanded their range of supply. *Juku* increasingly take on functions outside their original purview such as care, counseling, and guidance and thus achieve many of the *yutori* education goals that regular schools struggle to accomplish.

(2) Due to continuous changes, new types of *juku* have evolved particularly focusing on individual tutoring.

© Springer International Publishing AG 2018
S.R. Entrich, *Shadow Education and Social Inequalities in Japan*,
https://doi.org/10.1007/978-3-319-69119-0_8

215

(3) This industry shows continuous efforts to increase opportunities for socioeco-
    nomically disadvantaged students to participate in various types of lessons in
    the shadow and thus gain benefits from *juku*-lessons also.
(4) Families increasingly rely on *juku* as their primary contact in educational mat-
    ters, wherefore these schools gain further importance as educational gap-closer
    and authority in educational and social matters.

8.1   Problematic

In Western research, two prevalent views on the characteristics of Japanese education exist: The Japanese schooling system was repeatedly praised for its high academic outcomes, equality of opportunities and high quality by researchers,
international organizations, and governments across the world (e.g., Stigler and
Stevenson 1991; Stigler and Hiebert 1999; Akiba et al. 2007; OECD 2012).
However, this glorification of Japanese education is disturbed by the negative perception that schooling is too rigid and uniform (Cave 2001: 173) and possesses a
competitive exam culture (Zeng 1999) concomitant with the so-called examination
hell (e.g., Stevenson and Baker 1992). Dull root learning (Dierkes 2012), group
pressure, conformism, the opposition of creativity (e.g., Volker Schubert 1992,
Volker Schubert 1999; Volker Schubert 2005; Volker Schubert 2006; Kariya 2010;
Park 2013), and one of the highest enrolment rates in private "cram schools" in
international comparison (e.g., Bray 1999; Schümer 1999; Bray 2009; Bray and
Lykins 2012) are the identified results. The blending of equality of opportunities
and the prevailing competition led to the incredible success of the Japanese education system ("Japanese education miracle," Arnove and Torres 2007: 5), providing
the country with a highly trained workforce. In contrast, the excesses of the *gakureki shakai* (credentialist society) caused major problems for Japanese education
(Amano 1998: 162), in particular school disorder phenomena, such as school violence (*kōnai bōryoku*), bullying (*ijime*), psychic disorder, student suicides, vandalism, juvenile crimes, and school absenteeism or refusal leading to *gakkyū hōkai* (the
breakdown of school class discipline or class disruption). The rigid and uniform
system was thus believed to put Japanese schools and education in danger while
also contributing to a decline in academic achievement (*gakuryoku teika*) (Azuma
2002: 14, Fujita 2010: 22, Dierkes 2013: 3). As a consequence, far-reaching public
and political debates about the failing of the education system led to a new reform
course. Since the late 1990s, Japanese education has entered a state of crisis (*kyōiku
kiki*) and continuous reformation particularly emphasizing relaxation (*yutori*) and
internationalization (*kokusaika*) of education (see Chap. 10). The implemented
reforms caused major changes in the regular schooling system (Fujita 2010).

However, the ongoing debates often missed to acknowledge educational realities
besides formal education, in particular students' massive enrolment in paid-for,
extracurricular supplementary lessons outside of school. Even though the imple-

mented reforms were supposed to decrease the examination hell and by this mini-
mize the demand for shadow education services, it is not clear how the *juku*-industry
reacted to the reformation of the formal schooling system. In addition, demographic
developments have led to an ever-decreasing student population that not only negatively affects the regular schooling system, which continuously shrinks (MEXT
2017); the *juken sensō* ("entrance examination war," Rohlen 1980: 220) was
believed to stop due to fewer competitors and thus make shadow education superfluous (Okada 2012: 145). However, as the above quotation of a *juku* principal shall
illustrate, these changes seem to have not led to the disappearance of pressure on
students or competition between them.

This impression is further supported through the evaluation of the development
of the *juku*-industry's revenues and enrolment rates over the last two decades, which
reveals that the shadow remained surprisingly strong and stable. This further illustrates the persistence of this market, which seems largely unaffected by changes
(see Chap. 7). Even though there are increasing efforts to understand the role of
shadow education in Japan (e.g., Mori and Baker 2010; Watanabe 2013; Kataoka
2015; Mawer 2015) and an "increasing interest in trying to explain the expansion of
private tutoring systems" (Dawson 2010: 21), recently, previous research simply
missed to discuss how national shadow education systems manage to stay successful despite unfavorable conditions. This question is highly relevant, since a strong
dependence on shadow education has major implications for a national education
system in terms of educational quality and opportunities as well as social inequality
issues (Jones 2011). As I have extensively discussed in the preceding chapters,
shadow education in Japan is believed to strongly contribute to social reproduction
or even increase social inequalities. Families' increased insecurities concerning
educational credentials and their returns are one major cause for the persistence of
the high demand for additional support (see Chap. 7). However, insecurities alone
do not explain how the Japanese shadow education sector managed to overcome all
attempts to rob it of its very foundation: the *kyōiku kyōsō* (educational competition).
Also, the access to shadow education for socioeconomically disadvantaged families
is not automatically closed, as I was able to show empirically in Chap. 5. Accordingly,
the often overlooked high diversity within the Japanese shadow education industry
and its enormous range of supply provides a plausible explanation for the persistence of the highly institutionalized Japanese supplementary school system, due to
the provision of opportunities to participate for students from all social strata.
Unfortunately, only few researchers have pointed to the diversity within the *juku*-
industry (e.g., Komiyama 1993, 2000; Drinck 2006; Roesgaard 2006; Mawer 2015)
or carried-out quantitative analyses focusing on the differences within this vast market (e.g., Yuki et al. 1987). *Juku* are considered an "educational stopgap and market
gap" (Dierkes 2009); empirical evidence on how these schools deal with changes
that affect the education system as a whole is nonexistent.

Following New Institutionalist Theory (NIT), institutional change is caused by
individual actions (see Chap. 3). If students' educational needs have changed as a
result of vast educational and demographic change over the last 20 years, families'
demands concerning shadow education should have changed along with them. It

seems reasonable to assume that a further differentiation within the *juku*-industry occurred in response to changing educational realities over the last 20 years. Whether this possible evolution of the *juku*-industry contributes to more or less educational opportunities and thus the formation of new or the reduction of existing social inequalities will be content of this chapter.

In sum, this chapter addresses the question how Japanese shadow education managed to maintain strong despite steadily decreasing student populations and major changes in the formal education system and how change of this industry affect social inequalities in present Japan. To present reliable and new results, data of the 2013 *Juku Student and Teacher Survey* (JSTS) are analyzed using a mixed-method approach. Following a new institutionalist approach, recent changes in the highly diverse *juku*-industry are empirically explored. The results shed light on the structural and content transformation of the institutionalized shadow education industry over the last 20 years and allow drawing conclusions concerning socioeconomically disadvantaged students' opportunities to actually gain access to shadow education in present Japan.

8.2   Theoretical Framework: Shadow Education in an Era of Educational Change

Before introducing the hypotheses of this chapter, first, recent changes in the education system due to decreasing student populations and education reforms are discussed for their impact on the shadow, followed by an outline of the diversity of the *juku*-industry focusing on the specifics of major *juku*-types, before research hypotheses are generated based on the foregoing discussions.

8.2.1   Recent Changes to Japanese Education

Over the last two decades, Japanese education has undergone major changes due to two main developments: (1) steadily decreasing student populations and (2) the reorientation of education either placing greater emphasis on relaxation (*yutori*) or competition (*kyōsō*) as well as internationalization (*kokusaika*). The decrease in student populations is an outcome of steadily declining birth rates during the post-baby boomer phase (see Chap. 2, Fig. 2.3). Hence, since the mid-1980s, the enrolment ratios at primary, middle, and high schools entered a state of decline resulting in the shrinking of the mainstream schooling system. According to Bray and Lykins (2012), shadow education mimics (or shadows) the regular schooling system. Consequently, "[a]s the content of mainstream education changes, so does the content of the shadow. And as the mainstream grows, so does the shadow" (p. x). Hence, the shadow education sector is expected to shrink along with the mainstream education system (see also Bray 1999, 2009). Due to decreasing student populations, estimations in the 1990s predicted the abolition of the intense educational competition and the examination hell until 2009, due to fewer competitors in the education race. Not surprisingly, the *juku*-market was believed to vanish along with the examination hell, becoming superfluous (Okada 2012: 145). However, since the percentage of students aiming to enter university has been continuously increasing since the 1990s (see Chap. 7, Fig. 7.1), the total number of students taking the central university entrance exam (*sentā*) remained constant from 1995 to 2014 (see Chap. 10, Fig. 10.1).[1] Therefore, the competition between students and the demand for exam preparation has most likely only decreased partially. According to Kariya Takehiko, one of the leading Japanese educational sociologists, competition has actually decreased compared to 20 years ago. However, in present Japan, parents concentrate their efforts on the support of only one or maybe two children. Hence, families have more financial resources and willingly accept the high costs of shadow education, believing that such investments increase the chances of their children to get secure and prestigious jobs.[2] Consequently, conversely to general expectations, the still high enrolment in shadow education seems also to be an outcome of the low birth rates.

Based on the political consensus that the "overheated competition" for entrance to schools is making education dysfunctional (Azuma 2002: 14), reform measures targeting the formal schooling system were initiated since 1977 under the guiding principle *yutori kyōiku* (no-pressure education) (Tanabe 2004: 3). These reforms initially pursued the goal to decrease the prevalent intense competition between students, lessen the pressure on students and give them "more time to explore their own interests" (Okada 2012: 139) in order to contain examination hell. To achieve this goal, the *yutori* reforms reduced the overall compulsory school curriculum by 30% (see Chap. 10, Table 10.1) and shortened the school week from a six- to a five-day school week coming into effect in 2002 (Goodman 2003: 7). Against the background of long-lasting economic recession, progressing globalization, and an evolving world culture of education emphasizing new educational standards (Baker and LeTendre 2005; Baker 2014), concerns regarding the actual state and purpose of the education system and its supply function for the economy were raised as well (Azuma 2002: 14, Fujita 2010: 22). As a result, the believed need for stronger internationalization (*kokusaika*) in education led to a stronger promotion of individuality (*kosei*) and creativity (*sōzōsei*) (Goodman 2003: 16–18, Aspinall 2010). To create room to develop *kosei* and *sōzōsei* by augmenting teachers' influence on school curricula and encouraging students to follow their own study interests, the so-called *sōgōtekina gakushū no jikan* (integrated study period) was introduced as a new subject in compulsory school, coming into effect in 2002 (Bjork and Tsuneyoshi 2005). To abolish the *shiken jigoku* at the transition to high school and university, on the one hand, a new six-year secondary school type uniting middle and high school level thus eliminating entrance examinations for high school was introduced in

---

[1] Since the 1990s, of the approximately 600.000 new university entrants each year, 520.000 to 530.000 applicants took the test (DNC 2014c).

[2] Personal communication with Kariya Takehiko, November 2013.

1999 (Okada 2012: 121). On the other hand, universities were advised to strongly consider other criteria for university entrance besides entrance examinations to reduce exam hell at the end of high school.[3]

These radical reforms were launched despite the superficial international success of Japanese education and against a strong opposition. In particular, the reduction of study hours in school led to a national education discourse, fearing a decline in students' academic achievement (gakuryoku teika ronsō; Takayama 2008: 388). Besides politicians, leading Japanese sociologists expressed their concerns about the actual sense of these reforms (e.g., Sato 1999; Ono and Ueno 2001). Fujita (2000) went so far as to call the drastic curriculum reduction "educational disarmament" and pointed to the fact that Japan was changing its course against the global educational "rearmament" trend with the common goal to stay economically competitive (pp. 5–20). The nonsignificant but nevertheless observable drop in the performance of Japanese students in the following two PISA surveys of 2003 and 2006 was politically exploited to discredit the *yutori* reforms as contradicting the *kokusaika* intention of the national policy course, resulting in a realignment of Japanese educational policy. The MEXT then introduced new guidelines,[4] placing more weight on the "basics and fundamentals" of teaching and learning and aiming at ensuring that the academic achievement level of students would remain high while also fostering individuality and creativity (M. o. E. MEXT, Culture, Sports, Science and Technology 2005: ch. 1, part 5). To make Japanese education more competitive again, several new reforms were initiated with a stronger emphasis on *datsu-yutori* (de-relaxation) and *kokusaika*. Consequently, in 2008, the course of study was revised once more, resulting in a 10% increase of total study hours at the primary and middle school level, coming into effect in 2012 (see Chap. 10, Table 10.1), and aiming to increase academic achievement and incorporate "PISA-like competencies" (Breakspear 2012: 24). In addition, the time for the "integrated study period" was cut in favor of the core subjects Japanese, Mathematics, Science, Social Studies, and English (see Chap. 10, Table 10.1). Particularly English language skills of Japanese students were promoted, and therefore several attempts were made to increase quality and length of instruction in school.[5] By reintroducing a national achievement test in 2007, consisting of a traditional part (basic knowledge) and a new part (application skills, PISA related competencies; Breakspear 2012: 19), workload and competition are likely to have increased again (for a detailed descrip-

---

[3] Students can enter universities on the basis of the evaluation of practical tests, interviews, essays, and *suisen nyūgakkō* (a recommendation letter of a school principal). In addition, students' engagement in extracurricular activities, such as school clubs (*bukatsudō*) or volunteer activities (*borantia katsudō*), shall receive attention in the admission process (Aspinall 2005: 211–14).

[4] For example, a new education policy goal called *tashikana gakuryoku* (solid academic ability), a new education guideline called *manabi no susume* (exhortation towards learning), and a new general education reform plan entitled *Yomigaere Nihon!* ('Japan! Rise Again!') (Takayama 2008: 394).

[5] For example, the "English Education Reform Plan corresponding to Globalization" aiming to "enhance English education substantially throughout elementary to lower secondary school" (MEXT 2014).

tion of these reforms and their outcomes see Chap. 10). Even though the "examination competition problem" (*juken kyōsō no mondai*) was recognized for causing heavy cramming on a societal level (Roesgaard 2006: 2–3), higher workload and competition were reintroduced to the education system to maintain international competitiveness. Furthermore, former relaxation measures prove partly ineffective. The 6-year secondary schools particularly attracted students from privileged backgrounds and ergo missed to provide a real alternative for students to escape examination hell (Okada 2012: 135). More importantly, universities with low alternative admission rates continue to design and hold highly difficult entrance exams, wherefore educational competition in the access to universities has only decreased partially (Kinmoth 2005; Kariya 2013).

In conclusion, students are more than ever expected to do well in school, in entrance examinations, and in national and international achievement tests. In addition, students are supposed to demonstrate fluent English, develop their creativity, work autonomously, and gain new skills, which go beyond mere content reproduction, while being faced with increasing uncertainties concerning their future chances on the labor market. Regular schools are required to ensure adequate education to fulfill society's expectations for students but have much less room to accomplish this task due to generally reduced learning hours in school compared to the 1990s. Relaxation measures proved partly ineffective. However, the stronger emphasis on internationalization in education particularly promoting individuality and creativity describes major changes in the general orientation of Japanese education, which adapted to international guidelines in education. This results in changing educational demands for the mainstream and the shadow sector. Without adequately adapting to these new demands, the shadow education industry should have heavily diminished over the last two decades, especially against the background of constantly decreasing student populations. The question thus is how the *juku*-market maintains its success despite these changes.

8.2.2   Diversity in Supply: A Typology of Juku

One of the pioneers in comparative education, Sir Michael Sadler (1900), stressed that a national education system is like a "living thing" – it never stops to grow and change its shape. According to Bray and Lykins (2012), shadow education mimics the regular schooling system and changes its shape along with it (p. x). Since vast changes in the shadow education system of a country affect several serious issues in education, such as educational opportunity provision, social inequality in educational attainment, or children's well-being (ibid), all changes affecting the regular schooling system impact the size and shape of the shadow education system as well. In turn, the organization and overall influence of a national shadow education system on students' life shed light on the possible shortcomings of the regular schooling system (Roesgaard 2006). As Dawson (2010) has argued, "juku capitalize on those shortcomings, acting as a market which absorbs unmet demand" (p. 17).

Following this argumentation, vast changes in the public schooling system should affect the shadow education industry in a decisive way.

Following the rationale of NIT, which basically emphasizes the importance of institutions as connections between social structures and individual actors, the development and expansion of the Japanese *juku*-industry have to be understood as a result of rational actions of individuals whose uncoordinated, individual, own personal benefit-maximizing choices create institutions (Maurer and Schmid 2002: 21). Ultimately, the existence and development of the *juku*-market fundamentally depend on the needs of families, which represent the *juku*'s customer base. Families' demand for supplementary education is dominated by rational decisions. Hence, families need to decide whether investments in shadow education are necessary in general and assess what kind of shadow education is best suited to achieve their educational goals. Increasing differences in the demand for shadow education should result in a higher functional differentiation of the *juku*-industry.

In fact, during the *juku*-boom era in the 1970s, not only the number of *juku* increased drastically in response to increasing, but for the most part unmet educational demands in the course of educational expansion, *juku* became highly specialized (Dierkes 2010: 26). Hence, besides the three general organizational types of *juku* according to size and administration (ōte juku (major corporations), chūshō juku (juku of small or medium size), and kojin juku (small owner-operated juku); see Chap. 2, p. 54, Nishimura 2009: 15–16, METI 2010: 6), numerous specializations were established until the 1990s. Based on existing research, the following six main types of *juku* can be identified:

Yobikō	Specialize on university entrance examination preparation targeting high school students and so-called *rōnin*, high school graduates preparing for university or college entrance exams without formal affiliation to a school. These schools are more often frequented by high achievers. High tuition fees and big classes characterize this type of school. The success of these schools is based on their success rate (*gōkakuritsu*), i.e., the percentage of their students which successfully enter prestigious universities (Mamoru Tsukada 1988, Mamoru Tsukada 1991, Drinck 2006: 344).
Shingaku juku	Specialize on the transition from one school level to the next. The main focus thus lies on entrance exam preparation, mostly for high school. These schools are more often frequented by high achievers. Relatively high tuition fees and big classes characterize this type of school. The success of these schools is based on their success rate (*gōkakuritsu*). In these regard, *shingaku juku* are similar to *yobikō* but concentrate their services on students preparing for primary, middle, and high school entrance (Fukaya 1977, Rohlen 1980: 210, Roesgaard 2006: 34–37).
Hoshū juku	Specialize on supplementation of school lessons and catching up. Thus supplementary tuition implying remedial purposes are supplied, wherefore these schools are open for different kinds of

lessons, which primarily relate to school contents. Students with primarily average achievement level among all grades use lessons at these schools to prepare and go over school lesson contents. In addition, students encountering certain difficulties in school or *ochikobore* (students which cannot follow the pace in class) enter these *juku*. Relatively affordable tuition fees, small classes, and tuition based on a pedagogical idea (*kyōiku rinen*) characterize these schools (Komiyama 1993: 85, Roesgaard 2006: 37–40).

Kyūsai juku[6]   Specialize on remedial tuition for students with low achievement level. At these less numerous "salvation" schools, one-on-one tutoring (*kobetsu shidō*) or tutoring in small groups is prevalent to provide individual support for children who cannot follow the school curriculum (*ochikobore*), have specific learning problems, or even dislike school. The principals of such schools generally follow a pedagogic principle/idea (*kyōiku rinen*) and do not aim to simply give remedial teaching for students who cannot keep up in class. Individual student's problems are in the focus with the aim to identify causes for school disorder problems such as truancy or school phobia (*futōkō*) and possibly cure them. Hence, relatively affordable tuition fees and one-on-one tutoring characterize this kind of *juku* (Yuki et al. 1987; Komiyama 1993: 80–91; Roesgaard 2006: 41–42).

Doriru juku   Count as one of the most successfully operating *juku*-types, even though not much has been reported about these schools. At first glance, the *doriru* (drill) *juku* would be classified as *hoshū juku*, but there are several significant differences – Most obvious is the size. One popular example is the *Kumon Kyōshitsu*, the world's largest *juku*-corporation with approximately 4 million enrolled students in 48 countries. The most characteristic feature of Kumon and other *doriru juku* is found in their specialization on practicing ("drilling") basic skills in single subjects, such as English and mathematics. These schools are further characterized by relatively affordable tuition fees, big classes, and sometimes pedagogical principles (Roesgaard 2006: 40–41).

Sōgō juku   Follow a "comprehensive" approach, meaning that this type of *juku* combines features of several types of *juku* and has more than one study focus. Consequently, these schools miss a specific study focus as found at other types of *juku*. However, these schools are a logical outcome of families' differentiated demands: Students which have certain problems in one or more subjects and at the same time wish or need to prepare for entrance examinations, for example, are in a position to combine both their goals

---

[6]Roesgaard (2006) refers to these *juku* as *kyōsai* ('mutual support') *juku*, which sounds as if students are in a position to help themselves; wherefore, the traditional term *kyūsai* is preferred here.

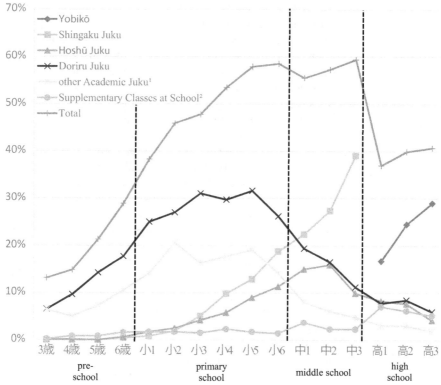

Abbreviations: 歳=years old; 小=primary school grade; 中=middle school grade; 高=high school grade.
[1] This category includes other *juku* without detailed description and *juku* focusing on the *soroban* (abacus),
calligraphy, computer skills and so on. Excluded are non-academic *juku* for arts, sports, music or cooking etc.
[2] This category consists of classes offered by schools after regular classes and at the weekends.

Valid responses: n(mothers)=15450

Fig. 8.1 Enrolment at different types of *juku*, according to age/grade, in %, 2013 (Benesse
Gakkōgaikyōikukatsudō ni kansuru Chōsa 2013, own calculation)

and achieve both. Relatively affordable tuition fees, big and small
classes, and sometimes pedagogical principles characterize these
schools (Komiyama 1993: 85–86).

In summary, *sōgō juku* provide the greatest range of supply in all general study
purposes and are possibly very attractive for students with several needs but still
have limitations of different sorts and may lack effectiveness or quality in one of the
fields compared to highly specialized *juku*-types, such as *yobikō* or *kyūsai juku*. This
general overview shows that what is believed to be known about the *juku*-industry
is mostly referring to *shingaku juku* and *yobikō*. This industry is often equated with
examination hell even though several *juku* without expensive preparatory lessons in
big classes focusing on entrance exams resulting in a highly competitive learning
atmosphere exist.

Empirical data concerning the distribution of students according to these *juku*-
types are scarce. Here only private corporations such as the Benesse Group carried

out surveys which provide us with additional data to close this gap (Fig. 8.1).[7] Accordingly, in 2013 particularly during primary school, most students enrolled at *doriru juku* (31.6% in 5th grade), since many students try to achieve basic learning strategies which may prove beneficial in their later school life. In addition, a high percentage of students was enrolled at other, nonspecified kinds of *juku* (20.6% in 2nd grade). *Shingaku* and *hoshū juku* were most frequently attended during middle school (*shingaku*, 46.2% in 9th grade; *hoshū*, 18.5% in 8th grade). During high school, a general decrease in *juku* attendance is obvious. Thus, following the first major transition in students' school life, *yobikō* become the major provider for shadow education lessons (29% in 12th grade). In addition, more students take the opportunity to join supplementary classes provided by their schools (3.1% in 10th grade).

The *juku*-industry's diversity reflects private operators' responses to changing educational premises and demands in postwar Japan. However, whereas the *juku*-boom era and its favorable conditions for *juku* lies long in the past, the question of how this industry managed to remain strong despite unfavorable conditions since the 1990s remains. The next section thus discusses recent educational developments in order to identify changes affecting the *juku*-industry since the end of the 1990s, before analyzing how *juku* actually have responded to these changes in part three.

8.2.3 Research Hypotheses: The Impact of Change on the Shadow Education Industry

The foregoing discussions can be summarized in one central question: Is the high diversity within the *juku*-industry the reason for this industry's continued success in spite of unfavorable developments, such as the continuously decreasing number of potential clients due to the low fertility rate and major changes in the national course of education? Following New Institutionalist Theory (NIT), the often overlooked but existing high diversity of the *juku*-industry and the decades of unbroken success support the argument that the Japanese shadow education system adapted to changing conditions and changing needs of its "customers" during the last wave of educational expansion over the last two decades. Hence, it seems reasonable to assume that the *juku*-industry is in no way rigid but flexible enough to recognize changes and respond to such changes thus managing to survive despite unfavorable circumstances. It is likely that this development has resulted in higher demands on the shadow to compensate for the perceived gap between expectations for students and actual provision of regular schools to meet these expectations. While the regular schooling system stagnates or even shrinks due to problems connected to the dilemma of the "ageing society" Japan, the second schooling system is still eager to

[7] My utmost gratitude for granting me access to the 2013 Benesse Gakkōgaikyōikukatsudō ni kansuru Chōsa ("Benesse survey on the expenses of out-of-school education") goes to Kimura Haruo and Mochida Seiko of the Benesse Educational Research and Development Institute. Also I would like to thank Prof. Emi Kataoka (Komazawa University) for her support and for introducing me to the representatives of this survey.

grow further. However, whether changes within this industry affect social inequalities in present Japan is difficult to assess. Based on the discussions, I argue that *juku*-operators have been expanding their range of supply and loosen access regulations recently, to ensure high enrolment ratios and attract more students despite decreasing student populations. In addition, *juku* were in need to adequately respond to international preferences as adapted in formal education, emphasizing individuality and creativity while promoting stronger competition. Based on these considerations, I formulate the following hypotheses:

[H1]   *Flexibility thesis:* To stay successfully in business, *juku* replace or expand their traditional specializations in favor of new specializations. Hence, new types of *juku* evolve.

[H2]   *Educational opportunity thesis:* Students which are affected by recent changes use shadow education as educational opportunity to increase their chances to achieve educational goals. Students from disadvantaged family backgrounds are more likely to gain access to *juku* that have expanded their supply and taken on more than one distinct study focus.

[H3]   *Adjustment thesis:* If considerable changes occur that affect education in general, the *juku*-industry adjusts its organization, programs, and regulations in response to these changes. This thesis can be specified into the following three sub-theses:

[H3–1] In response to *decreasing student populations*, *juku* place stronger emphasis on the individual student and his/her needs, thus expanding their range of supply and search for new potential client groups to keep their enrolment rates stable. To attract generally all potential clients, more opportunities for the participation of students with disadvantaged family backgrounds are created.

[H3–2] In response to the *reformation of the mainstream schooling system*, *juku*-operators identify and countermeasure shortcomings of the new education reform course through new programs.

[H3–3] In response to *changed demands of families* regarding the education of children, *juku*-operators place stronger emphasis on the individual student and his/her needs. As a consequence, teaching approaches and contents are adjusted and individual curricula for students are created.

8.3   Results: Diversity in Supply as Guarantor for Educational Opportunities?

To verify my research theses stated above, analyses are carried out with the aim to present new findings regarding *juku*-operators' responses to change in recent years and outcomes of these responses for social inequality formation in present Japan, lead on by a short introduction to data and methods. To obtain sound conclusions, I based my analyses on data from the *Juku Student and Teacher Survey* (JSTS) of the year 2013. Following a short introduction to the used variables and the methodical approach, three major analysis-strings follow in the results section: First, the *juku* of the JSTS sample will be classified based on characteristic indicators. Second, multinomial logistic regression analysis predicting students' likelihood to attend a certain *juku* is carried out. Finally, data of the JSTS teacher questionnaire survey and data from semi-structured interviews with the principals of the *juku* are analyzed using qualitative content analysis.

8.3.1   Data and Methods

To test my above-stated hypotheses and achieve convincing findings,[8] I choose a mixed-method approach, using a within-method triangulation model (Jick 1979: 602–611, Gürtler and Huber 2012). Hence, I base this chapter's calculations and evaluations on the *Juku Student and Teacher Survey* (JSTS) of 2013 instead of the earlier used HHSS surveys. I designed the JSTS to complement the existing data by targeting a different population: *jukusei*, students enrolled at private schools in the shadow education sector, as well as the operators of this industry, *jukuchō* (*juku* principals) and their teachers (*jukukōshi*). As introduced in Chap. 4, the JSTS includes quantitative data from two questionnaire surveys targeting students and teachers as well as qualitative data from open items of these two questionnaire surveys and additional interviews with the principals of the participating 20 *juku* schools.

In the following, first, the quantitative data of the student questionnaire survey and additional object characteristics are analyzed to classify the *juku* of my sample as a means to reveal whether classic *juku*-types still exist or not in regard to hypothesis [H1].

Second, the classification of *juku* will serve as dependent variable for a multinomial logistic regression analysis predicting students' likelihood to enter certain *juku*-types in accordance with hypothesis [H2]. This analysis focuses on the impact of parental educational background as a proxy for social origin and students' motives to pursue *juku*-lessons (including students' views on regular school instruction) as a proxy for unmet educational demands of families while also controlling for gender and school ranking variables (school ranking and type of administration). To reflect unmet demands (see Chap. 4, Fig. 4.11 and 4.12), individual support ("I can receive individual support from the *juku* teacher"), gap-closing ("I want to close gaps of knowledge"), teaching method ("the teachers teaching method is easy understandable"), learning environment ("the learning environment is better than in school"), non-regular contents ("things are taught beyond the school class level"), high ambitions ("I want to go to the best school possible hereafter"), help during class ("When I need help during class, the teacher helps me"), and instruction quality ("In general, class in school was not very good") will serve as explanatory variables in my upcoming analysis in part two of the results section.

---

[8] All data were translated from Japanese into English by the author.

Third, open questionnaire items of the teacher survey and semi-structured interviews of *jukukōshi* (including *jukuchō* and some staff members) are analyzed using qualitative content analysis to clarify how *juku* adjust to changing circumstances and whether more educational opportunities for students with disadvantaged family background are provided by certain *juku* in regard to hypothesis [H3]. Through the analysis of the quantitative part of the student and teacher data, conclusions regarding the state of the *juku* at the time of the data collection become possible, partly answering hypotheses [H1] and [H2]. However, only the additional analysis of qualitative data allows to further explore whether the found results of the quantitative data analysis are an actual outcome of recent changes or not. Hence, all three analysis-strings serve to achieve final conclusions.

8.3.2   Results of Analyses

8.3.2.1   A Typology of *Juku*

To carry out evidence-based analyses assessing whether *juku* have replaced or expanded existing specializations and thus new types of *juku* have evolved as assumed in hypothesis [H1], first measurable empirical indicators need to be identified to accurately empirically grasp the specifics of the introduced six main *juku*-types, before the *juku* of the JSTS sample will be classified according to these indicators. Hence, building on existing research and my own fieldwork, in the following characteristic indicators to classify *juku* according to their specialization are described and (re)arranged into strong empirical indicators and weak empirical indicators:

Strong empirical indicators are:

Scope of supply	In how many of the five major areas of study (Japanese, mathematics, science, social science, and English) are courses provided? Are there programs in other areas?
Focus of study	What is the main study specialization at this school? As stressed in an earlier work (Entrich 2014a: 94), the following five major study goals can be identified: (1) enrichment (focus on contents beyond school curriculum), (2) remedial (focus on catching up in school), (3) study skills (focus on basic and advanced study methods and learning strategies), (4) entrance exams (focus on high school or university entrance exam preparation), and (5) school exams (focus on school exam preparation).
Target group	Students of which grade and academic achievement level are primarily targeted?
Teaching approach	What kind of instruction style (class or individual instruction) is carried out at this school?

Relation to school	Do the attended courses follow regular schools' curricula or their own goals?
Tuition fees	How high is the relative level of investment costs to participate in programs at this school?
Advertising	What strategy is pursued to attract clients through advertisement?

Weak empirical indicators are:

Atmosphere	What kind of learning atmosphere is prevalent at this school?
Size	How many branches, teachers, and clients has this company have in total?
Teaching materials	Is studying based on regular schools' textbooks, commercial materials, or homemade materials?
Admission	Do students need to pass entrance exams to access this school or are all potential clients welcome?
Location	Where is this school (and its branches) located?

According to these indicators, based on a literature analysis including numerous sources (Kondō et al. 1963; Fukaya 1977; Rohlen 1980; Yuki et al. 1987; Mamoru Tsukada 1988; Mamoru Tsukada 1991; Komiyama 1993; Russell 1997; Zeng 1999; Komiyama 2000; Iwase 2005, 2006; Roesgaard 2006; Iwase 2007; Mimizuka 2007; Mizushima 2007; R. Watanabe 2007a, b; Iwase 2008; METI 2010; M. Watanabe 2013; Entrich 2014; Ota 2014), Table 8.1 shows a final *juku*-typology, consisting of six ideal types.

To test hypothesis [H1], the different *juku* of my sample will be classified on the basis of the described strong empirical indicators and compared to the original classification as given by the operators. Through this procedure, the actual specializations of *juku* in present Japan can be captured, before the later carried-out qualitative content analyses will show whether the found classification of *juku* is an outcome of recent developments or an unobserved error, meaning that these *juku* have given out wrong self-assessments regarding their classification and actually no change in their specialization has occurred.

Based on the analysis of JSTS data and the evaluation of additional object characteristics (for a detailed description of the data analysis building the foundation of the displayed results, see Appendix), a final classification of the sampled *juku* is presented in Table 8.2. According to my analyses, no *juku* of my sample perfectly matches all the requirements to be unambiguously classified as one of the six main *juku*-types. The characteristic features of the *juku* described in Table 8.1 describe ideal types of course.

This analysis shows that especially *kojin/chūshō juku* cannot afford to specialize on only one or two study foci but supply a wide range of courses to cover all possible needs of students. Therefore, students at all these *juku* can generally benefit from a combination of school-related, remedial programs and at the same time prepare for upcoming examinations. With the exception of JukuH, all *juku* offer lessons for students from more than one school type and across several age groups (at least 4 years coverage), while an academically highly heterogeneous student body with

Table 8.1 A typology of *juku*

Juku-types				Yobikō	Shingaku	Hoshū	Kyōsai	Doriru	Sōgō
Strong empirical indicators	Scope of supply			5	5	5	>5	1–2	5
	Focus of courses		Enrichment		x	x			x
			Remedial			x	x		x
			Study skills			x	x	x	x
			Entrance exams	x	x				x
			School exams		(x)	x			x
	Target group	School level	Primary school		x	x	x	x	x
			Middle school		x	x	x	x	x
			High school	x		(x)	x		x
		Academic performance	High	x	x			x	x
			Average		x	x		x	x
			Low				x	x	x
	Teaching approach		One on one				x		
			Small groups			x	x	x	x
			Big groups	x	x	x		x	x
			Video lessons	x					
	Relation to school		Strong			x			
			Little				x		x
			None	x	x			x	
	Tuition fees		High	x	x		x		x
			Mediocre		x	x		x	x
			Low		x	x		x	x
	Advertising		Commercial	x	x			x	x
			Success rate	x	x				x
			Pedagogy			x	x	(x)	x
			Word of mouth			x	x	x	x

Weak empirical indicators									
Atmosphere		Competitive	x	x			x			x
		Stimulating	x	x			x			x
		Supportive			x	x		x		
		Relaxing			x				x	
		Nurturing				x				
Size	Number of branches	>50	x	x			x		x	x
		Up to 50	x	x			x		x	x
		1		x	x		x			x
	Number of teachers	>50	x	x			x		x	x
		>10–50		x	x					x
		Up to 10		x	x	x	x		x	x
	Number of students	>1000	x	x			x		x	x
		>200–1000	x	x			x			x
		<200			x			x	x	
Teaching materials		Own texts	x	x			x		x	x
		Commercial	x	x	x	x	x		x	x
		School texts			x	x	x			x
Admission		Entrance exams	x	x		x	x			(x)
		Physical limits	x	x	x	x	x			x
		No limits	x						x	
Location		Urban	x	x	x	x	x		x	x
		Rural			x		x			x

x = applicable/existing; (x) partly applicable/existing

Table 8.2 Classification of the JSTS *juku*-sample on the basis of strong empirical indicators (JSTS 2013 Student, Teacher and interview data; object characteristics)

		Kojin/chūshō juku					Ōte juku		
		JukuA	JukuB	JukuC	JukuD	JukuE	JukuF	JukuG	JukuH
Scope of supply		5	5	5	5	>5	>5	>5	>5
Focus of courses	Enrichment	x	x	x	x	(x)	x	x	(x)
	Remedial	(x)	x	x	x	x	(x)	x	(x)
	Study skills	x	x	x	x	x	x	x	x
	Entrance exams	x	x	(x)	x	x	x	x	x
	School tests	x	x	x	x	(x)	(x)	x	
Target group	Grade	6–9	6–9	5–9	1–9	1–12	1–9	1–12	10–12
	High performer	x	x	x	x		x	x	x
	Average performer	x	x	x	x	x	x	x	
	Low performer		x	x	x	x		x	
Teaching approach	One on one			x	x	x	x	x	x
	Small groups					(x)	x		
	Big groups	x	x	x	x		x		
	Video lessons								x
Relation to school	Strong	x		x	x				
	Weak		x			x	x	x	x
	None								

Tuition fees	High	x	x		x	x	x	x
	Middle		x	(x)	(x)	x	x	
	Low			x	x	x	x	
Advertising	Commercial					x	x	x
	Success rate	x			x	x		x
	Pedagogy		x	x	x	x	x	
	Word of mouth	x	x	x	x		x	
Official classification according to operator		*Shingaku*	*Doriru*	*Sōgō*	*Hoshū*	*Shingaku*	*Shingaku*	*Yobikō*
Actual classification according to supply		*Sōgō*	*Sōgō*	*Sōgō*	*Sōgō*	*Kobetsu shidō sōgō*	*Shingaku Kobetsu shidō sōgō*	*Yobikō*

x = applicable/existing; (x) partly applicable/existing

For the computation of the strong empirical indicators, see Appendix high- and low-performing pupils is found. The majority of *juku* (five of eight) also offer individual tutoring (*kobetsu shidō*), wherefore classic teacher-centered teaching in large classes (*shudan shidō*) does not seem to play a major role anymore. At all *juku*, a more or less strong connection to the school curricula is found due to the wide range of supply. Even at JukuH, such a connection exists, even though this school is run as a *yobikō*. The level of tuition fees and the type of advertising still varies considerably between the schools. Small- and medium-sized *juku* basically have affordable tuition fees and acquire its student body largely through word of mouth. *Ōte juku* seem to generally charge higher tuition fees, even though some programs at JukuF and JukuG are found with low tuition as well. Chain *juku* generally rely on commercial advertising, often based on their success rate. In addition, nowadays also pedagogical ideas are highlighted (e.g., JukuF and JukuG). In summary, only small differences between organization and supply is found. This might be the result of increasing demands of students and the need of small *juku* to attract a larger proportion of potential clients while being limited in resources to meet students' demands. *Kojin* and *chūshō juku* generally consist of only one or maybe two schools and are limited to one specific area, have limited space, can only afford to hire a limited number of teachers, and thus need to expand their range of supply according to changing educational demands. In contrast, the *ōte juku* of my sample have no such physical and personnel limitations and show higher specialization. Here a clear advantage of chain *juku* becomes visible: promotion of most kinds of teaching approaches on a large scale. This is why only JukuF (*shingaku juku*) and JukuH (*yobikō*) are not classified as *sōgō juku*.

However, the *sōgō juku* of my sample show distinct features that deserve further attention. Whereas JukuA/B/D limit their instruction modes to group lessons (*shūdan shidō*), based on pedagogical ideas and a child-centered approach, JukuE and JukuG specialized on one-on-one tutoring (*kobetsu shidō*). In this regard, both *juku* share several features of *hoshū*, *shingaku*, and *kyūsai juku* without being limited to these features. Following a comprehensive approach, a wide range of courses in all main subject areas for students from 1st to 12th grade is provided. In conclusion, most modern *juku* seem to have expanded their range of supply as predicted by hypothesis [H1]. This development is accompanied by a stronger focus on individualization of services, which supports the national education strategy corresponding to globalization. Especially among *kojin/chūshō juku*, a new type seems to have emerged, the *kobetsu-shidō-sōgō juku*.

To evaluate whether this identified trend development in the *juku*-industry is a response to recent changes, in the following *juku*-operators' statements regarding the change of their institutions are analyzed.

8.3.2.2   Decision for a Certain Type of *Juku*

To test hypothesis [H2], multinomial logistic regression analysis is carried out to predict the impact of family background, schooling background, and students' perception toward school lessons as a proxy for unmet educational demands on the likelihood to enter *juku* of different specialization (Table 8.3). According to the findings presented in Table 8.2, the JSTS sample of *juku* can be subcategorized into four types of *juku*, ranging from highly restricted access (high tuition fees, high academic performer, i.e., entrance exams) to low restricted access (low tuition fees, low academic performer, i.e., no entrance exams) resulting in the following coding of the dependent variable: *yobikō* (1), *shingaku juku* (2), *kobetsu-shidō-sōgō juku* (3), and general *sōgō juku* (4). Again, Average Marginal Effects (AME) are displayed to make comparisons across these four groups possible. Depicted are the likelihoods to enter a certain *juku* (e.g., *yobikō*) in reference to entering any other type of *juku* (e.g., *shingaku, kobetsu-shidō-sōgō, or sōgō juku*).

Model 1 is a basic model measuring the general impact of gender, parents' highest education level, and school ranking on the participation in lessons at the different *juku*. According to my calculations, no gender differences are detected. Students from advantaged family backgrounds (at least one of both parents holds a university degree) are significantly more likely to enter *yobikō* (+19%) and *shingaku juku* (+12%), whereas students whose parents possess no tertiary education degrees are much more likely to enter general *sōgō juku*. In addition, the reputation of a school exerts a major impact on the likelihood to choose *yobikō* over *sōgō juku*. The probability to enter *yobikō* is also particularly increased for students from private schools (+38%), whereas students who attend public schools are more likely to enter *shingaku* or *sōgō juku* (+17% and +22%, respectively). Since only high school students attend *yobikō*, whereas the majority of middle school students attend *shingaku juku*, these differences result from a generally lower quality level of private schools at the high school level on the one hand and a higher quality level of private middle schools on the other hand. As for *kobetsu shidō sōgō juku*, the probability to enter does not significantly vary from the other types of *juku*. Neither family background nor school ranking determine access to these schools.

In Model 2, further covariates are included to measure the influence of unmet demands of students on the likelihood to enter different *juku*. In particular, students who are in need of individual support (+6%), have high ambitions (+9%), and rate the quality of regular schools' instruction as generally bad (+19%) have a higher likelihood to attend *yobikō*. This strong impact of the perceived insufficient instruction at regular school on the enrolment probability at *yobikō* should not be misinterpreted as to say that school instruction is generally bad and *yobikō* would provide better instruction than regular schools. The made statements clearly refer to students' need to be adequately prepared for university entrance exams – and in this field, *yobikō* seem to provide much better services than regular schools and comprehensive *juku*. The latter have no such primary focus but specialize in several fields. Therefore, students who demand better teaching methods (+9%), non-regular contents (+5%), and help during class (+7%) are more likely to enter *sōgō juku*. For

Table 8.3 Multinomial logistic regression analyses predicting students' likelihood to enter highly specialized in comparison to comprehensive *juku*, displaying AME (JSTS 2013, Student Survey)

		Specialized *juku*				Comprehensive *juku*			
		Yobikō		*Shingaku juku*		*Kobetsu shidō sōgō juku*		*Sōgō juku*	
		Ref: all respective other *juku*							
		Model 1	Model 2	Model 1	Model 2	Model 1	Model 2	Model 1	Model 2
Social origin	Gender								
	Male	0.01	0.04	−0.04	−0.03	0.01	0.00	0.02	−0.01
	Parents' highest education level								
	Graduate school	0.15	0.11	0.12	0.08	−0.04	−0.08	−0.22*	−0.11
	University	0.19**	0.15*	0.12**	0.05	0.00	−0.03	−0.32***	−0.17**
	College	0.20*	0.18*	−0.02	−0.07	−0.02	−0.04	−0.15+	−0.07
	Ref: no tertiary education								
School ranking	School reputation								
	High	0.33***	0.30***	−0.06	−0.08	−0.05	−0.08	−0.21**	−0.14*
	Average	0.27***	0.25***	−0.05	−0.06	−0.04	−0.07	−0.18**	−0.12*
	Ref: Low reputation								
	School administration								
	Public	−0.38***	−0.35***	0.17***	0.16***	−0.01	0.00	0.22***	0.19***
	Ref: Private school								

Unmet demands					
Motives	Individual support	0.06**	0.02	0.02+	-0.10***
	Gap-closing	-0.01	-0.02	0.01	0.02
	Teaching method	-0.06*	-0.03	-0.00	0.09***
	Learning environment	0.02	0.10***	-0.03	0.01
	Non-regular contents	-0.16***	0.08**	0.01	0.05**
	High ambitions	0.09**	-0.03	-0.04**	-0.02
General view on school instruction	Help during class	-0.02	-0.02	-0.03	0.07*
	Instruction quality	0.19***	0.06	0.03	-0.28***
	Ref: no				
N (valid cases)	432				
Model significance (chi²-test)		***	***	***	***
Pseudo R^2 (McFadden)		0.12	0.30	0.12	0.30

$***P < 0.001; **P < 0.01; *P < 0.05; +P < 0.10$

students to attend *shingaku juku*, particularly the learning environment is deemed better than in regular school, wherefore the likelihood to enter increases by 10%. Also, contents outside the school curriculum are another major factor that impacts whether students enter *shingaku juku* (+8%). In contrast, students who enter *kobetsu shidō sōgō juku* generally show no significant differences in their demands, except being partly more likely to wish for individual support (+2%) or are a little less ambitious (−4%).

Regarding the *educational opportunity thesis* [H2], students seem affected by recent changes and use shadow education as educational opportunity to increase their chances to achieve educational goals in accordance with earlier findings (see Chap. 6). This analysis additionally showed that students from disadvantaged family backgrounds are more likely to gain access to *juku* that have expanded their supply and taken on more than one distinct study focus, i.e., *kobetsu shidō sōgō juku* and *sōgō juku*. Such *juku* seem to employ more educational opportunities for their students.

8.3.2.3 *Juku*-Operators' Responses to Change

To test hypothesis [H3] and thus identify how *juku* have responded and will continue to respond to recent changes in the regular schooling system, the problem of decreasing student populations, and changing educational demands of families, I will draw on interview data and open items of the teacher questionnaire survey. In the latter, the following items were included to get first-hand information on how representatives of *juku* explain changes and general success of their schools:

- Q17: "Since you have started working at this juku, have you watched changes concerning the teaching methods toward students and the organization of classes (e.g., timetable, the reflection of students' needs, etc.)?"
- Q18: "Concerning the teaching methods toward students and the organization of classes (e.g., timetable, the reflection of students' needs, etc.), do you think changes will occur in the future?"
- Q19: "What are the aspects that make this juku most successful?"
- Q10: "Do you have a system at this juku that allows economically disadvantaged students to attend also?"

These items were analyzed using qualitative content analysis prioritizing the data according to significance of the *juku* respondent's position at the different *juku* from high (*jukuchō*) to low (staff member). In this way, the following main response categories were identified according to salience: (1) individualization, (2) expansion of supply, (3) access, (4) autonomy, (5) care, and (6) guidance. In the following, I will separately explore the contents of these six response categories by discussing *juku*-operators' responses to recent and ongoing changes in an exemplary way.

Individualization

In response to decreasing student populations, educational reforms, and changed educational demands of families, all *juku* of my sample emphasize an increased focus on individualization in several regards as suspected in hypotheses [H3-1], [H3-2], and [H3-3]. First of all, most *juku* of my sample recently changed the size of their classes "from big groups (about 30 students) to smaller groups (about 15)" (*jukuchō* 1006, JukuB, Q17). Some *juku* have even undergone extreme transformations over the past 20 years, such as the following:

> From lecturing classes to asking questions; from condescending lecturer-student relationships to a more eye-to-eye understanding; from big groups to small group class rooms; from a common curriculum and common progress to common menus and differentiated progress; from only public primary, middle and high school students to 50% private primary, middle and high school students.(*jukuchō* 1023, JukuE, Q17)

At JukuE, *kobetsu shidō* with not more than five students per group is now practiced exclusively. Teachers at this *juku* explain that individual instruction became a necessity, because the differences in students' academic achievement level have increased and so "the differences of all students' learning progress increased. To hold classes in groups became difficult" (*jukukōshi* 1022, JukuE, Q17). However, the individual teaching approach holds several implications for the teachers, who report that the curriculum has become highly individualized, and even though it is much easier to lecture only one or two students at a time compared to group lecturing, each lesson needs throughout preparation to support and challenge each individual student according to his needs (*jukukōshi* 1020, JukuE, interview September 2014).

The other small *juku* of my sample did not abandon class instruction, but nevertheless report that they feel an increasing demand for individual support. At JukuA the teaching approach has not changed. No individual lectures are provided and lessons are still only given in big groups. However, this former *shingaku juku* has expanded its curriculum and is now called *sōgō-shingaku juku*. According to the head and founder of this school, a strong focus on *shingaku* (transition to high school) is still given, but the range of class content and study goals were expanded to meet individual needs of the *jukusei* (*jukuchō* 1005, JukuA, interview June 2014). Meeting students' individual needs is understood as serving the main goal of placing students in prestigious high schools and staying successfully in business.

As for the *ōte juku*, JukuG was specially designed to meet individual needs of students and carries out *kobetsu shidō* exclusively. At this *juku*, at no time more than two students are supervised by one teacher. Teachers describe their approach as follows:

> Towards students we extensively ask questions such as 'What question did you not understand?', 'With which task or text do you want to proceed?', 'Inside and outside the study content, are there other things you want to ask?' in order to elicit thoughts (kotoba) out of the students. (*jukukōshi* 1078, JukuG, Q17)

At the *shingaku*-oriented JukuF, "the tendency towards individual correspondence has (also) become stronger" (staff 1052, JukuF, Q17). Besides implementing one-on-one tutoring, the teachers "also try to firmly see that each individual is cherished" (staff 1042, JukuF, Q17) during class sessions. A long-serving teacher shortly summarizes his experiences as follows:

> The importance to keep attention to some individuals has increased. I have the impression that the overall academic achievement level has decreased – just a little though. (*jukukōshi* 1063, JukuF, Q17)

The increased need for individual support and guidance is viewed as a result of the perceived decline in students' academic achievement level as a publicly feared outcome of the *yutori* reforms. JukuF reacted to this decline in achievement level by "increasing the number of tests" (*jukukōshi* 1085, JukuF, Q17) to grasp students' ability accurately and give feedback accordingly. In addition, classes were subdivided into A (tests are in the center of lessons) and B lessons (lectures are in the center). In these lessons, "for students with low ability level, we slowly proceed in the decided fields, and when their ability has improved, we deepen (the students' knowledge) in a wide range of fields" (*jukukōshi* 1036, JukuF, Q17). Also, the teaching approach within these lessons changed from "traditional" didactic teaching to classes where carrying out a distinct teaching method is central.

The promotion of individuality and creativity as major parts of the government's internationalization policy results in the deviation from classic specializations of *juku*-courses to respond to individual demands. The CEO of the parent company of JukuF and JukuG views this ongoing change as a positive development for Japanese education in general. According to this chairman, against the background of changing working conditions and increasing insecurity (see Chap. 7), parents nowadays are questioning the purpose of students' relentless cramming in particular. Once entrance to university is achieved, students often miss perspectives for their future, since they did not have the time to think about what they want to do with their life after having achieved this major step. Individual premises are not considered. Due to increasing internationalization, the rigidity of the school system is slowly crumbling. In addition, the fundamental achievement principle seems to become less important resulting in a greater openness of education and increasing educational opportunities. This CEO believes that *juku* will continue to make great contributions achieving this national goal (CEO JukuF/G, interview March 2013). According to my data, the general trend toward individualization will be continued. Most operators are eager to improve and expand individual tutoring programs. At *juku* where large class instruction is still prevalent such as JukuC, the size of classes will be reduced soon. Of the *ōte juku* of my sample, JukuF and JukuH report plans for a further subdivision of classes to better meet students' individual needs and support students with low academic achievement levels.

Expansion of Supply

As suspected in hypothesis [H3-1], due to decreasing student populations, *juku* expand their range of supply and search for new potential client groups to keep their enrolment rates stable to stay in business. Most small *juku* do not carry out advertisement but recruit new *jukusei* through word of mouth only. New clients are won based on parents' and students' satisfaction with received services. In contrast, big chain *juku* also produce commercial advertisement highlighting their success in placing students into prestigious high schools and universities (JukuF and JukuH) or promoting certain pedagogy (JukuG). Since these companies are partly very long in the business (more than 50 years), they often benefit from "a firm trust in the long history of the juku" (jukukōshi 1066, JukuF, Q19). In the case of JukuF and JukuG, which belong to the same parent company, over the years, the range of supply was extensively expanded and a "lifelong client concept" was developed:

> Besides educational coaching, we are able to provide services to meet needs across various ages and lesson styles such as the dream realization program, group lessons, individual instruction, early childhood education and yobikō. (*jukukōshi* 1050, JukuF, Q19)

By "uniformizing" "the educational 'line-up' from early childhood to adulthood" (*jukukōshi* 1057, JukuF, Q19), this company aims to keep students enrolled as long as possible. In the same way, smaller *juku* are eager to bind their students and emphasize "long-term learning, [through which] learning habits are developed" (*jukuchō* 1001, JukuA, Q19). However, the decrease in student populations is not without consequences. The head of JukuE explained that it has become increasingly difficult to stay in business for small *juku* due to chains such as JukuG (*jukuchō* 1023, JukuE, interview March 2013). Changes toward individual tutoring are also an outcome of increased competition between *juku*, which search for new ways to expand their supply. To further guarantee future success, JukuE has the following plans:

> The one-on-one instruction for private primary, middle and high school students will increase. In addition, practical English such as English conversations will be introduced. Also, we will enhance the science and social science courses to create a combined five subject course for the metropolitan high school exam. (*jukuchō* 1023, JukuE, Q18)

Juku search for ways to improve their English lessons to meet students' increased demands in this subject due to the national reform of English instruction as key toward stronger internationalization of Japanese education. To improve English language education, *juku*-operators across the country organize conferences and networks to discuss how they will proceed and profit from reforms of the regular schooling system.[9] In addition, at JukuD the supply will be further expanded to support students in their nonacademic activities, such as *bukatsudō* (Cave 2004). In general, the technicalization of class instruction will be further promoted by including new media such as electronic blackboards and tablets. Also, new clients shall be acquired by targeting students from combined public schools (6-year secondary school type) and by entering "different business sectors" (*jukukōshi* 1081, JukuF, Q18).

---

[9] *Juku* organize and take part in conferences such as the 2014 "Make the best of the English education reform by acquiring jukusei!" (*Eigo kyōiku kaikaku o jukusei kakutoku ni ikasu!*) conference.

Access

Besides the expansion of supply, access regulations for students from disadvantaged family background were loosened as suspected in hypothesis [H3-1]. Students across all social strata are targeted. JukuF shortened the time for one class period from 50 to 45 minutes and reduced the number of class periods with "the intention to reduce the financial burden" (*jukuchō* 1084, JukuF, Q17). In summary, "due to the decrease in the difficulty level of tasks in entrance examinations and the decreased competition rate, the time for classes and the apparent tuition fees went down" (*jukukōshi* 1054, JukuF, Q17). This reduction of tuition and test fees was explained as a direct outcome of changing demands of students and parents in accordance with hypothesis [H3-3]. Families are now able to compile their own *juku* timetable and thus decide on tuition fees individually. In addition to such formal changes, most *ōte juku* created some kind of discount or scholarship system to attract bright students who possess less financial resources. At JukuF, the following system exists:

> We have a tuition fee reduction and exemption system. This is a system that halves the tuition fee for students if several conditions are met, such as performance, economic background, the classroom head's recommendation etc. (*jukukōshi* 1067, JukuF, Q10)

In a similar way, JukuH offers a scholarship system for bright students, where "up to two courses (2x73500yen) are provided for free" (*jukuchō* 1016, JukuG, Q10). Students with a certain academic level are thus enabled to receive lessons free of charge for 2 months. In response to the 2011 disaster,[10] JukuF also created a discount for victims of natural disaster. *Kojin* and most *chūshō juku* generally cannot afford to offer such scholarships, but have nevertheless reacted to decreasing student populations and other changes by introducing discounts for siblings or self-study sessions. In the future, further possibilities for students with disadvantaged family background to attend *juku* shall be created:

> Given that students who are not blessed economically cannot attend, I think that it will be of central concern to meet the needs of the disadvantaged ten percent of students and parents instead of only letting a wide range of children participate together. (*jukukōshi* 1066, JukuF, Q18)

Autonomy

In accordance with hypothesis [H3-3], in addition to individual tutoring, the operators of several *juku* "started to realize the importance of self-study and therefore the self-study rooms have been improved significantly" (*jukukōshi* 1075, JukuG, Q17). The use of self-study rooms, "where students can raise their voice and receive instruction by a teacher while studying there" (*jukukōshi* 1073, JukuG, Q10), is

---

[10] I am referring to the earthquake and tsunami that struck Japan on March 11, 2011, and the following Fukushima Daiichi nuclear power plant disaster.

often comparably cheap or even free of charge, and so it is easier for students with disadvantaged background to attend a *juku* and benefit from professional care. Self-study sessions have become a regular feature at most *juku* and serve to nurture students' ability to autonomously study to achieve their study goals and evaluate their learning progress. In particular regarding homework, a self-study habit, autonomy and self-reliance are intended to be nurtured. At JukuA, students are obliged to use these rooms every day to become self-reliant, disciplined, and diligent students, who will proceed studying autonomously to accomplish their goals even after leaving the *juku*.

Members of the *yobikō* chain JukuH generally put strong emphasis on students' autonomy when studying. In this regard, the advantages of video lessons were highlighted, which are carried out extensively. Not only are these lessons viewed as very accurate; across the whole nation, "students can receive the same class over and over again" (*jukuchō* 1015, JukuH, Q19). Teachers let students work individually and "putting effort into studying is made into a habit. Accordingly, by "'making students study', it becomes probable that students 'put effort into studying due to their own intentions'" (*jukuchō* 1016, JukuH, Q19). In the same way, smaller *juku* emphasize the importance to encourage students to study autonomously to prevent the exertion of "excessive pressure on students" (*jukukōshi* 1021, JukuE, Q19).

Care

Somewhat in line with hypothesis [H3-2] and [H3-3], *juku*-operators try to counteract shortcomings of the regular schooling system in several regards. Hence, most *juku* students have the chance to have a say in the learning environment and study atmosphere. In particular at *kojin/chūshō juku*, operators find it important to create an "at home" atmosphere to make carefree learning possible. Teachers try to create a "sense of intimacy" in the relationship with their students, based on trust. This also applies for the *kobetsu shidō* chain JukuG, where one teacher explains how important a deep relationship with the students might prove for a school's success:

> We try to handle the distance between teachers and students. We are not only teachers, but persons for sorrow consultation, and because teachers function as someone whom students talk to, the relationship between teachers and students is deep. Consequently, for the student it is hard to quit. (*jukukōshi* 1075, JukuG, Q19)

At JukuF, one member of the administrative staff additionally pointed out, that "the juku is not only a place where instruction is received; it is also possible to listen and talk about the things which are not discussed with the guardians" (staff 1052, JukuF, Q19). According to the operators, their role as caretakers ensured long-lasting success of the chain. Many *juku* not only interpret their ongoing success and attractiveness as a result of their academic programs, but their role as caretakers by listening to students' concerns and problems. In this regard, JukuC finds it important that "even while adapting to the trend of times by using IT, the guidance of the heart (kokoro) is not neglected" (*jukukōshi* 1027, JukuC, Q19). JukuD emphasizes the importance to also take "good care outside instruction time" (*jukuchō* 1007, JukuD,

Q19) resulting in a large amount of additional time spent for "exercises and club activities etc. (and) the time when homework for school is done" (*jukuchō* 1007, JukuD, Q17).

Guidance

Even though JukuF is counted as *shingaku juku*, teachers admit that "it is not only about passing exams; study focusing on something beyond that point is carried out" (*jukukōshi* 1061, JukuF, Q19). Students are professionally supervised and guided by coaches who help them to identify their own study goals and work out strategies to achieve these goals. This "educational coaching" takes on regular schools' *shinro shidō* (placement counseling) function, where teachers strive to place all students in suitable schools by "constructing" their students' aspirations (LeTendre 1996). To support this program, teachers now have to ask themselves how they can "capture students' consciousness regarding their goals" (*jukukōshi* 1040, JukuF, Q17). *Juku*-operators take on the role of guidance counselors in order to help students achieve their goals. In accordance with hypothesis [H3-2], at the *yobikō*, JukuH teachers realized that by "attending the same class not everybody's achievement is improving" and thus "curriculum guidance to suit each individual student became necessary" (*jukuchō* 1015, JukuH, Q17). Hence, this school makes it its duty to prepare students for university entrance exams while paying attention to their school related responsibilities:

> We carry out instruction that directs the eye on school. If students who are still enrolled in high school while preparing for university entrance exams want to achieve their goal, it is severe to let them study only during their time at the yobikō. In order to still make an effort while attending school, we conduct events such as regular routine tests and study sessions and manage the integrated study time at school and the decline of academic achievement. (*jukuchō* 1016, JukuH, Q17)

This statement partly explains the discovered diversity of courses at this *juku* as shown in Table 8.2. Even though the difficulty level of university entrance examination exams has partly decreased, *yobikō* feel the need to counteract the apparent academic decline as caused by the curriculum reduction in regular schools and support students in their studies instead of just preparing them for exams. JukuH also intends to "manage" the integrated study time at school (*sōgōtekina gakushū no jikan*) as one prominent feature of the *yutori* reforms. Students are advised to use their integrated study period at school to make effort for exam preparation.

8.4 Discussion

Finally, the findings and implications of the presented analyses are summarized and discussed with respect to my formulated research theses.

Concerning [H1], the *flexibility thesis*: To stay successfully in business, *juku* replace or expand their traditional specializations in favor of new specializations. Hence, new types of *juku* evolve. As a result, the structural composition of the *juku*-

industry changed. *Sōgō juku* have become the prevalent type, in particular among small- and middle-sized *juku*, since a high specialization on only one or two distinct study goals has become unprofitable. Only large corporations possess the resources to still run schools with a distinct specialization, such as *shingaku*, for example. At these *ōte juku*, students are distributed to schools of different specialization according to their study goals. As a result of stronger individualization in this field, *kobetsu shidō*-oriented *sōgō juku* have emerged as a new type.

Concerning [H2], the *educational opportunity thesis*: For a high proportion of students, a major reason to enter *juku* are unmet educational demands. If the regular schooling system lacks quality or misses to address certain issues adequately due to recent changes, *juku*-lessons are viewed as an educational opportunity to achieve educational goals. In this regard, *juku* which follow a comprehensive approach seem best suited to serve students with several needs, whereas *juku* with higher specialization promise remedy for students which pursue certain goals. In addition, if formerly highly specialized *juku* have expanded their supply and taken on more than one distinct study focus, students from disadvantaged family backgrounds will be more likely to gain access to such *juku*. However, at the higher specialized *juku* which generally charge higher tuition fees, in order to maintain a high reputation based on students' success rate, a reduction of tuition fees or scholarships become possible for students from disadvantaged family backgrounds showing high academic performance. In summary, to attract generally all potential clients, more opportunities for the participation of students with disadvantaged family backgrounds are created. In present Japan, social inequalities are likely to be reduced under the condition that disadvantaged educational strata make use of educational opportunities inside and outside of school. One major predictor for such investments is high ambitions (see also Chaps. 5 and 7).

Concerning [H3], the *adjustment thesis* [H3-1] proved correct: the analyses show that the dependence on shadow education in Japan is not likely to vanish as a result of decreasing student populations. Even though the decreasing pool of potential clients represents a natural enemy to this private for-profit education industry, *juku* remained successful by increasing their bandwidth of supply and by targeting new client groups. In particular, large corporations constantly search for new niches where they can expand. To further attract new students, access regulations were loosened to enable economically disadvantaged students to participate through discounts or scholarships and self-study sessions. [H3-2] proved correct also: the reformation of the mainstream schooling system originally meant to counteract the major reasons for intense participation in shadow education in Japan, the *kyōiku kyōsō* and *shiken jigoku*. But, not only did these reforms partly fail to reduce the pressure and workload of students, due to the new education course toward stronger internationalization, new educational premises exist. Thus, subject contents (most prominent: English education) and teaching approaches are content of constant improvement. Independent of the size of *juku*, most schools also emphasize the increased importance to function as guidance counselors and caretakers/sorrow consultants. *Juku* take on functions of family and school which are of essence but no longer valued enough or carried out by these social institutions. Accordingly, by managing students' school life in a certain way and by changing the curriculum to meet students' changed demands, *juku* also countermeasure shortcomings of the new education reform course. [H3-3] proved correct as well: In response to changed demands of families regarding the education of children, *juku*-operators place stronger emphasis on the individual student and his/her needs. New individual demands to acquire competencies and creativity of students have led to the adjustment of teaching approaches and contents as well as create individual curricula for students. As a major consequence of increased individual demands, individual tutoring has become a frequent mode of instruction at most *juku*. Thus, in the future, it is likely that *kobetsu shidō* emphasizing *sōgō juku* will dominate the market.

In conclusion, this study expands our knowledge about *juku* as follows. The recent development of *juku* follows three trends: First, the structural composition of the *juku*-market changes. Second, the *juku*-curriculum becomes individually customized. Third, more educational opportunities for students of all social strata are created to keep enrolment rates stable. These trends favor students which pursue individual educational goals outside the classic spectrum of standardized entrance examination preparation or mere repetition of school lesson contents – including students from disadvantaged family backgrounds. The carried-out analyses show that the *juku*-industry is a highly diverse education market that has undergone major transformations since the 1990s and does not only function as general gap-closer in education anymore – it "goes beyond shadowing the formal system" (Dawson 2010: 17). The prevalent picture of *juku* as cram schools with stressed-out students sitting in large classes proves antiquated. *Juku* nowadays emphasize all sorts of teaching methods and learning environments. A wide range of educational opportunities for students across all social strata is provided. Shadow education in Japan has thus the potential to function as an instrument to neutralize disadvantaged family background.

In summary, the ongoing success and persistence of this industry has two major reasons:

1. Flexibility: *Juku* are in a position to identify and promptly respond to emerging educational demands and mismatches and thus fill all gaps in the formal schooling system. Besides functioning as gap-closer for academic support, *juku* increasingly take on functions outside their original purview such as care, counseling, and guidance and thus achieve many of the *yutori* education goals that regular schools struggle to accomplish. The created gap between demand on students and support in schools and at home is filled by *juku*. These schools thus help students to live up to increased societal expectations.
2. Indispensability: *Juku* have gained importance for students and families to achieve individual educational goals and contribute to achieving national education goals by supporting the internationalization of Japanese education. Besides having understood the importance to develop strategies promoting competency development of students outside the traditional purview of Japanese education, *juku* further expand their power in the education system and the lives of students of all ages ("lifelong-client concept") and all social classes. Families increasingly rely on *juku* as their primary contact in educational matters, wherefore these schools gain further influence on children's value formation and general attitude toward learning as well as individual educational life course formation.

Due to the apparently well-organized structure of the *juku*-industry, it seems appropriate to speak of a "national *juku*-system." Numerous associations and networks organize regularly held conferences across the country, where original research is discussed, strategies are developed to meet problems in education, improve the quality of teaching and learning, and create new educational opportunities for students.

Appendix

In the following, the basis for the classification of the JSTS *juku* sample as shown in Table 8.2 is outlined, separately describing the results for each of the strong empirical indicators.

1. Scope of Supply

To measure what kind of lessons students actually attend, the JSTS data included the following item: "Within one week, how much time do you spend at this juku? Please report all subject areas (e.g. Japanese, Mathematics, Science, English) in which you are taking lessons" (Q19, Student Survey). Where no data was provided by the students due to a missing sample (JukuC and JukuG), object characteristics and interviews delivered the needed information leading to the categorization shown in Table 8.4. Accordingly, at all *juku*, at least the five main subject areas are provided.

2. Focus of Courses

The focus of courses represents the strongest indicator to measure the specialization of a *juku*. The actual range of supply of the sample's *juku* was calculated based on students' responses to the following item: "What kind of course do you attend at this juku? Multiple answers are possible" (Q18, Student Survey). Students could choose between five general study goals, as stressed in an earlier work (see Entrich 2014: 94): (1) enrichment (focus on contents beyond school curriculum), (2) remedial (focus on catching up in school), (3) study skills (focus on basic and advanced study methods and learning strategies), (4) entrance exams (focus on high school or

Table 8.4 Scope of supply (JSTS 2013, Student Survey; object characteristics; interview data)

		Kojin/chūshō juku				*Ōte juku*			
		JukuA	JukuB	JukuC	JukuD	JukuE	JukuF	JukuG	JukuH
Distribution of students according to courses	Japanese	x	x	x	x	x	x	x	x
	Mathematics	x	x	x	x	x	x	x	x
	Science	x	x	x	x	x	x	x	x
	Social science	x	x	x	x	x	x	x	(x)
	English	x	x	x	x	x	x	x	x
	Other					(x)	(x)	(x)	x
	Total	5	5	5	5	>5	>5	>5	>5

Table 8.5 Focus of courses, in % (JSTS 2013, Student Survey)

		Kojin/chishō juku					Ōte juku		
		JukuA	JukuB	JukuC	JukuD	JukuE	JukuF	JukuG	JukuH
Distribution of students according to courses	Enrichment	93.3	78.9	–	46.7	38.7	74.7	–	32.0
	Remedial	26.7	81.6	–	66.7	77.4	31.3	–	43.7
	Study skills	95.6	97.4	–	95.0	87.1	62.6	–	52.3
	Entrance exams	48.9	63.2	–	55.0	45.2	84.8	–	82.9
	School tests	–	–	–	–	35.5	17.2	–	8.6
	Other	–	–	–	–	6.5	1.0	–	0.9
N (valid responses)		45	38	0	62	31	100	0	224
Official classification according to operator		*Shingaku*	*Doriru*	*Sōgō*	*Hoshū*	*Shingaku*	*Shingaku*	*Sōgō*	*Yobikō*
Actual classification according to supply		*Sōgō*	*Sōgō*	*Sōgō*	*Sōgō*	*Sōgō*	*Sōgō*	*Sōgō*	*Sōgō*

university entrance exam preparation), and (5) school exams (focus on school test/ exam preparation). Table 8.5 displays the final distribution of students according their responses.

Most students attend not only one but several courses at the same *juku*. As explained in Chap. 8, a strong focus on one or two of the five main study purposes would result in a classification as ideal *juku*-type (see Table 8.1). To be classified as *shingaku juku*, for example, students should generally attend entrance exam preparation lessons and additional enrichment lessons. However, the distribution of students according to courses also shows that all *juku* of our sample actually provide far more than the original classification according to the respective operator implies. In particular, smaller *juku* (JukuA to JukuE) show no clear main focus of courses.

Whereas almost all *jukusei* at these *juku* take classes where study skills are nurtured (a domain of *doriru juku*), differences are especially visible in the distribution of students to enrichment and remedial courses. Only at JukuA more students attend enrichment compared to remedial courses, even though preparation courses as the decisive feature of *shingaku juku* are attended by only 49% of the *jukusei*. In contrast, at *ōte juku*, a stronger specialization is found. At JukuF most students prepare for entrance exams and receive additional enrichment lessons, showing a strong focus on school transition preparation. Still, to classify this *juku* as *shingaku juku* would mean to overlook the high percentage of students who are actually receiving remedial and study skill lessons. The same applies for JukuH. According to this analysis, all *juku* of the sample show signs of a comprehensive approach and should be classified as *sōgō juku*.

3. Target Group

Whether *juku* generally target a certain group of students was indirectly measured by asking students the following question: "Which school do you currently attend? Please check only one box and fill in your current grade as well" (Q12, Student Survey). In addition, object characteristics served to gather data on the targeted student population, resulting in the overview shown in Table 8.6.

4. Teaching Approach

Table 8.6 Target group (JSTS 2013, Teacher Survey)

		Kojin/chūshō juku					*Ōte juku*		
		JukuA	JukuB	JukuC	JukuD	JukuE	JukuF	JukuG	JukuH
Target group	Grade	6–9	6–9	5–9	1–9	1–12	1–9	1–12	10–12
	High performer	x	x	x	x		x	x	x
	Average performer	x	x	x	x	x	x	x	
	Low performer		x	x	x	x		x	

x = applicable/existing

What kind of teaching approach *juku* actually provide was measured in the Teacher Survey by asking *juku* teacher and principals the following item: "Per month, how much does one class period cost at this institution? Please write the cost for one class period for every of the three options in the boxes below. If this institution does not offer any of the three options, please make a cross in column 2: 'We do not offer this'" (Q08a/b/c, Teacher Survey). Table 8.7 shows which kinds of instruction the *juku* of the sample provide. According to these data, most *juku* already provide individual tutoring (*kobetsu shidō*); JukuF and JukuG have even specialized on this instruction style. Only JukuA, JukuB, and JukuD continue to primarily rely on class instruction (*shūdan shidō*).

5. Relation to School

To find out whether there is a strong or weak connection to school curricular contents, on the one hand, the above described focus of courses proves meaningful, since students preparing for school tests and exams or with remedial needs generally need to receive instruction based on school curricula contents. In addition, personal observations, object characteristics, and interviews delivered the needed information leading to the categorization shown in Table 8.8. Accordingly, no *juku* of the sample has no relation to regular school.

6. Tuition Fees

One of the most interesting variables to measure the access to *juku* and their status is the level of tuition these schools charge. To measure this variable, the following item was included in the Teacher Survey: "Per month, how much does one class period cost at this institution? How much do you charge for one lesson (from … to …)" (Q08a/b/c, Teacher Survey).

According to these data, tuition fees vary considerably between the sampled schools. As shown in Fig. 8.2, the range of tuition fees for one course per month

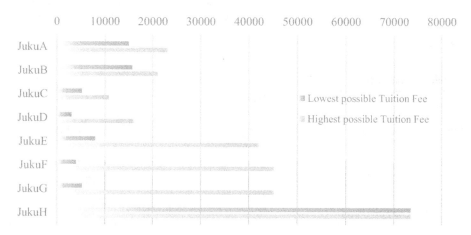

Fig. 8.2 Range of tuition fees for one course per month, per *juku*, in Yen (JSTS 2013, Teacher Survey)

Table 8.7 Teaching approach (JSTS 2013, Teacher Survey)

		Kojin/chūshō juku					Ōre juku		
		JukuA	JukuB	JukuC	JukuD	JukuE	JukuF	JukuG	JukuH
Teaching approach according to operators	One on one teaching approach			x		x	x	x	x
	Lessons in small groups (<8 students)					x	x		
	Lessons in larger groups (>8 students)	x	x	x	x		x		
	Video lessons								x
Primary teaching approach		*Sshūdan shidō*	*Shūdan shidō*	Mixed	*Shūdan shidō*	*Kobetsu shidō*	Mixed	*Kobetsu shidō*	Mixed

x = applicable/existing

Table 8.8 Relation to school (JSTS 2013, Teacher Survey)

		Kojin/chūshō juku					Ōte juku		
		JukuA	JukuB	JukuC	JukuD	JukuE	JukuF	JukuG	JukuH
Relation to school	Strong		x	x	x				
	Weak	x				x	x	x	x
	None								

x = applicable/existing

Table 8.9 Advertisement strategies (JSTS 2013, Teacher Survey)

		Kojin/chūshō juku					Ōte juku		
		JukuA	JukuB	JukuC	JukuD	JukuE	JukuF	JukuG	JukuH
Advertising	Commercial						x	x	x
	Success rate	x				x	x		x
	Pedagogy		x	x	x	x	x	x	
	Word of mouth	x	x	x	x	x			

x = applicable/existing.

varies significantly between the different *juku*. The lowest tuition fees are charged by JukuC and JukuD, whereas JukuA and JukuB charge generally fees at a mediocre level. JukuE to JukuG offer courses from low to high tuition fees. In comparison, JukuH is highly expensive.

7. Advertising

Data on the *juku*'s strategy to acquire students through advertisement is based on object characteristics, such as flyers, website information, etc., and interviews, leading to the categorization shown in Table 8.9. Based on this evaluation, there are general differences of the strategies used to acquire new students between by the *kojin/chūshō juku* and *ōte juku* of the sample. Whereas *kojin/chūshō juku* generally rely on word of mouth and a pedagogical approach, *ōte juku* rely primarily on commercial advertisement. *Juku* which understand themselves as *shingaku juku* or *yobikō* (JukuA, JukuE, JukuF, and JukuH) also place great importance on their success rate (*gōkakuritsu*), i.e., the percentage of their students which successfully enter prestigious schools.

References

Akiba, M., LeTendre, G. K., & Scribner, J. P. (2007). Teacher quality, opportunity gap, and national achievement in 46 countries. *Educational Researcher, 36*(7), 369–387.

Amano, I. (1998). Postwar Japanese education: A history of reform and counterreform. In E. R. Beauchamp (Ed.), *Education and schooling in Japan since 1945* (pp. 152–167). New York: Routledge.

Arnove, R. F., & Torres, C. A. [Hrsg.] (2007). *Comparative education: The dialectic of the global and the local*. Lanham/Boulder/New York/Toronto/Plymouth: Rowman & Littlefield.

Aspinall, R. (2010). *Education reform in Japan in an era of internationalization and risk*. Hikone: Center for Risk Research, Shiga University.

Azuma, H. (2002). The development of the course of study and the structure of educational reform in Japan. In G. DeCoker (Ed.), *National standards and school reform in Japan and the United States* (pp. 5–19). New York: Teachers College Press.

Baker, D. P. (2014). *The schooled society*. Stanford: Stanford University Press.

Baker, D. P., & LeTendre, G. K. (2005). *National differences, global similarities. World culture and the future of schooling*. Stanford: Stanford University Press.

Bjork, C., & Tsuneyoshi, R. (2005). Education reform in Japan: Competing visions for the future. *The Phi Delta Kappan, 86*(8), 619–626.

Bray, M. (1999). *The shadow education system: Private tutoring and its implications for planners*. Paris: UNESCO, International Institute for Educational Planning (IIEP).

Bray, M. (2009). *Confronting the shadow education system: What government policies for what private tutoring?* Paris: UNESCO International Institute for Educational Planning (IIEP).

Bray, M., & Lykins, C. (2012). *Shadow education: Private tutoring and its implications for policy makers in Asia*. Hong Kong: Comparative Education Research Center (CERC) and Asian Development Bank.

Breakspear, S. (2012). *The policy impact of PISA: An exploration of the normative effects of international benchmarking in school system performance* (OECD Education Working Papers, 71).

Cave, P. (2001). Educational reform in Japan in the 1990s: 'Individuality' and other uncertainties. *Comparative Education, 37*(2), 173–191.

Cave, P. (2004). "Bukatsudō": The educational role of Japanese school clubs. *Journal of Japanese Studies, 30*(2), 383–415.

Dawson, W. (2010). Private tutoring and mass schooling in East Asia: Reflections of inequality in Japan, South Korea and Cambodia. *Asia Pacific Educational Review, 11*, 14–24.

Dierkes, J. (2009). Privatschulen und privatwirtschaftliche Zusatzschulen in Japan: Bildungspolitische Lückenbüßer und Marktlücke [Private schools and private-sector supplementary schools: Education political stopgap and gap in the market]. *Zeitschrift für Pädagogik, 55*(5), 732–746.

Dierkes, J. (2010). Teaching in the shadow: Operators of small shadow education institutions in Japan. *Asia Pacific Education Review, 11*(1), 25–35.

Dierkes, J. (2012, March 2). Exam forces students to cram irrelevant facts. *Asahi Shimbun*. http://info.japantimes.co.jp/print/eo20120203a1.html

Dierkes, J. (2013). The insecurity industry: Supplementary education in Japan. In: J. Aurini, S. Davies and J. Dierkes (Eds.), *Out of the shadows: The global intensification of supplementary education* (International perspectives on education and society, Vol. 22, pp. 3–21). Bingley: Emerald Publishing.

Drinck, B. (2006). Leistung und Lernen im "überhitzten" Bildungssystem Japans [Performance and learning in the 'overheated' Japanese education system]. *Bildung und Erziehung, 59*(3), 337–352.

Entrich, S. R. (2014). Effects of investments in out-of-school education in Germany and Japan. *Contemporary Japan, 26*(1), 71–102.

Entrich, S. R. (2016). Der Bedarf nach Mehr: Erklärungen für die Persistenz der Juku-Industrie [The need for more: Explanations of the persistence of the Juku-industry]. *Bildung und Erziehung, 69*(2), 155–174.

Fujita, H. (2000). *Shimin shakai to kyōiku* [The civil society and education]. Kyoto: Seori Shobo.

Fujita, H. (2010). Whither Japanese schooling? Educational reforms and their impact on ability formation and educational opportunity. In J. A. Gordon, H. Fujita, T. Kariya, & G. K. LeTendre

(Eds.), *Challenges to Japanese education. Economics, reform, and human rights* (pp. 17–53). New York: Teachers College Press.

Fukaya, M. (1977). Shingakujuku to sono kinō: shūdan mensetsu chōsa o tegakari to shite [The Shingakujuku and its functions: Clues from a group interview study]. *Kyōiku Shakaigaku Kenkyū, 32*, 51–64.

Goodman, R. (2003). The why, what and how of educational reform in Japan. In R. Goodman & D. Phillips (Eds.), *Can the Japanese change their education system? Oxford studies in comparative education* (pp. 7–30). Oxford: Symposium Books.

Gürtler, L., & Huber, G. L. (2012). Triangulation. Vergleiche und Schlussfolgerungen auf der Ebene der Datenanalyse [Triangulation. Comparisons and conclusions at the data analysis level]. In M. Gläser-Zikuda, T. Seidel, C. Rohlfs, A. Gröschner, & S. Ziegelbauer (Eds.), *Mixed Methods in der empirischen Bildungsforschung* [Mixed methods in empirical educational research] (pp. 37–50). Münster: Waxmann.

Iwase, R. (2005). Shingaku juku ni okeru gakushū keiken no kōzō [The organization of learning experiences in a Shingaku Juku]. *Tōkyōdaigaku Daigakuin Kyōikugakukenkyūka Kiyō, 44*, 1111–1118.

Iwase, R. (2006). Shingaku juku ni okeru kodomo no kōi yōtai: Kodomo ni yoru chōsei ronri no keisei to sono sayō [The acting of children in Shingaku Juku: The formation of an arbitration logic by children and its effect]. *Tōkyōdaigaku Daigakuin Kyōiku Kenkyū-ka Nenpō, 8*, 69–78.

Iwase, R. (2007). Gendai nihon ni okeru juku no tenkai: Juku o meguru shakai-teki imi no hensen katei [The development of Juku in modern Japan: The transformation of the social importance of Juku]. *Tōkyōdaigaku Daigakuin Kyōikugakukenkyūka Kiyō, 46*, 121–130.

Iwase, R. (2008). Sōgō juku ni okeru jugyō katei no tokushitsu-teki yōtai to shakai-teki imi: Senku-teki jirei ni miru sōgō-ka to chūgaku juken to no kankei no kōsatsu [The social importance of Sōgō Juku and their specific teaching process aspects: Considering the relationship between middle school entrance exam and the pioneering case of synthetization]. *Tōkyōdaigaku Daigakuin Kyōikugakukenkyūka Kiyō, 48*, 81–91.

Jick, T. D. (1979). Mixing qualitative and quantitative methods – Triangulation in action. *Administrative Science Quarterly, 24*, 602–611.

Jones, R. S. (2011). *Education reform in Japan* (OECD Economics Department Working Papers 888).

Kariya, T. (2010). Views from the Japanese side. Challenges to Japanese education. In J. A. Gordon, H. Fujita, T. Kariya, & G. K. LeTendre (Eds.), *Challenges to Japanese education. Economics, reform, and human rights* (pp. 11–13). New York: Teachers College Press.

Kariya, T. (2013). *Understanding structural changes in inequality in education*. Paper presented at the DIJ-Workshop "Social Inequality in Japan: A Reassessment" DIJ Tokyo.

Kataoka, E. (2015). Gakkōgaikyōiku-hi shishutsu to kodomo no gakuryoku [Expenses for out-of-school education and academic achievement of students]. *Komazawadaigaku Bungakubu Kenkyū Kiyō, 73*, 259–273.

Kinmoth, E. H. (2005). From selection to seduction: The impact of demographic change on private higher education in Japan. In J. S. Eades, R. Goodman, & Y. Hada (Eds.), *The 'Big Bang' in Japanese higher education. The 2004 reforms and the dynamics of change* (pp. 106–135). Melbourne: Trans Pacific Press.

Komiyama, H. (1993). *Gakurekishakai to juku – datsu juken kyōsō no susume* [Credentialist society and Juku –stop the entrance examination competition!]. Tokyo: Shinhyōron.

Komiyama, H. (2000). *Juku: Gakkō surimuka jidai wo maeni* [Juku: before the era of downsizing schools]. Tokyo: Iwanami Shoten.

Kondō, M., Nogaki, Y., Harada, A., & Takahata, M. (1963). Shingaku junbi kyōiku no kenkyū. Gakushūjuku – kateikyōshinado ni kansuru chōsa hōkoku [A study of out-of-school education preparing for entrance examinations. Report of the Gakushū Juku and private tutoring survey]. *Kyōiku Shakaigaku Kenkyū, 18*, 239–355.

LeTendre, G. K. (1996). Constructed aspirations: Decision-making processes in Japanese educational selection. *Sociology of Education, 69*(3), 193–216.

Maurer, A., & Schmid, M. (2002). Die ökonomische Herausforderung der Soziologie? [The economic challenge of sociology?]. In: A. Maurer, & M. Schmid (Eds.), *Neuer Institutionalismus: Zur soziologischen Erklärung von Organisation, Moral und Vertrauen* [New institutionalism: Concerning a sociological explanation of organization, morale and confidence] (pp. 9–38). Frankfurt am Main: Campus.

Mawer, K. (2015). Casting new light on shadow education – Snapshots of Juku variety. *Contemporary Japan, 27*(2), 131–148.

METI, Ministry of Economy, Trade and Industry. (2010). *"Gakushūjuku kōshi ginō kentei shiken" no setsuritsu ni muketa – Gakushūjuku kōshi nōryoku hyōka shisutemu kōdo-ka jigyō* [Towards the establishment of an "Exam concerning the Ability of Juku Teachers" – The industry for the further development of the Juku teachers' ability evaluation system]. Retrieved from www.meti.go.jp/policy/servicepolicy/contents/management_support/H21%20gakusyujyuku%20report.pdf

MEXT, Ministry of Education, Culture, Sports, Science and Technology. (2005). *FY2005 white paper on education, culture, sports, science and technology – Educational reform and enhancement of the educational functions of communities and families.* Retrieved from http://www.mext.go.jp/b_menu/hakusho/html/06101913.htm

MEXT, Ministry of Education, Culture, Sports, Science and Technology. (2014). *English education reform plan corresponding to globalization.* Retrieved from: http://www.mext.go.jp/english/topics/1343591.htm

MEXT, Ministry of Education, Culture, Sports, Science and Technology. (2017). *Statistics.* Retrieved from http://www.mext.go.jp/english/statistics/

Mimizuka, H. (2007). Shōgakkō gakuryoku kakusa ni idomu: Dare ga gakuryoku o kakutoku suru no ka [Determinants of children's academic achievements in primary education]. *Kyōiku Shakaigaku Kenkyū, 80,* 23–39.

Mizushima, Y. (2007). *Shingaku juku fuyō-ron* [A theory concerning the unnecessity of Shingaku Juku]. Tokyo: Discover.

Mori, I., & Baker, D. P. (2010). The origin of universal shadow education – What the supplemental education phenomenon tells us about the postmodern institution of education. *Asia Pacific Educational Review, 11,* 36–48.

Nishimura, N. (2009). *Naze uchi no ko dake gōkaku suru no ka? Chūgaku juken 'kashikoi juku no tsukaikata'* [Why do only our children pass the test? The smart way to use Juku for middle school entrance]. Tokyo: Eijipress.

OECD, Organisation for Economic Co-operation and Development. (2012). *Strong performers and successful reformers in education: Lessons from PISA for Japan.* Retrieved from https://doi.org/10.1787/9789264118539-en

Okada, A. (2012). *Education policy and equal opportunity in Japan.* New York/Oxford: Berghahn Books.

Ono, S., & Ueno, K. (2001). *Gakuryoku ga abunai* [Educational achievement is in danger]. Tokyo: Iwanami Shoten.

Ota, T. (2014). *Shingaku juku to iu sentaku* [A choice called Shingaku Juku]. Tokyo: Nihon Keizai Shimbun Shuppan.

Park, H. (2013). *Re-evaluating education in Japan and Korea. Demystifying stereotypes.* London/New York: Routledge.

Roesgaard, M. H. (2006). *Japanese education and the cram school business: Functions, challenges and perspectives of the Juku.* Copenhagen: NIAS Press.

Rohlen, T. P. (1980). The Juku phenomenon: An exploratory essay. *Journal of Japanese Studies, 6*(2), 207–242.

Russell, N. U. (1997). Lessons from Japanese cram schools. In W. K. Cummings & P. G. Altbach (Eds.), *The challenge of eastern Asian education: Implications for America* (pp. 153–170). New York: State University Press.

Sadler, S. M. (1900). Study of foreign systems of education. Reprint with small deletions by George Z. F. Bereday (1964). *Comparative Education Review, 7*(3), 307–314.

Sato, M. (1999). *Kyōiku kaikaku o dezain suru* [Designing educational reform]. Tokyo: Iwanami Shoten.

Schubert, V. (1992). *Die Inszenierung der Harmonie. Erziehung und Gesellschaft in Japan* [The staging of harmony. Education and society in Japan]. Darmstadt: Wiss. Buchges.

Schubert, V. (1999). *Lernkultur – Das Beispiel Japan* [Learning culture – the example of Japan]. Weinheim: Deutscher Studien Verlag.

Schubert, V. (2005). *Pädagogik als vergleichende Kulturwissenschaft – Erziehung und Bildung in Japan* [Pedagogy as comparative cultural study – education in Japan]. Wiesbaden: VS Verlag für Sozialwissenschaften.

Schubert, V. (2006). Individualisierung und Konformität — Kontrastierende Modelle in Japan und Deutschland? [Individualisation and conformity — Contrasting models in Japan and Germany?]. In T. Schwinn (Ed.), *Die Vielfalt und Einheit der Moderne* [The diversity and unity of modernity] (pp. 185–197). Wiesbaden: VS Verlag für Sozialwissenschaften.

Schümer, G. (1999). Mathematikunterricht in Japan: Ein Überblick über den Unterricht in öffentlichen Grund- und Mittelschulen und privaten Ergänzungsschulen [Mathematics education in Japan: An overview of instruction in public elementary and secondary schools and private supplementary schools]. In V. Schubert (Ed.), *Lernkultur – Das Beispiel Japan* [Learning culture – The example of Japan] (pp. 45–76). Weinheim: Deutscher Studien Verlag.

Stevenson, D. L., & Baker, D. P. (1992). Shadow education and allocation in formal schooling: Transition to University in Japan. *American Journal of Sociology, 97*, 1639–1657.

Stigler, J. W., & Hiebert, J. (1999). *The teaching gap: Best ideas from the world's teacher's for improving education in the classroom.* New York: Free Press.

Stigler, J. W., & Stevenson, H. W. (1991). How Asian teachers polish each lesson to perfection. *American Educator, 15*(1), 12–20.

Takayama, K. (2008). The politics of international league tables: PISA in Japan's achievement crisis debate. *Comparative Education, 44*(4), 387–407.

Tanabe, Y. (2004). What the 2003 MEXT action plan proposes to teachers of English. *The Language Teacher, 28*(3), 3–8.

Tsukada, M. (1988). Institutionalised supplementary education in Japan: The Yobiko and Ronin student adaptations. *Comparative Education, 24*(3), 285–303.

Tsukada, M. (1991). *Yobiko life: A study of the legitimation process of social stratification in Japan.* Berkeley: Institute of East Asian Studies, University of California.

Watanabe, M. (2013). *Juku: The stealth force of education and the deterioration of schools in Japan.* North Charleston: CreateSpace Independent Publishing Platform.

Yuki, M., Sato, A., & Hashisako, K. (1987). *Gakushū juku – Kodomo, oya, kyōshi wa dō miteiru ka* [Academic Juku – How do children, parents, and teachers view them?]. Tokyo: Gyōsei.

Zeng, K. (1999). *Dragon gate, competitive examinations and their consequences.* London/New York: Cassell.

Chapter 9
Conclusion

Overcoming Social Inequality Through Shadow Education?

> *"Juku, which was long dismissed as 'cram school', [...] has made a significant contribution to the formation of a broad intelligent middle class in postwar Japan"*
>
> *('Juku: The Stealth Force of Education and the Deterioration of Schools in Japan', by Manabu Watanabe 2013: vii).*

結
論

Abstract This chapter summarizes the main findings of the book by addressing the central question underlying all prior analyses: Is there a possibility that shadow education is used as an instrument to neutralize a student's disadvantaged family background and thus serves as an explanation for high educational outcomes but low socioeconomic impact on these outcomes among Japanese students? Or does a high dependence on shadow education as found in Japan inevitably contribute to the reproduction or increase of educational and social inequalities? By bringing together the specific findings of the different chapters of the book, the following overall finding is presented: Shadow education in Japan enables students to neutralize their disadvantaged family background – if certain conditions are met. Based on this assessment, the conceptual implications stemming from the Shadow-Education-Inequality-Impact (SEII) Frame as introduced in Chap. 1 of this book and its specific outliers for the field of international shadow education are presented. Hence, researchers are encouraged to make use of the introduced SEII Frame for future research on shadow education in different settings, while treating the Japanese model of shadow education as exemplary role model for such research. Finally, some recommendations for politicians and researchers alike are made.

9.1 Overall Summary

With respect to my main research question concerning the possibility that shadow education is used as an instrument to neutralize disadvantaged family background and thus serves as an explanation for high educational outcomes but low socioeconomic impact of these outcomes among Japanese students, in the following, the theoretical and empirical parts of this work are shortly summarized. In particular the findings and implications of the different research dimensions as reflected in the four empirical chapters will receive detailed attention in order to achieve a synthesis of all research findings and accomplish final conclusions.

Following the general introduction with the aim to provide the reader with an understanding of the major political and societal relevance of the possible implications of shadow education for educational and social inequalities, the structure of the book was outlined stressing the importance to approach this issue from four different dimensions of general importance (*access*, *effects*, *continuity*, and *change*; see Chap. 1, Fig. 1.2) based on suitable data and applying adequate theoretical concepts and methods (Chap. 1). Only then, evolving patterns become visible and can be analyzed. To accomplish this task, first, the introduction of a general contextual frame, the Shadow-Education-Inequality-Impact (SEII) Frame, proved necessary. Second, contextual, theoretical and methodical sound approaches needed introduction and followed in Chaps. 2, 3 and 4.

Chapter 2 thus addressed the question how the formal and informal Japanese education sectors are connected. My discussions showed that shadow education in Japan is a major phenomenon that has to be understood as one major outcome of postwar educational expansion in Japan. The so-called *gakureki shakai* (credentialist society) was founded on an intense "diploma disease" taking the form of an entrance examination system that causes the high stratification of the upper secondary and tertiary education levels. To access advantageous schools, heavy educational competition between students and schools has become a regular feature in the lives of Japanese students and caused families' extraordinarily high demand for private supplementary lessons to achieve a competitive edge in the educational race. In addition, there seem to exist certain gaps in the regular schooling system's provision of education that further justify the existence of this vast supplementary education market. The Japanese shadow education system has reached a level at which not only all possible educational gaps of the schooling system are covered, supply beyond that point is offered. Also, the participation of most students in either one of the provided lessons in the shadow and the diversity of supply make it difficult to estimate whether shadow education in Japan contributes to social reproduction or the increase in social inequalities. I concluded that it is quite possible that a high percentage of students from disadvantaged social backgrounds are in a position to use shadow education as an instrument to neutralize socioeconomic disadvantages and achieve a high social status. The above quotation by Manabu Watanabe is meant to once more illustrate the actual position *juku* occupy in the Japanese education system. These schools are more than "cram schools." It is even highly questionable whether the "Japanese education miracle" (Arnove and Torres 2007: 5) would have been possible without the *juku*-industry, which seems to provide more educational opportunities than former research would admit. The postulated equality of educational opportunities in Japanese education hinged on the educational opportunities provided by the shadow education industry.

Following this contextual background, theoretical concepts to approach this issue were introduced (Chap. 3), which understand the demand for shadow education as a result of rational cost-benefit considerations of forward-looking individuals, whereas the outcomes of such investments are believed to inevitably foster social inequalities. To be able to approach this issue adequately and produce reliable findings, well-suited data and appropriate methods are essential. Hence, in Chap. 4, the later used data and methodical specifics were introduced. Finally, I approached the issue from four theoretical angles in Part II (Chaps. 5, 6, 7 and 8), focusing on the four main research dimensions outlined in the SEII Frame. To draw overall conclusions, the findings of each of the four empirical chapters are briefly summarized in the following, with respect to my main research question.

9.1.1 Concerning SEII Dimension 1: The Access to Shadow Education

Chapter 5 aimed to clarify who decides to invest in shadow education and how strong such an investment depends on social origin. Based on my theoretical discussions primarily drawing on and extending Rational Choice Theories (RCT) and Shadow Education Investment Theory (SEIT; see Chap. 3) thus introducing a multiple actor decision model for the Japanese context (see Chap. 5, Fig. 5.1), I hypothesized that the decision for shadow education is the cumulative outcome of parents' and students' preferences, stressing that students gain considerable influence on such a decision with higher age [H1]. Hence, high school students' influence on these decisions becomes critical implying an alteration of social origin determination [H2]. In addition, socioeconomically disadvantaged students find ways to participate in shadow education thus possibly achieving a different education level than predicted by classic RCT [H3] (see Chap. 5).

My analyses revealed that whether students gain access to shadow education in present Japan is generally restricted by socioeconomic background, thus supporting existing international as well as Japanese research on the subject. However, by understanding shadow education as an investment that is based on families' rationality when making educational decisions, considerable differences in the determinants concerning the decision for shadow education across different social strata in Japan were disclosed. In particular, post-high school graduation goals of families proved decisive for such decisions. However, by separately measuring the impact of fathers', mothers', and students' educational aspirations on the likelihood to participate in shadow education, significant differences between the three decision-making parties were found. Whereas fathers' influence on such decisions remains insignificant, mothers' involvement proves decisive for their children's likelihood to enter the shadow – at least until they grow older. During high school, students gain the upper hand in the decision-making process.

However, we have to be aware that the decision to seek shadow education is not a zero-sum game between parents and students. Only when controlling for contextual background, such as school ranking, administration type and location, and previous experience with shadow education, the actual impacts of social origin and educational aspirations become visible and allow us to verify whether this impact is significant against the structural background in which decisions are made. I found that highly ranked public high schools in metropolitan areas assemble a higher proportion of students who feel the need to invest in shadow education during high school. These schools push their students to enter highly ranked universities and thus ensure that their own prestige stays high. The influence of students' social origin thus decreases when they are enrolled at such a highly ranked institution. However, if we believe that these schools determine where their students end up, students' own aspirations would not show the strong impact found in my analyses. Thus, even against the backgrounds of strong social origin and school influence, a clear and strong effect of students' own aspirations remained throughout all analyses.

In particular during high school, the student might see the need to invest in shadow education to improve his or her chances to follow a desired pathway, even if the mother is not convinced. Students thus prove very resilient when they have decided to follow a certain path. In particular, if a mother has not made a clear decision for her child's future career or if the student is unaware of her choice, the student might use this freedom to increase his or her chance of entering a high-ranked university by attending a *juku* during high school. The differences in the decision to seek a distinct type of shadow education reflect this freedom as well. Whereas enrolment in *juku* is still much more affected by social origin, the educational aspirations of parents, and school background, a decision to take correspondence courses is generally neither affected by social origin nor by parental aspirations but mostly depends on students' own aspirations. Students thus do not depend as much on their parents' resources and approval to purchase these courses. In addition, students intending to enter a first-class university via entrance exam proved to be most likely to attend shadow education. These students simply convinced their parents of the importance of participating in shadow education for their future career, and they may also make different decisions concerning shadow education investments.

In regard to my main research question, the analyses of Chap. 5 further differentiated whether students come from advantaged or disadvantaged family backgrounds. Significant differences between social strata concerning the choice for shadow education of different types were verified. Whereas ambitious students from advantageous socioeconomic backgrounds generally increase their chance to enter shadow education in high school independent of their parents' wishes regarding their future educational pathway, the choice to invest in shadow education among disadvantaged social strata remained primarily with the mothers. Whereas top quarter social strata base their decisions very much on contextual background, such as school ranking, for bottom quarter social strata, the decision depends primarily on aspirations. A differentiation of my analyses according to shadow education type found similar effects for *juku*-choice and the decision to receive correspondence courses, with the exception that bottom quarter social strata students have significant say in the decision for correspondence courses also. Hence, ambitious students are in a position to benefit from shadow education such as correspondence courses despite disadvantageous socioeconomic background and independent of the attended school.

In sum, the findings in Chap. 5 provide a strong argument to not overlook students as actors who might choose divergent educational pathways and thus impact educational decisions and social inequality formation in several contexts. Students' roles in decision-making could very possibly alter the potential impact of social origin – students could counteract social reproduction by getting involved themselves. The analyses carried out verified that shadow education does not automatically reproduce social inequality. There are different types of shadow education, and not every type depends heavily on social origin, as found in the case of correspondence courses. Hence, students from disadvantaged family backgrounds might have the chance to achieve academic resiliency by deciding for shadow education – under the condition that the chosen shadow education investment strategies prove equally effective across social strata. This major condition was further explored in Chap. 6.

9.1.2 Concerning SEII Dimension 2: The Effects of Shadow Education

Chapter 6 aimed to scrutinize whether shadow education inherits the power to enhance all students' chances to achieve a high education level independent of socioeconomic status, contrary to Seiyama's (1981) Shadow Education Investment Theory (SEIT; see Chap. 3). Hence, by extending SEIT thus introducing a differentiated investment strategy and outcome model for the Japanese context (see Fig. 6.1), I hypothesized that whether investments in shadow education in Japan lead to significant advantages depends on the type of lesson (private tutors, *juku*-classes, or correspondence courses), the length of investment (short term vs. long term), and the study purpose (transition: *shingaku*; supplementation: *hoshū*; or a combination of both: *sōgō*). My central assumption was that significant differences in investment strategies and their outcomes would be found for students from advantaged in comparison to disadvantaged family backgrounds. More specifically, I hypothesized that disadvantaged ESCS students would only gain significant advantages for school transition and thus their educational career from such investments, if they would make short-term investments in *juku*-classes or correspondence courses following a *shingaku* or *sōgō* study purpose (hypotheses [H2-2] and [H3-2], see Chap. 6).

The carried-out analyses verified that all social strata gain significant returns from investments in shadow education, even though families pursue very different investment strategies (in terms of duration, type, and study focus of the lessons) according to socioeconomic background. Students from advantaged socioeconomic backgrounds gain significant advantages for transition to university if they make long-term investments in private tutoring and *juku*-classes with a *shingaku* focus, whereas investments in correspondence courses lead to no advantages for these students. In contrast, students from disadvantaged ESCS backgrounds gain similar advantages from long-term investments in *juku*-classes with *shingaku* or *sōgō* study focus, but no significant advantages for school transition from investments in private tutoring, in accordance with my hypotheses. Correspondence courses are a special case, as they prove very effective for increasing disadvantaged strata students' chance to enter high-ranked high schools and show high AME for the transition to top universities as well. However, due to a too small number of students participating in correspondence courses, no significance of effects could be verified for the latter scenario. These results show that shadow education is possibly used as an instrument of social closure as long as students from advantaged strata have easier access to shadow education and make more use of the opportunities provided by the shadow compared to other strata. However, taking into account the findings of Chap. 5, students from disadvantageous family backgrounds find ways to participate in shadow education and through such investments potentially increase their final education level also. Therefore, shadow education is an effective strategy to achieve a competitive advantage and gain a high education and thus social status for all social strata. These findings make clear that adjustments to the SEIT proved necessary, since inequalities in educational outcomes also largely depend on whether students from disadvantageous backgrounds join the competition and make goal-oriented and purposeful investments. Consequently, shadow education is very possibly one major explanation for students' academic resiliency due to the provision of opportunities outside of the regular schooling system, which are partly accessible by disadvantaged socioeconomic strata also.

However, since competitive advantages of shadow education for disadvantaged social strata students were found for *juku*-classes with a *shingaku* or *sōgō* study focus only, differences in the access and opportunities to enter the *juku*-industry could not be shown. To achieve a full understanding concerning the influence of shadow education on social inequality formation in present Japan, recent changes affecting education in general and the demand for shadow lessons need to be taken into account as well. Only then will we be able to clarify whether the achieved findings are actually positive or not. Only viewed in relation to the developments of the Japanese shadow education sector in terms of access and effects, the discussed findings achieve their final meaningfulness. Chaps. 7 and 8 thus addressed such continuity and change of the shadow education industry from the 1990s to the 2000s.

9.1.3   Concerning SEII Dimension 3: The Continuity of Shadow Education

Chapter 7 aimed to show that the continuous high dependence on shadow education in Japan is a result of changed rationales in educational decision-making, which is affected by insecurities. I argued that by nourishing itself on such insecurities among Japanese families regarding the worth of educational credentials, the persistence of the Japanese shadow education industry would have to be understood as one of the unintended consequences of educational expansion since the 1990s. However, since this development might have contributed to increasing educational and thus social inequalities, by extending Rational Choice Theory (RCT), focusing on Subjective Expected Utility Theory (SEUT) and Relative Risk Aversion Theory (RRAT; see Chap. 3), I introduced an insecurity decision-making model (see Chap. 7, Fig. 7.3). Based on this model, I hypothesized that insecurities have increased since the 1990s, wherefore advantaged and disadvantaged educational strata make investments in shadow education either to maintain their status position or advance socially. I assumed that if students from disadvantaged educational strata have high ambitions (social advancement motive) or are uncertain, they would be more likely to invest in shadow education compared to the 1990s (hypothesis [H1-2]). I further assumed that these students would gain significantly higher advantages from their investments today than in the 1990s (hypothesis [H2-2]), consequently resulting in a decrease of educational inequalities through shadow education (see Chap. 7).

Comparative calculations based on the HHSS surveys of 1997 and 2011 revealed, however, that social inequalities are unlikely to be reduced due to recent developments. In present Japan, parents' education status strongly impacts whether shadow education is pursued during middle school, whereas the impact of students' university aspirations on their likelihood to pursue such lessons during this period of time generally decreased. In comparison to the 1990s, students who intend to stay in the education system following high school graduation and enter university have become less likely to pursue shadow education, whereas students who are unsure which educational pathway to follow have still about the same likelihood to attend classes in the shadow in reference to students who will enter the labor market following high school graduation. However, models differentiating for educational strata showed that students from advantaged educational strata continue to use shadow education as a security strategy to avoid downward social mobility. In contrast, students from disadvantaged educational strata, who follow the social advancement motive aiming at higher educational credentials (university or college aspirations) or are uncertain which future pathway they should pursue, have become much more likely to use shadow education as a strategy to achieve upward social mobility since the 1990s, thus verifying [H1-2]. This would support the assumption that social inequality has not increased due to shadow education.

However, my analyses further showed that students from advantaged educational strata, which continue to primarily follow the status maintenance motive or are uncertain about their future educational pathway and have participated in shadow education prior to the transition to high school, continue to gain considerably higher advantages from shadow education investments for high school transition than highly ambitious students from disadvantaged educational strata in present Japan compared to the 1990s. In addition, the probability to achieve entrance to Academic A high schools for students from disadvantaged educational strata, who have high aspirations and made investments in shadow education during middle school, is still significantly higher compared to the reference population, but this likelihood decreased drastically. In total, students from disadvantaged strata are less likely to enter top-ranked schools in present Japan if compared to the 1990s. In stark contrast to hypothesis [H2-2], these results support the assumption that social inequality in present Japan has actually increased.

Since advantaged educational strata constantly strive for ways to preserve their status by achieving a competitive advantage, the ranking of schools within the same track (e.g., academic high schools or university) takes on the role of allocating students to different societal positions thus providing advantaged social strata with opportunities of social closure. Even though there seem to exist opportunities to access shadow education for all social strata, only if more students from disadvantaged social strata exploit this opportunity and gain advantages from their investment, social inequalities will be significantly reduced. However, whether students gain such advantages highly depends on the investment strategy employed. Hence, not only the before-discussed actual opportunities to gain access to shadow education in spite of a limited amount of resources (Chap. 5) prove essential if students attempt to use shadow education as an educational strategy to neutralize disadvantaged family background, they need to also make purposeful, effective investments with the resources and opportunities they are given.

As discussed in Chaps. 6 and 7, students of all social strata are in a position to gain significant advantages from investments in shadow education. Chaps. 5 and 7 further stressed that opportunities to enter the Japanese shadow education system seem to exist for disadvantaged social strata, but indicated that a decreasing percentage of such students actually pursues shadow education with the intention to achieve a higher social status compared to the 1990s. Also, the ways in which students gain access to different kinds of lessons are still unclear. Besides stressing the importance of insecurities concerning educational credentials in accordance with the status maintenance motive regarding families' continued investments in shadow education, the findings of Chap. 7 also imply trends toward the devaluation of educational credentials and a foreseeable, at least temporary end of educational expansion. Both these trends might either lead to a gradually decreasing dependence on shadow education in Japan or new educational demands from families searching for new ways to achieve competitive advantages and preserve their status through additional investments in education, consequently increasing demands on the shadow industry. Only if the Japanese shadow education industry successfully adapts to such changes, its ongoing persistence could be justified and even a further increase in enrolments might become possible. The question whether social inequality is affected and will continue to be affected by changes in education in general and in the shadow education system in particular is of high relevance and was further analyzed in Chap. 8.

9.1.4 Concerning SEII Dimension 4: The Change of Shadow Education

Chapter 8 aimed to clarify how Japanese shadow education managed to maintain strong despite unfavorable changes since the 1990s and how this affects educational opportunities for disadvantaged educational strata. By applying New Institutionalist Theory (NIT; see Chap. 3) to the development of the institutionalized shadow education market in Japan, I hypothesized that the *juku*-industry managed to stay successfully in business due to the high flexibility of the market, which allows to expand or replace traditional specializations of *juku* by new specializations [H1]. Also, I assumed that recent educational changes affect students and their families, which then turn to *juku* for help. In particular, students from disadvantaged family backgrounds make use of *juku* with an expanded course menu and thus use shadow education as an educational opportunity [H2]. Furthermore, I assumed that the *juku*-industry would adjust its organization, programs, and regulations in response to considerable changes that affect education in general [H3], such as decreasing student populations, the reformation of the regular schooling system, and changed demands of families (see Chap. 8).

According to my analyses, *juku* have proven very flexible in adjusting to educational changes of all sorts. To stay successfully in business, *juku* replace or expand their traditional specializations in favor of new specializations, and new types of *juku* evolve. On the one hand, *juku* following a comprehensive approach (*sōgō juku*) have become the prevalent type, since a high specialization on only one or two distinct study goals has become unprofitable, especially for small- and middle-sized *juku*. Only large corporations possess the resources to still run schools with a distinct specialization. On the other hand, the stronger individualization of education led to the emergence of *kobetsu shidō*-oriented *sōgō juku* as new type of *juku*. In response to decreasing student populations, the reformation of the mainstream schooling system, and changed educational demands of families, *juku* constantly increase their bandwidth of supply, target new client groups, and adjust and possibly improve subject contents and teaching approaches. Besides functioning as gap-closer for academic support, *juku* increasingly take on functions outside their original purview such as care, counseling, and guidance and thus achieve many of the *yutori* education goals that regular schools struggle to accomplish. In particular, the individual student and his/her needs have become one major concern of the operators of this industry. To enable students to acquire new competencies and creativity, teaching approaches were adjusted and individual curricula created. As the major consequence of increased individual demands, individual tutoring has become a frequent mode of instruction at most *juku*. Thus, in the future, it is likely that *kobetsu shidō* emphasizing *sōgō juku* will dominate the market. *Juku*-operators have not only understood the importance to develop strategies promoting competency development of students outside the traditional purview of Japanese education but successfully made themselves indispensable. Families increasingly rely on *juku* as their primary contact in educational matters, wherefore these schools gain further influence on children's value formation and general attitude toward learning as well as individual educational life course formation. *Juku* even gained importance for students and their families to achieve individual educational goals and contribute to achieving national education goals by supporting the internationalization of Japanese education.

From families' point of view, *juku*-lessons are viewed as an educational opportunity to achieve educational goals. In this regard, *juku* which follow a comprehensive approach seem best suited to serve students with several needs, whereas *juku* with higher specialization promise remedy for students who pursue one distinct goal. In addition, if formerly highly specialized *juku* have expanded their supply and taken on more than one distinct study focus, students from disadvantaged family backgrounds will be more likely to gain access to such *juku*. However, at the higher specialized *juku*, which generally charge higher tuition fees in order to maintain a high reputation based on students' success rate, a reduction of tuition fees or scholarships becomes possible for students from disadvantaged family backgrounds showing high academic performance. In summary, to attract generally all potential clients, more opportunities to enable students with disadvantaged family backgrounds to participate are created. In present Japan, social inequalities are likely to be reduced under the condition that disadvantaged educational strata make use of educational opportunities inside and outside of school. One major predictor for such investments are high ambitions, as I have shown earlier (see Chaps. 5 and 7).

Hence, the recent development of *juku* follows three trends: First, the structural composition of the *juku*-market changes. Second, the *juku*-curriculum becomes individually customized. Third, this industry shows continuous efforts to increase opportunities for socioeconomically disadvantaged students to participate in various types of lessons in the shadow to keep enrolment rates stable. These trends favor students which pursue individual educational goals outside the classic spectrum of standardized entrance examination preparation or mere repetition of school lesson contents – including students from disadvantaged family backgrounds. The carried-out analyses showed that the *juku*-industry is a highly diverse education market that has undergone major transformations since the 1990s and does not only function as general gap-closer in education anymore – it "goes beyond shadowing the formal system" (Dawson 2010: 17). A wide range of educational opportunities for students across all social strata is provided.

9.2   Final Conclusion

Taking into account the findings of Chaps. 5, 6, 7 and 8, we have to conclude that shadow education in Japan inherits the potential to function as an instrument to neutralize disadvantaged family background – if certain conditions are met.

First of all, students from disadvantaged family backgrounds and their families have to develop high ambitions concerning the child's future educational pathway and realize that investments in shadow education can make the difference between failing and succeeding. Only if students intend to enter high-ranked universities and are determined to actually achieve such high set goals while being aware of the consequences of such choices, the chance to achieve a high social status becomes realizable. Given that the last wave of educational expansion in Japan is gradually coming to a halt as implied by MEXT statistics (see Chap. 7, Fig. 7.1) and supported by the results of Chap. 7, it seems that more and more families follow a status maintenance motive instead of trying to achieve higher educational credentials. Whereas this seems natural for high educated strata, for low educated strata, higher ambitions are necessary to counteract social reproduction. If parents do not possess such high aspirations, students need to make up their minds themselves, i.e., become resilient, and consider to pursue shadow education even against their parents' wishes.

Second, families need to make purposeful and goal-oriented investments in shadow education at the major transition points in school life course in order to maximize the possible effects of such an investment. Hence, early investments in shadow education prove meaningful if the student encounters difficulties in certain study areas. Further investments in shadow education prior to the transition to high school prove necessary to increase the chance to enter a high-ranked high school and thus increase the chance to also enter a higher-ranked university afterwards. Whereas it might become too expensive to choose entrance to a highly specialized *juku* (*yobikō, shingaku*) or private tutoring, by adequately making strategical use of lessons at *sōgō juku* or correspondence courses, the effects of shadow education investments might prove equally – if not more – beneficial.

Third, to make the best use of the limited amount of resources, students from disadvantaged family backgrounds need to generally study very hard at home. This way, shadow education is only used where certain challenges occur or professional support is needed to achieve the same level of preparation as students from advantaged family backgrounds, who can afford to pursue such lessons more often and with a higher intensity. In particular, at the transition to high school and university students might particularly profit from *shingaku*-style lessons that represent the best possible preparation for entrance exams and might provide them with a competitive advantage in the educational race for educational credentials. In addition, students should make more use of educational opportunities provided by the regular schooling system as well, such as alternative methods to enter university by recommendation, etc., and complement their alternative goals with shadow education focusing on *sōgō*-style lessons, so as to maximize their chances of gaining entrance to high-ranked universities through alternative entrance methods while receiving sufficient preparation for entrance exams as well.

Fourth, students should make extensive use of fee reduction and exemption programs provided by major *juku*-corporations and use discounts and tuition-fee-free study rooms where possible. Particularly eager students will have better chances to receive scholarships from *juku* and by this gain access to the best instruction the market has to offer.

Finally, in present Japan, social inequalities in educational attainment will only decrease if a high percentage of students from disadvantaged social strata meet these conditions and thus make use of the positive features of the shadow education market. If families have realized that shadow education is an effective educational strategy to realize social upward mobility, purposeful investments of a high proportion of families with disadvantaged background would contribute to a decrease in social inequalities in present Japan. Until now, however, it seems as if the increased opportunities in the shadow are only seldom used by students which would need them the most: students from disadvantaged strata. Hence, it is not the existence of shadow education per se that causes the still existing and increasing educational and social inequalities, the differences in the utilization of the provided opportunities according to social strata cause inequality in educational attainment. These results lead us to certain implications for future research and recommendations for future policy approaches toward this phenomenon.

9.3   Implications and Recommendations: Acknowledging Evolving Patterns

Based on the foregoing discussions and findings, two solutions to the problem of educational and social inequalities as an outcome of shadow education investments can be identified: A real decrease in inequalities can only be achieved if the demand for shadow education is abolished (best solution) or if disadvantaged social strata gain equal access to all kinds of shadow education services and make more use of the provided opportunities to actually neutralize their peers' advantages (second best solution) (for a similar argument, see Schlösser and Schuhen 2011: 377). Both solutions stem from the belief that something can be done to decrease the impact of shadow education on class-specific disparities – even in a system such as the Japanese one – where a high degree of flexibility in the shadow is apparent. This flexibility produces evolving patterns that need notice. The change dimension introduced in the SEII Frame cannot be underestimated but did not receive much attention in research and politics yet. Only if change within the shadow is understood and evolving patterns are identified, promising measures to contain the negative outcomes of shadow education become possible.

Since simply banning shadow education is unlikely to lead to the disappearance of the *juku*-industry – as the example of South Korea shows (see Dawson 2010) – to accomplish the first solution in present Japan, the root of the educational competition and the *shiken jigoku*, the *gakureki shakai*, needs to change. However, such fundamental societal change is hardly implementable through political instruments. Politicians should concentrate on modifying the excesses of this credentialist society and target the competition-generating entrance examination system. As LeTendre (1994: 134) already argued, the "problems in Japanese education stem from the system of tracking in high schools and beyond." Of course, the abolition of the entrance examination system and thus the extensive tracking it produces is no easy task at all and might lead to unintended consequences if not carried out by considering all parts of the education system in debates about education. Public, private, and *juku* schools have to be involved when change is supposed to happen. Simply banning entrance examinations and high school ranking for public schools might prove insufficient, since well-off parents will still try to get their children a competitive educational advantage by sending them to private schools[1] and make additional investments in shadow education. As Amano and Poole (2005: 694) argued, all reforms targeting entrance examinations may just be useless in a society where the brand of a product is more important than its content, wherefore the "labelization" (*gakkōreki*) of schooling institutions is unlikely to stop. To achieve the goal of reducing the intensified competition between students, which causes families to consider investing vast amounts of time, effort, and money for shadow education lessons, more opportunities in the regular secondary and tertiary education systems have to be introduced or rather existing opportunities need more consequent enforcement. For example, the *yutori* reforms introduced alternative methods of admission to university and created a 6-year combined secondary school. Both measures were meant to provide more options and spare students the examination hell at the transition to high school and university but proved partly ineffective (as further discussed in Chap. 10). Hence, such attempts should be further encouraged and supported. In addition, a stronger regulation of the entrance examination system itself and the contents needed to achieve a high score in these exams proves necessary. Students should be able to achieve entrance to high-ranked high schools and universities without needing additional preparation in the shadow education sector. The formal schooling system should at least provide students with the needed armamentarium to survive in the entrance examinations. Therefore, entrance examinations cannot be allowed to include contents outside the school curriculum, for example. Also, the central, state-recognized entrance exams (such as the *sentā*) need to become an obligatory instrument for all high schools and universities, whether public or private. The same applies to the *niji* exam. Only then the same chances exist for all students.

The best possible and most realistic solution would be the introduction of equal access to shadow education for all social strata. The introduction of private tutoring programs at regular schools, which would compensate for the shortcomings of regular classes and provide students with the care and support they supposedly need, is one popular attempt to achieve this goal. Whether such programs would actually become a legitimate alternative to shadow education is questionable, though. On the one hand, these additional courses would need financing, personal, etc. These resources already exist in the shadow and are hardly replaceable. On the other hand, as the examples of South Korea (see, e.g., Dawson 2010) or the United States (see Mori 2013) show, the success of such programs might not come overnight nor is foreseeable whether these programs will be accepted as a legitimate alternative to lessons at *juku*. In both these countries, supplementary lessons are provided by the state to support weak performers with remedial assistance after school. In the United States, this is part of the "No Child Left Behind Act." Even

---

[1] This is exactly what happened in the prefectures Kyōto and Kōchi in the early 1950s. Here the best students enrolled in private instead of public schools due to the abolishment of tracking, i.e., entrance exams and high school ranking (Kariya and Rosenbaum 1999: 216).

though this kind of free of charge tutoring for low-income families was created, the participation rate of those eligible to apply for the state-funded "supplementary education services" remains quite low. According to a 2009 survey of the US Department of Education, many parents are unwilling to send their children to additional tutoring just because they have below-average grades (Mori 2013: 202). The possibility of stigmatizing children as having problems in school might also play its part in the decision-making process for applying for such lessons, because only low-income students with low grades are eligible to apply. State subsidy systems to support private tutoring for students from disadvantaged family backgrounds are another, more passive strategy to deal with shadow education. One example for such a pure voucher system is Germany. In Germany families can apply for financial aid to pay for shadow education if the student shows low academic performance and comes from a low-income family. This makes sense in an education system that does not rely on shadow education for enrichment or preparation purpose (see Entrich 2014, Entrich and Lauterbach 2017). For Germany and the United States, many problems in accessing vouchers or lessons by those eligible to access them are also reported. Therefore not many of those with need for remedial or other support actually receive help through these measures. Contrasting to these both countries, in South Korea, public-private tutoring programs at schools were introduced for all students alike, with the difference that these supplementary lessons are free of charge (using vouchers) only for those students from low-income families. Other families have to pay for these services depending on the income level of parents (Dawson 2010: 19). The described measures might help mitigate the impact of shadow education on social inequalities but are unlikely to result in an abolishment of the private tutoring industry. All these attempts to deal with shadow education do not reduce the need for supplementary education in the slightest. There is only a partial shift of these lessons from shadow to school and in the way lessons are funded. As long as individual actors feel the need for additional support and try to find the best possible support, private initiators will be there to help them get it. Families with more financial resources and high educational aspirations will make most use of these services, and thus inequalities will not vanish. Hence, families will most likely continue to rely on supplementary services. As the flexibility of the *juku*-industry has illustrated (see Chap. 8), the Japanese shadow education system is eager and able to adapt to changing circumstances. At this point, the abolition of the *juku*-industry seems hardly possible anymore. The same is true for many other shadow education systems across the world.

A better way to achieve equal access to shadow education would be the provision of information on the opportunities outside regular schools in regular schools and measures toward a stronger integration of the *juku*-industry into the formal schooling system through cooperations or amalgamations of schools and *juku* (see Dierkes 2009, Kuroishi and Takahashi 2009). Until now, only few such cooperations or merger actually exist and are tolerated by local boards of education. Most of these schools are state-recognized but profit-oriented private schools, which have either emerged from *juku* or have a *juku* affiliated to them. Such cooperations with *juku* are still more of an exception in the case of public schools. Even though some conservative politicians actively pursue the stronger integration of *juku* in the regular school-ing system, the central institution in education in Japan, the MEXT, does neither officially recognize such cooperations nor approve of them (Dierkes 2009: 744–745). First governmental attempts toward a new supplementary education policy are visible in the *mirai juku* ("future *juku*") movement (Yamato and Zhang 2017). These new types of *juku* are funded by the government and communities, providing free of charge lessons for economically disadvantaged students. This is an example of how private and public partnerships help to legitimize shadow education. As a conse-quence, the general public and political acceptance of *juku* grows, making shadow education a formal part of mass schooling. Such cooperations between the formal and informal education sectors in Japan would contribute to more equality in edu-cational opportunities and make it possible for Japanese officials to make use of the educational potential of the *juku*-market for achieving national education goals. It would also allow stronger regulation and observation of the development of the market, which could be used to also reduce the pressure on students, by adjusting the curricula and timetables of regular and *juku* schools to fit each other, for exam-ple. In addition to the stronger incorporation of *juku* into the regular schooling sys-tem, state subsidies should be created to enable economically disadvantaged students to pursue additional lessons as well – independent of their academic records.

Another important step toward this direction would be the formal recognition of the *juku*-industry by MEXT officials, classifying *juku* as schools, because that is what they are: institutions where students receive education. An incorporation of this industry into formal education seems logical and promising. Only then would education policy have the power to change education in a way that allows to achieve set goals, such as the reduction of inequality in educational opportunities. The *juku*-system has already become a solid part of the education system – an institution (in several regards) that is not likely to vanish. What might further diminish if nothing changes is the trust in public education. This implies that the power of education will continue to shift into private hands. International research on shadow education showed that these educational markets are generally under-regulated. An often found political strategy is to ignore this private education sector (Bray and Kwo 2014: viii) – a strategy that the Japanese government pursued for decades. Whether changes affecting the mainstream impact the size and shape of the Japanese shadow education system has not been on any political agenda, vast changes in the shadow education system of a country affect several serious issues in education, such as educational opportunity provision, social inequality in educational attainment, or children's well-being. Consequently, by not adequately evaluating, regulating, or controlling what is going on in the shadow, official sources might not only run the risk of making far-reaching political decisions without considering the impact of shadow education on educational reality, but miss the opportunity to profit from the second schooling system's potential when trying to achieve national or international educational goals. Governments across the globe would do well to learn from the Japanese example and recognize and try to further incorporate and thus regulate the shadow of their education systems.

9.4   Conceptual Implications

The conception of this study underlies a simple logic: A general analytic frame is necessary to identify and structure analyses meant to understand the phenomenon of interest. In this case, shadow education and how this kind of education affects the formation of educational and social inequalities was in the center of attention. As there are no formalized frames to approach this subject, I developed the *Shadow-Education-Inequality-Impact* (SEII) Frame to logically structure the way in which the field should be approached.

Second, to achieve sound conclusions based on reliable findings, a focus on one specific case is recommended. The focus on Japan is exemplary in two ways: (1) It illustrates how such analyses can be brought forth using the SEII Frame, and (2) it shows how much we can actually learn from an advanced shadow education model such as the Japanese one. In addition, this study also stresses the importance of embedding analyses into a certain context, which is not rigid but ever-changing and evolving. As comparative educationalist Sir Michael Sadler (1900) argued, we should not forget that "things outside the schools matter even more than the things inside the schools, and govern and interpret the things inside" (p. 310). This is still a major point that should not be underestimated. The context in which (shadow) education takes place is thus extremely important for our understanding of why it takes place in the way it does. Specifically, the change of this context needs to be taken into consideration to grasp ever-evolving patterns of shadow education thus allowing to understand the real implications of shadow education on certain phenomena, e.g., social inequality. Due to this way of approaching the issue, the conceptual implications of this work for similar topics in other national settings are significant. As illustrated using the Japanese example, the implications of educational reforms in the regular schooling system and decreasing student populations need to be evaluated for their impact on the shadow education industry in high- and low-intensity shadow education countries, for example. Modern, especially developed, countries all suffer from the outcomes of low fertility rates and demographic change. These "schooled societies" (Baker 2014) also experience the (un)intended outcomes of educational expansion. Education as an institution needs to adapt to these changes. However, if governments across the world believe that excesses of educational expansion and competition between students would vanish as a result of decreasing student populations, the Japanese example clearly shows that this might not necessarily be the case. Another point the Japanese example illustrates is that the evaluation of the development of a country's shadow education system allows conclusions about the state of progress and sense of educational reformation and changes in social inequality issues. Reforms supporting the expansion of private for-profit educational services should be questioned as to whether they are making actual sense or more harm than good.

The third highly important issue that was addressed in the book is the importance of applying existing theories or even developing new concepts suited to capture the causes and implications of shadow education investments for social inequalities.

The theoretical concepts applied in this book can be used in numerous settings, but might need to be adjusted in order to make sure to which degree a certain concept applies. The demand for shadow education in this work was primarily understood as a result of rational cost-benefit considerations of forward-looking individuals, who then cause social reproduction through their investments. Future research would do well to find different theoretical approaches and possibly produce different insights. For example, besides understanding shadow education investments as rational decisions, it is possible to apply a more structuralist viewpoint, where constraints urge individuals to make such decisions. Also, the consequences of shadow education development as part of mass educational expansion should be taken up. Hence, new theoretical viewpoints should be brought into the discussion and used to analyze the four major dimensions outlined in the SEII Frame.

Another important implication of conceptual nature concerns the data basis and the methods applied. It is highly important to base all analyses on well-suited data and appropriate methods. It has to be noted that new statistical methods and models should be considered to develop our knowledge on shadow education. However, the explanatory power of the carried-out analyses very much depends on the quality of the data. The above recommended focus on case studies also stems from the experience that it is hard to achieve comprehensive insights about a system of education and its outcomes by using large-scale assessment studies or other studies comparing multiple cases at one time. Such direct comparisons are helpful to get a general understanding about certain overall connections or correlations between main variables, such as social origin, performance, and educational attainment – if the used items are adequately defined and translated. However, these studies often have data limitations as they overlook national characteristics in education, culture, and society, allowing for analyses in a rigid frame only. This often leads to oversimplification of relationships and remains superficial in its explanatory power. From such analyses, we know that social origin exerts a general impact on shadow education participation and that investments in shadow education are related to academic performance (e.g., Baker et al. 2001, Entrich 2014). What actually goes on behind the scenes is not examined through such analyses. Another problem concerns the causality between variables, as most such studies are cross-sectional studies. Future research should strongly consider using longitudinal data to analyze the phenomenon and further identify causal connections between shadow education investments and social origin as well as educational success. Particularly interesting would be the impact of shadow education experience of different sorts and durations in a long-term perspective, e.g., modeling the impact of such investments on future job opportunities or actual occupation and income. Hence, more shadow education research should emphasize a life course perspective.

Finally, future research in comparative education should strongly concentrate on empirically analyzing the impact of transnational and national political and institutional forces on the development of shadow education systems across the globe and draw conclusions about the implications of these developments for the state of education, educational opportunity provision, and social inequalities in the analyzed countries. This is also why research on advanced systems such as the Japanese *juku-*

industry should be on top of the list of educationalists concerned with the outcomes of globalization, educational expansion, inequality formation, student performance, demographic change, educational reformation, and so on.

References

Amano, I., & Poole, G. S. (2005). The Japanese university in crisis. *Higher Education, 50*(4), 685–711.

Arnove, R. F., & Torres, C. A. (Eds.). (2007). *Comparative education: The dialectic of the global and the local*. Lanham/Boulder/New York/Toronto/Plymouth: Rowman & Littlefield.

Baker, D. P. (2014). *The schooled society*. Stanford: Stanford University Press.

Baker, D. P., Akiba, M., LeTendre, G. K., & Wiseman, A. W. (2001). Worldwide shadow education: Outside-school learning, institutional quality of schooling, and cross-national mathematics achievement. *Educational Evaluation and Policy Analysis, 23*(1), 1–17.

Bray, M., & Kwo, O. (2014). *Regulating private tutoring for public good. Policy options for supplementary education in Asia*. Hong Kong: Comparative Education Research Center (CERC).

Dawson, W. (2010). Private tutoring and mass schooling in East Asia: Reflections of inequality in Japan, South Korea and Cambodia. *Asia Pacific Educational Review, 11*, 14–24.

Dierkes, J. (2009). Privatschulen und privatwirtschaftliche Zusatzschulen in Japan: Bildungspolitische Lückenbüßer und Marktlücke. [Private schools and private-sector supplementary schools: Education political stopgap and gap in the market]. *Zeitschrift für Pädagogik, 55*(5), 732–746.

Entrich, S. R. (2014). Effects of investments in out-of-school education in Germany and Japan. *Contemporary Japan, 26*(1), 71–102.

Entrich, S. R., & Lauterbach, W. (2017). Shadow education as an instrument of social closure? Contradicting findings from the German LifE study. *Comparative Education Review*, submitted.

Kariya, T., & Rosenbaum, J. E. (1999). Bright flight – Unintended consequences of detracking policy in Japan. *American Journal of Education, 107*, 210–230.

Kuroishi, N., & Takahashi, M. (2009). Gakkō kyōiku to juku sangyō no renkei ni tsuite no ichikenkyū: Genjō no bunseki to kongo no tenbō [A study on collaborations between the cram-school industry and public education: From present circumstances to future proposals]. *Kyōiku Sōgō Kenkyū, 2*, 1–14.

LeTendre, G. K. (1994). Distribution tables and private tests: The failure of middle school reform in Japan. *International Journal of Educational Reform, 3*(2), 126–136.

Mori, I. (2013). Supplementary education in the United States: Policy, context, characteristics, and challenges. In J. Aurini, S. Davies, & J. Dierkes (Eds.), *Out of the shadows: The global intensification of supplementary education* (pp. 191–207). Bingley: Emerald Publishing.

Sadler, S. M. (1900). Study of Foreign Systems of Education. Reprint with small deletions by George Z. F. Bereday (1964). *Comparative Education Review, 7*(3), 307–314.

Schlösser, H.-J., & Schuhen, M. (2011). Führt Nachhilfe zu Wettbewerbsverzerrungen? [Does private tutoring result in distortions of competition?]. *Empirische Pädagogik, 25*(3), 370–379.

Seiyama, K. (1981). Gakkōgai kyōiku tōshi no kōka ni kansuru ichikōsatsu. [A Study of the Effects of Out-of-school Educational Investment]. *Hokudai Bungakubu Kiyō, 30*(1), 171–221.

Watanabe, M. (2013). *Juku: The stealth force of education and the deterioration of schools in Japan*. North Charleston: CreateSpace Independent Publishing Platform.

Yamato, Y., & Zhang, W. (2017). Changing schooling, changing shadow: Shapes and functions of juku in Japan. *Asia Pacific Journal of Education, 37*(3), 329–343.

Chapter 10
Excursus

Recent Changes to Japanese Education: The *Yutori* Reforms

日
本
の
教
育
の
変
化

*"Introduction of these [yutori] policies
raised the possibility that a system
known for its resistance to change
would undergo major restructuring."*

('High Stakes Schooling', by
Christopher Bjork 2016: 2)

Abstract This chapter outlines the causes and outcomes of the *yutori* (relaxation) education reform as the major shift in contemporary Japanese education, specifically addressing the question whether the *yutori* reforms have actually changed Japan's regular schooling system so as to reduce competition for high credentials and thus possibly reduce the demand for shadow education. Based on a literature review and the analysis of Ministry of Education (MEXT) reports, the following main findings are presented:

(1) The *yutori* reforms have not lessened the pressure on students to do well in school nor have they reduced the competition in the educational race significantly.
(2) Internationalization (*kokusaika*) of Japanese education has become the major goal of Japanese politicians and MEXT officials, even at the cost of reintroducing major competition into the system and sacrificing the idea of *yutori*. Based on these findings, the demand for shadow education is unlikely to be reduced as an outcome of educational reformation. Instead, new demands were created over the last two decades, which are likely to be filled by the Japanese *juku*-industry.

© Springer International Publishing AG 2018
S.R. Entrich, *Shadow Education and Social Inequalities in Japan*,
https://doi.org/10.1007/978-3-319-69119-0_10

10.1   Problematic

The millennium was "marked by many changes that fall under the rubric of globalization" (Rohlen 2002: 195). Japan is only one example where this change can be
documented, but a very good and, of course, a special one. The major outcomes of
globalization on national systems of education are far-reaching, as not only borders
have lost importance in favor of a world economy, consequently shifting competition for (certain) jobs from a national to an international level; education itself is
fundamentally affected. Education across the world and particularly in highly
industrialized, "schooled societies" (Baker 2014) such as Japan is increasingly
affected by transnational forces, which describe the global influence on the shaping
of "essential educational activities of curricula, teaching, and administration [which]
is becoming more obvious in all categories of nations" (Baker and LeTendre 2005:
xi). These transnational forces massively influenced the institution of education
worldwide, creating an institutional world model of education characterized by several cross-border features of mass schooling, such as the "world curriculum," meaning similar core subjects exist in schools across the globe including English as a
dominant foreign language instruction (Lenhardt 2008: 1020–1021). Global governance is practiced by international organizations such as the OECD, UNESCO,
World Bank, IEA, and others, with the aim to control the development and shape of
the global education market, as the examples of PISA, TIMSS, and other major
assessments illustrate (Sellar and Lingard 2013, Sellar and Lingard 2014). Also,
increasing privatization of education and private investments by families in formal
and informal or supplementary schooling, i.e., shadow education and study abroad,
has become apparent. These developments, of course, affect many dimensions of
schooling and its outcomes, including social inequalities.

Even though former Anglo-American research on Japan tended to speak of Japan
as the "exception" from global restructuring, Takayama (2009) showed that educational reform in Japan is strongly influenced by global developments in education.
However, the paradox of high efficiency and quality on the one hand, and the negative stereotypes associated with Japanese education, such as the high dependence on
shadow education, on the other hand, is not without consequences. Although Japan
was praised for its education system due to Japanese students' high performance in
international large-scale assessments such as PISA or TIMSS, in Japan itself, a
completely different view on education is found: for decades, education has been
content of political and public debates leading to several reforms of the existing
system. Various concerns finally led to a call for change in education, to meet challenges of the future and reduce the burden of the youngsters (Cave 2016: 1–2).
Whether real change in Japanese education occurred and actually reduced competition and workload of students is of question, though.

This chapter sheds light on how Japanese education policy has struggled between
the impact of transnational forces as reflected in the national political goal of inter-
nationalizing Japanese education and the national goal to reduce pressure on students and decrease competition in education (*yutori*). Hence, Japanese politicians
and educationalists alike have been focusing on two major strategies to improve

education over the last decades: (1) *yutori*, with the aim to tackle the problems within Japanese education, such as competition, school disorder, and examination hell; and (2) *kokusaika*, internationalization of education as a means to stay economically competitive in a globalized world. It seems, however, that both tasks cannot be achieved at the same time. As the above quotation by Christopher Bjork shall illustrate, the Japanese education system is known for its resistance to change. Even though Japanese education policy constantly changed its orientation during its modern history, essentially only two main emphases are apparent: (1) "control and competition" and (2) "freedom and choice" (Amano 1995, Shimizu 2001). The *yutori* reforms were a clear move towards more "freedom and choice," with the aim to reduce pressure on students to do well in school, increase freedom of choice, reduce competition, and make school more enjoyable again. This kind of relaxation policy should have reduced the dependence on shadow education significantly, too. However, as discussed in Chaps. 2, 7, and 8, the shadow remains strong in Japan. This implies that the carried-out reforms did not achieve their goal of reducing competition between students and schools. The findings of Chap. 7 further support the assumption that the recent reformation of the formal schooling system in Japan failed to increase equality of educational opportunities, rather the opposite. Hence, whether social inequalities in contemporary Japan have grown or not also very much depends on the outcomes of the education policy course of the last two decades. Which reform measures were actually carried out with what intention and how this changed Japanese education will be content of this chapter.

This chapter addresses the question whether the *yutori* reforms have actually changed Japan's regular schooling system in a way that reduced competition for high credentials and thus possibly reduced the demand for shadow education. To approach this issue, based on a literature review and the analysis of Ministry of Education (MEXT) reports, first, the causes of the *yutori* (relaxation) education reforms are outlined. Second, the main *yutori* reform measures are introduced. Third, the outcomes of the *yutori* reforms are critically analyzed with the aim to identify whether these reform measures have possibly reduced pressure and competition in education, thus reducing the demand for shadow education also. Fourth, the failure of the *yutori* reforms and the reintroduction of heavy competition through *datsu-yutori* (anti-relaxation) measures are discussed, showing where Japanese education is headed. A final concluding summary then discusses what all the reforms mean for Japanese education, its formal and informal or shadow parts.

10.2 *Yutori Kyōiku*: An Attempt to Decrease the Educational Competition?

In order to decrease the prevalent intense competition between students and lessen the pressure on them as well as give students "more time to explore their own interests" (Okada 2012a: 139), reform measures targeting the formal schooling system were initiated since 1977 under the guiding principle *yutori kyōiku* (no-pressure education; Tanabe 2004: 3). However, even though the "examination competition problem" ("*juken kyōsō no mondai*") was recognized for producing heavy cramming on a societal level (Roesgaard 2006: 2–3), adequate reforms were not initiated until the 1990s. This third major wave of educational reformation in Japan not only originated from the belief that students' school life was too much a burden for children and needed to become more enjoyable again (Fujita 2010: 19). Whereas this reason seems to be the most obvious one, the changing context in which Japanese education takes place has to be considered also when discussing the upcoming of this major education reform wave in Japan. In summary, three major causes for the initiation of the *yutori kyōiku* reforms can be identified:

1. *Overheated Competition*: The intense *kyōiku kyōsō* including the *shiken jigoku* caused by the entrance exam system (Azuma 2002: 14) and dull root learning (Bjork and Tsuneyoshi 2005: 625) in conjunction with the rigidity of the schooling system and the comparatively lax university system (Goodman 2003: 9) conveyed the need to lessen students' workload and change the entrance examination system to encourage students' learning interest.
2. *School Disorder*: The "school disorder" phenomena were believed to put Japanese schools and education in danger (Central Council on Education 1998, cited in Azuma 2002: 14, Fujita 2010: 22, M. o. E. MEXT, Culture, Sports, Science and Technology 2012a: part 1, SF 1: sect. 1, ch. 4).
3. *Internationalization*: Against the background of the "drastic slowdown of the economy" (Motani 2005: 309) and the need to stay competitive internationally due to progressing globalization and evolving new educational standards, concerns regarding the actual state and purpose of the education system and its supply function for the economy were raised (Azuma 2002: 14, Fujita 2010: 22). In particular, the perceived decline in students' academic achievement (*gakuryoku teika*) caused long-lasting debates (Takayama 2008: 388). This resulted in the perceived need for stronger internationalization (*kokusaika*) (Goodman 2003: 18, Aspinall 2010), which in turn led to increasing demands on students to do better in school and the need for a new approach in education to encourage individuality (*kosei*) and creativity (*sōzōsei*) (Goodman 2003: 16–18, Jones 2011: 13, Cave 2016).

First of all, if we speak of *yutori* education, meaning no-pressure or relaxed education, this automatically implies that this reform's major goal would be to get the pressure out of the classrooms by counteracting the existing examination hell and reducing the workload, even though the official translation would rather be something like "liberal, flexible and comfortable school life" (Kariya and Dore 2006: 151). However, besides this sound explanation for the radical reforms that followed, there are other, more often discussed, reasons. On the one hand, the schooling system was criticized for being too rigid, while at the same time, the field of higher education was criticized in the opposite way (Goodman 2003: 9). In particular, representatives of major corporations and conservative politicians criticized the universities for their lack of cooperation with the economy by not training students according to the economies' needs. Universities have traditionally strived to keep their independence in teaching and research matters. Companies thus needed to develop their own intern training systems (OJT, on-the-job training; see Demes and Georg 2007: 290) to train college and university graduates. This led to the intense *shūkatsu* (job-hunting) period of fourth year university students who are in need to expand their job application skills. Consequently, major company representatives demanded to reform higher education in order to stay internationally competitive by making universities the provider of the twenty-first-century workforce. Due to the drastic decrease in youth population and thus potential university applicants, criticism of the existing university system was also raised within the university system, in particular by private universities (Amano and Poole 2005: 694–697). According to estimations in the 1990s, the low fertility rate was believed to put an end to the examination hell until 2009, meaning the tough competition for university entrance would just stop due to fewer competitors. Without competition and too little demand for higher education, private universities would automatically be affected by financial difficulties (ibid: 700). But this was not the case (Okada 2012a: 145). However, the believed "2009 crisis," as it was called (Goodman 2003: 11), led to considerable rethinking among professors and whether stronger emphasis should be laid on "teaching" as the new primary objective, taking the place of the former preference "research" (Amano and Poole 2005: 700).

Secondly, one of the most cited reasons for the perceived need to change the ongoing system are violent incidents and other phenomena of school disorder, which occurred in Japan more frequently since the 1970s and received major attention by the press (Fujita 2010: 22). Every now and again, the press would pick up violent incidents such as *ijime* (bullying) at school and discuss them by questioning the functionability of the schooling system. Besides the problems of school disorder, especially cases of student suicides received major attention by the media. Often suicides were believed to be directly related to either school disorder within the school, such as *ijime*, or the intense competition caused by the *shiken jigoku*. In 2007, *The Japan Times* concluded that Japan has now it's "[w]orst student suicide rate yet" (The Japan Times 2007) and that "problems at school" as mentioned in students' suicide notes were at a record high. In particular "pressure because of poor performance records [and] [b]ullying" are believed to be main causes for student suicides (ibid). However, it is well known that school disorder phenomena are not at all limited to Japan, but found in all modern societies, because "[w]hen the society becomes richer and becomes more generous, the general trend is that you will relax discipline in the society" (Kajita 2013: 1). The 1970s were such a time for Japan, which enjoyed economic recovery and wealth during this time. From a comparative point of view, concerns about school disorder in Japan seem exaggerated, considering that it was proven that Japan is still and has always been one of the countries with only minor school disorder problems in international comparison. The case of student suicides is another story, though. The relation to the *kyōiku kyōsō* is an actual strong argument for a relaxation policy. Until today, politicians still use incidents related to school disorder or student misbehavior to legitimate further reform attempts by concluding that the Japanese school system is in danger.

Thirdly, during the 1990s, education in Japan became to be understood as the "key to international economic competition" (Cave 2001: 173). However, the way in which the Japanese attempted to increase their economic competitiveness through education is actually not only the most important reason for the implementation of the *yutori* reforms but also the most paradox reason when considering the view on Japanese education from outside of Japan. As I mentioned earlier (Chaps. 1 and 8), Japanese education was repeatedly praised for its excellence in academic achievement and high level of equality of educational opportunities. Japan's officials decided on a new education course at a time when most Western countries began to favor the opposite approach. However, as Bjork (2016) recently discussed, Japan's East Asian neighbors with similar education systems and problems, including an above-average dependence on shadow education, such as China, South Korea, and Singapore, followed similar paths. The *yutori* reforms were an actual attempt to change the ways of teaching, to change from the classical, objectivist approach of teaching towards a new constructivist approach, which was believed to be more effective in increasing academic performance outcomes. Whereas the classical approach favored functional literacy (discipline- and subject-based knowledge, knowledge accumulation) and mastery learning (transmission and accumulation, repetition and memorization), the new approach laid greater emphasis on a generative ability (generic skills and competence, critical and creative thinking abilities) and exploratory learning (child-centered participatory and interdisciplinary learning) (Fujita 2010: 27) as demanded by international education standards. Both approaches overlap and are not explained in detail here. What is of importance is the general change towards a more individualized approach to teaching and learning. The goal behind this course change was basically to stronger westernize Japanese education by creating "*jiritsu shita kojin*"– independent individuals (Kariya 2010: 12) on the basis of the principles "individuality, internationalisation, lifelong learning and information technology" (Jones 2011: 13). There was a strong belief that students required more than "the traditional drills and skills" (Bjork and Tsuneyoshi 2005: 621) and would thus have to acquire "new abilities." These new abilities would especially have to concentrate on creativity and critical thinking skills to finally catch up with Western standards in education – just as Japan has catched up with the West in economic terms in the 1970s (Fujita 1997: 73).

10.3 Carrying Out the Idea of *Yutori*: Good Intentions

To achieve the major goals of reducing academic pressure and increasing students' motivation to learn as well as creativity and critical thinking abilities, not only the entrance examination system was targeted and changed with the introduction of the *sentā shiken* in 1989 (see Chap. 2) but also "the restructuring or reorganization of all aspects of school education: opportunity structure, curriculum, teaching practices, educational governance, educational administration, and school management"

(Fujita 2010: 18). In short, the most important fields targeted by the *yutori kyōiku* reforms can be summarized in the following two spheres of major concern:

1. *Relaxation (yutori):* To decrease the *kyōiku kyōsō* and school disorder, the *yutori* reforms targeted:

   (a) The overall curriculum: The overall compulsory school curriculum was reduced by 30%, whereas the school week changed from a 6- to a 5-day school week (Goodman 2003). In addition, innovative instructional practices were introduced, and more opportunities for students were created by expanding the number of elective courses, for example (Bjork 2016: 7–8).

   (b) Classroom management: Teachers were advised to refrain from physically punishing students and instead compassionately mentor their students in order to reduce school disorder phenomena (Bjork 2016: 8–9).

   (c) The structure of the schooling system: A new 6-year secondary school type was introduced to the school system in 1999 in order to eliminate the *shiken jigoku* at the transition to high school (Okada 2012a: 121, MEXT 2017a: school system).

   (d) The university entrance examination system: Universities were advised to stronger consider other criteria for entrance to make it easier for students to enter a university (under certain circumstances) without taking an entrance examination (Amano and Poole 2005, Aspinall 2005, Jones 2011).

2. *Internationalization (kokusaika):* Change of schooling guidelines to stronger promote:

   (a) Individuality (*kosei*), creativity (*sōzōsei*), and "international sensitivity" (in the sense of *kokusaika*) to enable Japan to "survive in an era of global competition" (Azuma 2002: 14). To create room to develop *kosei* and *sōzōsei* by augmenting teachers' influence on school curricula and encouraging students to follow their own study interests, the so-called *sōgōtekina gakushū no jikan* (comprehensive or integrated study period) was introduced as a new subject in compulsory school (Bjork and Tsuneyoshi 2005: 621, Bjork 2016: 7).

   (b) The curriculum contents and teaching methods at universities were targeted with the aim to better "serve" students according to their demands (Amano and Poole 2005: 697). According to a 1998 report of the university council, universities should be reformed in order to "allow individuality to shine in the competitive environment of the 21st century" (M. o. E. MEXT, Culture, Sports, Science and Technology 2012a: part 1, SF 1: sect. 1, ch. 4).

   (c) Further key directions to match international demands on education were the development towards a life-long learning society (*shakai kyōiku*), information technology (*jōhōka*), and liberalization (*jiyūka*) (Okada 2012a: 109). Under the keyword *jiyūka* actual school choice was introduced to the system, enabling parents to choose between different schools of the same type (Goodman 2003: 18–19).

The most outstanding and visible reform measure of the *yutori* reforms was the drastic reduction of regular study hours at school. This reduction reached its climax with the implementation of the 1998 announced cut of the school curriculum by no less than 30%, coming into effect in 2002. Even though the *yutori* reform course was launched in the 1980s, it did not show an overall reduction of the school curriculum until 2002. However, due to the possible increase in electable lessons, other subjects were partly reduced already. Actually, first reforms in this direction were initialized in the 1970s, where the reduction of school contents started (Bjork and Tsuneyoshi 2005: 620). These changes did not affect the general curriculum, but they show the course to which Japanese education was beginning to head. In 1998 the Central Council on Education (CCE) came to the conclusion that "Japanese education inclined to be one-way teaching of knowledge and tended to downplay the ability for independent learning and thinking. Also, having been preoccupied with equality in education, sufficient attention has not been given to the variety of student personalities" (CCE 1998, cited in Azuma 2002: 14). To increase individualization (*kosei*) and promote creativity (*sōzōsei*), the so-called *sōgōtekina gakushū no jikan* (integrated study period) was introduced as a new subject for students from grade 3 to 12 in 1998, coming into effect in 2002.

In primary school, 105 to 110 hours were laid down for the integrated or comprehensive study subject, whereas this subject varied from 70 up to 130 hours in middle school. Hence, schools were pretty flexible regarding the length and number of class periods, but also regarding their instructional content. To incorporate students' interest into lessons and thus foster students' learning motivation and creativity, teachers, who could not rely on official textbooks for this subject, were advised to encourage their students to share their own ideas and develop projects (Bjork and Tsuneyoshi 2005: 621). However, in order to introduce this new subject and make room for students' individual development or rather personalization of contents, existing subjects had to be cut additionally.

In summary, the *yutori* curriculum reforms led to a drastic decrease of instruction time not only for the academic subjects, such as Japanese Language (approximately 35 hours per grade), Social Studies (up to 35 hours in grades 3, 7, 8, 9), Mathematics (up to 35 hours in grades 8 and 9), Science (up to 35 hours in grade 3), and Electives, generally meaning English Language classes (approximately 5 hours per grade in middle school), but also for the nonacademic subjects, such as Music (up to 25 hours in grade 7), Fine Arts (up to 25 hours in grade 7), Physical Education (approximately 15 hours per grade), Industrial Skills (up to 15 hours in grade 6), and Special Activity Lessons (up to 35 hours for grades 4–9) (see Appendix, Table 10.1).

The only subject that remained unaffected by the new course was Moral Education, a subject that was often used to catch up on lessons in other subjects anyway (Goodman 2003: 10). Of the 1998 curriculum following the introduction of the new *yutori* curriculum guidelines, only 60% (7th grade) to 66% (9th grade) are academic (Fukuzawa and LeTendre 2001: 11). In addition to these curriculum reductions, the school week was reduced from six to five days, banishing school on Saturdays (Jones 2011: 13). Even though the MEXT believed that the *yutori* reforms were a chance to finally basically reform English education as the central skill for more *kokusaika* (Goodman 2003: 18) and even though English became its own subject and was no longer only a category of Electives, the allocated time for English lessons did not increase. The desirable shift of the first English lessons to the primary school level was also not accomplished until the next curriculum guidelines were out in 2008.

Another aspect with possible major implications for students' school life is found in the liberalization (*jiyūka*) policy. Until the new millennium, parents' and students' options to pick a school were very limited. In general, primary and middle school students were allocated to a public school in their neighborhood. Only private schools offered an alternative – a more expensive alternative. However, due to school disorder problems, dissatisfaction with the quality of teaching and leadership, the resistance of schools to listen to parents' demands, dissatisfaction with educational standardization, and schools' unwillingness to reform, parents raised concerns about sending their children to certain schools without having any say in the decision and thus demanded more choice. In addition, representatives of government, educational institutions, and the media critiqued the public schools without much evidence and thus contributed to the belief that public schools' quality has suffered (Dierkes 2008: 232–234). Even though the new *jiyūka* is generally limited to metropolitan areas such as Tōkyō, it allows parents and students to choose between different public schools in the district (*ku*) the students are living in (Goodman 2003: 19). This reform was believed to bring more freedom of choice to families and more healthy competition between schools to the system and encourage unpopular schools to carry out reforms and improve their quality (Dierkes 2008: 232–234). In addition to school choice, the newly introduced 6-year secondary school was created to provide more options and spare students the examination hell at the transition to high school (Okada 2012a: 121). Of course, this liberalization attempt can be understood as an attempt to confer more self-determination to the people, but there are negative consequences to this "freedom" as well, as I will discuss in the following subchapter.

The last point of major importance is the reform of higher education. Beginning in the 1990s, the first true reformation of Japan's universities started with the aim to adjust university education according to new goals and standards in education. Especially private universities were under a lot of pressure to change their courses of study to attract more applicants from a shrinking pool of graduates. To achieve this goal, new faculties with stronger emphasis on *kokusaika*-related studies were established, e.g., departments of international or cultural studies; the curriculum was changed and syllabuses were introduced; teaching methods were supposed to become more innovative; and evaluations of classes were introduced (Amano and Poole 2005: 697). Besides these impressive challenges, the MEXT raised demands to change the admission procedures, to lessen the *kyōiku kyōsō*. Until recently, only performance is counted for getting access to high schools and universities, with very few exceptions. Thanks to the *yutori* reforms, different ways to successfully enroll at these institutions have become possible, which "are better suited to the wishes of the individual candidates and to the needs of the particular faculties and departments to which they are applying" (Aspinall 2005: 210). Hence, students are now allowed to enter universities on the basis of the evaluation of practical tests, interviews, essays, and *suisen nyūgakkō* (a recommendation letter of a school principal). In addition, students' engagement in extracurricular activities, such as clubs (*bukatsudō*) or volunteer activities (*borantia katsudō*) shall be acknowledged as well. Especially private universities responded positively to these demands and set up so-called admission offices (AO) following the example of Keio university, which started its first AO in 1990 to consider more students based on qualities besides academic performance in entrance examinations. In addition, students who still take the entrance examinations for universities (*sentā* and *niji*) have the opportunity to take varying tests according to the demands of their later enrolled major in university and thus do not necessarily have to take tests in all core subject areas, but sometimes only two or three (ibid: 210–212).

10.4   The Outcomes of *Yutori*: Reversing the Course

As argued earlier, the radical *yutori* reforms were launched despite the superficial success of Japanese education and a lot of opposition. In particular the reduction of study hours in school led to a national education discourse concerned with the feared decline in academic achievement (*gakuryoku teika ronsō*) (Takayama 2008: 388). Besides politicians, leading Japanese sociologists explained their concerns regarding the actual sense of these reforms. Fujita (2000) even went so far as to call the drastic curriculum reduction "educational disarmament" and pointed to the fact that Japan was changing its course against the global educational "rearmament" trend with the common goal to stay economically competitive. After the publication of the first PISA results in December 2001, the opposition to *yutori* began to gain the upper hand in the debates, and even the MEXT had to give in three months before the actual implementation of the reforms. The MEXT then began to follow a new education policy goal: the *tashikana gakuryoku* (solid academic ability) and launched the *manabi no susume* (exhortation towards learning) education guideline (Takayama 2008: 394). This new guideline placed more weight on the "basics and fundamentals" of teaching and learning again and aimed to ensure that the academic achievement level of students would remain high while also fostering individuality and creativity (M. o. E. MEXT, Culture, Sports, Science and Technology 2005: ch. 1, part 5). Consequently, new reform measures to reverse the 1998 initiated *yutori* reforms were already well underway when the predicted *kyōiku kiki* (education crisis) was somehow confirmed by the 2003 PISA results as announced in December 2004. In the following, I will first review the reasons for the missing opposition to what I would like to call the "anti-*yutori*" reform course in education – even though the new reform measures were still marked as *yutori* – before discussing the actual changes following this course change in the next subchapter.

Many have argued that particularly parents would have an interest to reduce the pressure on their children and would therefore advocate for these reforms (Goodman 2003: 21). They would make their demands heard by involving themselves in school politics through their representatives in the PTA (parent–teacher association), for example. This organization is quite powerful, since it represents the parents' views and wishes on the local and prefectural boards of education. Hence, it is not unreasonable to consider the PTA having "teachers running for their suits and bowing a whole lot [while the] PTA chief is usually [...] on a nearly equal social level as high government officials" (Martin 2012). Parents are therefore a powerful force in the discussion about educational reforms and would get their concerns taken seriously. Unfortunately, the opposite is true: *yutori* has never been popular among parents (Takayama 2008: 399), who viewed the reduction of the curriculum and the shortening of the school week as not in the interest of their children and opposed them mostly. The truth is most parents fear that a school system with less pressure will only result in an achievement gap which they would have to compensate by paying for extracurricular lessons outside of school (i.e., shadow education). Clearly most parents are not "prepared to take risks with their own children's education" (Goodman 2003: 21). In this regard, parents raised their voices and made demands on the government. According to the media, these demands were too high to live up to, whereas the media was fast to speak of "monster parents" (Kataoka 2014). Nevertheless, a political response was achieved: former (and actual) prime minister Shinzo Abe felt obliged to implement the so-called *Education Rebuilding Council* in 2006, with the aim to work out possible reforms (Yamashita and Okada 2011: 39).

Besides parents, politicians and the industry opposed such aspects of *yutori* education based on the argument that Japan's economy would fail in international competition due to the expected and, as they saw it, the proven *gakuryoku teika*, referring to Japanese 15-year-olds' decline in PISA reading performance. Even the MEXT, which remained the lone advocate of its reforms, had to change the course of education to survive politically (see Takayama 2008). In conclusion, after the 2003 PISA results were out, the first and perceived major goal of the three major reasons for the implementation of the *yutori* reforms with the aim to finally counteract the examination hell (as outlined in the preceding subchapter) vanished in favor of *kokusaika* (internationalization) and the stronger adaptation to international education standards. When evaluating the outcomes of the 1998 reforms, the change of the course seems somehow reasonable, as the following discussions regarding the main points that were implemented in 1998 shall illustrate:

First of all, there were problems with the actual implementation of the *yutori* reforms. In particular the content of the newly introduced Integrated Studies were not concretely defined and left teachers only with guidelines to accomplish the task to develop students' creative thinking ability (Bjork and Tsuneyoshi 2005: 621). Not surprisingly, the private industry already produced a number of unofficial textbooks shortly after the implementation of the new subject in 2002 (Goodman 2003: 10). The fear that this new subject would be used to cover other contents, as argued by Goodman (ibid), was partly verified in Chap. 8. In general, many teachers raised complaints following the implementation of the *yutori* reforms, since they felt too much pressure on themselves now – pressure raised by the government, the media, and parents. On the one hand, teachers needed to fulfill their duty towards the MEXT by nurturing students according to the new agenda. On the other hand, teachers felt a need to compensate for the reduced study time in school towards the parents, who were worried about their children's academic skills, which they thought their children needed in their later life course (Bjork and Tsuneyoshi 2005: 623).

Second, free school choice was highly debated. Although the different types of school choice remained locally or regionally limited, until 2004, 8.8% of the municipalities with more than one school introduced free school choice for primary and 11.1% for middle schools (Dierkes 2008: 234). This percentage increased to 15.9% for primary schools and 16.3% for middle schools in 2012 (M. o. E. MEXT, Culture, Sports, Science and Technology 2012b: 3, 9). School choice thus became more individualized, but at what costs? For once, competition between compulsory public schools increased through school choice thus contributing to the perceived decline in the quality of public education and a possible ranking of public primary and middle schools in certain districts. This, in turn, possibly results in a more unequal distribution of educational opportunities and more limited access to schools for students with disadvantaged family background (Dierkes 2008: 236). The same concerns were expressed by Okada (2012a, b), regarding the introduction of the 6-year secondary school. Okada argues that *jiyūka* (liberalization) was used as a catchphrase while conservative forces aimed to establish a more diversified meritocratic educational structure by reversing the single-track education system structure aiming to create a national elite. In order to do that, the revision of Article III of the Fundamental Law of Education (*kyōiku-kihon-hō*) was targeted, as it guaranteed all children equal opportunities in education "according to their ability" – thus bearing room for interpretations. Conservatives used these words to promote *nōryokushugi* – the "ability first principle." The promoted *jiyūka* actually turned out to be *tayōka* (diversification) resulting in an increased inequality of educational opportunities. One of the outcomes directly following the implementation of the *yutori* reforms was thus "ability grouping" in primary and middle schools. In 2002, 60% of all compulsory schools had already adopted this grouping system and thus began to put students into different groups according to their aptitude (Bjork and Tsuneyoshi 2005: 623). Consequently, Okada interprets the growing inequality in life chances in present-day Japan as a direct consequence of the conservatives' success over the egalitarian concept, because the newly favored principle of *nōryokushugi* and parents' freedom of choice contribute to social class inequalities.

Third, the reform of higher education, in particular regarding the admission procedures, has to be evaluated regarding its success in actually decreasing the *kyōiku kyōsō*. In addition to the initiated reforms, the low fertility rate was believed to put an end to the *shiken jigoku* until 2009, meaning the tough competition for university entrance would just stop due to fewer competitors (Okada 2012a: 145). In particular private universities feared for their existence, since they heavily depend on tuition fees. But, since the percentage of students aiming to enter university is steadily increasing (see Chap. 2, Fig. 2.2), the total number of students taking the *sentā shiken* remained constant from 1995 to 2014 (Fig. 10.1).

This is a quite surprising finding considering the reported new admission possibilities to university. In order to finally get rid of the examination hell, the number of examinees taking the *sentā shiken* each year should have decreased drastically by

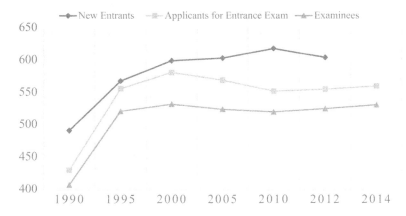

Fig. 10.1 Annual number of university entrants, applicants for the *sentā shiken* and actual examinees, in 1000, 1990–2014 (M. o. E. MEXT, Culture, Sports, Science and Technology 2012d; Daigaku-Nyūshi-Sentā 2014a, b)

now, in particular considering that by 2002 the new method to enter by recommendation was already very popular (Aspinall 2005: 210). However, things seem to be quite as they used to be, when considering that neither the number of applicants for the *sentā*, the actual number of students who took the *sentā* (examinees), nor the number of new entrants has considerably changed from 1995 to 2014.

While there are approximately 600,000 new university entrants each year, the number of *sentā* examinees also remained between 520,000 and 530,000 each year since 2000. This shows that most university applicants still take the central entrance examination, even though a higher percentage of students enters university by alternative entrance methods. Whereas in the year 2000 65.8% of new entrants entered university in the traditional way by taking the entrance examination, in 2012 still 56.2% did so. In contrast, in 2000 approximately 31.7% of all new entrants had entered by recommendation, and in 2012 this share reached 34.8% – a percentage that was already reached in 2002 (34.1%) and thus remained constant for 10 years. An actual increase in alternative admission is only found for the AO systems – admission through the newly set up admission offices. Whereas in 2000 only 1.4% of all new entrants entered through the AO, in 2012 8.5% of new all students enrolled through the AO system (M. o. E. MEXT, Culture, Sports, Science and Technology 2012c: 1, 4). What has to be noted here is the fact that even though national and public universities have responded to the MEXT's demands to increase the percentage of students who enter by alternative methods, most students (more than 90%) who manage to enter a university by recommendation actually enter private institutions. This is no new phenomenon though, since a recommendation system existed long before the introduction of the *yutori* reforms, but was limited to students who managed to enroll in high schools attached to universities (Watanabe 2013: 151). In 2012, still 84.1% of all new national university entrants and 73.3% of all new public university entrants had to take the entrance examination to enter a university. In contrast, every second new private university entrant has entered by recommendation or through the AO system (50.5%) (M. o. E. MEXT, Culture, Sports, Science and Technology 2012c: 1–29). What is also of concern here is the fact that "many private universities are advised to take the [entrance examination] scores into consideration when selecting prospective students in either the AO (Admissions Office) screening or by school recommendation" (Mina 2013). In general, since the implementation of the *yutori* reforms, private universities have been very successful in attracting students to enroll.

As a result, since the 1990s the number of private universities increased (Kariya 2013, MEXT 2017b), leaving only 169 non-private institutions out of the currently existing 770 universities (M. o. E. MEXT, Culture, Sports, Science and Technology 2014c). Even though some researchers even went so far as to say that the distinction function of the entrance exams is not necessary anymore, due to a steadily increasing number of universities and other institutions in the tertiary education sector leading to the possibility to enroll despite low academic achievement (e.g., Mori 2002), the entrance examination system has not yet lost its power as the central instrument of allocation. Only the difficulty level of entrance examinations at certain high schools and universities is believed to have decreased. Universities with low alternative admission ratios thus have still highly difficult entrance exams. In addition it has to be noted that students who might have entered without taking the entrance examination often have to take extra lessons provided by universities to ensure students have the required basic skills (Aspinall 2005: 211). According to Amano Ikuo, one of the leading Japanese sociologists, the competition for access to university is only going into a new direction, which led him to create a new ranking of universities consisting of three major groups: highly selective universities, mildly competitive universities, and non-competitive or "F-rank" (free-pass) universities (Amano and Poole 2005: 694, 706). The last category has become more popular recently, due to the steady increase of the number of private universities (Kariya 2013). To enter such an F-rank university, students still need to pass entrance examinations. According to the major preparatory schools (*yobikō*) such as Kawaijuku, universities and colleges which are categorized as F-rank have a take-up rate of 65% or higher. However, students mostly apply to several universities and use these institutions as a security strategy (Kinmoth 2005: 119). This means, even though admission might be almost guaranteed, most students do not want to enter a third-rate, expensive private university but still try to get into higher-ranked, prestigious institutions.

Consequently, despite the new ways of entrance besides the entrance exam, admission to higher-ranked universities is still fierce. If a student is not recommended based on outstanding school efforts, he would still have to succeed in the highly difficult entrance exams. Moreover, for students with high aspirations, the passing of high-ranked universities' entrance examinations remains decisive to achieve a competitive edge and thus a status advantage. Due to the MEXT's new privatization policy (*dokuritsu hōjinka*) resulting in a decrease in state subsidies for the national and public universities which started in April 2004, national and public universities also have to think more about how to attract the brightest students to remain on top of the university ranking and ensure constant demand. This introduces even more competition between students into the system than before, partly explaining the still high enrolment via entrance examinations at national and public universities.

Foreseeing that, in 1999 Amano already concluded that "in a society that places more importance on the name of the school from which one graduates […] students will continue to strive to enter a small number of 'top-tier' or 'brand-name' universities, and the severe entrance examination war will not disappear" (Amano and Poole 2005: 694). It appears that although the university entrance examination system was criticized for decades because of the extraordinary high competition it produces, all initiated reforms in higher education do not yet show satisfying results. Competition between students remains fierce and has only decreased partially.

As I have discussed in Chap. 2, the transition to university depends very much on the rank of the attended high school (Okada 2012b: 122), shifting the competition for university entrance to the high school entrance level. There is, however, a big difference between university and high school entrance. Whereas the percentage of students entering university or junior college reached 56% in 2012, since the 1970s, almost every student enters high school (see Chap. 7, Fig. 7.1). Hence, the transition to high school determines the later given educational options and makes the transition to high school crucial. Even though entrance to a university has gotten easier if a student does not aim too high, to enter prestigious universities, a profound preparation is still indispensable. Because of that, for high schools, only minor modifications of the admission procedure are visible. High schools are still functioning as allocation institution for tertiary education and labor market, showing a hierarchical ranking. In general, students still have to take an entrance examination to get into the high school of their choice. This does not mean that other references such as students' middle school GPA (grade point average) are not taken into consideration in the admission process, but this is not new and thus the academic achievement test remains crucial. To succeed in this examination, solely performance counts. In conclusion, entrance examinations are still "central to the allocation process" (Stevenson and Baker 1992: 1640), because the "labelization" (*gakkōreki*) of schooling institutions has not stopped, as Amano predicted (Amano and Poole 2005: 694).

10.5   Anti-*yutori* Course: Making Japanese Education Competitive Again

In summary, there seem to be several adequate reasons to further develop the *yutori* reforms or even reverse them to some degree, but what was actually done in the years since 2002 seems to not have eased the workload of students or the examination hell. As Bjork (2016) recently concluded, "post-2002 revisions of the Course of Study undercut many of the changes aimed at reducing academic intensity in the schools" (p. 214). The actual causes for the reverse of the *yutori* education course were the education in crisis (*kyōiku kiki*) debates, particularly discussing the decline in academic achievement (*gakuryoku teika ronsō*) in conjunction with the 2004 PISA shock. But, since the reformation of Japanese education is far from being complete, the often asked question "whither Japanese education," as asked by many scholars following the reversion of the *yutori* course (Goodman 2005, Fujita 2010, Kobayashi 2013), remains an important issue. Japanese education remains under constant change. Results of large-scale assessments such as PISA and TIMSS are exploited to justify the anti-*yutori* course. This new course laid stronger emphasis on the *kosei* (individuality) component of the reform, distancing itself from the *yutori* component. "Relaxed" education was no longer believed to be effective in any way and would contradict the *kokusaika* intention of the national policy course. To get back on track and make Japanese education more competitive again, several new reforms were initiated following the *kyōiku kiki*, *gakuryoku teika*, and PISA shock discussions, which can be summarized as follows:

1. *Relaxation (yutori)*: In the sense of *yutori*, the reduction of pressure on students was carried out, resulting in:

    (a) 2005: Financial support for private schools with the aim "to maintain and improve these schools' educational and research conditions and reduce the financial burden of learning for students and pupils enrolled there" (M. o. E. MEXT, Culture, Sports, Science and Technology 2012a: part 2, ch. 5)

    (b) 2006: Establishment of the Education Rebuilding Council with "a focus on compulsory education and the issue of bullying" (ibid: part 1, SF 1: sect. 1, ch. 7)

    (c) 2010: Program for "free tuition fee at public high schools" and introduction of the "high school support fund" (ibid: part 2, ch. 3)

    (d) 2011: Lowering of class size of first grade primary school classes to 35 students and introduction of a flexible class size determination (ibid)

    (e) 2012/2013: increase of teaching staff at schools (ibid)

2. Anti-relaxation (*datsu-yutori*): To counteract previous *yutori* reform measures following the guiding policy goal *tashikana gakuryoku* (solid academic achievement), several changes aimed at increasing the workload and pressure on students again:

    (a) 2002: The *manabi no susume* (exhortation towards learning) education guideline was an attempt to get back to basics while also fostering individuality and creativity (M. o. E. MEXT, Culture, Sports, Science and Technology 2005: ch. 1, part 5).

    (b) 2004: Announcement of the new general education reform plan entitled "*Yomigaere Nihon!*" ("Japan! Rise Again!") with the aim to improve students' academic achievement level (MEXT 2017a: elementary and secondary education, reform of compulsory education).

    (c) 2008: Revision of the course of study resulting in a 10% increase of total study hours at the primary and middle school level, coming into effect in

2012, with the aim to increase academic achievement and incorporate "PISA-like competencies" (Breakspear 2012: 24). In addition, the time for the subject "Integrated Studies" was cut in favor of the five core subjects (see Appendix, Table 10.1).

3. *Internationalization (kokusaika)/diversification (tayōka)*: To further promote *kokusaika* and create a more diversified education according to the principles of *jiyūka* and *tayōka* (Okada 2012a: 109), the following additional reforms were carried out or announced:

(a) 2003: Implementation of the "Action Plan to cultivate Japanese students' English aptitude" (Sage 2007: 2)

(b) 2005: Revision of the Private Schools Act "so that [...] private schools will respond appropriately to the rapid changes in social circumstances in recent years and voluntarily and flexibly address different issues. [In summary,] private schools are expected to create unique and attractive schools that respond to people's requests" (M. o. E. MEXT, Culture, Sports, Science and Technology 2012a: part 2, ch. 5)

(c) 2006: Revision of the Fundamental Law of Education (*kyōiku-kihon-hō*) with the intention to nurture "strong-willed Japanese people with the strength of mind to lead the way in the 21st century" and newly stipulate "that the government shall formulate a basic plan [...] to comprehensively and systematically advance policies to promote education" (ibid: part 1, SF 1: sect. 1, ch. 6)

(d) 2007: Reintroduction of a national achievement test consisting of a traditional part (basic knowledge) and new part (application skills, PISA-related competencies) (Ninomiya and Urabe 2011, Breakspear 2012: 19, Sato, et al. 2013)

(e) 2008: Enhancement of foreign language education from primary to high school coming into effect in 2011 (M. o. E. MEXT, Culture, Sports, Science and Technology 2012a: part 2, ch. 3)

(f) 2009: Update of the 2008 course of study to increase the weight of English instruction, coming into effect in 2011 to 2013 (M. o. E. MEXT, Culture, Sports, Science and Technology 2009)

(g) 2009: Revision of the "Ordinance for Enforcement of the School Education Act" to make enrolment at university more flexible by abolishing "the principle of April enrolment" (M. o. E. MEXT, Culture, Sports, Science and Technology 2012a: part 1, SF 1: sect. 1, ch. 7)

(h) 2014: Introduction of the new "English Education Reform Plan corresponding to Globalization" with the aim to "enhance English education substantially throughout elementary to lower/secondary school" (M. o. E. MEXT, Culture, Sports, Science and Technology 2014a)

(i) 2016: Implementation of the new "National University Reform Plan" with the aim to "maintain competitiveness and create new added-value ideas by building a structure in which each university makes optimum use of its strengths and characteristics and encourages independent and autonomous improvement and development" (M. o. E. MEXT, Culture, Sports, Science and Technology 2014d)

(j) 2020: Planned realization of the national education goal of "upgrading the Japanese society and its citizen" against the background of the 2020 Olympics in Japan (M. o. E. MEXT, Culture, Sports, Science and Technology 2014b)

The above shown overview illustrates the strong emphasis on further promoting internationalization as one of the constants of education policy on the one hand and the gradual warding off from *yutori* on the other hand. Attempts to relax students' school life are hardly found anymore, and thus it is of question whether "these changes portend the gradual abandonment of the goals of relaxed education or [whether] the reforms continue to exist in a slimmer form" (Bjork 2016: 215). The introduction of a flexible class size determination and lower class sizes beginning in primary school is no guarantor that classes in middle and high school will not extend to 40 students per class again. Furthermore, a class size of 35 is still high in international comparison – especially for primary schools. To actually ensure that the number of students in class will not exceed 35, additional teaching staff is required, resulting in an increase of personnel in 2012 and 2013, also with the aim to better deal with school disorder issues. This increase in teaching staff is, however, planned for primary school grades one and two only. Special attention is still given to the issue of bullying (*ijime*) in Japanese classrooms, pointing to the still existing prevalence of some school disorder problems, possibly also a result of insufficient measures to stop the *shiken jigoku*. Another positive aspect would be the reduction of tuition fees at private and public schools, in particular high schools. This is a necessary step to create opportunities for students from disadvantaged economic backgrounds to be able to apply at high-ranked schools with high tuition fees. This is a generally very positive development that only misses to include private schools in the shadow education sector. To succeed in the competition for entrance to high schools, which starts long before tuition fees at these schools have to be paid, expensive preparation is often unavoidable. Students who cannot afford sufficient preparation in the shadow education sector are often unable to enter their school of choice and are thus unable to benefit from these changes. If the main criterion to get admission to these support programs is academic achievement, students from socioeconomic advantaged backgrounds are more likely to get supported and thus increase their advantages, consequently fostering inequality of educational opportunities instead of counteracting such inequalities.

In contrast to the relaxation measures, the *datsu-yutori* measures aimed at increasing the academic achievement level of Japanese students and thus resulted in a recurring increase of workload and competition. Shortly after the 2002 *manabi no susume* guideline and its request to lay stronger emphasis on the fundamentals of teaching and learning again, in 2004 a new education reform plan was announced by Minister of Education Nariaki Nakayama entitled "*Yomigaere Nihon!*" ("Japan! Rise Again!"). It has to be noted that this reform plan was announced in November 2004, just a month before the publication of the 2003 PISA results (MEXT 2017a:

elementary and secondary education, reform of compulsory education). This plan aimed to create an "education that will raise children who engage in friendly rivalry and have the 'spirit of challenge'" (ibid), consisting of five reform proposals: (1) "amendment of the Fundamental Law of Education"; (2) "improvement of academic ability"; (3) "improvement of the quality of teachers"; (4) "placing importance on education on the ground"; and (5) "reform of the system of national treasury's share of compulsory education expenses" (ibid). This marked the beginning of the reversion of the *yutori* course, since the promotion of competition (*kyōsō*) and diversity (*tayōsei*) were put back on the agenda. Of special importance are points one and two. The amendment of the Fundamental Law of Education (FLE) meant a major interference in the fundamentals of modern Japanese education but was nevertheless implemented in 2006. The revised version of the FLE includes a newly added paragraph saying that financial assistance should be provided for those who, "in spite of their ability, encounter difficulties in receiving education for economic reasons" (M. o. E. MEXT, Culture, Sports, Science and Technology 2006), in accordance with the ability-first principle. This created the possibility to support the formation of a national elite, as actively pursued by conservative political forces. In addition, the concept of "Lifelong Learning" was included (Article 3) and private schools were acknowledged as being of "public nature" and fulfill an "important role in school education" and shall thus be promoted and supported through subsidies "by the national and local governments" while respecting their autonomy (ibid). To improve students' academic ability, it was decided to stronger benchmark and evaluate by measures such as nationwide surveys (i.e., reintroduction of a national achievement test), marking the clear output steering character in education.

With the publication of the second PISA results in December 2004 and the outbreak of what was labeled "PISA shock" in Japan, the opposition to *yutori* finally outweighed their proponents. In particular Minister Nakayama used PISA as an instrument of argumentation and justification of the following anti-*yutori* course. Nakayama demanded that the time for Integrated Studies would be reduced drastically, school on Saturdays be reintroduced, and school vacation be cut to increase students' study time again (Takayama 2008: 398). Following the minister's demands, the revised course of study as announced in 2008 showed an overall study time increase of 10%. The MEXT increased the study time in the five core academic subjects Japanese, Social Studies, Mathematics, Science, and English by placing special emphasis on PISA-related competence fields "to foster future generations of specialists in science and technology and improve each citizen's basic scientific knowledge [by] attracting students' interest in science, technology and mathematics" (M. o. E. MEXT, Culture, Sports, Science and Technology 2012a: part 2, ch. 3). This is the first time in decades that the instruction time at school was actually increased again. However, besides the five core subjects, only the time for Physical Education was increased. The Integrated Study Period was partly heavily decreased, while Electives were deleted completely, leaving students no choice whether they want to study English or not. English education was extended to primary school grades five and six and shall be further expanded to grades three and four soon. In

general, more importance was attached to academic skills related to PISA competency fields and English education. Critical thinking ability and communication
skills were laid stronger emphasis on.

The formerly criticized rigidity of the school system was restored by these measures. One new component of the system, the strong emphasis on internationalization (*kokusaika*), gained importance as a result of the PISA shock debates.
Henceforth, ideals like individuality (*kosei*) and creativity (*sōzōsei*) remained
important, even though the actual subject meant to foster students' *kosei*, *sōzōsei*,
and critical thinking ability as demanded by the OECD, the Integrated Study Period,
was reduced again. The "back to basics" claim of 2004 led to a concentration on the
PISA-related subjects in general and English language. Hence, the MEXT's new
major concern was the promotion of English education, resulting in the 2003
"Action Plan to cultivate Japanese students' English aptitude" (Sage 2007: 2).
However, according to a study by Lockley, et al. (2012), the demands of the Action
Plan were only met partially. The reason for these great concerns regarding Japanese
students' English is the fact that students were continuously found to lack English-
speaking skills – much more than students from their Asian neighbors South Korea,
Taiwan, or China, for example. Newspapers have frequently discussed this topic
and argued that the problem is caused by the entrance examination system, specifically the contents of the English section of these exams, where no speaking ability
is examined. Consequently, English lessons concentrate on grammar and translation
only, failing to foster students' ability to actually use their English skills in real-life
conversations (Yonedzu 2013, Yoshida 2013, Clavel 2014). This problem is known
for a long time. Japanese students are always behind in international rankings on
English proficiency. In 2007, Japan ranked only place 136 of 161 countries in the
"Test of English as a Foreign Language" or TOEFL (Knüsel 2011). Hence, Takaki
Yoshiaki, the new Minister of Education, stressed that in order to meet the demands
of globalization, "the Japanese people must develop a refined sense of cosmopoli-
tanism, with powers of expression that they can utilize on the world stage confi-
dently, articulating their principles and beliefs clearly. MEXT intends to achieve
this objective by enhancing foreign language education" (Takaki 2011: 1). However,
real measures to increase the state of English education in Japan were not taken
until after the PISA discussions. And the results have only become visible recently:
first with the introduction of English instruction to primary schools with the reversed
course of study, which came into effect 2011, and second with the Commission on
the Development of Foreign Language Proficiency's "Five Proposals and Specific
Measures for Developing Proficiency in English for International Communication"
(M. o. E. MEXT, Culture, Sports, Science and Technology 2011) also in 2011.
Following this, the new "English Education Reform Plan corresponding to
Globalization" (M. o. E. MEXT, Culture, Sports, Science and Technology 2014a)
was launched in 2014.

Whereas the reversed course of study is an actual measure, the 2011 proposals
remain proposals of course but were seriously taken into consideration by the Abe
government. The five proposals recommended to stronger assess and verify students' actual attainment level are as follows: proposal 1, to promote students'

awareness of the "necessity of English in the global society"; proposal 2, to provide students "with more opportunities to use English"; proposal 3, to reinforce "English skills and instruction abilities of English teachers"; proposal 4, to improve English education at "schools and communities"; and proposal 5, to modify the university entrance exams "towards global society" (M. o. E. MEXT, Culture, Sports, Science and Technology 2011). For Japanese school students, this last proposal is of special relevance here, since it targets a long discussed and criticized issue caused by the entrance examination system: these exams force students "to cram irrelevant facts" (Dierkes 2012). Memorization is of essence to succeed in these examinations. Of course, in the case of English proficiency, to cram vocabulary and grammar cannot be helped, but what worth will come of it if students have memorized whole sentences in English but cannot produce their own ones? English communication is often misunderstood as memorization (Chavez 2014). The Commission on the Development of Foreign Language Proficiency finally acknowledged this problem and concluded that "English entrance exams in universities do not always aim at English skills required by the global community including speaking ability. The entrance exams must be modified so as to involve not only listening and reading skills stipulated by the Courses of Study but also speaking and writing, with all the four skills tested at proper balance" (M. o. E. MEXT, Culture, Sports, Science and Technology 2011: 12).

With the announcement that Japan would carry out the Olympics in 2020, new national goals for 2020 were formulated in 2014 (M. o. E. MEXT, Culture, Sports, Science and Technology 2014b) and have even increased the pressure on students to get better at English: the MEXT has made English one of the most important skills as a means to adequately represent a high national academic level and stay internationally competitive – as well as to ensure that the Japanese people will be able to welcome the visitors in English. To achieve this goal, English instruction in schools is under constant change. Following the revised course of study guidelines of 2009, in high schools English instructions are held in English since 2013. The same shall be implemented in middle schools. For primary school students, the start of English lessons was shifted to third grade beginning 2014. By April 2020, English will become a formal subject taught three times a week, while all third graders shall be instructed in English (Abe 2013: 7, 13, Japan Today 2013, Kameda 2013, Knüsel 2013). Of course, it has to be asked whether these measures can actually be carried out. Even though there is a new program that allows up to 200 teachers to stay abroad for three months in order to improve their own English skills (Abe 2013), more foreign teachers will get hired and the *eiken* (Test in Practical English Proficiency) shall get utilized to certify Japanese English teachers' actual English-speaking ability (Japan Today 2013). Nevertheless, the progress in English education highly depends on teacher education. The problem with English proficiency is not one of schools only but remains an issue in university. Students who have never needed to use their English skills will continue to avoid using English in university as well. Hence, the English level at a university is often considerably low also (Gattig 2012). Universities are still generally criticized by the government and industry for not providing Japan with the workforce needed to meet the challenges

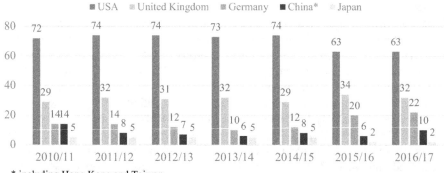

* including Hong Kong and Taiwan

Fig. 10.2 Number of universities in the top 200 of the Times Higher Education world university ranking, 2010–2017 (THE 2017)

of the twenty-first century. International or transnational skills are viewed crucial in this regard. In a society that still places more weight on the name of a university based on its prestige, the ranking of institutions has reached a new level. Universities are no longer only compared inside the country only but internationally. Consequently, the World International Ranking of the Times Higher Education (THE 2017) received major attention in the Japanese media as well. In recent years, only few Japanese universities made it to the top 200 in international ranking, as Fig. 10.2 illustrates.

Whereas the United States and the United Kingdom dominate the rankings since the first implementation of these rankings in 2004, Western countries such as Germany are represented by an increasing number of universities as well. Even China, which had just began to further promote higher education, succeeded in placing several universities among the top ranks (including Hong Kong and Taiwan). Japan, with its more than 700 universities, is underrepresented with five universities on average (in 2016 and 2017, only two universities made it into the top 200: the universities of Tōkyō and Kyōto). When the 2010/2011 results were out, debates reached its climax because Japan's number one university *Tōdai* (Tōkyō University), which had been on top of the Asian rankings for some time, was displaced by the University of Hong Kong. In 2017, *Tōdai* only ranked 7th place among all Asian universities. In addition, it has to be noted that even the *Tōdai* did not make it into the top 20 of all universities since the rankings started, where approximately 75% are constantly coming from the United States with the universities of Harvard, Stanford, and Princeton and the California Institute of Technology on top; only challenged by the United Kingdom with the universities of Oxford and Cambridge. Even though within the World Reputation Rankings the *Tōdai* was often found in the top 10 (2017, rank 11), in the World University Rankings, *Tōdai* only made it into the top 30 at best (2017, rank 39).

These and other reasons as discussed earlier led to the ongoing criticism of university education in Japan and the further pressure for stronger internationalization.

In addition to already initiated reform measures, the government under the regency of Prime Minister Abe presented the so-called "Abeducation" policy approach. Following the popular term "Abenomics" (the direction of economics under the Abe government), these new education direction were Prime Minister "Abe's growth strategy for education to develop human resources that can 'prevail on the world stage'" (Kakuchi 2013a). The Minister of Education Hakubun Shimomura summarized the goal of Abeducation as enhancing "the globalisation of our higher education institutions [and] to transform Japanese universities to world universities so they can be placed within the top ranking" (ibid). Prime Minister Abe even went so far as to announce the establishment of the "internationally competitive 'Super Global University' [and] 'Super Global High School'" (Abe 2013: 23) by stronger adapting education to globalization and create more opportunities for "able young people" to study abroad (ibid). According to Abe's plans, within the next decade "ten or more Japanese universities will be ranked in the top 100 universities in the world" (ibid: 50). Further measures are the creation of possibilities to "send young Japanese English-language teachers to the United States, as well as high school students who aspire to study abroad. Additionally, [...] we will promote high quality international student exchange programs, backed by quality assurances from each university" (Takaki 2011: 1). To realize these reforms, Abeducation depends on the "power of the private sector," which Abe intents to unleash "to the fullest extent" (ibid: 3), meaning increased support of private schools and universities and a stronger emphasis on deregulation and devolution to strengthen competition – the perceived engine of a higher academic performance level of students. These measures will again increase *jiyūka* (liberalization), or more precisely, *tayōka* (diversity), since the increase of the role private organizations play in the education system will not only lead to more freedom of choice but also more inequality of educational opportunities. In this regard, following the principles of Abeducation, the Council for the Implementation of Education Rebuilding examines the "modality of the school system (6-3-3-4 system)" (M. o. E. MEXT, Culture, Sports, Science and Technology 2012a: part 1, SF 1: sect. 3, ch. 5) in order to find new ways for diversification by stressing the major importance of stronger internationalization of Japanese education.

These attempts target the current entrance examination system as well. Through the revision of the "Ordinance for Enforcement of the School Education Act" in 2009, the enrolment at university has already become more flexible, since universities are allowed to set up entrance examination dates besides April (ibid: part 1, SF 1: sect. 1, ch. 7). High school graduates can now apply for university admission more than once a year, thus increasing the chance of avoiding the *rōnin* life if they fail to enter a university at first try. In addition, since 2012 the Council for the Implementation of Education Rebuilding as launched by Prime Minister Abe in 2006 was "discussing connections between high school education and university education, and the modality of university entrance examinations" (ibid: part 1, SF 1: sect. 3, ch. 5). Instead of a central test at the end of high school, several assessments at different points in time are recommended. The new test shall consist of two parts:

a basic test to ensure students' academic level is sufficient to enter university and one test to replace the current *sentā shiken*. The new *sentā* shall be designed to not give scores only, but "place students in several academic levels. Universities will be asked to make a decision from these levels, along with wider (and, let's admit it, more subjective) variety of criteria such as essays, interviews and extracurricular activities" (Mina 2013). Through this measure, students will have more than one opportunity to take the entrance examination and do not need to stake everything on one chance, and thus the number of students who become *rōnin* and have to wait one year without status to take the entrance examination again the following year might be reduced. However, the overall goal of the reformation of the *sentā shiken* will be to "raise the academic ability of students," said Masashi Kudo, an official at the Ministry of Education (Masashi Kudo, in Kakuchi 2013b). In addition, to raise English proficiency, tests such as the TOEFL shall be introduced to the entrance examinations starting in 2015 (Abe 2013: 23, 52). This change in the entrance examination system will lead to an increase of the examination hell again, predicts one of the Benesse corporation's education experts, Kazuo Maruyama, who said that since "the new test would focus heavily on academic achievement [students] will have to study harder to get better scores to enter good universities" (Kazuo Murayama, in Kakuchi 2013b). Concerns were also raised by high school teachers, who fear that the flexibility to take a university entrance exam already during the second or third year of high school would only result in students who "will be studying only for the test" (Ryoichi Oikawa, head of the National Association of Upper Secondary School Principals, in Kakuchi 2013b). What is overlooked is the before stressed importance of raising learning interest and motivation as well as creativity. The focus is clearly back on scores, whereas the actual well-being of students as taken into consideration when promoting *yutori kyōiku* seems to have been sacrificed in favor of competition and rigidity to foster economic competitiveness.

10.6   Conclusion

Summarizing the above discussions with respect to my initial research question, it becomes quite clear that *yutori* education was in no position to actually prevail and live up to its expectations. Many educationalists and politicians soon came to favor internationalization of Japanese education with the result that competition for high credentials and workload have only partly decreased at best. In his recent work, Cave (2016) concluded that the carried-out reforms of the last two decades have brought "only limited changes to this assessment and selection system" (p. 192). But this is only partly true. As Amano (1995) showed, Japanese education policy was under constant change during its modern history, always shifting between "control and competition" and "freedom and choice." Whereas *yutori* was a move towards "freedom and choice," in the aftermath of the *gakuryoku teika ronsō* and the PISA shock Japanese education policy moved back to laying its main emphasis on competition (see also Shimizu 2001: 198). However, we have to acknowledge that there is no clear-cut in this shift towards stronger competition. Central control was mostly given away by devolution policy while freedom of choice remained. The combination of both inherits new implications for students' school life and the private supplementary education market as well. In summary, the new *yutori* education reform course is now stronger emphasizing "such guiding ideas or ideologies as excellence, efficiency, and accountability; neoconservatism, neoliberalism, and market fundalism; postmodernism and post-Fordism; consumerism, privatization, and marketization (choice and competition); deregulation, devolution, and new public management [...]; testism, inspectionism, and performance-based evaluation or outcome-based education" (Fujita 2010: 18–19). This means, the reversed course has brought back the fundamental basics of Japanese teaching and learning principles and again increases the pressure on students, while students are supposed to possess skills and abilities besides what traditional approaches to learning actually support. Hence, in addition to traditional expectations towards students to perform well in school and in entrance examinations, students are pressured to develop a high level of academic competencies as required by national and international achievement tests. Furthermore, the international dimension of skill development has become a major concern in education policies, wherefore students are supposed to demonstrate fluent English, develop their creativity, work autonomously, and gain new skills, which go beyond mere content reproduction, while being faced with increasing uncertainties concerning their future chances in the labor market.

This development affects the Japanese shadow education industry in a decisive way. As I have shown in Chap. 8, the shadow is very flexible and fast in adapting to these changes and the new demands on students. The dependence on shadow education in Japan is thus unlikely to vanish as an outcome of recent reforms. In fact, the increased demands on students are more likely to further increase the role of *juku* in education. This, of course, has major implications for the interdependence of *juku* and schools (see Chap. 2), which might even grow, thus seriously affecting students' well-being, personal and educational development as well as careers. The implications of shadow education for social inequalities have been the major focus of the book, and it remains an exciting topic against the background of this ongoing change.

Appendix

Table 10.1 Curriculum changes in compulsory school, in total hours per grade, 1977–2008

Subject/year of implementation		Grades									
		小1	小2	小3	小4	小5	小6	中1	中2	中3	Trend
Japanese	1977	272	280	280	280	210	210	175	175	175	–
	1989	306	315	280	280	210	210	175	140	140	↑
	1998	272	280	235	235	180	175	140	105	105	↓
	2008	306	315	245	245	175	175	140	140	105	↑
Social Studies	1977	68	70	105	105	105	105	140	140	105	–
	1989	–	–	105	105	105	105	140	140	70–105	(↓)
	1998	–	–	70	85	90	100	105	105	85	↓
	2008	–	–	70	90	100	105	105	105	140	↑
Mathematics	1977	136	175	175	175	175	175	105	140	140	–
	1989	136	175	175	175	175	175	105	140	140	–
	1998	114	155	150	150	150	150	105	105	105	↓
	2008	36	175	175	175	175	175	140	105	140	↑
Science (*Living Environment Studies*)	1977	68	70	105	105	105	105	105	105	140	–
	1989	102	105	105	105	105	105	105	105	105–140	↑
	1998	102	105	70	90	95	95	105	105	80	↓
	2008	102	105	90	105	105	105	105	140	140	↑
Music	1977	68	70	70	70	70	70	70	70	35	–
	1989	68	70	70	70	70	70	70	35–70	35	(↓)
	1998	68	70	60	60	50	50	45	45	35	↓
	2008	68	70	60	60	50	50	45	35	35	↓
Fine Arts	1977	68	70	70	70	70	70	70	70	35	–
	1989	68	70	70	70	70	70	70	35–70	35	(↓)
	1998	68	70	60	60	50	50	45	35	35	↓
	2008	68	70	60	60	50	50	45	35	35	–
Health and Physical Education	1977	102	105	105	105	105	105	105	105	105	–
	1989	102	105	105	105	105	105	105	105	105–140	(↑)
	1998	90	90	90	90	90	90	90	90	90	↓
	2008	102	105	105	105	90	90	105	105	105	↑
Industrial Arts/ Homemaking	1977	–	–	–	–	70	70	75	75	105	–
	1989	–	–	–	–	70	70	70	70	70–105	↓
	1998	–	–	–	–	60	55	70	70	35	↓
	2008	–	–	–	–	60	55	70	70	35	–

(continued)

Table 10.1 (continued)

Subject/year of implementation			Grades									Trend
			小1	小2	小3	小4	小5	小6	中1	中2	中3	
Moral Education		1977	34	35	35	35	35	35	35	35	35	–
		1989	34	35	35	35	35	35	35	35	35	–
		1998	34	35	35	35	35	35	35	35	35	–
		2008	34	35	35	35	35	35	35	35	35	–
Special Activities		1977	34	35	35	70	70	70	70	70	70	–
		1989	34	35	35	70	70	70	35–70	35–70	35–70	(↓)
		1998	34	35	35	35	35	35	35	35	35	↓
		2008	34	35	35	35	35	35	35	35	35	–
Electives (English)	Total	1977	–	–	–	–	–	–	105	105	140	–
	Total	1989	–	–	–	–	–	–	105–140	105–210	105–280	↑
	English	1998	–	–	–	–	–	–	105	105	105	–
	Others		–	–	–	–	–	–	0–30	50–85	105–165	↓
	English	2008	–	–	–	–	35	35	140	140	140	↑
Integrated Study		1998	–	–	105	105	110	110	70–100	70–105	70–130	–
		2008	–	–	70	70	70	70	50	70	70	↓
Total		1979	850	910	980	1015	1015	1015	1050	1050	1050	–
		1989	850	910	980	1015	1015	1015	1050	1050	1050	–
		1998	782	840	910	945	945	945	980	980	980	↓
		2008	850	910	945	980	980	980	1015	1015	1015	↑

Monbushō (1977a, b, 1989a, b, 1998a, b) and M. o. E. MEXT, Culture, Sports, Science and Technology (2008, 2010)

References

Abe, S. (2013). *Japan Revitalization Strategy – JAPAN is BACK. Policy Directive of the Prime Minister of Japan and his Cabinet.* Retrieved from: http://japan.kantei.go.jp/96_abe/documents/2013/index.html

Amano, I. (1995). *Kyōiku kaikaku no yukue – jiyūka to koseika o motomete* [The future of education reform – Seeking liberalization and individualization]. Tokyo: University of Tokyo Press.

Amano, I., & Poole, G. S. (2005). The Japanese university in crisis. *Higher Education, 50*(4), 685–711.

Aspinall, R. (2005). University entrance in Japan. In J. S. Eades, R. Goodman, & H. Yumio (Eds.), *The 'Big Bang' in Japanese higher education. The 2004 reforms and the dynamics of change* (pp. 199–218). Melbourne: Trans Pacific Press.

Aspinall, R. (2010). *Education reform in Japan in an era of internationalization and risk.* Hikone: Center for Risk Research, Shiga University.

Azuma, H. (2002). The development of the course of study and the structure of educational reform in Japan. In G. DeCoker (Ed.), *National standards and school reform in Japan and the United States* (pp. 5–19). New York: Teachers College Press.

Baker, D. P. (2014). *The schooled society.* Stanford: Stanford University Press.

Baker, D. P., & LeTendre, G. K. (2005). *National differences, global similarities. World culture and the future of schooling*. Stanford: Stanford University Press.

Bjork, C. (2016). *High stakes schooling – What we can learn from Japan's experience with testing, accountability & education reform*. Chicago/London: The University of Chicago Press.

Bjork, C., & Tsuneyoshi, R. (2005). Education reform in Japan: Competing visions for the future. *The Phi Delta Kappan, 86*(8), 619–626.

Breakspear, S. (2012). *The policy impact of PISA: An exploration of the normative effects of international benchmarking in school system performance* (OECD Education Working Papers 71).

Cave, P. (2001). Educational reform in Japan in the 1990s: 'Individuality' and other uncertainties. *Comparative Education, 37*(2), 173–191.

Cave, P. (2016). *Schooling selves. Autonomy, interdependence, and reform in Japanese junior high education*. Chicago: The University of Chicago Press.

Clavel, T. (2014, May 1). English fluency hopes rest on an education overhaul. *The Japan Times*. http://www.japantimes.co.jp/community/2014/01/05/general/english-fluency-hopes-rest-on-an-education-overhaul/#.Ut1U2rQwcYA

Chavez, A. (2014, October 1). Teachers must Nurture Critical Thinking, Confidence in English for a Shot at 2020 Goals. *The Japan Times*. Retrieved from: http://www.japantimes.co.jp/community/2014/01/10/our-lives/teachers-must-nurture-critical-thinking-confidence-in-english-for-a-shot-at-2020-goals/#.U-SH4WOOz3

Daigaku-Nyūshi-Sentā. (2014a). *Heisei 26-nendo daigaku nyūshi sentā shiken jisshi kekka no gaiyō* [Overview of the final results of the National Center Test for University Admissions]. Retrieved from: http://www.dnc.ac.jp/data/shiken_jouhou/h26/

Daigaku-Nyūshi-Sentā. (2014b). *Shigan-sha-sū jukenshasū-tō no suii* [Changes in the number of applicants and examinees]. Retrieved from: http://www.dnc.ac.jp/data/suii/suii.html

Demes, H., & Georg, W. (2007). Bildung und Berufsbildung in Japan [Education and vocational training in Japan]. In K. Bellmann, & R. Haak (Eds.), *Der japanische Markt – Herausforderungen und Perspektiven für deutsche Unternehmen* [The Japanese market – Challenges and perspectives for German companies] (pp. 267–300). Wiesbaden: Deutscher Universitätsverlag.

Dierkes, J. (2008). Japanese shadow education: The consequences of school choice. In M. Forsey, S. Davies, & G. Walford (Eds.), *The globalisation of school choice?* (pp. 231–248). Oxford: Symposium Books.

Dierkes, J. (2012, March 2). Exam forces students to cram irrelevant facts. *Asahi Shimbun*. http://info.japantimes.co.jp/print/eo20120203a1.html

Fujita, H. (1997). *Kyōiku kaikaku: Kyōsei jidai no gakkō-dzukuri* [Education reform: Building schools in an era of symbiosis]. Tokyo: Iwanami Shoten.

Fujita, H. (2000). *Shimin shakai to kyōiku* [The civil society and education]. Kyoto: Seori Shobo.

Fujita, H. (2010). Whither Japanese schooling? Educational reforms and their impact on ability formation and educational opportunity. In J. A. Gordon, H. Fujita, T. Kariya, & G. K. LeTendre (Eds.), *Challenges to Japanese education. Economics, reform, and human rights* (pp. 17–53). New York: Teachers College Press.

Fukuzawa, R. E., & LeTendre, G. K. (2001). *Intense years: How Japanese adolescents balance school, family and friends*. New York: Routledge.

Gattig, N. (2012, November 13). Failing students: Japanese universities facing reckoning or reform. A day at the 'Circus' offers harsh lessons about Japan's higher education system and its low English levels. *The Japan Times*. http://www.japantimes.co.jp/community/2012/11/13/issues/failing-students-japanese-universities-facing-reckoning-or-reform/#.Ut1zkLQwcYA

Goodman, R. (2003). The why, what and how of educational reform in Japan. In R. Goodman & D. Phillips (Eds.), *Can the Japanese change their education system?* (Oxford studies in comparative education, pp. 7–30). Oxford: Symposium Books.

Goodman, R. (2005). W(h)ither the Japanese university? An introduction to the 2004 higher education reforms in Japan. In J. Eades, R. Goodman, & Y. Hada (Eds.), *The 'Big Bang' in Japanese higher education. The 2004 reforms and the dynamics of change* (pp. 1–31). Melbourne: Trans Pacific Press.

Japan Today (2013, December 15). Education Ministry proposes radical English education reform. *Japan Today*. http://www.japantoday.com/category/national/view/education-ministry-proposes-radical-english-education-reform

Jones, R. S. (2011). *Education reform in Japan* (OECD Economics Department Working Papers 888).

Kakuchi, S. (2013a, March 27). Abeducation – A new Push for Higher Education Internationalization. *University World News.* http://www.universityworldnews.com/article.php ?story=20130627113411208

Kakuchi, S. (2013b, November 14). Reform of University Entrance Exam Sparks Debate. *University World News.* http://www.universityworldnews.com/article.php?st ory=20130913114950164

Kajita, E. (2013). *The decline in the academic level of Japanese children and the development of educational reform.* Paper presented at the Japan Information & Culture Center, Washington.

Kameda, M. (2013, December 31). English to get 2020 push but teachers not on same page. Exposure to start in third grade for basic communication ability by junior high. *The Japan Times.* http://www.japantimes.co.jp/news/2013/12/31/national/english-to-get-2020-push-but-teachers-not-on-same-page/#.Ut1UxbQwcYA

Kariya, T. (2010). Views from the Japanese side. Challenges to Japanese education. In J. A. Gordon, H. Fujita, T. Kariya, & G. K. LeTendre (Eds.), *Challenges to Japanese education. Economics, reform, and human rights* (pp. 11–13). New York: Teachers College Press.

Kariya, T. (2013). *Understanding structural changes in inequality in education.* Paper presented at the DIJ-Workshop "Social Inequality in Japan: A Reassessment" DIJ, Tokyo.

Kariya, T., & Dore, R. (2006). Japan at the meritocracy frontier: From here, where? *The Political Quarterly, 77*(1), 134–156.

Kataoka, E. (2014). Dare ga kyōshi o shinrai shite iru no ka – 'monsutā pearento' gensetsu no kenshō to kyōshi e no shinrai [Sociological analysis of parental trust in school teachers and the "Monster Parent" phenomenon in Japan]. *Komazawa Shakaigaku Kenkyū, 46,* 45–67.

Kinmoth, E. H. (2005). From selection to seduction: The impact of demographic change on private higher education in Japan. In J. S. Eades, R. Goodman, & Y. Hada (Eds.), *The 'Big Bang' in Japanese higher education. The 2004 reforms and the dynamics of change* (pp. 106–135). Melbourne: Trans Pacific Press.

Knüsel, J. (2011, April 3). Englisch zum Schulanfang. *Asienspiegel.* http://asienspiegel.ch/2011/04/ englisch-zum-schulanfang/

Knüsel, J. (2013, December 13). Englisch sprechen lernen. *Asienspiegel.* http://asienspiegel. ch/2013/12/englisch-sprechen-lernen/

Kobayashi, V. (2013). Afterword – Change upon change: Whither Japan, Whither Japanese education? In G. DeCoker & C. Bjork (Eds.), *Japanese education in an era of globalization: Culture, politics, and equity* (pp. 183–188). New York: Teachers College Press, Columbia University.

Lenhardt, G. (2008). Vergleichende Bildungsforschung. Bildung, Nationalstaat und Weltgesellschaft [Comparative education research. Education, National State and World Society]. In W. Helsper & J. Böhme (Eds.), *Handbuch der Schulforschung* [Handbook of school research] (pp. 1009–1028). Wiesbaden: VS Verlag.

Lockley, T., Hirschel, R., & Slobodniuk, A. (2012). Assessing the action plan: Reform in Japanese high school EFL. *Electronic Journal of Foreign Language Teaching, 9*(2), 152–169.

Martin, B. (2012, May 28). The PTA in Japan. More things Japanese. http://morethingsjapanese. com/the-pta-in-japan/

MEXT, Ministry of Education, Culture, Sports, Science and Technology. (2017a). *Education.* Retrieved from: http://www.mext.go.jp/english/introduction/1303952.htm

MEXT, Ministry of Education, Culture, Sports, Science and Technology. (2017b). *Statistics.* Retrieved from: http://www.mext.go.jp/english/statistics/

MEXT, Ministry of Education, Culture, Sports, Science and Technology. (2005). *FY2005 White Paper on Education, Culture, sports, science and technology – educational reform and enhancement of the educational functions of communities and families.* Retrieved from: http:// www.mext.go.jp/b_menu/hakusho/html/06101913.htm

MEXT, Ministry of Education, Culture, Sports, Science and Technology. (2006). *Basic act on education. Act No. 120 of December 22, 2006.* Retrieved from: http://www.mext.go.jp/english/ lawandplan/1303462.htm

MEXT, Ministry of Education, Culture, Sports, Science and Technology. (2008). *Shōgakkō gakushū shidō yōryō* [Elementary school curriculum guidelines]. Retrieved from: http://www.mext.go.jp/a_menu/shotou/new-cs/youryou/syo/

MEXT, Ministry of Education, Culture, Sports, Science and Technology. (2009). *Yōchien kyōiku yōryō, ko-chūgakkō gakushū shidō yōryō-tō no kaitei no pointo* [Pre-school education and primary and middle school course of study guidelines revision points]. Retrieved from: http://www.mext.go.jp/a_menu/shotou/new-cs/youryou/1304385.htm

MEXT, Ministry of Education, Culture, Sports, Science and Technology. (2010). *Chūgakkō gakushū shidō yōryō* [Middle school curriculum guidelines]. Retrieved from: http://www.mext.go.jp/a_menu/shotou/new-cs/youryou/chu/index.htm

MEXT, Ministry of Education, Culture, Sports, Science and Technology. (2011). *Five proposals and specific measures for developing proficiency in English for International Communication. By the Commission on the Development of Foreign Language Proficiency.* Retrieved from: http://www.mext.go.jp/english/elsec/1319701.htm

MEXT, Ministry of Education, Culture, Sports, Science and Technology. (2012a). *2012-Nen monbu kagaku hakusho* [2012 white paper on education, culture, sports, science and technology]. Retrieved from: http://www.mext.go.jp/b_menu/hakusho/html/hpab201301/1338525.htm

MEXT, Ministry of Education, Culture, Sports, Science and Technology. (2012b). *Ko-chūgakkō ni okeru sentaku-sei no jisshi jōkyō ni tsuite* [Concerning the status of the implementation of school choice for primary and middle schools]. Retrieved from: http://www.mext.go.jp/a_menu/shotou/gakko-sentaku/index.htm

MEXT, Ministry of Education, Culture, Sports, Science and Technology. (2012c). *Kōdai setsuzoku tokubetsu bukai (dai 4-kai) haifu shiryō – shiryō 1: AO nyūshi-tō no jisshi jōkyō ni tsuite* [Special group concerned with the connection between high school and University education (4th Meeting). distribution material – Material 1: Concerning the implementation of the AO entrance]. Retrieved from: http://www.mext.go.jp/b_menu/shingi/chukyo/chukyo12/shiryo/1329266.htm

MEXT, Ministry of Education, Culture, Sports, Science and Technology. (2012d). *Statistical abstract 2012, edition 1.9, Universities and junior colleges.* Retrieved from: http://www.mext.go.jp/english/statistics/1302965.htm

MEXT, Ministry of Education, Culture, Sports, Science and Technology. (2014a). *English education reform plan corresponding to globalization.* Retrieved from: http://www.mext.go.jp/english/topics/1343591.htm

MEXT, Ministry of Education, Culture, Sports, Science and Technology. (2014b). *JAPAN vision 2020 ~intensive discussion on a future vision of Japan.* Retrieved from: http://www.mext.go.jp/english/topics/1345958.htm

MEXT, Ministry of Education, Culture, Sports, Science and Technology. (2014c). *Kōritsu daigaku ni tsuite* [Concerning public Universities]. Retrieved from: http://www.mext.go.jp/a_menu/koutou/kouritsu/index.htm

MEXT, Ministry of Education, Culture, Sports, Science and Technology. (2014d). *National University reform plan.* Retrieved from: http://www.mext.go.jp/english/topics/1345139.htm

Mina. (2013). National Center Test for University Admissions to be replaced by new achievement test in five years. *Japan Trends* (2013-10-31). Retrieved from: http://www.japantrends.com/national-center-test-for-university-admissions-to-be-replaced-by-new-achievement-test-in-five-years/

Monbushō, Ministry of Education. (1977a). *Chūgakkō gakushū shidō yōryō* [Middle school curriculum guidelines]. Retrieved from: http://www.nier.go.jp/yoshioka/cofs_new/s52j/index.htm

Monbushō, Ministry of Education. (1977b). *Shōgakkō gakushū shidō yōryō* [Elementary school curriculum guidelines]. Retrieved from: https://www.nier.go.jp/guideline/s52e/index.htm

Monbushō, Ministry of Education. (1989a). *Chūgakkō gakushū shidō yōryō* [Middle school curriculum guidelines]. Retrieved from: http://www.nier.go.jp/yoshioka/cofs_new/h01j/index.htm

Monbushō, Ministry of Education. (1989b). *Shōgakkō gakushū shidō yōryō* [Elementary school curriculum guidelines]. Retrieved from: http://www.nier.go.jp/yoshioka/cofs_new/h01e/index.htm

Monbushō, Ministry of Education. (1998a). *Chūgakkō gakushū shidō yōryō* [Middle school curriculum guidelines]. Retrieved from: http://www.mext.go.jp/a_menu/shotou/cs/1320061.htm

Monbushō, Ministry of Education. (1998b). *Shōgakkō gakushū shidō yōryō* [Elementary school curriculum guidelines]. Retrieved from: http://www.mext.go.jp/a_menu/shotou/cs/1319941.htm

Mori, R. (2002). Entrance examinations and remedial education in Japanese higher education. *Higher Education, 43*(1), 27–42.

Motani, Y. (2005). Hopes and challenges for progressive educators in Japan: Assessment of the 'Progressive Turn' in the 2002 educational reform. *Comparative Education, 41*(3), 309–327.

Ninomiya, A., & Urabe, M. (2011). Impact of PISA on education policy – The case of Japan. *Pacific-Asian Education, 23*(1), 23–30.

Okada, A. (2012a). *Education policy and equal opportunity in Japan.* New York/Oxford: Berghahn Books.

Okada, A. (2012b). Education reform and equal opportunity in Japan. *Journal of International and Comparative Education, 1*(2), 116–129.

Roesgaard, M. H. (2006). *Japanese education and the cram school business: Functions, challenges and perspectives of the Juku.* Copenhagen: NIAS Press.

Rohlen, T. P. (2002). Concluding observations: Wider contexts and future issues. In G. DeCoker (Ed.), *National standards and school reform in Japan and the United States* (pp. 177–205). New York: Teachers College Press.

Sage, K. (2007). MEXT's 2003 action plan: Does it encourage performance assessment? *Shiken: JALT Testing & Evaluation SIG Newsletter, 11*(2), 2–5.

Sato, H., Urabe, M., Ninomiya, A. & Sasaki, T. (2013). *A comparative study of the PISA's impact on education policies: With viewpoint of global governance.* Paper presented at the XV World Council on Comparative Education Societies, University of Buenos Aires.

Sellar, S., & Lingard, B. (2013). PISA and the expanding role of the OECD in global educational governance. In H.-D. Meyer & A. Benavot (Eds.), *PISA, power, and policy: The emergence of global educational governance.* Oxford: Symposium Books.

Sellar, S., & Lingard, B. (2014). The OECD and the expansion of PISA: New global modes of governance in education. *British Educational Research Journal, 40*(6), 917–936.

Shimizu, K. (2001). The pendulum of reform: Educational change in Japan from the 1990s onwards. *Journal of Educational Change, 2*, 193–205.

Stevenson, D. L., & Baker, D. P. (1992). Shadow education and allocation in formal schooling: Transition to university in Japan. *American Journal of Sociology, 97*, 1639–1657.

Takaki, Y. (2011). *Education in a New Era.* Global Media Inc. http://www.foreignaffairs.com/about-us/sponsors/japan-education-in-a-new-era

Takayama, K. (2008). The politics of International League Tables: PISA in Japan's achievement crisis debate. *Comparative Education, 44*(4), 387–407.

Takayama, K. (2009). Is Japanese education the "exception"?: Examining the situated articulation of neo-liberalism through the analysis of policy keywords. *Asia Pacific Journal of Education, 29*(2), 125–142.

Tanabe, Y. (2004). What the 2003 MEXT action plan proposes to teachers of English. *The Language Teacher, 28*(3), 3–8.

THE, Times Higher Education. (2017). *World university rankings.* Retrieved from: https://www.timeshighereducation.com/world-university-rankings

Watanabe, M. (2013). *Juku: The stealth force of education and the deterioration of schools in Japan.* North Charleston: CreateSpace Independent Publishing Platform.

Yamashita, J., & Okada, S. (2011). Parental attitudes toward public school education in Tokyo. *Social Science Japan Journal, 14*(1), 39–54.

Yonedzu, K. (2013, March 23). Naze Ajia de nihonjin dake itsu made mo eigo o hanasenai no ka? Hirogaru machigatta benkyō-hō. *Business Journal.* https://blogs.yahoo.co.jp/karnak_s/11706737.html

Yoshida, R. (2013, October 23). Required English from third grade eyed. *The Japan Times.* http://www.japantimes.co.jp/news/2013/10/23/national/required-english-from-third-grade-eyed/#.Ut1U1LQwcYA

Glossary of Japanese Terms

Bukatsudō	部活動	Club activities at school
Chūgakkō	中学校	Middle school (7th to 9th grade)
Chūshō juku	中小塾	Small- and middle-sized *juku*
Doriru juku	ドリル塾	Supplementary schools focusing on "drill" of basic learning contents and strategies
Fubyōdō shakai	不平等社会	Inequality society
Furītā	フリーター	Freeter is a 15- to 34-year-old free "Arbeiter" (German for worker); freeter is a part-time jobber or comparable work and is generally not affiliated with an educational institution or work at home
Fuzoku kōtōgakkō	付属高等学校	Private high schools attached to private universities
Gakkōgaikyōiku	学校外教育	Education outside of school, often used in the same way as shadow education
Gakureki shakai	学歴社会	Credentialist society
Gakushū juku	学習塾	Academic *juku*
Gakkyū hōkai	学級崩壊	The breakdown of school class discipline
Gōkakuritsu	合格率	Success rate: rate of students which gain admission to certain (high-ranked) schools/universities
Hensachi	偏差値	Scores derived from the results of *mogi shiken* at *juku* showing the relative chances to achieve admission to certain schools; these scores are used to create school and university rankings indicating the needed performance level to gain admission to schools
Hoshū juku	補習塾	Supplementary schools focusing on remediation and "supplementation" of school curriculum
Juken jigoku	受験地獄	Examination hell
Juken kyōsō	受験競争	Entrance examination competition
Juken sensō	受験戦争	Entrance examination war
Juku	塾	Private for-profit school offering all sorts of instructions in academic as well as nonacademic fields

Jukuchō	塾長	Head of a *juku*, *juku* principal
Jukukōshi	塾講師	Teachers at *juku*
Jukusei	塾性	Students enrolled at a *juku*
Kakusa shakai	格差社会	Differentiated society or society of social gaps
Katei kyōshi	家庭教師	Private home teacher
Karyū shakai	下流社会	Lower-class society
Keizai kakusa	経済格差	Economic inequality
Kobetsu shidō	個別指導	Individual guidance or instruction
Kojin juku	個人塾	Individually managed *juku*
Kosei	個性	Individuality
Kōtōgakkō	高等学校	High school (10th to 12th grade)
Kōtōsenmongakkō	高等専門学校	Colleges of technology
Kyōiku kyōsō	教育競争	Educational competition
Kyūsai juku	救済塾	Supplementary schools focusing on remediation emphasizing "mutual support"
Mogi shiken	模擬試験	Mock exam showing students what schools they have a high pass probability when taking the entrance exam
Naishinsho	内申書	Internal report card concerning students' motivation, effort, conduct, scores, etc., which builds the basis for recommendations for certain middle and high schools
Naraigoto	習い事	Things concerned with learning, meaning afternoon activities including *bukatsudō* and certain drill lessons on school grounds or at *juku*, which are generally extra paid
Niji shiken	二次試験	Second-stage entrance examination following the national *sentā shiken*; in contrast to the *sentā*, the *niji* is designed by each university independently
Ochikobore	落ちこぼれ	Students which cannot keep up with the pace in class
Ōte juku	大手塾	Major *juku* corporation
Rōnin	浪人	Students who prepare for university or college entrance but have already graduated from high school and are thus without official affiliation; this term originates from masterless *samurai* of the feudal era
Shijuku	私塾	Private *juku*; this term describes the private schools of the Tokugawa era
Shiken jigoku	試験地獄	Examination hell
Shingaku juku	進学塾	Supplementary schools focusing on school "transition"
Shinro shidō	進路指導	Placement counseling at school
Shiritsu gakkō	私立学校	Private schools
Shōgakkō	小学校	Primary school (1st to 6th grade)
Shūdan shidō	集団指導	Group or class guidance/instruction
Shūshyokukatsudō	就職活動	Job hunting (short, *shūkatsu*)

Sentā shiken	センター試験	Short for *daigaku nyūshi sentā shiken*, "University Entrance Center Examination"; often only called the *sentā* ("center")
Sōgō juku	総合塾	Supplementary schools following a "comprehensive" approach
Sōgōtekina gakushū no jikan	総合的な学習の時間	Integrated study period; a new subject meant to provide room to concentrate on contents outside the classic spectrum of the curriculum
Sōzōsei	創造性	Creativity
Suberidome	滑り止め	Insurance principle: things done to ensure security
Suisen nyūgakkō	推薦入学校	Recommendation letter of a school principal
Tanki daigaku	短期大学	Junior college (short-term university)
Tsūshin tensaku	通信添削	Correspondence courses
Yobikō	予備校	"Preparatory schools" for university entrance examinations
Yūshōreppai	優勝劣敗	Survival of the fittest
Yutori kyōiku	ゆとり教育	No-pressure education